"Sophia A. McClennen's new book is a fantastically readable analysis of why ironic comedy has become so important in politics today. It confirms what I witnessed myself as a political comedian in Egypt during the Arab Spring: The crazier the politicians get, the more valuable political comedy becomes for the public. As I learned myself and as this book proves, when absurd politicians take power, it is hard to use reason against them, but it can be easy to use satire. McClennen convincingly shows how satirical comedy helps reason triumph over political repression. Even better, *Trump Was a Joke* reminds us that when you're laughing, you can't be afraid."

—**Bassem Youssef**, the "Jon Stewart of Egypt" and author of *Revolution for Dummies: Laughing Through the Arab Spring*

"*Trump Was a Joke* offers the best, most-comprehensive guide yet to the power of political satire in shaping public opinion during turbulent political times. It is a must-read account of how political satire has come to play such a dominant role in contemporary politics, especially in the era of populist leaders and the global war on truth. It does an excellent job of explaining how being seriously funny can have serious impact on keeping us sane and it shows us how satire can work as a powerful political tactic."

—**Srdja Popovic**, author of *Blueprint for Revolution: How to Use Rice Pudding, Lego Men, and Other Nonviolent Techniques to Galvanize Communities, Overthrow Dictators, or Simply Change the World*

TRUMP WAS A JOKE

Written by a scholar of satire and politics, *Trump Was a Joke* explains why satire is an exceptional foil for absurd political times and why it did a particularly good job of making sense of Trump.

Covering a range of comedic interventions, *Trump Was a Joke* analyzes why political satire is surprisingly effective at keeping us sane when politics is making us crazy. Its goal is to highlight the unique power of political satire to encourage critical thinking, foster civic action, and further rational debate in moments of political hubris and hysteria. The book has been endorsed by Bassem Youssef, who has been referred to as the "Jon Stewart of Egypt," and Srdja Popovic, author of *Blueprint for Revolution*, who used satirical activism to bring down Serbian dictator Slobodan Milosevic.

With a foreword by award-winning filmmaker, satirist, and activist Michael Moore, this study will be of interest to readers who follow politics and enjoy political comedy and will appeal to the communications, comedy studies, media studies, political science, rhetoric, cultural studies, and American studies markets.

Sophia A. McClennen is Director of the Center for Global Studies and Professor of International Affairs and Comparative Literature at Pennsylvania State University, State College, PA.

Routledge Advances in Theatre & Performance Studies

This series is our home for cutting-edge, upper-level scholarly studies and edited collections. Considering theatre and performance alongside topics such as religion, politics, gender, race, ecology, and the avant-garde, titles are characterized by dynamic interventions into established subjects and innovative studies on emerging topics.

Rechoreographing Learning
Dance As a Way to Bridge the Mind-Body Divide in Education
Sandra Cerny Minton

Politics as Public Art
The Aesthetics of Political Organizing and Social Movements
Martin Zebracki and Zane McNeill

Lessons for Today from Shakespeare's Classroom
The Learning Benefits of Drama and Rhetoric in Schools
Robin Lithgow

Notelets of Filth
An *Emilia* Companion Reader
Laura Kressly, Aida Patient, and Kimberly A. Williams

Transcultural Theater
Günther Heeg

Shakespeare and Cultural Appropriation
Vanessa I. Corredera, L. Monique Pittman, Geoffrey Way

For more information about this series, please visit: www.routledge.com/Routledge-Advances-in-Theatre-Performance-Studies/book-series/RATPS

TRUMP WAS A JOKE

How Satire Made Sense of a President Who Didn't

Sophia A. McClennen
With a foreword by Michael Moore

LONDON AND NEW YORK

Cover image: The Yale Center for British Art, Paul Mellon Collection

First published 2023
by Routledge
4 Park Square, Milton Park, Abingdon, Oxon OX14 4RN

and by Routledge
605 Third Avenue, New York, NY 10158

Routledge is an imprint of the Taylor & Francis Group, an informa business

© 2023 Sophia A. McClennen

The right of Sophia A. McClennen to be identified as author of this work has been asserted in accordance with sections 77 and 78 of the Copyright, Designs and Patents Act 1988.

All rights reserved. No part of this book may be reprinted or reproduced or utilised in any form or by any electronic, mechanical, or other means, now known or hereafter invented, including photocopying and recording, or in any information storage or retrieval system, without permission in writing from the publishers.

Trademark notice: Product or corporate names may be trademarks or registered trademarks, and are used only for identification and explanation without intent to infringe.

British Library Cataloguing-in-Publication Data
A catalogue record for this book is available from the British Library

ISBN: 978-1-032-27803-2 (hbk)
ISBN: 978-1-032-27801-8 (pbk)
ISBN: 978-1-003-29417-7 (ebk)

DOI: 10.4324/9781003294177

Typeset in Bembo
by Apex CoVantage, LLC

*In memory of my mother,
Honey Hope (1939–2017),
who taught me the power of laughter,
and to Remy Maisel,
who's been the perfect accomplice in satire.*

CONTENTS

Acknowledgments   *x*
Foreword by Michael Moore   *xiii*
List of Figures   *xvi*

1   This Can't Be Good, Or How I Learned to Stop Worrying and Love Satire   1

2   Trump Was a Joke, But It Wasn't Funny   23

3   It's Hard to Make a Joke Out of a Joke   52

4   The First Media-Created President   85

5   "Let's Make Donald Drumpf Again"   127

6   The Joke's on You: The Power of Satire   214

7   The Last Laugh: Satire's Secret Weapon   247

Works Cited   265
Index   287

ACKNOWLEDGMENTS

This book posed plenty of challenges for me, not least of which was the satirical subject matter. It wouldn't have made it into final form without a lot of help and support.

I have dedicated the book to the memory of my mother, whom I value more and more for her sense of humor and what it taught me about how to handle challenges and adversity, and to Remy Maisel, who has been an ally throughout my study of satire. She and I wrote *Is Satire Saving Our Nation* in 2014 when Jon Stewart and Stephen Colbert both had back-to-back shows on Comedy Central, and that work continues to ground a lot of how I think about the power of political satire today. Her wit, insight, sarcasm, and support have been a constant source of encouragement.

Over the years I have also had the immense good fortune to connect with a lot of satirists, and there is no question that those relationships have offered a lot to my work. I can't thank Michael Moore enough for his support, camaraderie, and creativity. I have deeply valued our conversations and the chance to witness some of his most exciting work reach the public. I have also been greatly honored to have connected with Bassem Youssef, whose work as a satirist continues to be one of the most significant examples of the power of satire to date. Srdja Popovic—the man who taught me to think about not just creative political satire but also directly active political satire—has become one of my most important collaborators. Our *Pranksters vs. Autocrats* shows what happens when you pair an activist and a scholar to study the political effects of laughtivism.[1] That project is currently expanding into a far larger study.

Over this time, I also had the chance to connect with Jordan Klepper and Sara Taksler, along with writers for *The Daily Show* and *Late Night with Seth Meyers*, and with an amazing group of political cartoonists, including Mike Thompson, Joel

Pett, Steve Sack, and Matt Wuerker, each of whom allowed me to reproduce their work in this book. I am grateful to all of them for the creative ways that they use satire to help us make sense of the world.

I've also had numerous academic colleagues, from friends to virtual acquaintances, whose thoughts about satire matter a lot to me. They are far too numerous to thoroughly account for, but I want to give special thanks to Caty Borum Chattoo, Stephen Duncombe, Lauren Feldman, Julie Webber, and Dannagal Young: their work has been a source of inspiration and insight. Then there are the colleagues who don't particularly work on satire, but who have also been great sounding boards– an even harder group to fully recognize. Jon Abel, Jose Alvarez, Jeffrey Di Leo, Peter Hitchcock, Gina Stinnett, and Chris Zorn deserve special thanks.

I had a great group of readers, including Larry Boggess, Mark Leiren Young, and Hugh Murray. They offered a lot of valuable suggestions for which I am most grateful.

I also have to thank my research assistant support, especially Trey Fields, who really helped track down a lot of material for this book, and Oliviah Gearhart, who helped to get it into shape to go to press. Eric Spielvogel and Tamara Knoss used their creative talents to produce graphics used in the book, and I am thankful for their talent and vision.

I started working on the effects of political satire when I published *Colbert's America: Satire and Democracy* with Palgrave in 2012. Readers of this book will note that some of the ideas I developed there, as with *Is Satire Saving Our Nation* and my many columns for Salon.com and other outlets, appear here as well. I also want to thank B. Ruby Rich and *Film Quarterly* for offering me a chance to preview some of the arguments made here in an essay published in their Winter 2021 issue.[2] I also am grateful to Jody Baumgartner and Amy Becker for offering me a chance to contribute to their edited volume *Political Humor in a Changing Media Landscape: A New Generation of Research*. My essay for that volume focused on the risks of satire, and many of those ideas appear in this book as well.[3]

I remain appreciative of my time on the *Harvard Lampoon* and the role that experience played in helping me to understand and value satire. It was fun to cite Dan Greaney, for instance, who was president of the *Lampoon* when I was on the staff and then went on to write for *The Simpsons*. I also enjoyed the fact that other *Lampoon* alums, like Andy Borowitz and Colin Jost, have work that appeared in this book too. It's been a satire community that I appreciate more and more as the years go on.

My book writing always requires a network of family and friends, and I have had the benefit of a strong base of support. I want to give special thanks to my Aunt Stephania for her constant intellectual engagement with my work and the various ways that her generosity and thoughtful nature support me. My kids, Isabel and Henry, each have their own distinct senses of humor, both of which amaze, delight, and, more often that I'd like to admit, outwit me. I am also grateful for Mark, who came into my life after much of this book was written, but who offered support and encouragement as I worked to get this book into your hands.

Notes

1 Popovic, Srdja and Sophia A. McClennen. *Pranksters vs. Autocrats: Why Dilemma Actions Advance Nonviolent Activism*. Cornell University Press, 2020.
2 McClennen, Sophia A. "Trump's Ironic Effect on Political Satire." *Film Quarterly*, vol. 75, no. 2, 2021, pp. 27–37, https://doi.org/10.1525/FQ.2021.75.2.27.
3 McClennen, Sophia A. "The Joke Is on You: Satire and Blowback." *Political Humor in a Changing Media Landscape: A New Generation of Research*, ed. Jody C. Baumgartner and Amy B. Becker. Lexington Books, 2018, pp. 137–156.

FOREWORD

I first met Trump in 1991. At a reproductive rights fundraiser he was co-hosting. He couldn't have cared less about women's rights. I'm guessing he was just trying to impress his daughter. Which made the whole thing both disgusting and sad.

Back when everyone thought he was just an entertaining freak show, I knew he was dangerous, I knew he meant business, and I was convinced he would win the election. Nobody wanted to hear that. I was booed! After all, it simply wasn't possible. America was not going to turn its beloved country over to a crazed, bombastic, absurd buffoon, a reality TV host who bragged about grabbing (assaulting) women by their genitals. A professional liar who called those who served to defend the country in our volunteer Army "losers," a comment that surely would have ended any politician's career.

Yet the more outrageous he got, the more the public couldn't turn away. And that's the thing about Trump. It was almost impossible to ridicule him, because how do you make a joke out of someone when that someone is making the joke about himself first? The audience—the voters—had never experienced such self-ridicule from a person they were also being asked to take seriously. He may have had a reality TV show, but it often felt like there wasn't anything real about him at all.

That's the challenge of Trump. He didn't seem real, but he was *very* real, scary real. Like really, really, really set-the-world-on-fire real. His hatred, racism, misogyny, and basic disrespect for everything that could make this country great was grotesquely beyond real.

So how exactly do you deal with a guy like that? How could we communicate the threat his presidency posed, while also keeping ourselves energized and positive? How could we challenge him without letting him be the center of the show? When I watched the media obsess over him and much of the public mock him, I worried we were not prepared for what was to come. We weren't getting it, and it wasn't going to go well.

I'd like to remind everyone that his entire presidential campaign started off in June of 2015 as a media hoax because he was jealous of how he believed his fellow NBC primetime star Gwen Stefani was getting more attention from the network and that her show (*The Voice*) was considered more successful than his. So, he decided one day to create a media spectacle and rode down his golden escalator to a cheering throng below. Only later did we find out that much of the throng was paid "extras." In the days and weeks after, much to his surprise, his fake announcement that he was running took off like wildfire—and before we knew it, Trump was rising in the polls, and the future of our democracy was falling.

That's the thing about Trump. He has pretty much always been a joke *and* a threat. Absurd *and* terrifying. Sure, we've had scary presidents and we've had odd ones. But never, ever, ever did we have a president who combined such extremes, at the same time, all the time.

That's what makes this book important. Sophia A. McClennen shows us that it was the extremes of Trump that made it really difficult for the traditional media to take him seriously. Her book expertly analyzes why satire played such an important role in making sense out of a president who seemed like a bad joke and a weird nightmare. While the mainstream news was busy putting together panels of experts, the political comedians got right down to the business of showing us what Trump was up to. As you'll learn in this book, at exactly the moment when we needed to take the threats to our nation seriously, it turns out that satire came to the rescue.

That was what I was thinking back in 2016 when I suggested we needed "an army of comedy" to go after Trump. Comedy serves as a disruption. And with Trump it meant not letting him control the story and not letting him set the terms. Even better, each time we mocked him, it bothered him. It showed us all that his thin skin was a sign of his thin grip on his overblown ego.

One of the reasons I loved reading this book is that throughout my career I've spent a lot of time trying to figure out the secret sauce of satire and how best to use it. On these very pages Sophia has asked and answered the basic existential question of political humor. Can satire help convince an audience to take something serious seriously? Is it helpful to advance a cause or, if done wrong, is it distracting? Does the biting edge of satire, if condescending or patronizing, hurt our chances for winning people over and building a common vision? Or, perhaps, is satire the most powerful nonviolent weapon available to all citizens to speak truth to power, to bring down an autocrat or a bully, to expose the cruelty exacted upon a population that has no other defense to fight back? In other words, what better way to bring down the powerful and the elites than to laugh them right out of town?

So, this is why this book matters. It shows us how satire works and what effect it has on us and other people. Sophia A. McClennen has studied this like no one else I know. While our job may be to make (or film) the jokes, hers is to analyze their real-life impact—and she does a great job of it.

But there's another, more important, way this book matters. *Trump Was a Joke* teaches us that what we think of as the success of creative activism needs a broader definition. I mean, just because the court jester didn't lead to the end of the king's reign, that doesn't mean it didn't make a difference. Right? Each and every one of you reading this right now was born with a funny bone. I'm not saying you're all stand-up comedians or the next Borat. But each of us has a sense of humor. What's important in these dark times is not that you can *tell* a joke—it's that you *get* the joke. And when tens of millions get the joke that is Ted Cruz or Rudy Giuliani or Fox News, that's when their power becomes deflated and neutered. That's when they can't hurt people anymore. Because it's hard to do damage to those who are laughing their asses off at YOU.

This book explains the various ways that satire stepped up and helped us make sense of the most confounding and catastrophic president of all time. It shows us how satire builds communities, keeps us from falling into a catatonic state of depression, and helps us think in more advanced ways about how to handle crises. It even shows us how satire can work to defend democracy when politicians and the media don't.

I've learned a lot from this book and hope you will too.

Keep laughing my friends, all the way to the polls!

Michael Moore
Labor Day, 2022

FIGURES

1.1	What is satire?	3
1.2	Cover image from *The Atlantic* of May 2017 shows the public interest in Trump satire.	6
1.3	This meme is just making fun of Trump's hair, which tended to get mocked quite a lot, making the joke even less critically powerful.	7
1.4	This cartoon from the *Detroit Free Press*' Mike Thompson is a perfect example of the use of irony in satirical comedy to point out hypocrisy.	8
1.5	Trump tweets a complaint about Alec Baldwin and *Saturday Night Live*, showing that he was paying attention to the show.	9
1.6	Trump complains about late-night hosts not being fair to him.	9
1.7	Alec Baldwin tweets after retiring his Donald Trump impersonation.	10
1.8	Three tweets critical of Michelle Wolf's 2018 WHCAD roast.	11
1.9	An example of an average citizen using ironic sass to respond to a Trump tweet.	12
2.1	Trump presidential run timeline.	27
2.2	Trump jokes by the decade.	30
2.3	A 2017 tweet revisits a *Mad Magazine* roast of Donald Trump as lying about his business successes.	32
2.4	Sacha Baron Cohen interviews Trump in character as Ali G.	33
2.5	Trump lies about his experience with Sacha Baron Cohen.	33
2.6	*Doonesbury* comic strips keyed into Trump as a blustering megalomaniac.	35
2.7	A timeline of the various times that *SNL* included Trump or impersonations of Trump.	36
2.8	*Doonesbury* mocks the long history of Trump campaigning to boost his celebrity.	39

2.9	John Oliver apologizes for the time when he begged Donald Trump to run while guest hosting *The Daily Show*.	40
2.10	Trump delivers his rebuttal and has the final word at the Comedy Central roast.	42
2.11	Jimmy Kimmel mocks Trump for worrying about comedians.	46
3.1	Atamaniuk as Trump on *The President Show*.	54
3.2	Baldwin as candidate Trump.	56
3.3	The first time Trump tweets an attack on *SNL* and Alec Baldwin.	57
3.4	Alec Baldwin's Top Ten impersonations of Trump on *SNL*.	60
3.5	Matt Damon as Brett Kavanaugh for an *SNL* Cold Open.	63
3.6	Jimmy Fallon's Trump impersonation falls flat.	64
3.7	Sarah Cooper's impersonations offered both her own reaction to Trump's words as well as her rendition of his facial expressions.	65
3.8	Melissa McCarthy as Sean Spicer on *SNL*.	66
3.9	Helen Mirren and Sarah Cooper re-enact the 2005 *Access Hollywood* tape.	67
3.10	Trump mocks a disabled reporter.	69
3.11	How to tell the difference between a satirist and a jerk.	71
3.12	Samantha Bee goes after Ivanka.	73
3.13	Trump tweets nonsense about wiretapping.	74
3.14	Just one example of the many ways that protest signs use ironic wordplay to mock Trump.	75
4.1	Trump tweets about "covfefe."	86
4.2	Trump notes the power of his tweet.	86
4.3	One of many tweets that mocked the president's tweet.	87
4.4	Merriam-Webster piles on the Trump tweet.	87
4.5	Jimmy Kimmel adds to the mocking of Trump's typo.	88
4.6	Image from the August 23, 2010, debate on *The Daily Show* between John Oliver and Wyatt Cenac.	89
4.7	The fake *Time* Donald Trump cover.	97
4.8	This graph illustrates the huge gap between Trump's paid versus earned media in comparison with other candidates.	98
4.9	Breakdown of percentage of news reports about each candidate.	99
4.10	This tweet by reporter Matthew Chapman illustrates the double standard of the news media's treatment of Obama versus Trump.	100
4.11	Jake Tapper with Kellyanne Conway in what appears to be yet another publicity stunt of feigned outrage.	102
4.12	Gallup finds a stark political divide on trust in the news media.	102
4.13	This cartoon by Pulitzer Prize–winning cartoonist Joel Pett shows how satire used puns to help make sense of Trump's version of fake news.	110
4.14	Jon Stewart makes fun of Wolf Blitzer's coverage of the missing Malaysian Airlines flight.	111

4.15	Pew showed that viewers of *The Daily Show* and *The Colbert Report* score higher on knowledge of the news than viewers of most traditional news outlets.	112
4.16	Pew found greater fragmentation among most admired news figures; Jon Stewart placed surprisingly high on the list.	113
4.17A,B	The Stewart Top Ten.	114
4.18	Stewart and O'Reilly go head-to-head at their debate.	116
4.19A,B	The Colbert Top Ten.	117
4.20	Colbert announces the launch of @RealHumanPraise on *Twitter*.	118
4.21	One of the many times that Trump attacked *SNL* as though it were a news media outlet.	120
5.1	John Oliver reminds viewers of a previous *Twitter* exchange with Donald Trump.	128
5.2	John Oliver compares Trump's regard for the truth to a lemur's interest in the Supreme Court vacancy.	128
5.3	The "Satire League" to the rescue.	132
5.4	Satirical cartoonist Matt Wuerker suggests that Trump will destroy centuries-old institutions in this cartoon that came out shortly after the fire at Notre Dame.	135
5.5	"Ministry of Satire" ID card for John Oliver.	140
5.6	Oliver's Trump-era highlights.	141
5.7	Mr. Nutterbutter tells Bob Murray to "eat shit," highlighting the way that Oliver blends satirical punch with all-out silliness.	145
5.8	"Ministry of Satire" ID card for Stephen Colbert.	146
5.9	Colbert's Trump-era highlights.	149
5.10	Colbert delivers yet another monologue critiquing Trump.	151
5.11	"Ministry of Satire" ID card for Samantha Bee.	153
5.12	Bee's Trump-era highlights.	156
5.13	Samantha Bee calls Ivanka Trump a "feckless c@#t" for not intervening in her father's politics concerning migrant families.	157
5.14	"Ministry of Satire" ID card for Seth Meyers.	159
5.15	Meyers' Trump-era highlights.	161
5.16	Meyers goes after Trump's tweets on another segment, which lists one weekend of topics.	163
5.17	"Ministry of Satire" ID card for Jimmy Kimmel.	164
5.18	Kimmel describes how he got into a *Twitter* feud with the president's son.	166
5.19	Kimmel's Trump-era highlights.	167
5.20	Kimmel taunts Trump with a meme mocking his childish refusal to accept the election results.	169
5.21	"Ministry of Satire" ID card for Trevor Noah.	170
5.22	*The Daily Show with Trevor Noah*'s Trump-era highlights.	172
5.23	Trevor Noah eviscerates the civility argument.	175

5.24	"Ministry of Satire" ID card for Hasan Minhaj.	177
5.25	Minhaj's Trump-era highlights.	179
5.26	Minhaj is amazed by a high school Steve Miller.	181
5.27	"Ministry of Satire" ID card for Lee Camp.	182
5.28	Camp's Trump-era highlights.	183
5.29	Lee Camp points to all of the military bases surrounding Iran.	186
5.30	"Ministry of Satire" ID card for Andy Borowitz.	186
5.31	Borowitz' Trump-era highlights.	189
5.32	"Ministry of Satire" ID card for Michael Moore.	190
5.33	Moore's Trump-era highlights.	192
5.34	The Trump team tweets a doctored clip from *Trumpland*.	193
5.35	Donald Trump, Jr., reinforces the idea that the right doesn't get irony.	194
5.36	This cartoon by Steve Sack perfectly illustrates the twisted logic of the Trump administration and shows how satire is effective at exposing the Trump team's hypocrisy.	198
5.37	This cartoon by Joel Pett clearly suggests that Trump is a threat to both a free press and cartoonists.	199
5.38	This photo shows the increase in sarcasm and sass at protests.	200
5.39	This billboard calls out Paul Ryan for "running" from his constituents.	201
5.40	Silly tweet mocking Trump.	202
5.41	Satirical tweet mocking Trump.	202

1
THIS CAN'T BE GOOD, OR HOW I LEARNED TO STOP WORRYING AND LOVE SATIRE

The 2016 election was a watershed moment for U.S. politics: Donald Trump won the presidency with more experience on reality TV than in politics; the rise of fake news on social media allowed ridiculous stories to circulate broadly at unprecedented levels; and we learned more about current events from satirical comedians than we did from the mainstream television news media.

None of that sounds good.

But it is the last part of my opening sentence that really causes some of us to worry. It makes perfect sense to question whether political satire, much of which is on cable, can possibly be a productive and positive force in shaping the political climate. I mean, how could comedians who make a lot of money prancing around for audiences and cracking jokes be helping strengthen democracy?

I've spent much of my academic career studying the social effects of political satire, and even I understand that the arguments I am about to make are, if not mind-boggling, at least counterintuitive. Even those of us who enjoy consuming political satire are likely reluctant to acknowledge that it may be one of the most powerful weapons supporting our democracy today. So, I get it; I understand the assumption that satire can't possibly be helping and that perhaps it is even hurting political discourse.

This book will prove that those worries are off base and that satire, in fact, has played a productive and positive role in promoting a healthy democracy in the United States. *Trump Was a Joke* explains why satire was better at exposing the absurdity of the Trump presidency than traditional news outlets, and it considers whether the increasing power of satire is healthy for democracy. While satire has played a larger and larger role in shaping public debate since 9/11/2001, the Trump presidency ushered in an era when comedians have been increasingly successful in helping us understand serious issues. From John Oliver to Stephen Colbert, from Samantha Bee to Seth Meyers, and from Michael Moore to Alec Baldwin as Donald Trump and Melissa McCarthy as Sean Spicer, a wide range of political comedians worked to rescue the American public from the insanity of Trump and everything he represented.

Satirists have pretty much always wanted to rescue their audiences from the madness of the moment, and lovers of political satire know that critical comedy has a long and complicated history. Without doubt, some of what we witnessed in the Trump presidency has direct ties to the long history of political comedy both in the United States and across the globe. The impersonation of Trump by Alec Baldwin for *Saturday Night Live* (*SNL*), for example, would likely never have existed without our nation's own long history of the impersonation of powerful politicians. And yet, there is a decidedly different context for satire today. Regardless of whether you like it or not, you can't dispute the fact that political comedy occupies a central part of political discourse. Think about the fact that you couldn't even sum up the story of Trump without referring to at least a few examples of comedy covering the issues and framing the debates.

This is all to say that the presence and power of political comedy when Trump held office from 2017 to 2021 were truly "unpresidented," to trope on one of Trump's infamous mis-tweets. Anyone interested in figuring out how and why that happened will want to read this book. Is the answer that we are all a bunch of media-consuming drones who prefer frivolous entertainment to serious political debate? Or is the answer that so-called serious political debate got pretty silly and stupid leading up to the 2016 election, so much so that it was the comedians who actually seemed to make the most sense?

One way or the other it seems important to document this story and critically analyze it. Tracing a range of exemplary satire moments both before and after the election, especially focusing on Trump's first two years in office, *Trump Was a Joke* offers both a roadmap to the rising importance of political satire in our nation and an analysis of its effects on civic action. Its core argument is that the Trump presidency ushered in one of the least logical moments in U.S. political history, and it is precisely because Trump was literally a joke that satire became an even more important tool for analyzing political discourse than ever.

Let me illustrate this point by way of a telling anecdote. But before I do that, let's get a couple of the core terms—satire and irony—used in this book sorted out.

Satire is dedicated to exposing human folly, and its goal is to inspire critical thinking and reasoned social engagement.[1] It is often accompanied by irony, parody, and wordplay. It is regularly confused with mockery, cynicism, and sarcasm. Frequently, these different comedic and critical modes exist side by side, meaning that a comedian may make a sharp satirical point one moment to turn around and sarcastically attack someone the next. One of the essential elements of satire is that, through the performance of scrutiny and critique, the audience is asked to perform its own scrutiny and critique. Thus, one key characteristic of satire is its call for an active audience that needs to analyze the satirical joke. Another key feature of satire is that it asks the audience to question sources of authority and to refuse to take the status quo for granted. The idea is to ask the audience to reflect on how

How I Learned to Stop Worrying and Love Satire 3

What is satire?

As my co-author Remy Maisel and I defined it in our 2014 book, *Is Satire Saving Our Nation?*, satire is dedicated to exposing human folly and its goal is to inspire critical thinking and reasoned social engagement. Satire uses wit (less often laugh out loud humor) to call attention to abuses of power, folly, vices, lies, BS and stupidity. Basically, satire sees something it doesn't like in the world or something that doesn't make sense and it uses satirical wit to help you see it too.

FIGURE 1.1 What is satire?

Source: Cristina Bernazzani, "Recharge the Mind," https://stock.adobe.com/search/images?filters%5Bcontent_type%3Aillustration%5D=1&hide_panel=true&k=satire+brain&search_type=suggested search&asset_id=103908055. License free image.

the world has been presented to it and ask whether that representation makes sense, is fair, is just, or is right. What makes satire even more powerful is the fact that it asks the audience to think critically while being highly entertaining and pleasurable. In contrast with dry, literal, political commentary, satire communicates with a broader, often younger, public. Combining silliness with seriousness, satire shows that commonly accepted truths require reconsideration and resistance.

One complication to understanding satire is its relationship to irony. Almost all satire uses irony, but not all irony is satirical. So, let's unpack the meaning of irony because it may actually be a term that is even less understood than satire. Irony has three dominant modes: (1) Situational irony, in which what is expected to happen doesn't happen or in which reality doesn't make sense. For example, the least qualified person wins an election. (2) Dramatic irony, in which the audience knows more about the situation than the characters. This type of irony, though, can happen in the real world and not only in stories. For example, when the public knows that the nation is heading into a public health crisis and it is being led by a president who doesn't believe in science. (3) Rhetorical irony, or what I prefer to call creative irony because it may not only be expressed rhetorically, in which an artist or comedian or everyday person represents something one way but means something else. Most satire is the third mode. At a basic level, rhetorical irony means saying something and meaning something else, like Stephen Colbert on *The Colbert Report* asking a guest, "George Bush: great president or greatest president?" when he does not support Bush at all.[2] Sean Hall explains that "irony is about opposites."[3] So, when people say the opposite of what they mean, "they are expressing a belief or feeling that is at odds with what they are saying on the surface."[4] And they often indicate that they are being ironic by using either extreme understatement or extreme overstatement. The key to creative irony, then, is the double layer between what is expressed and what is meant.

What this book will show is that Trump complicated irony because he embodied all three types at the same time. In Trump, the United States had elected an actual reality TV president (situational irony), who was also a parody of one (creative irony), and, in being elected, he acquired an immense amount of power he was entirely ill-equipped to handle (dramatic irony). It tends to be true that most creative irony is in fact aimed at exposing situational irony. An autocrat, for example, says their policies are in the public interest, and the satirist critical of the autocrat uses sarcasm to point out that autocracy in and of itself isn't in the public interest.

Most satire uses irony to help reveal the absurdity of a situation. In this way, creative irony, in which what is said is not what is meant, is used to expose situational irony, in which things don't make sense or aren't just, fair, or right. As mentioned, the least qualified person winning an election is situational irony. Sarcastically saying that one is "excited" that the least qualified person won an election is using figurative irony to expose situational irony. One of the core arguments of this book is that when the situation is extremely ironic, as it often was during the Trump presidency, then creative, figurative irony does an exceptional job at exposing how absurd reality has become.

OK, now back to my anecdote about how weird the connection got between satire and politics under Trump.

In June 2021, almost six months after Trump had reluctantly left the White House and Joe Biden took up office, the story broke that, when Trump was president, he had asked advisers and lawyers to investigate whether the Department of Justice could probe sources of satirical late-night comedy, like *SNL*, that made fun of him.[5] The fact that Trump would melt down, usually on *Twitter*, after he saw satire critical of him had been surprising enough. Typically, it is autocrats, not democratically elected leaders, who display such thin skin. In fact, one common trait of many U.S. presidents has been the capacity to launch self-deprecating jokes, a move that often undercuts any similar jokes lobbed at them.[6] Ronald Reagan made jokes about his age. Jimmy Carter quipped after leaving the White House, "My esteem in this country has gone up substantially. It is very nice now when people wave at me, they use all their fingers."[7] But before, during, and after Trump was in office, he displayed none of that good-natured self-mocking.

In fact, quite the opposite. Seth Meyers once reflected on working with Trump as a guest host of *SNL* and wondered if Trump even had the capacity to process comedy.[8] Regardless of whether Trump could "get" a joke, though, one thing is clear: he didn't like being the butt of one. Throughout his 2016 campaign and after, Trump made a habit of complaining about jokes he felt were critical of him, regularly taking to *Twitter* to grouse after seeing a joke on late-night comedy.

One *SNL* skit from December 2018 parodied *It's a Wonderful Life* (Frank Capra, 1946).[9] In it, everyone has a better life if Trump isn't in office; unsurprisingly, Trump wasn't amused. His *Twitter* response to the skit revealed, though, that Trump wanted to go further than just complain about jokes; he wanted to shut them down:

> A REAL scandal is the one-sided coverage, hour by hour, of networks like NBC & Democrat spin machines like Saturday Night Live. It is all nothing less than unfair news coverage and Dem commercials. Should be tested in courts, can't be legal? Only defame & belittle! Collusion?[10]

Trump's anxieties led to debates over how conservatives could defend themselves against liberal bias in late-night comedy.[11] But the critical point is that Trump did more than complain; he actually looked into whether he could find avenues to censor political comedy targeting him.[12]

As this book will show, the story of Trump's relationship to satire is not just filled with similarly surprising anecdotes; rather, the ironic complexities of the Trump figure itself created an unusual situation for satire, one that required it to adapt and change in novel ways. Because Trump was both absurd and terrifying, because he was both parody and credible threat, he created a unique situation for satirists, one in which many of the common tools they carry in their comedic tool kit didn't work.

If the satirists' invective is their hammer, how were they to use it on a figure who was already a bombastic bully? If another of their skills is parody, what to make of someone who already was parodic? After Trump was elected, *New Yorker* satirical columnist Andy Borowitz explained, "We're living in an age that defies satire."[13] Think, for example, of Trump's suggestion that drinking bleach might offer protection from the coronavirus.[14] Such a claim was deeply tragicomic: Trump—the deranged buffoon—threatens the health of the nation but does so in a way that is so absurd that it is darkly comedic. The dramatic irony is also situational. The audience watching Trump handle the crisis knows that the ending won't go well but also knows that it is stuck with him in the same play. It's ironic, but not funny.

Trump defied satire. Yet, as I will argue, the effect was not the end of irony but, rather, a reinvention of satire's primary mode of representational defiance. In fact, the most significant Trump effect on satire was to produce ironic irony. If satire is always an ironic representation, then under Trump it became an ironic representation of an ironic representation. The power of satire tends to lie in the gap between figurative representation and intended meaning. Yet, Trump's own bizarre, uncanny, embodied reality presented figurative representation with an ironic dilemma: how to make the bizarre real while also revealing how bizarre reality had become? The catch, however, is that this ironic house of mirrors upended traditional representational layers of irony. The best way to see what was being reflected in the Trumpian house of mirrors was to hold up the ironic mirror of satire, because any attempt to explain Trump in traditional literal ways simply didn't do him justice.

In these ways, Trump presented a unique challenge to irony, one requiring a wholly new satirical aesthetic. Satirical irony of Trump was not a matter of irony everywhere or ironic post-truthiness. Rather, this book explains that when Trump satire was at its best, it worked in two competing, yet intertwined, representational directions: a return to sincerely using irony to reveal the truth while also using irony to demonstrate the extent to which that reality had become grotesquely and ironically absurd. Although there were multiple types of satirical aesthetics aimed at Trump, the most effective was this new satirical form, which was at once an exaggeration of an exaggeration and also an earnest use of irony to deflate the lies, bigotry, and bias that defined the Trump presidency.

The catch, though, was how to create a satirical critique of Trump that could cut through the performative noise and extreme spectacle surrounding his presidency and how to mock someone who had already been so regularly mocked. Recall that, even before he announced his candidacy, Trump was a figure well-known to comedians. As Tom Bissell pointed out for *Harpers*, few people have been impersonated on *SNL* more often or by more actors—six, at last count—than Donald Trump.[15] Trump, Bissell notes, "is the rare novelty guest to have hosted twice: once in 2004, to promote *The Apprentice*, his reality television show, and again in late 2015, to soften perceptions of a presidential campaign widely seen as alarming."[16]

In May 2017 *The Atlantic* released an issue called "Can Satire Save the Republic?" which resembled the title of an earlier book I co-wrote called *Is Satire Saving Our Nation?*[17]

Featuring a photo of Baldwin putting on his Trump impersonation makeup, the issue opened with the observation that "Alec Baldwin has become America's deflator in chief, a weekly pinprick in Trump's balloon."[18] But Baldwin was just

FIGURE 1.2 Cover image from *The Atlantic* of May 2017 shows the public interest in Trump satire.

Source: The Atlantic. © 2017 The Atlantic Monthly Group, LLC. All rights reserved. Used under license.

one among many comedians who took aim at Trump. In fact, as Graydon Carter put it in *Vanity Fair*, "It can reasonably be said that our dear leader is now the most ridiculed man on the planet. In fact, he may well be the most ridiculed man in history."[19]

Just about every comedian has their own impersonation of Trump—a level of caricature rarely seen in the history of mocking presidents. What's critical to understand, though, is that not all impersonations offer the public valuable material to critically process. One of the reasons why satire can get a bad rap is because many critics of political comedy can't tell the difference between mockery and satire. As I'll explain throughout this book, not all comedy is equal and some is simply derogatory and divisive, even if it can be funny for some. Satire, though, is designed less to make fun of how someone looks and more to go after their beliefs, actions, arguments, and ideas. To illustrate the difference, consider the following two Trump jokes. One is just mockery;[20] the other is ironic satire.[21]

Most of the critics of satire don't fully understand the degree to which it is a unique comedic genre, and they base their critiques on a much larger umbrella of comedy, missing the distinctively powerful role that irony and nuance play in satirical comedy. Some impersonations, for example, are just pure mockery—making fun of a chubby, orange-faced buffoon. Think, for instance, of Jimmy Fallon's Trump—a

FIGURE 1.3 This meme is just making fun of Trump's hair, which tended to get mocked quite a lot, making the joke even less critically powerful.

Source: "Who Wore it Better," https://www.litromagazine.com/usa/wp-content/uploads/sites/3/2021/08/1.-Who-Wore-It-Better-1.jpg. License Free Image.

8 How I Learned to Stop Worrying and Love Satire

FIGURE 1.4 This cartoon from the *Detroit Free Press*' Mike Thompson is a perfect example of the use of irony in satirical comedy to point out hypocrisy.

Source: Mike Thompson. https://www.litromagazine.com/usa/wp-content/uploads/sites/3/2021/08/1.-Who-Wore-It-Better-1.jpg. Used with permission.

silly, but not particularly powerful or even memorable impersonation. Those types of caricatures deflate the aura of Trump and diminish his imposing power, but they don't add much to the political debate of his character or his policies.

Not so with Baldwin's Trump, which spurred a major amount of public commentary and which also offered viewers a window into a private, anxious, immature Trump that the public likely hadn't imagined. While some worried that allowing Trump to host *SNL* in 2015 normalized him, there seems little doubt that Baldwin's impersonations of Trump framed the candidate as a blustering, ill-prepared, immature, attention-craving, narcissistic paranoiac. But perhaps even more interesting is the fact that Baldwin didn't just offer a potent parody of a man who already seemed like a mockery; he also caught the attention of Trump himself.[22]

Trump's late-night tweets whining about Baldwin served to prove that satire was playing a prominent role in shaping political discourse. And his lumping of *SNL* within a general category of "media" he felt were "rigging the election" also showed that, for Trump, there was no difference between the *SNL* coverage of him and that of CNN.[23]

But that was only the beginning. As more and more late-night comedians roasted Trump, calling him completely unhinged,[24] a moron,[25] and a lying racist,[26] he started to claim that it was unfair that comedy was coming after him.[27]

While the tweets show that Trump has zero understanding of either the Fairness Doctrine, which called for balanced political coverage and was repealed by

FIGURE 1.5 Trump tweets a complaint about Alec Baldwin and *Saturday Night Live*, showing that he was paying attention to the show.

Source: https://abcnews.go.com/video/embed?id=42863149. License free image.

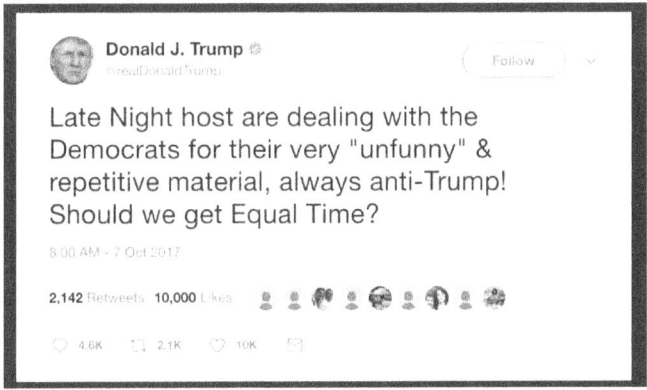

FIGURE 1.6 Trump complains about late-night hosts not being fair to him.

Source: @realDonaldTrump, *Twitter* 7 October 2017, https://pbs.twimg.com/media/DLi7pKEWAAAy vKf?format=jpg&name=large. License free image.

Republicans in 1987, or the Equal Time rule, which only applies to political candidates, they also reveal that the relationship between Trump and political comedy was truly unparalleled. Not only were comedians at the center of political critique, but Trump also fueled the fire by paying so much attention to them.

While Baldwin's impersonations didn't keep Trump out of office, there is significant evidence that satire did, in fact, help the U.S. public deal with the absurdity of Trump's election, just as it helped the public make sense of the George W. Bush administration's unsubstantiated arguments in favor of the Iraq War. To drive home my point, after the 2020 election was called for Joe Biden, Alec Baldwin appeared on *SNL* holding up a sign stating, "You're Welcome."[28] Later, on *Twitter* he shared a similar photo and added, "It's been fun."[29]

Trump's special relationship to satire is only one part of the story of how his presidency changed the role of political comedy in our nation. The other critical shift took place in how the news media covered Trump and how that coverage was different from what happened on satire news shows, in political cartoons, and in snarky internet memes. Once Trump announced his plans to run for office, the

FIGURE 1.7 Alec Baldwin tweets after retiring his Donald Trump impersonation.

Source: @ABFalecbaldwin, *Twitter* 8 November 2020, https://www.aceshowbiz.com/news/view/00162283.html. License free image.

news media scrambled to figure out how to take him seriously, but satire never bothered to do that. The satirists saw the joke and put it on display, again and again, while the news media wavered between playing it straight, getting caught up in the sensationalism, and getting frustrated. Too often the news media let the Trump team frame the angle to their coverage by making the news react to yet another sensationalized tweet or statement. Meanwhile, the satirists, making no apologies for their ironic takedowns or their entertainment value, used their jokes to get at substantive critical issues. When the mainstream news wondered if it needed to cover "all sides" of an issue and allowed yet another Trump crony to take up airtime, satire focused on calling out BS and exposing Trump team lies.

Consider, for example, the meltdown the press had after Michelle Wolf did the comedy roast at the 2018 White House Correspondents' Association Dinner (WHCAD). The fuss related to the idea that Wolf had crossed the line, especially in being too mean in her jokes about then Press Secretary Sarah Huckabee Sanders. While I'll go into detail later in this book about the significance of that annual event for framing political debate—starting with Stephen Colbert's epic roast of George

W. Bush in 2006 and then leading to Seth Meyers' roast of Trump in 2011—the fallout from Wolf's performance is a perfect example of the press getting it all wrong. Beyond not finding her funny and even considering her nasty, especially in relation to jokes that referenced Huckabee Sanders' looks, the real story here is that many members of the press felt Wolf should apologize for her jokes, jokes that called out the Trump team for lying and the press for profiting from coverage of those lies.[30]

The fact that former White House Press Secretary Sean Spicer, who regularly lied to the press and the public, was in unison with news personalities like NBC commentator Andrea Mitchell and MSNBC host Mika Brzezinski is a telling example of how the press had appeared to lose its moral compass in the Trump era. Suddenly it was Wolf who had offended and not the Trump team, despite the fact that at the very same time she was delivering her roast, Trump himself was at a rally in Michigan referring to the press as "dishonest" and suggesting that it didn't even have sources for its fake news stories.[31] At that same event, Trump referred to the press by saying, "these people, they hate your guts."[32] Yet, it was Wolf who would take flak for her caustic tone, especially from members of the media themselves. Regardless of whether one liked her performance, it served to underscore the sheer hypocrisy of the press, which found her roast more offensive than that of a president actively seeking to sow public distrust in the very work it does. In fact, that dynamic explains why, during the Trump era, satirists earned more of the public's trust than the news media. By 2020, 60 percent of the U.S. public expressed little to no trust in the news media at all.[33] Meanwhile, trust in satirists was on the rise so much that journalists were even aware of it. Back in 2015, Univisión journalist Jorge Ramos told John Oliver, "You have more credibility than most journalists in the United States."[34]

It isn't just that the public trusts comedians more than journalists, it also seems to learn more from political comedy than cable news. Poll after poll and research

FIGURE 1.8   Three tweets critical of Michelle Wolf's 2018 WHCAD roast.

Source: Jason Reed, 30 April 2018, https://www.dailydot.com/upstream/white-house-correspondents-dinner-takes/. License free image.

study after research study show that satire consumers score higher when questioned about current issues than most news viewers.³⁵ One of the critical goals of this book is to show how it came to be that consumption of satire helps to inform the public more than consumption of straight news. The facts are in on this one—but my goal is to help explain why that has happened. The satirists have been so good at their comedic coverage of issues that they are now often a source of the news itself, rather than just a commentary on it.

★★★

The story of satire in the Trump era allows us to delve into the very specific ways that the Trump presidency marked a rapidly changing media landscape, one in which satire was more effective at challenging propagandistic fake news and alternative facts than traditional news, and one in which the quick, nimble sass of satire was able to successfully engage with Trump and his supporters' use of social media.

FIGURE 1.9   An example of an average citizen using ironic sass to respond to a Trump tweet.

Source: @TheSWPrincess, *Twitter* 1 May 2018, https://twitter.com/TheSWPrincess/status/991508154482651138. License free image.

Not sure you believe me? Try this for fun. Search the archived comments that followed any given Trump tweet.[36] Sure, there were supporters cheering him on, but, overall, the bulk of replies were critical, and the majority of those critiques were satirical and ironic. In one fun example shown here, an average citizen responded to a Trump boast with sarcastic sass.[37]

The Trump presidency marked a real shift in the typical flow of information from a White House administration to the public. Unwilling to wait and uninterested in being managed, Trump was the first president in U.S. history to constantly take his message straight to the people via a social media platform—*Twitter*.[38] Sure, presidents in the past had made press announcements, given speeches, and addressed the public via the radio, but there is no question that Trump radically adjusted the role of the news media as a conduit for his message. It wasn't just his ability to have an immediate audience that was new, though, it was the fact that when he did connect with the public, he often did so with bluster, lies, alternative facts, and hyperbole. His baseline mode of communication was extreme—a reality that made it hard to parody because he already seemed so absurd. But, as I've explained, that's the catch. Because Trump was such a hyperbolic figure, it turned out that the comedic register of satire was better suited to make sense of him than straight news.

So, what exactly did happen to the news media during the Trump presidency? While it would be fun to blame the decline of political discourse entirely on Trump, that would be a mistake. Well before he was a candidate, the nation was moving steadily toward greater and greater political polarization, and the news media were moving more and more steadily toward favoring sensation, scandal, and punditry over information and serving the needs of their corporate owners more than the needs of an informed citizenry. This shift matters because we saw a substantial part of the public in the 2016 election fall for fake news that often confirmed its existing biases. While the term "fake news" has several registers, made even more confusing by the fact that Trump himself called any negative news about him "fake," here I mean specifically news created to misinform the public, heighten conflict, and influence politics, otherwise known as propagandistic fake news. In the 2016 election, propagandistic fake news stories held the attention of the public to such a great degree that some analysts worried that fake news affected the outcome of the election. This book will trace the role of propagandistic fake news in shaping public opinion, and it will show that, contrary to what one might imagine, satire turns out to be one of the best defenses against that type of fake news—both in terms of attention getting and in terms of how it helps the brain think critically. Because satire is ironic and absurd, it is uniquely suited to serve as a foil for illogical, propagandistic fake news, as well as for irrational, hyperbolic political speech.

At the end of the day, it may be that the real story of the Trump era is the way in which it ushered in a moment in U.S. history during which critical thinking, rational arguments, facts, evidence, and clear logic were truly under threat. Most of the intellectual debates among thinking citizens in the wake of the Trump election circled around how to understand what had happened. Were Trump's voters pissed, angry, bigoted, or just stupid? One thing seemed clear: the nation's collective ability to process reality seemed under threat. How else to make sense of the idea that a reality TV celebrity had beaten one of the most experienced presidential candidates? This book isn't going to answer the question of why Trump won or, even more to the point, why Hillary Clinton lost. But it is going to prove that, even though satire didn't keep Trump out of office, it did some extremely valuable work toward helping keep its audience sane, politically engaged, socially informed, and collectively connected.

★★★

There remains little doubt that the ascendancy of Trump was a head scratcher. But one of the really odd outcomes of the Trump win was the way in which a number of cultural critics chose to blame satirists like Jon Stewart, who stepped down as host of *The Daily Show* in 2015 during the primaries, for the rise of Trump. It is one thing to resist my argument that satire has been politically productive; it's altogether another one to blame satire as the culprit.

Now, to be sure, satire wasn't alone in being blamed for the rise of Trump. Fingers were pointed at Bernie Sanders and his supporters, misogynists who didn't want a female president, narcissistic and clueless millennials, and the desperate white working class.[39] Of course, the Russians occupied their own special place as villains too, especially Russian fake news. But, in my view, the weirdest twist on the blame game was the way in which several publications blamed satire, especially the satire of Jon Stewart and Stephen Colbert, who left his position as host of *The Colbert Report* in 2014 to host *The Late Show*, a more mainstream late-night comedy show.

Even weirder, Stewart and Colbert were not blamed for ending their host roles on *The Daily Show* and *The Colbert Report*, respectively, at a time when our country may have needed their refreshing brand of comedy most; they were blamed for hosting their shows in the first place. In one example of many, Lee Siegel wrote a piece for *The Columbia Journalism Review* on "How Jon Stewart, Stephen Colbert blazed a trail for Trump."[40] In another, Steve Almond described the idea that political satire is good for democracy as a "Bad Story."[41]

While Baldwin's impersonations and all the other satire that went along with his work didn't keep Trump out of office, there is significant evidence that satire did, in fact, help the U.S. public deal with the absurdity of Trump's election. One of the thorny questions that haunts the study of satire and politics is, what can it do? Malcolm Gladwell, for instance, has been another outspoken critic of satire. Satire, according to Gladwell, is an analgesic that helps placate the public, distracting those who should engage in rebellion.[42] According to him, leaders are laughed at rather than meaningfully challenged.[43] "It's not the respectful voice that props up the status quo," Gladwell notes, "it is the mocking one."[44] For Gladwell satire has been "institutionalized."[45] Other critics of satire have wondered if satire has actually played a role in further dividing our nation.

While I'll devote some real space to the criticism of satire in the pages to come, let's walk through a few of the critiques launched by Siegel and Almond because they help to explain some of the ways I'll approach the arguments in this book and because the assumption that satire can't be good for democracy has become commonplace. Siegel claims that Stewart and Colbert "helped create the atmosphere of 'fake news' (formerly known as gossip, rumor, dis- or misinformation) that helped elect Trump, and that currently has the media up in arms."[46] Siegel makes an interesting point—because it is true that satirical fake news and propagandistic fake news both distort the truth. But he misses the fact that there is a substantial difference between satirical fake news that depends on irony, critical thinking, and questioning the status quo and misinforming fake news that preys on fear, bias, and sensationalist hyperbole. Satirical news and fake news literally access different parts of the brain. Not only do they require entirely different cognitive work, but they also yield completely different outcomes. If you read a fake news headline that Hillary Clinton founded a child sex-trafficking ring, and you believe it, you will feel outrage. If you read a *New Yorker* headline that reads "Americans Startled by Spectacle of President Who Can Speak English" shortly after French President Emmanuel Macron addressed the U.S. Congress, you'd be amused, but only after you processed the ironic joke that Macron was able to speak more educated English than our own president at the time.[47]

Sure, to decide between propagandistic fake news and satire news can be messy at times. We have all fallen for a fake news hook, but that's the challenge. If you can't tell the difference between Andy Borowitz and Alex Jones, then you need to hone your reasoning skills, and satire is one of the few readily available sources of media that will help do that.

That's the crazy part of these anti-satire attacks. They often woefully lack any real logic or nuance themselves—a fact made more ironic by their critique of irony. Siegel blurs Colbert's truthiness with Trump's post-truth.[48] He suggests that the public has an inability to discern the difference between irony and idiocy. What's really odd is that he misses the fact that, with a reality TV president in office, we needed to get even better at those skills, not give up on them. Siegel went on to accuse Stewart and Colbert of negatively influencing the news media, leading it to dangerously confuse comedy, mockery, and straight-faced reporting.[49] He misses the point, though, that both shows repeatedly called out the news media for their failures to provide the U.S. public with much-needed information. Who can forget Stewart's appearance on CNN's *Crossfire* in 2004 when he called out the show, especially conservative commentator Tucker Carlson, for dumbing down political debate?[50] In fact, as a sign of his impact, Stewart's intervention led to the cancellation of *Crossfire*.

This means that many critics of satire like Siegel invert cause and effect. The corporate news media were already a circus devoted to scandal and sensationalism well before Stewart and Colbert took the helm on their shows. Colbert and Stewart rose to fame precisely because they filled a gap the media had left open. Their viewers were repeatedly ranked as more informed than those of traditional news outlets because the news media had already dropped the ball.

Critics like Almond make similar mistakes in their arguments. But, with Almond, the critique of satire is that it treats our democracy as a farce.[51] Following in the footsteps of those critics who think that satire leads to a cynical distrust of everyone and everything and thus shuts down citizen engagement with politics, Almond suggests that Stewart and Colbert caused their audiences to distract themselves with laughter when they needed to be actively engaged and serious about issues. He writes about the pre-midterm election rally that Stewart and Colbert held on the National Mall in 2010, "Far from challenging the quacks, Stewart and Colbert proved to be invaluable allies. Their shows insulated viewers from feelings of distress that were an appropriate and necessary response to our historical moment."[52] Almond thinks that Stewart and Colbert helped to usher in an era of "unseriousness" that made the U.S. public disinclined to engage with political debates to a sufficiently significant degree.

What really amazes in these anti-satire critiques is the fact that they tend to be lodged from a position of pure speculation. These anti-satire critics are some of our sharpest cultural critics, and yet, for some reason, they completely ignore the reams of academic scholarship, much of which will be referenced throughout this book, that refute their arguments. They have no proof of what they are saying—but it feels right to them to go after satire.

As mentioned when I started this introduction, it does make sense to wonder whether the rise of satire as a player in shaping political discourse is a good thing. Instincts suggest it can't be good. But that's what research is for. We have a hunch, and then we seek evidence to see if the hunch is right. At a moment when expertise is under attack, it is astonishing to see the anti-satire critics come after political comedy without any real proof, simply because they suspect it is doing damage to our country.

It is also telling that the anti-satire pundits are quick to ascribe power to satire, but only negative power. It is hard to draw a direct line from satire to political action, for instance, but this book will offer several specific examples. Data on the behavior of satire viewers are extensive, and research on the cognitive effects of the consumption of satire is also pretty clear—and both areas of work show specific ways in which satire performs a valuable social role. In order to really uncover the power of satire, the last chapter of *Trump Was a Joke* examines the effects of satire on the brain. Referencing research on the cognitive effects of sarcasm, snark, satire, and irony, this book shows how satire plays a productive role in helping to foster critical thinking, advanced cognitive skills, and rational debate. While the nation has long suffered from a dumbing down of political debate, it is fair to say that the vapid 24/7 cable news cycle, the rise of fake news, the proliferation of extremist views, heightened political polarization, and echo chambers, and the election of Trump marked a low point in the collective intelligence of our democracy. Satire's clear connection to advanced critical-thinking skills is a powerful antidote to collective brain rot. In fact, one of the effects of satire that we can prove without any doubt is the role it plays in engaging high-order thinking.

And yet the anti-satire critics don't seem to have bothered to consult any of that research. So, what might explain that knee-jerk reaction? And what might it tell us about the decline of critical commentary on the left and the right? Almond's book, for example, argues that "bad stories lead to bad outcomes."[53] His theory is that there were lots of "bad stories" circulating in and around the 2016 election that helped to usher in the age of Trump because folks were too attached to narratives that didn't serve the public good. I think he is likely right, but his argument is diminished by the fact that, in many of his examples of "bad stories," he basically has no evidence of any kind. Ironically, he writes that bad stories are "fraudulent either by design or negligence"—yet his own argument about the dangers of satire neglects the facts.

I suspect that there is something in the fun of satire that simply doesn't feel politically authentic to these critics, given the fact that they return again and again to the idea that the pleasure and entertainment of satire are the problem. Yet there is actual evidence that these instincts are wrong. We have proof of the ways that satire viewers are educated on issues and that they are not just more informed but also more engaged in political action. And we have proof that they are smarter, more creative, and more socially connected than those who can't or won't process irony. We have proof that when political actors are having fun, they are more likely to stay engaged and that information presented through comedy helps folks to better remember it. So that's yet another part of the story this book hopes to address. How did some of our most visible cultural critics get so clueless about what satire does?

And that leads me to one of the best examples of political satire in our nation's history and the film title referenced for the title of this chapter. *Dr. Strangelove, Or How I Learned to Stop Worrying and Love the Bomb* was released in 1964 and quickly drew criticism for its biting satire of military culture, Cold War logic, and Texan masculinity.[54] When the film was released, it produced anxiety that it would lead audiences to lose faith in our nation's institutions and cause them to question authority. As John Patterson writes, "There had been nothing in comedy like Dr. Strangelove ever before."[55] Today, though, it is considered to be one of the best films of all time and one of the best examples of how political satire can productively shape public opinion. Patterson describes it as "a comic masterpiece that's also deeply serious and perceptive about the mad military mindset of those times."[56] The point is, when *Dr. Strangelove* was released, folks freaked out that it would harm the nation. Now they see how it offered a smart and insightful take on military mentalities and political hawks—a perspective that was surely valuable when the United States decided to dramatically increase involvement in Vietnam only a few years after the film came out. Rather than do damage to the republic, the film created iconic parodic personas that provided a "good story," to invert Almond, through which to think about pressing political issues.

Dr. Strangelove mocked a ridiculous system and, while it was released in an era that had plenty of political satire—*The Smothers Brothers Comedy Hour* would be launched in 1967, for instance—the presence of satire in the 1960s pales in comparison to what happened in the United States in the Trump era. Research shows that satire emerges in force in moments of crisis, and that may well explain why in the Trump era satire didn't just flourish, it actually became a larger part of the public media landscape than ever before in U.S. history. *Trump Was a Joke* argues that the ongoing power of satire reflects a much broader series of social changes that are connected to shifts in the media, in voting demographics, and in public perceptions of the role of entertainment in political behavior. Satire does more than serve a court jester function of poking fun at a broken system. It invigorates active citizenship and engaged debate of social issues. And, most importantly, it makes sense when politics doesn't.

★★★

The following chapters of this book will trace the core themes outlined in this introduction. "Trump Was a Joke, But It Wasn't Funny" begins by recounting the events of the Washington Correspondents' Association Dinner in April 2011 when both Barack Obama and Seth Meyers made jokes at Trump's expense. Covering the speculation that the jokes that night may well have spurred Trump to decide to run, the chapter offers a history of Trump jokes that date from before his campaign announcement, and it analyzes the "special relationship" Trump has to satire.

The next chapter, "It's Hard to Make a Joke Out of a Joke," opens by looking at the series of *SNL* impersonations that helped to launch the *Twitter* war between Trump and comedians. The chapter then analyzes how the bluster and hyperbole of Trump forced political comedy to use different tactics in its jokes, ones that still used irony, but struggled with the challenge of how to exaggerate an exaggeration. Comedians found themselves often playing it straight and serious to Trump and his team's farce, an inversion that has had a big impact on the way in which these comedians are seen as trustworthy sources of information by the public.

Further analyzing the way in which the Trump era changed the media landscape, the chapter on "The First Media-Created President" delves directly into the ways in which the Trump campaign changed political media coverage. From Trump's tweets, to his relationship to alt-right media, to the rise of propagandistic fake news, the 2016 primaries greatly transformed political media in our country. On broadcast news, Trump so often set the tone and content for coverage that many viewers turned to satirists for more balance and nuance.

The next chapter, "Let's Make Donald Drumpf Again," refers to a line from a February 2016 episode of John Oliver's HBO show *Last Week Tonight*. "Donald Trump is America's back mole," Oliver said.[57] "It may have seemed harmless a year ago, but now that it has gotten frighteningly bigger it is no longer wise to ignore it."[58] The episode focused particularly on Trump's attacks on truth and on logical thinking. Oliver didn't just reframe the conversation; he offered the public a much-needed outlet to vent its frustrations. Thus, this chapter highlights the work of a series of some of the most important Trump-era satirists and analyzes their impact on public dialogue. It then highlights how satire responded to the way in which Trump and his team seemed determined to destroy many of our core democratic institutions, often by taking on the role of conservators of the public good. This trend had begun during the George W. Bush years, but it took on more urgency and became more common after the Trump election.

"The Joke's on You: The Power of Satire" looks at the downside of satire, especially its potential to heighten boundaries between social groups. This chapter surveys the core critiques of satire's social influence. Drawing on the latest research on the social impact of satire, this chapter surveys the scholarship and explains the real risks and rewards of political satire in the current political and media landscape. The chapter surveys a range of critiques of satire, some of which are unsubstantiated by research, and some of which expose its serious risks.

The final chapter, "The Last Laugh," shows how satire is uniquely suited to serve as a foil for the brain rot brought on by much contemporary political discourse. Presenting a range of research from cognitive science to neuroscience, it shows how satire helps to engage the brain in high-order thinking, attention to nuance, analytical reasoning, and contextual reasoning—all skills we need today more than ever. It also shows how the pleasure of the laughs we get from satire may well provide an important antidote to the stress of contemporary politics. It argues that, in the end, the risks to the Trump presidency may have been more cognitive than political, and, if that is true, it means satire has an even greater role to play in saving our democracy than we may have first imagined.

Notes

1 These term descriptions have been lightly modified from my previous co-authored book, McClennen, Sophia A. and Remy Maisel. *Is Satire Saving Our Nation? Mockery and American Politics*. Palgrave Macmillan, 2014.
2 McClennen, Sophia A. "Stephen Colbert Schooled Fox News Hard: Comedy, Bill O'Reilly and the Exposure of Right-Wing Patriotism Lies." *Salon*, Salon.com, December 12, 2014, www.salon.com/2014/12/12/stephen_colbert_schooled_fox_news_hard_comedy_bill_oreilly_and_the_exposure_of_right_wing_patriotism_lies/.
3 Hall, Sean. *This Means This, This Means That*. Laurence King Publishing, 2007, p. 44.
4 Ibid.
5 Suebsaeng, Asawin and Adam Rawnsley. "Trump Wanted His Justice Department to Stop 'SNL' from Teasing Him." *The Daily Beast*, June 22, 2021, www.thedailybeast.com/trump-wanted-his-justice-department-to-stop-snl-from-teasing-him.
6 McAndrew, Frank T. "Politicians Don't Seem to Laugh at Themselves as Much Anymore." *The Conversation*, August 21, 2019, https://theconversation.com/politicians-dont-seem-to-laugh-at-themselves-as-much-anymore-122103. This study shows that making self-deprecating jokes elevates the audience's opinion of a politician. In contrast, jokes that mock a politician can negatively influence the audience's view. Baumgartner, Jody C., Jonathan S. Morris and Jeffrey Michael Coleman. "Did the Road to the White House Run Through Letterman? Chris Christie, Letterman, and Other-Disparaging Versus Self-Deprecating Humor." *Journal of Political Marketing*, vol. 17, no. 3, 2018, pp. 282–300, www.tandfonline.com/doi/abs/10.1080/15377857.2015.1074137.
7 Berman, Lea and Jeremy Bernard. "The Best Joke George W. Bush Ever Told in Office." *Time*, January 9, 2018, https://time.com/5094914/president-jokes/.
8 Dovere, Edward-Isaac. "Meyers, Trump Wanted Me to Apologize On-Air for Making Fun of Him." *Politico*, May 8, 2018, www.politico.com/magazine/story/2018/05/08/seth-meyers-trump-whcd-jokes-apologize-218323/.
9 Flood, Brian. "SNL Is Tougher on Trump Than Past Presidents, But NBC Won't Let Up Anytime Soon, Experts Say." *Fox News*, December 7, 2018, www.foxnews.com/entertainment/snl-is-tougher-on-trump-than-past-presidents-but-nbc-wont-let-up-anytime-soon-critics-say.
10 Balluck, Kyle. "Trump: 'Unfair' Coverage Should Be Tested in Courts." *The Hill*, December 16, 2018, https://thehill.com/homenews/administration/421574-trump-unfair-coverage-should-be-tested-in-courts.

11 Schneider, Christian. "Conservatives Should Not Surrender in Entertainment Wars." *Milwaukee Journal Sentinel*, June 14, 2018, www.jsonline.com/story/opinion/columnists/christian-schneider/2018/06/14/conservatives-should-not-surrender-comedy-war/701802002/.
12 Skolnik, Jon. "Trump Tried to Get Justice Department to Stop 'SNL' and 'Jimmy Kimmel Live' from Mocking Him: RPT." *Salon*, June 22, 2021, www.salon.com/2021/06/22/trump-tried-to-get-justice-department-to-stop-snl-and-jimmy-kimmel-live-from-mocking-him-rpt/.
13 Giuliani-Hoffman, Francesca and Andy Borowitz. "We're Living in an Age That Defies Satire." *CNN Money*, June 12, 2017, https://money.cnn.com/2017/06/12/media/andy-borowitz-interview-reliable-sources-podcast/index.html.
14 "President Trump Suggests 'Injecting Disinfectant as Coronavirus Cure | NBC New York'." *YouTube* video, 0:45, posted by NBC New York on April 23, 2020, www.youtube.com/watch?v=zicGxU5MfwE.
15 Bissel, Tom. "The Tragicomedy of Donald Trump on Saturday Night Live." *Harper's Magazine*, September 13, 2017, https://harpers.org/archive/2017/10/whos-laughing-now/.
16 Ibid.
17 McClennen, Sophia A. and Remy Maisel. *Is Satire Saving Our Nation? Mockery and American Politics*. Palgrave Macmillan, 2014.
18 Jones, Chris. "Alec Baldwin Gets Under Trump's Skin." *The Atlantic*, May 2017, www.theatlantic.com/magazine/archive/2017/05/alec-baldwin-gets-under-trumps-skin/521433/.
19 Carter, Graydon. "A Joke Certainly, but No Laughing Matter." *Vanity Fair*, April 2017, https://archive.vanityfair.com/article/2017/4/a-joke-certainly-but-no-laughing-matter.
20 "120 Funny Donald Trump Jokes." *Humoropedia*, August 8, 2016, https://humoropedia.com/funny-donald-trump-jokes/.
21 Thompson, Mike. "Trump Jumps into the Affirmative Action Fight in Detroit Free Press." *Gannett*, 2017, www.gannett-cdn.com/-mm-/97165843b42a5ce77f7fe8b92940526a7fb616f8/c=53-28-1200-890&r=x513&c=680x510/local/-/media/2017/08/02/DetroitFreeP/DetroitFreePress/636372941952956487-MTEDP1-08-04-17forweb.jpg.
22 "Donald Trump Tweets 'SNL' Spoof Was a 'Hit Job'." *ABC News*, October 16, 2016, https://abcnews.go.com/video/embed?id=42863149.
23 Ibid.
24 De Moraes, Lisa. "Jimmy Kimmel: President Donald Trump Is Completely Unhinged." *Deadline*, Penske Media Corporation, August 15, 2017, https://deadline.com/2017/08/jimmy-kimmel-donald-trump-unhinged-news-conference-charlottesville-neo-nazis-white-supremacists-video-1202149926/.
25 Segarra, Lisa Marie. "Stephen Colbert to Rex Tillerson: 'Nobody Calls Our President a Moron Except Me'." *Time*, October 5, 2017, http://time.com/4970357/stephen-colbert-to-rex-tillerson-nobody-calls-our-president-a-moron-except-me/.
26 Barton, Chris. "Seth Meyers Calls Trump a 'Lying Racist' Over His Charlottesville News Conference." *Los Angeles Times*, Tribune, August 1, 2017, www.latimes.com/entertainment/la-et-entertainment-news-updates-august-seth-meyers-calls-trump-a-lying-1502978870-htmlstory.html.
27 *The Hill*. "Trump Wants 'Equal Time' on TV to Respond to 'Anti-Trump' Jokes." *Twitter*, October 17, 2017, https://twitter.com/thehill/status/916688843239313411/photo/1.
28 Alter, Rebecca. "Alec Baldwin Holds Up a 'You're Welcome' Sign on *SNL*." *Vulture*, Vox Media, November 8, 2020, www.vulture.com/2020/11/no-thanks-alec-baldwin-holds-a-youre-welcome-sign-on-snl.html.
29 "Alec Baldwin 'Overjoyed' to Stop Playing Donald Trump." *Aceshowbiz*. November 9, 2020, www.aceshowbiz.com/news/view/00162283.html.

30. Covucci, David. "Hell Is the Aftermath of the White House Correspondents Dinner." *The Daily Dot*, April 30, 2018, www.dailydot.com/layer8/white-house-correspondents-dinner-takes/.
31. Forgey, Quint. "Trump Vilifies 'Dishonest' Press at Michigan Rally." *Politico*, April 28, 2018, www.politico.com/story/2018/04/28/trump-michigan-rally-media-press-559197.
32. Pengelly, Martin. "'They Hate Your Guts': Trump Attacks Democrats and Media at Michigan Rally." *The Guardian*, April 29, 2018, www.theguardian.com/us-news/2018/apr/29/donald-trump-michigan-rally.
33. Brenan, Megan. "Americans Remain Distrustful of Mass Media." *Gallup*, September 20, 2020, https://news.gallup.com/poll/321116/americans-remain-distrustful-mass-media.aspx.
34. White, Rose. "Do We Trust Comedians More Than Journalists?" *Mediums*, June 12, 2016, https://medium.com/@rosekellywhite/do-we-trust-comedians-more-than-journalists-1a4b46a6588b.
35. See, for example, National Annenberg Election Survey. "*Daily Show* Viewers Knowledgeable About Presidential Campaign." September 21, 2014, www.naes04.org and www.techdirt.com/articles/20141113/06034829128/yet-another-study-shows-us-satire-programs-do-better-job-informing-viewers-than-actual-news-outlets.shtml.
36. You can access the full archive of Trump tweets here: www.thetrumparchive.com/.
37. Trump, Donald J. "The White House Is Running Very Smoothly Despite Phony Witch Hunts etc. There Is Great Energy and Unending Stamina, Both Necessary to Get Things Done. We Are Accomplishing the Unthinkable and Setting Positive Records While Doing So! Fake News Is Going 'Bonkers!'" *Twitter*, April 30, 2018, 4:02PM, https://twitter.com/realDonaldTrump/status/99109037341715251 with reply by @TheSWPrincess.
38. Trump was later banned from the platform in January 2021 and responded by creating his own platform, but during his candidacy and virtually all of his presidency, *Twitter* was his main source of social media attention.
39. Watkins, D. "Dear Hard-Working White People: Congratulations, You Played Yourself." *Salon*, Salon Media Group, November 20, 2016, www.salon.com/2016/11/20/dear-hard-working-white-people-congratulations-you-played-yourself/.
40. Siegel, Lee. "How Jon Stewart, Stephen Colbert Blazed a Trail for Trump." *Colombia Journalism Review*, Colombia University, December 22, 2016, www.cjr.org/special_report/trump_jon_stewart_stephen_colbert.php.
41. Almond, Steve. *Bad Stories: What the Hell Just Happened to Our Country*. Red Hen Press, 2018.
42. Gladwell, Malcolm. "Being Nice isn't Really so Awful." *The New Yorker*, December 10, 2013, www.newyorker.com/books/page-turner/being-nice-isnt-really-so-awful.
43. Ibid.
44. Ibid.
45. Ibid.
46. McClennen, Sophia A. "Don't Blame Jon Stewart for Donald Trump: Comedy Central Didn't Make America Fall for 'Fake News' and 'Post-truth'." *Salon*, Salon.com, December 31, 2016, www.salon.com/2016/12/31/dont-blame-jon-stewart-for-donald-trump-comedy-central-didnt-make-america-fall-for-fake-news-and-post-truth/.
47. Borowitz, Andy. "Americans Startled by Spectacle of President Who Can Speak English." *The New Yorker*, April 25, 2018, www.newyorker.com/humor/borowitz-report/americans-startled-by-spectacle-of-president-who-can-speak-english.
48. Keane, Erin. "From Truthiness to Post-Truth, Just in Time for Donald Trump: Oxford Dictionaries' Word of the Year Should Scare the Hell Out of You." *Salon*, Salon.com, November 19, 2016, www.salon.com/test/2016/11/19/from-truthiness-to-post-truth-just-in-time-for-donald-trump-oxford-dictionaries-word-of-the-year-should-scare-the-hell-out-of-you/.

49 McClennen, Sophia A. "Don't Blame Jon Stewart for Donald Trump: Comedy Central Didn't Make America Fall for 'Fake News' and 'Post-truth'." *Salon*, Salon.com, December 31, 2016, www.salon.com/2016/12/31/dont-blame-jon-stewart-for-donald-trump-comedy-central-didnt-make-america-fall-for-fake-news-and-post-truth/.
50 "Jon Stewart on Crossfire." *YouTube* video, 7:40, posted by Alex Felker, www.youtube.com/watch?v=aFQFB5YpDZE.
51 Almond, Steve. *Bad Stories: What the Hell Just Happened to Our Country*. Red Hen Press, 2018, p. 146.
52 Ibid., p. 150.
53 Ibid.
54 Kubrick, Stanley, dir. "Dr. Strangelove, Or How I Learned to Stop Worrying and Love the Bomb." 1964, https://www.imdb.com/title/tt0057012/.
55 Patterson, John. "Dr. Strangelove: No. 6 Best Comedy Film of All Time." *The Guardian*, October 18, 2010, www.theguardian.com/film/2010/oct/18/dr-strangelove-kubrick-comedy.
56 Ibid.
57 "Donald Trump: Last Week Tonight with John Oliver (HBO)." *YouTube Video*, posted by Last Week Tonight on February 29, 2016, www.youtube.com/watch?v=DnpO_RTSNmQ.
58 Locker, Melissa. "John Oliver Takes on Donald Trump on Last Week Tonight." *Time*, February 29, 2016, http://time.com/4240734/john-oliver-donald-trump-last-week-tonight/.

2
TRUMP WAS A JOKE, BUT IT WASN'T FUNNY

Celebrity businessman Donald Trump arrived at the glitzy White House Correspondents' Association Dinner in April 2011. He mingled with the celebrities, journalists, and politicians who typically attend the event, often dubbed as "nerd prom." He made his way to his table, a guest of Lally Weymouth, journalist, socialite daughter of Katharine Graham, and longtime publisher of *The Washington Post*.[1] The night promised to offer him a chance to build his celebrity cache.

And then it started.

The White House Correspondents' Association Dinner (WHCAD) gathers folks together annually to poke fun at the president, the press, and often other celebrities. The mocking is meant in good fun and celebrates the First Amendment, especially our nation's commitment to free speech and a free press. It typically begins with a comedic monologue by the president and then is followed by a roast of the president by a comedian. As President Barack Obama addressed the audience that night, it quickly became clear that he planned to focus his remarks on Trump, who had recently mentioned he might be interested in running for president in 2012, and who had spent the previous months claiming that there was no evidence that Obama was a U.S. citizen, suggesting he was actually born in Kenya and demanding that Obama produce his birth certificate. He subsequently offered large sums of money in return for Obama's compliance.[2] Just before the dinner, Obama had finally decided to release his birth certificate, which meant, Obama quipped to the audience, that Trump could "finally get back to focusing on the issues that matter. Like: Did we fake the moon landing, what really happened in Roswell, and where are Biggie and Tupac?"[3] He went on to ridicule Trump's gaudy taste and his frivolous TV show, *Celebrity Apprentice*.

But that wasn't all.

Next up was Seth Meyers, the comedian host of *Late Night* on NBC. After Meyers remarked that now that all of his Obama birth certificate jokes were no good,

DOI: 10.4324/9781003294177-2

he, too, went after Trump, who was still bristling from Obama's three-minute roast: "Donald Trump has been saying he will run for president as a Republican, which is surprising," Meyers remarked, "since I just assumed he was running as a joke."[4]

Trump first responded to the barbs with a smile and a wave of the hand, but as the mocking went on and the laughter mounted, his expression became a "frozen grimace."[5] Warm and gracious on his way into the gala, he left looking bruised and determined. Maggie Haberman and Alexander Burns noted, "That evening of public abasement, rather than sending Mr. Trump away, accelerated his ferocious efforts to gain stature within the political world."[6] They suggest that at his core Trump wants "to be taken seriously."[7]

What if, as Chuck Todd remarked in an interview with Meyers one month before the 2016 election, it was that evening of ridicule that gave Trump the drive to prove everyone wrong and run?[8] In fact, not long after Trump announced his decision to run for president on June 16, 2015, a number of commentators speculated that it had been that night of public humiliation that had given Trump the resolve to announce his candidacy.

As Trump's candidacy gained more and more steam, Meyers would be repeatedly called to task as though he were single-handedly responsible for Trump deciding to run in the first place. Meyers, for his part, seemed to enjoy the attention, even quarreling with Jimmy Fallon in February 2017 over which of the two comedians had played a bigger role in getting Trump elected. In contrast to Meyers, who had been criticized for being too harsh on Trump, Fallon had been lambasted for being too soft when he had interviewed candidate Trump on NBC's *The Tonight Show* and mussed his hair. Fallon not only came under fire for not being tougher on Trump—a weird accusation considering he is a comedian after all—but he also saw his ratings drop. He fell from the top slot in his late-night comedy category to the bottom, ceding his spot to Stephen Colbert's *The Late Show* on CBS, which had taken to offering far sharper comedic bite in its treatment of Trump during the campaign.

Fallon would later express regret over his softball treatment of Trump—a move that would then lead Trump to excoriate Fallon publicly via *Twitter*. After hearing of Fallon's regrets, Trump tweeted that Fallon is "now whimpering to all that he did the famous 'hair show' with me (where he seriously messed up my hair), & that he would have now done it differently because it is said to have 'humanized' me." The president then told Fallon to "be a man."[9] Fallon reacted by telling his audience on *The Tonight Show* that he had planned to tweet back at the president right away, but instead realized that he had "more important things to do." "Then I thought, 'Wait, shouldn't he have more important things to do?'" Fallon said to laughs. "He's the president! What are you doing? Why are you tweeting at me?"[10]

Fallon nailed it. Why didn't Trump have better things to do? Why did he get into *Twitter* exchanges again and again with comedians?

The thing is that, over the Trump presidency, this sort of behavior became so common that it was easy to lose sight of exactly how bizarre it was. But in this brief anecdote, I've shown that there really was something different about how Donald Trump dealt with comedy, especially satirical comedy.

One of the curious features of Trump's relationship to comedy during and after his campaign was the way in which he regularly engaged in public battles with comedians over their jokes about him. Sometimes he whined about unfair treatment. Other times he attacked them for not being funny. Still other times he claimed that they were all constantly trying to get him to appear on their shows and that they only went after him when he refused. But no matter which tack his bristling took, he didn't seem to be able to simply ignore the barbs and focus on his work as most presidents do. In fact, the most common tendency for a mocked president is either to ignore the joke, to laugh with it, or to make an even more self-deprecating joke in return—a move that is proven to deflate the initial joke.[11]

It was Trump's constant petulant engagement with comedians over their treatment of him that likely fueled the speculation that the 2011 Meyers roast influenced Trump's decision to run. So, is it possible that the Meyers roast really was the reason why Trump ran for office?

The quick answer is not likely, but it may have served as an extra push.

Let's start with why it isn't likely that that night altered Trump's plans in any way. First, we need to go back and revisit that "fateful" night in a bit more detail. Roxanne Roberts, writing for *The Washington Post*, suggests that most of the conjecture about Trump's response to his public roasting overblows the story.[12] She reminds readers that, before the events of the evening began, reporters already expected Trump to be the subject of jokes.[13] Shortly after he arrived at the event—and before any of the public ribbing had begun—they asked him if he was ready to take some heat. Sure, he told them, "I'm fine with this stuff."[14]

Roberts explains that she was seated behind Trump that night, which made it a bit hard for her to giggle at the jokes lobbed his way. She notes that he took the teasing by Obama in stride but seemed significantly more uncomfortable when Seth Meyers went after him. "The president was making jokes about me," he would later explain.[15] "I was having a great time. I was so honored. I was actually so honored. And honestly, he delivered them well."[16] But as for Meyers: "I didn't like his routine. His was too nasty, out of order."[17]

When Trump appeared on Fox News the next day to discuss the event, as headlines of his humiliation aired constantly in the press, he reiterated that he had found the Meyers jokes unpleasant: "I didn't know that I'd be virtually the sole focus, and I guess when you're leading in most of the polls, that tends to happen," he told *Fox & Friends*.[18] "I thought Seth Meyers, frankly, his delivery was not good—he's a stutterer and he really was having a hard time."[19]

There does seem to be little doubt that the Meyers roast got under his skin. Four years after the 2011 event, Meyers ran into Trump at the *Saturday Night Live* (*SNL*) 40th anniversary special in February 2015, only a few months before the real estate developer's presidential campaign launched. Meyers explains that he used the occasion to ask whether Trump would appear as a guest on *Late Night*, and that at first Trump seemed receptive to the idea.[20] But apparently the proposition was shut down once Meyers refused a demand made by Trump's lawyer at the time, Michael Cohen. According to Meyers, Cohen said that Trump would only appear on the show if Meyers would use it as an opportunity to publicly apologize for making fun of Trump at the WHCAD four years earlier. When Meyers refused to do that, Trump's offer to appear on his show was rescinded.

So, what was it about the Meyers roast that seemed to get to Trump? What did Meyers say that made all of the other jokes about Trump different? We could read a lot into the Meyers roast if it had been a unique experience, but it wasn't. Well before Meyers' 2011 jokes, Trump had regularly been the subject of some pretty brutal roasting. Making fun of him simply was nothing new.

Due to his celebrity status, blustering personality, gaudy style, and weird hair, he was often the subject of jokes. But before we run down jokes that predate the Meyers roast in 2011, it is also important to recall that one of the reasons why Trump was so often a butt of jokes was because he had been talking about running for president since the 1980s, despite having no political credibility whatsoever. Besides being an over-the-top celebrity businessman, some of the reasons why comedians loved to mock Trump were specifically because of his arrogant hubris and his cocky way of suggesting that he knew how to fix the world's problems, despite personally having failed multiple times in his own business dealings. Also critical to remember is that Trump's blustery behavior included repeated mentions that he might run for the highest office in the land.

Below is a timeline of Trump's suggestions that he wanted to run for president to help us put the Meyers-Trump story into perspective.[21] [22]

As NPR reports, it is not just that Trump had spent over 30 years talking about running for president; it is that, for the most part, when asked his thoughts on the matter, he stayed fairly consistent with the same messaging we saw in the 2016 campaign.[23] When you go back and watch old clips of Trump talking about his ideas for the country, you find young Donald Trump sounding very much like the old Trump. In those conversations, he repeated common themes he regularly invoked in his 2016 run—that trade isn't fair, that the world has long laughed at America for not being stronger, and that countries have taken advantage of U.S. generosity while refusing to pay their "fair share."[24]

Talking to Larry King in 1987, he said,

> I was tired, and I think a lot of other people are tired of watching other people ripping off the United States. This is a great country. They laugh at us. Behind our backs, they laugh at us because of our own stupidity.[25]

In that interview, Trump told King that he had accepted an invitation to appear in New Hampshire, understanding full well what that would imply for his potential desire to run for president.[26]

> **The Trump Presidential Run Timeline**
>
> **1987-1988**: Trump considers a run for president, while simultaneously juggling large debts, which stem from his purchase of the Taj Mahal casino.
>
> **October 1999**: Trump announces that he is forming a presidential exploratory committee for the 2000 election.
>
> **2000**: Trump enters the presidential race as a Reform Party candidate and receives more than 15,000 votes in the party's California primary.
>
> **2003-2004**: Trump begins hosting the reality show *The Apprentice* on NBC, which he also executive-produces. He mulls a run for president again but eventually decides not to join the race.
>
> **2010**: Trump suggests he may run for president.
>
> **March 2011**: A *Wall Street Journal*/NBC News poll shows Trump leading all presidential contenders, including Mitt Romney.
>
> **April 2011**: Amid more research, polls indicate that he would be the preferred Republican presidential candidate among voters. Trump repeatedly calls for President Obama to release his long-form birth certificate, questioning whether Obama was actually born in the United States– Obama eventually complies and releases the birth certificate. This is the polling Trump mentions when appearing after the WHCAD on *Fox & Friends*.
>
> **May 2011**: Trump officially announces that he has decided not to run for president.
>
> **February 2012**: Trump publicly endorses Republican candidate Mitt Romney for president.
>
> **2013**: Trump forms a presidential exploratory committee and, despite strong backing from Republican voters, eventually announces that he has no interest in running for governor of New York in 2014.
>
> **February 2015**: Trump decides not to renew his contract for *The Apprentice*, fueling speculation that he's mulling a run for president.
>
> **June 2015**: Trump formally announces that he's running for president in a speech delivered from Trump Tower in New York City.

FIGURE 2.1   Trump presidential run timeline.

In 1988 on *The Oprah Winfrey Show*, Oprah asked him if he'd run, and he replied,

> I just probably wouldn't do it, Oprah. I probably wouldn't, but I do get tired of seeing what's happening with this country, and if it got so bad, I would never want to rule it out totally, because I really am tired of seeing what's happening with this country, how we're really making other people live like kings, and we're not.[27]

He then went on to say,

> I think I'd win. I tell you what; I wouldn't go in to lose. I've never gone in to lose in my life. And if I did decide to do it, I think I would be inclined—I would say, I would have a hell of a chance of winning.[28]

In a 1999 interview with Larry King that took place 12 years after the one just referenced, Trump stated,

> So I am going to form a presidential exploratory committee, I might as well announce that on your show, everyone else does. But I'll be forming that, effective, I believe, tomorrow, and we'll see. We're going to take a very good, strong look at it.[29]

That same year he told Tim Russert on *Meet the Press* that he was serious about running.[30]

This history certainly casts doubt on the idea that it was the roasting by Meyers (and also Obama) in 2011 that gave Trump the idea to run. Clearly, he had been bouncing the idea around for decades. But perhaps what is most curious about this backstory is the fact that a series of commentators had asked Trump to opine on a candidacy. From Oprah to King to Russert, it apparently made sense to these interviewers to ask Trump whether he might run and what his policies might be. And while it would be convenient to wonder whether these questions were just lobbed at him for sport, if you go back and watch the interviews, it is not entirely clear that the questions to Trump about his thoughts on the future of the country were meant to offer him a chance to make a fool of himself. In fact, when we look back on those interviews, it could be argued that it was the pundits and commentators who "normalized" Trump and suggested he was president material. Certainly, these sorts of questions could have given Trump the idea that the public wanted to hear his thoughts on how best to run the country. So, maybe, if anyone is to blame for giving Trump the impetus to launch a campaign, it isn't Seth Meyers but rather Oprah Winfrey, Larry King, and/or Tim Russert. The point, as I'll dig into more in the chapter on Trump as a media-created president, is that part of the reason Trump ran was because the news media had offered him a platform to talk about his policy positions and, rather than treat him as a celebrity, they treated him as a politician. It was that blurring of the lines that then carried over into his presidency itself. Before, during, and after his run, Trump was always a bizarre public figure, one steeped in the spectacle of celebrity. He seemed like such a joke but kept being taken seriously.

The other part of the story that has begun to emerge with more clarity is the fact that the Democrats under Obama actually sought to elevate Trump's visibility. In memoirs from Obama insiders and leaked emails, we now have a fuller picture of the specifically strategic ways that the Democrats and the Obama team sought to turn public attention more directly to Trump. For instance, David Plouffe, Obama's campaign manager and later senior advisor, stated,

> There was strategy. Lifting up Trump as the identity of the Republican Party was super helpful to us. The president went out in the briefing room to present his long-form birth certificate, [but] really to continue the dance with Trump. Our view was lifting Trump up at the White House Correspondents' Dinner, you know, as kind of the example of the Obama opposition. There was a strategy behind the material and the amount of time we spent on Trump. *Let's really lean into Trump here. That'll be good for us.*[31] [32]

We now know that the Democrats' strategy was to elevate Trump because, they thought, he would be an easier opponent to vanquish. Clearly, they didn't see how serious the joke (i.e., Trump) could be.

So, at the very least, maybe before we get too focused on Seth Meyers as the reason the United States found itself with Donald Trump as president, we should take a broader, more nuanced perspective on the various times that political players and the media focused on Trump and encouraged (or provoked) him to run.

Now, let's get back to Trump jokes. Was it possible that the Seth Meyers roast truly got under Trump's skin? And, if so, why? We know that Trump did not seem as upset by Obama's remarks at the 2011 WHCAD. Both right after and for years following the event, Trump wouldn't seem to let go of his outrage over Meyers' performance that night. And, while he seems to be miffed by many comedians, it does appear clear that he really was unnerved by the Meyers performance. So, what made it different?

Before we can process what might have made the Meyers' jokes different for Trump, we have to take a look back at the long history of Trump jokes—especially those that emerged well before April of 2011. It is in looking back at previous Trump mockery that we can begin to grasp the full extent to which this man has regularly been the butt of the joke. Even more importantly, as I noted in the introduction to this book, once Trump became a political candidate, he almost immediately became the most mocked politician of all time. But, in order to understand the Trump-as-politician jokes, we need to appreciate the type of mockery he endured well before then. What we will see as we look back is that the jokes about politician Trump build on the types of jokes that were in place for decades.

While Trump jokes have recurring themes, like his ridiculous hair, taste in women, and undeserved swagger, it is possible to go back and map Trump jokes according to the ridiculous Trump personalities that comedians choose to feature in their jokes. Most Trump jokes focus on the following Trump personas: *The Bragging Businessman, The Reality TV Buffoon, The Birther Conspiracy Theorist,* and *The Absurd Politician.*

The post-2015 Trump jokes often combine a variety of these personas to create a hybrid persona that is the butt of the joke and overlays various over-the-top personality features. One of the things that is critical to note, then, is the fact that the

Trump Was A Joke

From failed businessman to reality TV celebrity and conspiracy theorist to President of the United States

The Bragging Businessman (1988-1992): *Spy Magazine* and *Mad Magazine* taunt real estate mogul Donald Trump for his business failures, bravado, and sensitivities about manhood.

The Future Flop (1999-2000): Darrell Hammond portrays Trump for the first time on SNL, Doonesbury satirizes his future campaign bluster, and *The Simpsons* predict a future President Donald J. Trump who runs the country into the ground.

The Reality TV Buffoon (2004-2010): Trump hosts NBC's *The Apprentice*, later morphing into *The Celebrity Apprentice*, which runs for a total of 185 episodes. Trump's braggadocious business persona becomes part of the cultural landscape and the butt of jokes.

The Birther Conspiracy Theorist (2011-2012): Trump becomes the face of the "birther conspiracy," calling on President Obama to prove he was born in the U.S. Late-night comedians like Jon Stewart, Steven Colbert, and Bill Maher rail against both the conspiracy theory and Trump himself. Seth Meyers and Obama humiliate Trump at the 2011 White House Correspondents' Dinner.

The Absurd Politician (2015-2020): Donald Trump announces that he will seek the Republican nomination for president. His rollercoaster campaign full of controversies and missteps resulted in a surprising general election victory. Alec Baldwin portrays the candidate and new President on SNL and wins a Primetime Emmy Award.

FIGURE 2.2 Trump jokes by the decade.

jokes tend to mock him both as a performance and as a real (real estate) person. The fact that the jokes already flagged his persona as embodying a figurative and literal significance is critical to understanding the ways in which comedy worked to expose both the Trump reality and the Trump spectacle, which, importantly, were never separate modes of his persona.

Another common theme across decades of Trump jokes is the fact that Trump already was an exaggerated, hyperbolic parody of a man. This matters because comedy generally depends on taking an image of a person and exaggerating it. We can note, for example, a number of times that comedians have exaggerated the exaggeration, turning Trump into a total caricature of a human being, as seen for instance in the *Spy* magazine cover from 1990 that depicts Trump as a crying baby businessman—a theme that reappeared with the angry baby Trump balloon that was flown in London when Trump visited there in July of 2018.[33] But, in other examples, the comedian doesn't really elaborate on or exaggerate the already absurd hyperbolic Trump persona, as takes place in a number of the *Doonesbury* cartoons that featured Trump over the years and that have basically "quoted" him in ways that are totally believable.

Many Trump jokes focus on his poor reasoning skills, weak command of the English language, megalomaniacal ego, toxic and fragile masculinity, constant need for attention, bullying racism and sexism, tendency to exaggerate and speak in hyperbole, and extraordinary lack of self-awareness. Jokes that focus on his appearance and demeanor highlight his coiffed hair, orange face, small hands, ill-fitting suits and overly long ties, bizarre hand gestures, awkward facial expressions, bumbling physicality, and accent. Jokes that highlight these physical features are consistent features of jokes about him, regardless of the Trump persona or personas highlighted.

It has to be pointed out that not all Trump comedy is equal. That is, some is just derogatory mocking that makes fun of his small hands or orange face. That kind of humor may be fun in the moment, but it doesn't have much, if any, productive critical or political impact. Most of the examples I'll outline here are satire—the type of comedy that is the focus of this book. Satire depends on irony and helps the audience to think critically about the butt of the joke, while also having a laugh. Those types of jokes help to expose Trump's hypocrisy, hubris, and blustery, bullying behavior. And they do it using sarcasm and irony, wherein they create a figurative representation of Trump that is meant to help reveal the persona by exposing the gap between the joke and the man. But as will also be clear in the types of jokes I'll outline here, many jokes do, in fact, simply make fun of Trump's physicality. This happens frequently because his own ridiculous appearance makes it easy to mock him in that way and because he also is so crass in his assessment of others—regularly calling people ugly or fat, for example.

The Bragging Businessman (1980s–Today)

The first wave of Trump jokes can be categorized as going after his businessman bravado. For the most part, these jokes blend a mockery of Trump's massive ego, his spoiled privilege, his gaudy style, his overconfidence in his business acumen, and his spectacular failures.

Probably one of the best examples of the jokes from this era comes to us from the now defunct *Spy* magazine, which published a satirical advertisement for Trump's book *The Art of the Deal*.[34] In the fake ad from 1988, Trump is referred to as a "Short-Fingered Vulgarian"—an insult that was used 12 more times over the next eight years. In 2016, Senator Marco Rubio, a rival for the Republican nomination, would seize on the small hands bit while mocking Trump.

Trump took such offense to *Spy*'s barbs at his hands that, according to the editors, he sent over a copy of his book *The Art of the Deal* with his hand outlined in bright gold on the cover to prove that he wasn't, in fact, short fingered. He then added a note promising, "If you hit me, I will hit you back 100 times harder."[35] So, then, as now, Trump often threatened those who mocked him. He didn't just attempt to discredit his comedic critics; he often went after them legally. He threatened *Spy* with lawsuits repeatedly.

32 Trump Was a Joke, But It Wasn't Funny

FIGURE 2.3 A 2017 tweet revisits a *Mad Magazine* roast of Donald Trump as lying about his business successes.

Source: @ablington, *Twitter* 16 June 2017, https://twitter.com/ablington/status/875888121635844100. License free image.

Mad Magazine jumped on the mocking-Trump-as-a-successful-businessman bandwagon in 1992.[36] In that issue, Sam Viviano and Mike Snyder ridiculed Trump for his businessman bravado in a cartoon that asked, "When should we believe Donald Trump?" and offered two possible choices: "When he writes a book telling us what a financial genius he is? Or when he has to beg his bankers to 'restructure' his debt because he is broke?"[37] The joke was a brilliant example of how satirical comedy can expose hypocrisy and faulty logic. The cartoon resurfaced when it was tweeted in June of 2017.[38]

One of the most hilarious examples of mocking Trump's businessman bravado persona came from Sacha Baron Cohen who interviewed Trump in character as Ali G for his *Da Ali G Show* in 2003.[39] Cohen's character regularly made his guests uncomfortable by becoming increasingly more ridiculous. In the segment he did with Trump, Trump is visibly uncomfortable. He also makes a total fool out of himself. When Cohen asks him about the history of business, Trump explains that business is as old as human life itself, "Hundreds of millions of years ago, people

FIGURE 2.4 Sacha Baron Cohen interviews Trump in character as Ali G.

Source: Smarty Max, "Ali G donald trump sacha baron Cohen interview," https://www.youtube.com/watch?v=sP5ElraFHHE. License free image.

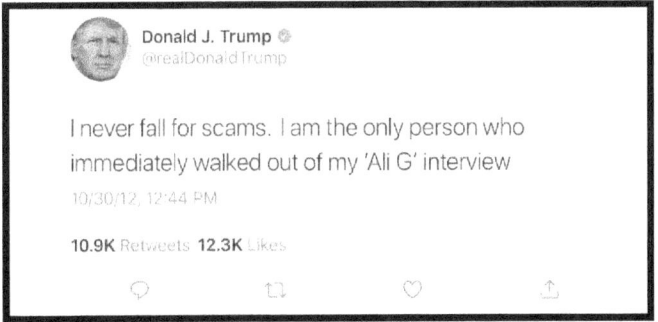

FIGURE 2.5 Trump lies about his experience with Sacha Baron Cohen.

Source: @realDonaldTrump, *Twitter* 30 October 2012, https://twitter.com/realDonaldTrump/status/263335564412076032. License free image.

were doing business, trading in rocks and stones."[40] Eventually Cohen tries to mock Trump's alleged business acumen by pitching an idea for "ice cream gloves."[41]

Trump would later claim that he had walked out on the interview, but it actually lasted almost two minutes—quite long for those types of segments on Cohen's show.[42]

Trump's feud with Sacha Baron Cohen would later be revived as Cohen launched a new show on Showtime titled *Who Is America*, in which he played five different roles and attempted to uncover the absurdities of U.S. society under President Trump. Prior to its debut on July 15, 2018, Cohen aired a few teasers reviving more of his ongoing feud with Trump and suggesting that Trump would be targeted again on the new show.

The Reality TV Buffoon (2004–Today)

After suffering a series of business setbacks in the 1990s (many of which were documented by *Spy*), Trump began to shift from building businesses to licensing his name and profiting from that. He then launched Trump University in 2005, which was largely a scam operation to get people to sign up for workshops and mini courses to learn how to get rich quick in real estate. At the same time that Trump was pivoting in his business dealings, reality TV was taking off as a form of entertainment. Shows like *Survivor* and *American Idol* both topped ratings in the early 2000s. This was the context that led producer Mark Burnett to approach Trump to see whether he would be willing to coproduce a show with Burnett that would be premised on the idea of the "ultimate job interview" in the "ultimate jungle."[43] Burnett suggested that on the show Trump would appear as himself, "a successful businessman with a luxurious lifestyle."[44]

The Apprentice catapulted Trump's media visibility—with his catchphrase "You're fired!" becoming part of the public lexicon. It also led to the emergence of the term "Trumponomics," a

> portmanteau of Donald Trump and economics initially spelled "Trump-Onomics" (2004), [which] started out as a bland managerial concept on cable TV, meant to convey the notion that "impressing the boss" was the only way to "climb the corporate ladder."[45]

This twist in Trump's history offered much fodder for comedians. Every part of his businessman bravado was now exaggerated even further by its transformation into reality TV hubris and spectacle. Trump had now been given a platform to increase his swagger, to have a mass public hang on his every blustery word, and to reinforce the idea that he was the perfect role model of the successful leader.

Gary Trudeau's *Doonesbury* comic offers one of the first examples of a satirist who made jokes about Trump as a politician from very early on in the history of Trump jokes. Trudeau has strips mocking candidate Trump dating back to 1987.[46] Trudeau made a habit of featuring Trump in his comic strips, and his ridicule of Trump covers the full gamut of Trump personas. Beginning in 2004, when *The Apprentice* first aired, Trudeau ran a series of comics that parodied Trump's *Celebrity Apprentice* persona as embodying a blustering megalomaniac.[47]

His strips also did an excellent job of highlighting the way in which Trump demanded that anyone near him be a total and absolute sycophant. And, of course, he made fun of Trump's hair.

The reality TV buffoon identity was mocked regularly by Darrell Hammond in his Trump impersonation for *SNL*. A few of the bits it did parodied Trump's promos for NBC. In a couple of these mock promos, *SNL* makes fun of Trump's need to feel like he's in charge. Hammond's Trump refused to follow directions or chose to follow them but only after taking credit for what they wanted him to do. They also made fun of Trump's constant need to exaggerate his successes and seem

FIGURE 2.6 *Doonesbury* comic strips keyed into Trump as a blustering megalomaniac.

Source: Doonesbury, "Yes, Mr. Trump," © 2004 G. B. Trudeau. Reprinted with permission of Andrews McMeel Syndication. All rights reserved.

important. In one example, Hammond says, "I need to get back to shooting the *Celebrity Apprentice*, which by the way, is getting huge post-air DVR rating hits in the 30- to 35-year-old white male douche demographic."[48]

Trump's reality TV persona would continue to be a feature of jokes launched about him even well after he was not on his show. And it would be this persona that continued to be used to suggest that Trump was not a person to be taken seriously. Those same themes would be present, for instance, in a roast Jimmy Kimmel did of Trump's meeting with North Korean dictator Kim Jong Un on his ABC late-night talk show in 2018.[49] Kimmel mocked Trump's unwillingness to listen to advisors who cautioned that meeting with an unstable dictator was not likely to lead to valuable results. Kimmel, though, reminds his audience that Trump was more about ratings and spectacle than actual statesmanship: "Trump wanted to make it look like he did something big, whether he did something big or not. He was not leaving this summit without claiming he made a deal."[50]

The Birther Conspiracy Theorist (2011–Present)

Rumors that Barack Obama was not eligible to be president because he was not a natural-born U.S. citizen dogged him from the moment that he launched his 2008 campaign. Trump would take up the mantle in 2011 in a particularly spectacular way. In March of that year on *Good Morning America*, Trump mentioned that he was seriously considering a run for president. In that interview, he said that he was a "little" skeptical of Obama's citizenship and that someone who shares this view should not be so quickly dismissed as an "idiot."[51] He went on to say, "Growing up no one knew him"—a claim that was patently false.[52] Trump then went on *The View* and ramped up his comments saying, "I want him to show his birth certificate."[53] Trump speculated that "there's something on that birth certificate that he doesn't like." Then, in an NBC interview broadcast on April 7, 2011, Trump said he would not drop the issue, because he was not satisfied that Obama had proven his citizenship.[54] Because of Trump's relatively high profile, his jumping on the birther bandwagon ramped it up a notch and allowed the conspiracy theory to gain visible traction at a much higher level.

Later, after Obama released his long-form birth certificate on April 27, 2011, Trump decided to consider it a win: "I am really honored and I am really proud, that I was able to do something that nobody else could do."[55] As Trump took credit for forcing Obama to release his long-form birth certificate, he refused to acknowledge that the document proved that he, himself, had been spouting nonsense for almost two months.

Saturday Night Live and Trump 1988 - 2021

The impersonations of Donald Trump on Saturday Night Live (SNL) span three decades and offer an excellent glimpse into the full range of Trump personas that comedians have chosen to highlight. His own two hosting appearances only add to the mix.

Phil Hartmann (1988-90): Hartmann's Trump focused on two key aspects of his persona— his opulent lifestyle, which was totally disconnected from the real world, and his womanizing. A skit from 1988 has him celebrating Christmas with Ivana as they sip Champaign and gift each other diamonds. In the second set of sketches from 1990, the focus is on Trump's headline-making divorce from Ivana and his tabloid-attracting relationship with Marla Maples.

Darrell Hammond (1999-2011, 2015-16): In the first set of skits, Hammond appears as Trump the absurd politician. In one skit where he faces off with Ross Perot (played by Cheri Oteri), Perot explains that they need a new leader to the reform party: "Apparently, fellas, I wasn't insane enough for the American people. What we need is a real nut bag." Then he tries to decide which leader would be better— Trump or Pat Buchanan. Later in that skit, Hammond as Trump makes a comment about immigrants that seems eerily familiar: "They steal and talk funny." Then he goes on to describe how he will glitz up the White House.

Trump as Trump (2004): Trump hosts in 2004 during the first season of *The Apprentice*. "It's great to be here on *Saturday Night Live*, but I'll be completely honest, it's even better for *Saturday Night Live* that I'm here," Trump boasts during his monologue. "Nobody's bigger than me, nobody's better than me; I'm a ratings machine." He then tells the audience, "Television is really just a hobby for me. I'm primarily occupied by my real estate holdings, my best-selling books, and making love to women who have won prizes for their beauty." Hammond as Trump later appeared on stage alongside Trump.

Jason Sudeikis (2012): Sudeikis appears as Trump to mock him as the birther conspiracy theorist. The skit aired shortly after Trump's offer to give $5 million to charity if Obama released his college transcripts on a *Fox and Friends* skit. "I have it on good authority from an African national that I met at a Rainforest Café that President Obama has been texting with some of the world's top terrorists, including Abu Nazir, Jafar, and The Riddler," Sudeikis as Trump says.

Taran Killam (2015): Killam as Trump appeared on the season opener Cold Open alongside Cecily Strong as Melania. The pair welcomes viewers to their "humble gold house." The bit references Trump's alleged sexism, anti-immigrant statements, and other controversies that had emerged during his quest for the Republican presidential nomination.

Trump as Trump (2015): Killam and Hammond helped make a Trump trifecta during his monologue as then-candidate Trump touched on his feud with Rosie O'Donnell. Offering a self-mocking view of his aggressive bullying style, Trump said in the opening, "People think I'm controversial, but the truth is, I'm a nice guy. I don't hold grudges against anybody."

FIGURE 2.7   A timeline of the various times that *SNL* included Trump or impersonations of Trump.

The comedians jumped all over Trump when he publicly joined the birther movement—and of course the notorious roast by Meyers at the 2011 WHCAD falls into this exact category.

But that wasn't the end of it after all. Despite the release of Obama's long-form birth certificate, Trump wouldn't drop his obsession with the idea that Obama was duping the U.S. public. On October 24, 2012, Trump released a web video that was broadcast on various media outlets. In it, he offered to donate $5 million to the charity of Obama's choice if Obama would produce his college transcripts and passport applications before October 31, 2012.[56] Trump suggested that his efforts were in the "public interest."[57]

That Trump stunt was simply too ridiculous for the comedians to ignore. Jon Stewart and Stephen Colbert, who hosted back-to-back shows on Comedy Central at the time, both immediately went after Trump. In the bit by Stewart, he runs down Trump's offer and tells his audience he will show them the clip of it, but what the audience sees is just a gorilla eating shit.[58] It was a classic example of how satire can use an analogy to expose something completely ridiculous. A key feature of Stewart's coverage of Trump's stunt was the way he used it to call out the media—a constant theme in his satire. He reminded viewers that perhaps the dumbest part of the story was the fact that the media covered Trump's offer like it was news. Stewart mocked the media's enthusiastic attention to Trump's stupidity and pointed out that Trump was turning the media into a joke—a line of critique from comedians about the failures of the news media that continues today.

Colbert's mocking of Trump was even more over-the-top. Recounting Trump's $5 million offer to Obama, Colbert offered one in return. He'd give Trump $1 million if he could "dip his balls in his mouth."[59] The absurdity of Colbert's offer served to highlight the absurdity of Trump's. Trump had characterized his offer as a way to raise money for charity, and so, too, did Colbert. Colbert's gross over-the-top offer drew attention to how crass Trump's was as well. Colbert held up an ironic mirror to Trump, one that helped make it easier to see Trump's stunt in its full-blown ridiculous reality.

But the real prize for mocking Trump as a birther conspiracy theorist goes to Bill Maher. Riffing off the absurdity of Trump's offer, during an interview in January 2013 with Jay Leno on *The Tonight Show*, Maher offered to donate $5 million to charity if Trump provided a copy of his birth certificate proving that he was not "spawn of his mother having sex with an orangutan."[60] That seemed like a pretty obvious joke, but Trump took him seriously and actually sent him a copy of his birth certificate and a list of charities he wanted to receive the money. When Maher didn't pay up, Trump sued him.

Maher responded to the lawsuit with this retort: "This is known as parody, and it's a form of something we in the comedy business call a joke," Maher said. "Just like we're the gun country, we're the joke country. We love our free speech, and we love celebrities getting taken down a peg. So, Don, just suck it up like everybody else."[61] Trump later dropped the suit, having been publicly shamed for even bringing it to begin with.

On September 16, 2016, as the Republican Party presidential nominee, Trump conceded, "President Barack Obama was born in the United States. Period."[62]

Despite the fact that he had claimed to put the controversy to rest five years prior, then reinitiated it, he chose once again to suggest that acknowledging a well-documented fact was a win for him, and he gave himself credit for resolving it. Despite finally conceding the point, comedians continued to mock him for his birtherism and penchant for conspiracy theories.

The Absurd Politician (1987–Present)

Mocking Trump as a politician has a long pre–candidate Trump history too. The first well-known example comes from a *Doonesbury* cartoon in 1987. Since then, comedians have mocked the idea of Trump as a politician, president, and statesmen repeatedly.[63] *Doonesbury*, in fact, has repeatedly made the same joke, mocking Trump's endless need for attention. The core of these types of jokes is the idea that Trump is woefully unprepared to lead, yet somehow has been given the chance to do it. Many of these jokes, then, are aimed as much at a society mesmerized by spectacle as they are at the spectacle itself.

In one noteworthy example of this type of joke from well before Trump had formally entered into politics, *The Simpsons* did an episode imagining the future titled "Bart to the Future." In that episode from 2000, Lisa Simpson has been elected president succeeding the presidency of Donald Trump.[64] Lisa is being briefed on the economy and learns that she has an economic disaster to correct that she inherited from President Trump.[65] As producer Dan Greaney explained it,

> What we needed was for Lisa to have problems that were beyond her fixing, that everything went as bad as it possibly could, and that's why we had Trump be president before her. That just seemed like the logical last stop before hitting bottom. It was consistent with the vision of America going insane.[66]

The entire episode was meant, he explains, as "a warning to America."[67]

In another example from 2013, when John Oliver was guest hosting *The Daily Show* while Jon Stewart was off, Oliver shows a clip of a news program mentioning that Trump is considering a run for president in 2016. Oliver responds by forcefully saying to Trump, "Do it. Look at me. Do it."[68] He then goes on to try to encourage him more, "I will write you a check right now on behalf of this country, which does not want you to be president, but which badly wants you to run."[69]

Oliver would later rerun that clip in a November 2016 episode of *Last Week Tonight*, apologizing for his "responsibility" for Trump's candidacy.[70]

The jokes about politician Trump follow a similar set of themes: that he is a celebrity and not a politician, that he has no clue about politics, that he is too much of a narcissist to be a good leader, and that a Trump campaign will be nothing but a media circus. Of course, one key feature of the pre-2016 jokes is that they often presume that Trump could never win—a factor that makes revisiting them today especially interesting. In the jokes that surfaced before Trump announced he really would run, comedians mocked him hard because they didn't take him seriously at

FIGURE 2.8 *Doonesbury* mocks the long history of Trump campaigning to boost his celebrity.

Source: Doonesbury, "Our thanks to the caller," © 2015 G. B. Trudeau. Reprinted with permission of Andrews McMeel Syndication. All rights reserved.

FIGURE 2.9   John Oliver apologizes for the time when he begged Donald Trump to run while guest hosting *The Daily Show*.

Source: "Last Week Tonight," episode 88, HBO, November 7, 2016.

all. As this book will show, after he was elected, the tables turned, with comedians recognizing the serious risks posed by a Trump presidency often well before the news media did. Their jokes about Trump as president then were meant to help reveal that he may be a joke, but it wasn't funny.

The Roast of All Roasts: The 2011 Comedy Central Trump Special

I've run down the long, complex history of Trump jokes that predate the 2011 WHCAD. That backstory helps to establish a number of things: that Trump had long been the subject of some fairly vicious mockery, that there was a range to the type of Trump personas that comedians targeted, and that the jokes tended to mock his massive ego, braggadocio, personal failures, ridiculous appearance, gaudy style, lack of ethics, hypocrisy, sexism, bigotry, privilege, and incompetence. We've also touched on the fact that Meyers was not the first comedian to get to Trump. Trump attempted to sue Bill Maher, threatened *Spy* magazine with various lawsuits, and also publicly insulted comedians who had targeted him well before the April 2011 event.

But before we decide what made the Meyers roast potentially different, there is one more example of Trump mockery that predated that night that needs to be examined. In March of 2011, only a little over a month before the WHCAD when Obama and Meyers mocked Trump, Comedy Central aired a 90-minute celebrity roast of Trump.[71] As the tagline to the show put it, "Real estate mogul, *The Apprentice* host and helmet-hair aficionado Donald Trump gets roasted by Seth MacFarlane, Snoop Dogg, Lisa Lampanelli, The Situation and more."[72] The show also included Jeffrey Ross, Marlee Matlin, Larry King, and future producer of the Trump-supporting *Roseanne* revival, Whitney Cummings.

The roast opens by framing a day in Trump's life, from his point of view. The images in the opening include a branded helicopter and a ride with a young blonde who shares his limo to Trump Tower, where deals are struck and campaign posters approved. As Trump departs, he gets a kiss from a beauty queen. Then as the show actually starts, Trump himself enters on stage in a golden golf cart flanked by sash-wearing models amidst a shower of cash. Trump then takes the stage personally to initiate the roast. At the time, he is clearly not just on board with the joke, he is reveling in it.

The Comedy Central roast remains, thus far, one of the most scathing takedowns of Trump to date, not only because the jokes keep coming at him for 90 minutes, but also because the jokes are delivered with a brutal edge. He's mocked for his opulence, his treatment of women, his incestuous attraction to his daughter, his business failures, his braggadocio, his absurd political ambitions, his sexism and racism, and, of course, his hair—all while not only he, but also Melania, Ivana, and his daughter Ivanka are all in attendance. "As a developer, Donald Trump has done so much damage to the New York skyline, instead of calling him 'The Donald' they should call him the 20th hijacker," joked comedian Gilbert Gottfried.[73]

What folks who focus on the Meyers roast forget is that many of the Comedy Central roast jokes made fun of Trump's political ambitions as well. Seth MacFarlane made a joke far more brutal and edgy than Meyers' "I just thought he was running as a joke" comment. MacFarlane stared right at Trump and delivered this massively insulting line: "It's pronounced, 'I am fucking delusional' not, 'I am running for president.'"[74] Snoop Dog, who Trump would later tussle with on *Twitter* after he was elected, also pulled no punches when he made fun of Trump's presidential ambitions: "Donald says he wants to run for president and move on into the White House. Why not? It wouldn't be the first time he pushed a black family out of their home."[75]

When Comedy Central decided to air the roast seven years later on the exact same weekend that Michele Wolf delivered her scathing Trump roast at the 2018 WHCAD to a room absent the president, the *LA Times* wondered what had happened to the man who could take a joke.[76] Pondering whether it was age, power, or repeated exposure to ridicule that wore Trump's skin down, the *Times* pointed out that

> at one point the future president appeared on some level to be in on the joke—or at least willing to pretend to be so in the name of furthering his wealth, his fame or, as referenced numerous times during "The Roast," his political ambitions.[77]

But there is more to the story, and it may provide the evidence we need to understand why Meyers' roast got to Trump so badly. On October 11, 2016—less than a month before the election—*Huffington Post* ran a story that explained a lot more about why Trump was apparently ok with the Comedy Central roast.[78] *Huffington Post* interviewed most of the key figures involved with planning the roast, and it even obtained copies of draft jokes marked up by Trump with a black Sharpie.

Apparently, well before any jokes were written, Trump's team made it known that two subjects were off-limits: Trump's past bankruptcies and any suggestion that he was not as wealthy as he claimed to be. Trump's assistant Rhona Graff also made it clear that roasters should address Trump only as "Mr. Trump." (Snoop Dog, as noted earlier, did not follow this rule).

One of the critical features of a roast is the rebuttal—the moment when the roastee gets a chance to joke back. Because Trump wasn't a comedian, the roasters drafted his text for him. The writers forwarded a draft to Trump in early March. A week later, he responded with his first set of edits, which can be found linked to the *Huffington Post* article. It quotes one of the writers, who mentioned in surprise that Trump had actually blacked out the punchlines of jokes. Scrapping punchlines, he added, represents "a classic lack of an understanding of how a joke works."[79]

Trump's edits were all over the place. He took out crass comments but added them in elsewhere. He changed punchlines to other ones that were far less funny. Trump also suggested a slam against the entire dais: "Their all losers and I like associating with loser because it makes me feel even better about myself." (The grammar mistakes are Trump's.) Even more revealing, Trump seemed to need to boost himself any chance he got. He changed a line that read, "I'm sorry, I must go now and make a million dollars somewhere else," to a "billion" dollars.[80]

What all of this shows is that Trump needed to feel like he was in control—even if he clearly wasn't. Trump had a hard time understanding the comedic elements of the roast but focused instead on the lines in a more literal way. And he needed the

FIGURE 2.10 Trump delivers his rebuttal and has the final word at the Comedy Central roast.

Source: Comedy Central Facebook status, 29 April 2018, https://www.facebook.com/watch/?v=10156217619054030. License free image.

jokes to work to elevate his celebrity, which is why he agreed to the roast to begin with. "So many people are initially intrigued by the idea and then it starts to cook in the brain and then they pass," said Rick Austin, who served as producer for the Trump roast.[81] "The more that we learned about Donald Trump along the way, the more it became obvious that Donald Trump is up for anything, so long as you are talking about him."[82]

It's worth pointing out that a roast, by nature, only happens to someone important, visible, and publicly interesting. Average people are not roasted. The concept of the roast is that a well-known, recognizable figure with a larger-than-life personality is made fun of. The jokes are designed to show that they are good natured and that a good ribbing won't affect their status. Thought of this way, it is not that surprising that Trump agreed to the roast. It was free publicity. As the show closes, Trump the politician has the last word. Suggesting a possible run that never materialized in 2012, he promises the crowd, "You will have the great pleasure of voting for the man that will easily go down as the greatest president in the history of the United States: Me."[83] Trump had the last word—and he used it to brag and campaign. What was not to like?

Back to the Meyers 2011 Roast

This is all to show that the real reason why Meyers may have gotten to Trump was because Trump was not in control of Meyers' bit. He didn't feel in on the joke (even if in the past when he did feel in on it, he was the butt of it). And even more importantly, the jokes did not help to elevate him. As Meyers explained to *Politico*, when he first worked with Trump on the 2004 *SNL* episode that Trump hosted, it seemed like Trump couldn't understand comedy. "He did not strike me as somebody who had ever even processed if something was funny or not," Meyers said.[84] "If the joke was about him being handsome or rich, he liked it. If the premise was based on his looks or his success, he would say, 'Oh, I like that.' But he wouldn't laugh or smile."[85] Meyers then went on to describe a sketch that Trump wanted to scrap for the 2004 *SNL* episode. According to Meyers, once Trump could see that the audience liked the bit, he got more and more into it—in much the same way that he would learn to repeat catchphrases that fired up his audiences at his campaign rallies.

These observations make assessing Trump's connection to comedy relatively simple: if Trump thinks he can get good attention because of the joke, he likes it. If he feels threatened by it, he doesn't. And that is why Meyers bothered him so much and the Comedy Central roast didn't.

The Meyers performance also bothered Trump's supporters. In one epic example, then Trump insider Omarosa Manigualt told PBS after Trump was elected that those who laughed at Trump's expense the night of the 2011 WHCAD would now have to respect the fact that he had won: "Every critic, every detractor, will have to bow down to President Trump. It's everyone who's ever doubted Donald, whoever disagreed, whoever challenged him. It is the ultimate revenge to become the most powerful man in the universe."[86]

And, in the end, that is also a critical part of the story. For Trump and his supporters, some jokes spark a need for revenge. For the *New Yorker*'s Adam Gopnik, who was present at the 2011 WHCAD, it seems clear that that was the night that changed everything:

> On that night, Trump's own sense of public humiliation became so overwhelming that he decided, perhaps at first unconsciously, that he would, somehow, get his own back—perhaps even pursue the presidency after all, no matter how nihilistically or absurdly, and redeem himself.[87]

Even though Gopnik misses the fact that Trump had long signaled his interest in running, he may well be right that there was an element of revenge that motivated Trump to prove those who laughed at him wrong.

One thing is clear: for a man who has a high opinion of himself, Trump is laughed at a lot. As Graydon Carter puts it, "For a preening narcissist who takes himself terribly seriously, being the butt of the joke heard round the world has got to hurt."[88]

This is one of the greatest challenges of understanding Trump's special relationship to comedy. He isn't just the most mocked politician of all time—racking up a solid three decades of jokes to date and a post-2016 election global footprint of jokes that is truly astonishing—he is particularly absurd and extremely easy to make fun of. The way he looks and speaks, the ideas he espouses, his behavior, his faulty logic, his penchant for bullshit and attachment to lying—all of this and more make it extremely easy to lob jokes his way. "[Trump] turned himself into an object of ridicule," Meyers pointed out, explaining why so many comedians were targeting him.[89] "This is a case of judo, where you're using someone else's momentum against them. It's not like we're attacking. We're just sort of like steering his weight and letting him take himself down."[90] Later, when confronted by Van Jones in a 2018 CNN interview about whether his 2011 jokes caused Trump to run, Meyers turned serious and explained that his comedy is designed to target hypocrisy wherever and whenever he finds it.[91] Trump, Meyers explains, simply just offers lots of opportunities for that.[92]

So, the story here is not just that Trump has been a joke for decades; it is also that the comedians have also been extremely good at highlighting his absurdities and offering the public the chance to unpack the various ridiculous Trump personas. Certainly, Larry King, Oprah Winfrey, and Tim Russert weren't able to find a way to deflate Trump's bluster when they interacted with him on their shows; if anything they amplified it. This is why during the 2016 campaign and after, the news media regularly treated comedians like major players in shaping the public's view on politics. The humorous analyses of Trump were often just much better at exposing the truth of Trump than straight news. This trend had started earlier when Jon Stewart and Stephen Colbert hosted their back-to-back satire news shows on Comedy Central regularly targeting Fox News, but by the time of Trump's run, it had become even more common for comedians to be taken as serious players in shaping public opinion. After the election, Colbert on CBS's *The Late Show* shot past NBC's *Tonight Show* with Jimmy Fallon in TV ratings once Colbert turned his focus to using his comedy to trash Trump. Every major news outlet covered Alec Baldwin's impersonations of Trump. ABC's Jimmy Kimmel became a national sensation when he broke into tears while talking about his infant son's heart surgery and what it taught him about needing to fight Trump's desire to destroy Obamacare.[93] Suddenly goofball Kimmel was making headlines in the *New York Times*.[94] And that's just a small set of examples of how comedians were setting the national conversation about the Trump presidency.

So, just as the biggest joke was elected president, the comedians who made fun of him were taken the most seriously.

Even since he lost the 2020 election, Trump jokes show no sign of waning. Comedians like Jimmy Fallon, who tried to play it soft with Trump at first, have jumped into the Trump joke fray. According to Bill Carter, political humor in the Trump era sailed into "absolutely uncharted" territory.[95] "There's no example of any kind of sustained attack like this on a politician."[96]

But here's the thing. Wounded ego aside, Trump really was a joke. His candidacy, his presidency, and his refusal to honor the results of the 2020 election, otherwise known as the "big lie," have all been absolutely absurd on every level. Trump was elected president without ever serving the nation in any capacity at all. This was a man with no military service, no political experience, and only the flimsiest understanding of what the three branches of government even do. He speaks at a fourth-grade level, and he was elected president of the United States. Even worse, once he was elected, he surrounded himself with a gaggle of inept idiots, a group I described before he even took office as a *kakistocracy*—government by the worst.

As Meyers explained for *Vox*, "The White House has the best writers' room in comedy."[97] Trump and his team kept churning out the absurdities, and the comedians kept using jokes to make sense of them. The more insane the presidency was, the more sense the comedians made when they made fun of it. While traditional news scrambled to appear balanced and to offer views from "all sides," it was the comedians who were able to target the farce and folly of Trump in ways that were both satisfying and smart for their audiences.

But here's the really weird part. Before Trump was elected, if I had told you that a billionaire reality TV star with no political experience and a blustering, uneducated manner would be elected to the highest office in the land, you would have thought that I was joking. And yet, here we are. The Trump era turned everything on its head. What seemed like a joke was real, and what should be serious became ridiculous. Trump ushered in an era of cognitive dissonance, and that is why satire, which often uses critical irony as its dominant communicative mode, did such a good job of sorting it out. "Trump may be a joke," Carter remarks, "but the chaos and destructive forces around him are not."[98]

This means that Trump was a joke, but it wasn't funny.

And, for what it is worth, the idea that we are even discussing whether a joke led to the most ridiculous president in U.S. history is also a joke. So, while Seth

Meyers likely does not deserve credit (or castigation) for getting Trump to run, there is little doubt that Trump had such a highly unusual connection to comedy that the jokes about him may well have made history.

But, as this book will make clear, Trump may well have been a joke, and he may well have led to a new type of satirical comedy designed to help make sense of him, yet everything about Trump as a joke was serious. Not only did Trump have a special relationship to comedy that then led comedy to play a unique role in the Trump era, but it was also satirical comedy that became the most successful communicative mode for making sense of the absurd nature of the Trump presidency. Satire is a unique form of comedy that aims to educate, inform, and call bullshit. Sure, it likes to entertain and get laughs, but that is not its primary goal or, at least, that is never its entire goal. When the president lies, makes things up, regularly twists the truth, and doesn't understand how to run a government, satirical comedy is able to use jokes to get at the truth. And in Trump's case, political comedians had been doing that for decades.

To add to the irony of my point about the increasing power of comedy in the Trump era, Trump himself repeatedly suggested that comedians play a powerful role in shaping political views. In a tweet from October 7, 2017, almost a year after he was elected, meaning that the Equal Time rule for media no longer applied because there wasn't a campaign in place, Trump said, "Late Night hosts are dealing with the Democrats for their very 'unfunny' & repetitive material, always anti-Trump! Should we get Equal Time?"[99] To which Jimmy Kimmel replied, "Excellent point Mr. President! You should quit that boring job—I'll let you have my show ALL to yourself #MAGA."[100]

While Kimmel's suggestion was funny, it turns out that the last thing we would have ever wanted was for the comedians to leave their jobs and stop helping to make sense of the biggest and most disturbing joke our nation has ever known. The rest of this book will explain why.

FIGURE 2.11 Jimmy Kimmel mocks Trump for worrying about comedians.

Source: @jimmykimmel, *Twitter* 7 October 2017, https://twitter.com/jimmykimmel/status/ 916674867734355968. License free image.

Notes

1. Haberman, Maggie and Alexander Burns. "Donald Trump's Presidential Run Began in an Effort to Gain Stature." *The New York Times*, March 12, 2016, www.nytimes.com/2016/03/13/us/politics/donald-trump-campaign.html.
2. "President Obama Roasts Donald Trump at White House Correspondents' Dinner!" *YouTube* video, 5:33, from the White House Correspondents' Dinner on MSNBC on April 30, 2011, posted by "SuchIsLifeVideos" on April 30, 2011, www.youtube.com/watch?v=k8TwRmX6zs4.
3. Teague Beckwith, Ryan. "Watch President Obama Troll Donald Trump in 2011." *Time*, August 10, 2015, https://time.com/3991301/donald-trump-barack-obama/.
4. "Seth Meyers Slams Donald Trump at White House Correspondents' Dinner!" *YouTube* video, 3:27, from the White House Correspondents' Dinner on the Place for Politics on April 30, 2011, posted by "SuchIsLifeVideos" on May 1, 2011, https://youtu.be/Mv4MzaGk2VI.
5. Haberman, Maggie and Alexander Burns. "Donald Trump's Presidential Run Began in an Effort to Gain Stature." *The New York Times*, March 12, 2016, www.nytimes.com/2016/03/13/us/politics/donald-trump-campaign.html.
6. Ibid.
7. Ibid.
8. "Seth Meyers Offers 'Sincerest Apologies' for Trump | MTP Daily | MSNBC." *YouTube* video, posted by MSNBC on October 10, 2016, www.youtube.com/watch?v=wvDlMxGNe74.
9. Trump, Donald J. "@jimmyfallon Is Now Whimpering to All That He Did the Famous 'Hair Show' with Me (Where He Seriously Messed Up My Hair), & That He Would Have Now Done It Differently Because It Is Said to Have 'Humanized' Me-He Is Taking Heat. He Called & Said 'Monster Ratings.' Be a Man Jimmy!" *Twitter*, June 24, 2018, 5:01 p.m., https://twitter.com/realDonaldTrump.
10. Pallotta, Frank. "Jimmy Fallon Responds to Trump: 'Why Are You Tweeting at Me?'" *CNNMoney*, June 26, 2018, https://money.cnn.com/2018/06/26/media/jimmy-fallon-trump-response/index.html.
11. McAndrew, Frank T. "Politicians Don't Seem to Laugh at Themselves as Much Anymore." *The Conversation*, August 21, 2019, https://theconversation.com/politicians-dont-seem-to-laugh-at-themselves-as-much-anymore-122103. This study shows that self-deprecating jokes elevate the audience's opinion of a politician. In contrast, jokes that mock a politician can negatively influence the audience's view. Baumgartner, Jody C., Jonathan S. Morris and Jeffrey Michael Coleman. "Did the Road to The White House Run Through Letterman? Chris Christie, Letterman, and Other-Disparaging Versus Self-Deprecating Humor." *Journal of Political Marketing*, vol. 17, no. 3, 2018, pp. 282–300, www.tandfonline.com/doi/abs/10.1080/15377857.2015.1074137.
12. Roberts, Roxanne. "I Sat Next to Donald Trump at the Infamous 2011 White House Correspondents' Dinner." *The Washington Post*, April 28, 2016, www.washingtonpost.com/lifestyle/style/i-sat-next-to-donald-trump-at-the-infamous-2011-white-house-correspondents-dinner/2016/04/27/5cf46b74-0bea-11e6-8ab8-9ad050f76d7d_story.html?noredirect=on&utm_term=.0ca400193f5f.
13. Ibid.
14. Ibid.
15. Ibid.
16. Ibid.
17. Ibid.
18. Donovan, Laura. "Trump on WHCD Jokes Against Him: 'Is There Anyone Else They Could Talk About?'" *Yahoo News*, May 1, 2011, https://news.yahoo.com/news/trump-whcd-jokes-against-him-anyone-else-could-203203408.html.
19. Ibid.

20 Dovere, Edward-Isaac. "Meyers: Trump Wanted Me to Apologize On-Air for Making Fun of Him." *Politico Magazine*, May 8, 2018, www.politico.com/magazine/story/2018/05/08/seth-meyers-trump-whcd-jokes-apologize-218323.
21 "Here's a Timeline of Every Time Donald Trump Ran for President | TV Guide." *TVGuide.com*, July 28, 2015, www.tvguide.com/news/donald-trump-presidential-campaign-timeline/.
22 "Superior Court of California: County of Los Angeles, Plaintiff Donald J. Trump Complaint for: (1) Breach of Contract, Donald J. Trump v. William Maher, Scott S. Balber." *The Hollywood Reporter*, February 4, 2013, www.hollywoodreporter.com/sites/default/files/custom/Documents/ESQ/Trump_Maher.pdf.
23 Gonyea, Don and Domenico Montanaro. "Donald Trump's Been Saying the Same Thing for 30 Years." *NPR*, January 20, 2017, www.npr.org/2017/01/20/510680463/donald-trumps-been-saying-the-same-thing-for-30-years.
24 Ibid.
25 "Donald Trump: 'I Don't Want to Be President'—Entire 1987 CNN Interview (Larry King Live)." *YouTube* video, 19:21, from CNN from September 2, 1987 on May 9, 2016, https://youtu.be/A8wJc7vHcTs.
26 Ibid.
27 Campbell, Colin. "'I Think I'd Win': Donald Trump Teased a Presidential Run on Oprah in 1988." *Yahoo News*, Yahoo, September 11, 2015, www.yahoo.com/entertainment/s/donald-trump-told-oprah-striking-144055581.html.
28 Ibid.
29 Gonyea, Don and Domenico Montanaro. "Donald Trump's Been Saying the Same Thing for 30 Years." *NPR*, January 20, 2017, www.npr.org/2017/01/20/510680463/donald-trumps-been-saying-the-same-thing-for-30-years?t=1562266080485.
30 "Transcript for February 22th." *NBCNews.com*, February 23, 2004, www.nbcnews.com/id/4304155/ns/meet_the_press/t/transcript-feb-th/#.XR5KIy2B0_U.
31 Abrams, Brian. *Obama: An Oral History*. Little A, 2018, p. 215.
32 This same strategy would be also implemented by the Clinton campaign. They called Trump a "pied piper candidate" and wanted the press to take him seriously (www.salon.com/2016/11/09/the-hillary-clinton-campaign-intentionally-created-donald-trump-with-its-pied-piper-strategy/).
33 Feirstein, Bruce. "Trump's War on 'Losers': The Early Years." *Vanity Fair*, August 12, 2015, www.vanityfair.com/news/2015/08/spy-vs-trump.
34 Ibid.
35 Ibid.
36 Even, Dan. "Fact Check: Did MAD Magazine Lampoon Donald Trump in 1992?" *Snopes.com*, June 28, 2017, www.snopes.com/fact-check/did-mad-magazine-publish-a-trump-cartoon-in-1992/.
37 "MAD Magazine Did Run a Satirical Donald Trump Cartoon in 1992." *The Associated Press*, October 19, 2018, https://apnews.com/article/fact-checking-2360472598.
38 Allison, F. "My Son Found This Mad Magazine from 1992 That We Had Kicking Around." *Twitter*, June 16, 2017, https://twitter.com/ablington/status/875888121635844100.
39 "Sacha Baron Cohen Recalls the Ali G – Donald Trump Interview." *YouTube* video, 3:09, posted by Seif Soudani on January 31, 2017, www.youtube.com/watch?v=W_ref_Xly7Y.
40 "Ali G Donald Trump Sacha Baron Cohen Interview." *YouTube* video, posted by Smarty Max on November 6, 2016, www.youtube.com/watch?v=sP5ElraFHHE.
41 Ibid.
42 Trump, Donald J. "I Never Fall for Scams: I am the Only Person Who Immediately Walked Out of My 'Ali G' Interview." *Twitter*, October 30, 2012, 10:44 a.m., https://twitter.com/realDonaldTrump/status/263335564412076032.
43 "The Apprentice (U.S. TV Series)." *Wikipedia*. June 6, 2019, https://en.wikipedia.org/wiki/The_Apprentice_(U.S._TV_series).

44 Firzli, Nicolas J. "Understanding Trumponomics." *Analyse Financiere*, January 26, 2017, http://analysefinanciere.org/2017/01/26/understanding-trumponomics/.
45 Ibid.
46 "Doonesbury Comic Strips by Garry Trudeau." *The Washington Post*, 1993, http://doonesbury.washingtonpost.com/strip/set/89.
47 "Doonesbury by Garry Trudeau." *GoComics*, October 1, 2004, www.gocomics.com/doonesbury/2004/10/01.
48 "NBC Promos—Saturday Night Live." *YouTube* video, 4:03, from Saturday Night Live on March 7, 2009, posted by Saturday Night Live on September 3, 2013, www.youtube.com/watch?v=2XMVNV98Vbw.
49 De Moraes, Lisa. "Jimmy Kimmel Mocks Donald Trump's Reality TV Pact with Kim Jong Un." *Deadline*, June 13, 2018, https://deadline.com/2018/06/jimmy-kimmel-donald-trump-kim-jong-un-summit-video-1202409518/.
50 Ibid.
51 Marr, Kendra. "Donald Trump, Birther?" *Politico*, March 17, 2011, www.politico.com/story/2011/03/donald-trump-birther-051473.
52 Ibid.
53 "Donald Trump on *The View*, March 23, 2011, Trump Wants to See Obama's Birth Certificate." *YouTube* video, 7:33, from *The View* on March 23, 2011, posted by "trumprulezdotcom" on March 25, 2011, www.youtube.com/watch?v=emkDpm_vQDg.
54 Ibid.
55 Scherer, Michael. "Birtherism Is Dead, But the Birther Industry Continues." *Time*, April 27, 2011, http://swampland.time.com/2011/04/27/birtherism-is-dead-but-the-birther-industry-continues/.
56 Goldman, Russell. "Donald 'Bombshell' Fails to Blow Up." *ABC News*, October 24, 2012, http://abcnews.go.com/Politics/OTUS/donald-trump-fails-drop-bombshell-offers-cash-obama/story?id=17553670.
57 "Superior Court of California: County of Los Angeles, Plaintiff Donald J. Trump Complaint for: (1) Breach of Contract, Donald J. Trump v. William Maher, Scott S. Balber." *The Hollywood Reporter*, February 4, 2013, www.hollywoodreporter.com/sites/default/files/custom/Documents/ESQ/Trump_Maher.pdf.
58 *The Daily Show with Jon Stewart*, Season 18, Comedy Central, October 24, 2012.
59 "Donald Trump's October Surprise—The Colbert Report (Video Clip)." Comedy Central, October 24, 2012, www.cc.com/video-clips/ifrr4g/the-colbert-report-donald-trump-s-october-surprise.
60 "Bill Maher's Offer to Donald Trump," *Politico*, January 10, 2013, www.politico.com/video/2013/01/bill-mahers-offer-to-donald-trump-009594.
61 Gardner, Eriq. "Donald Trump Withdraws Bill Maher Lawsuit." *The Hollywood Reporter*, September 12, 2019, www.hollywoodreporter.com/thr-esq/donald-trump-withdraws-bill-maher-432675.
62 Pramuk, Jacob. "Trump: 'President Barack Obama Was Born in The United States. Period'." *CNBC*, September 16, 2016, www.cnbc.com/2016/09/16/trump-president-obama-was-born-in-the-united-states-period.html.
63 *Doonesbury*. "Our Thanks to the Caller." April 5, 2015, http://i.cbc.ca/1.377 0163.1474374775!/fileImage/httpImage/image.jpg_gen/derivatives/original_620/doonesbury.jpg.
64 "Simpsons Predicted Donald Trump Presidency." *YouTube* video, 3:28, from *The Simpsons*, posted by Report al MID on March 18, 2016, www.youtube.com/watch?v=L-m_WxGPpOU.
65 Ibid.
66 Parker, Ryan. "'Simpsons' Writer Who Predicted Trump Presidency in 2000: 'It Was a Warning to America'." *The Hollywood Reporter*, June 26, 2019, www.hollywoodreporter.com/live-feed/simpsons-writer-who-predicted-trump-876295.

67 Ibid.
68 "John Oliver Regrets Begging Donald Trump to Run for President." *The Hollywood Reporter*. November 7, 2016, www.hollywoodreporter.com/news/john-oliver-donald-trump-president-944682.
69 Ibid.
70 "*Last Week Tonight*." Episode 88, HBO, November 7, 2013.
71 "Roast of Donald Trump—Roast of Donald Trump." Comedy Central, March 15, 2011, www.cc.com/episodes/a85pxi/roast-of-donald-trump-roast-of-donald-trump-season-1-ep-101.
72 Ibid.
73 Ibid.
74 Ibid.
75 Ibid.
76 Barton, Chris. "Revisiting Comedy Central's 'Roast of Donald Trump,' When 'President Trump' Was a Punchline and Trump Could Take a Joke." *Los Angeles Times*, April 27, 2018, www.latimes.com/entertainment/tv/la-et-donald-trump-roast-20180425-story.html.
77 Ibid.
78 Libit, Daniel. "The Inside Story of Donald Trump's Comedy Central Roast Is Everything You Thought It Would Be." *The Huffington Post*, October 11, 2016, www.huffingtonpost.com/entry/the-inside-story-of-donald-trumps-comedy-central-roast-is-everything-you-thought-it-would-be_us_57fbed42e4b0e655eab6c191.
79 Ibid.
80 Ibid.
81 Ibid.
82 Ibid.
83 Ibid.
84 Dovere, Edward-Isaac. "Meyers: Trump Wanted Me to Apologize on Air for Making Fun of Him." *Politico*, May 8, 2018, www.politico.com/magazine/story/2018/05/08/seth-meyers-trump-whcd-jokes-apologize-218323/.
85 Ibid.
86 Mazza, Ed. "'Every Critic, Every Detractor, Will Have to Bow Down to President Trump'." *The Huffington Post*, September 23, 2016, www.huffingtonpost.com/entry/omarosa-bown-to-president-trump_us_57e47e34e4b0e80b1ba15296.
87 Gopnik, Adam. "Trump and Obama: A Night to Remember." *The New Yorker*, June 19, 2017, www.newyorker.com/news/daily-comment/trump-and-obama-a-night-to-remember.
88 Carter, Graydon. "The Trump Presidency Is Already a Joke." *Vanity Fair*, March 22, 2017, www.vanityfair.com/news/2017/03/graydon-carter-trump-presidency-is-already-a-joke.
89 Blanc, Jarrett and Jeff Greenfield. "Meyers: Trump Wanted Me to Apologize On-Air for Making Fun of Him." *Politico*, May 8, 2018, www.politico.com/magazine/story/2018/05/08/seth-meyers-trump-whcd-jokes-apologize-218323.
90 Ibid.
91 "Seth Meyers Full Explosive Interview with Van Jones." *YouTube* video, 18:53, from Seth Meyers interview on June 16, 2018, posted by Ed Sanora on June 16, 2018, www.youtube.com/watch?v=oMRJDVuLems.
92 Ibid.
93 "Jimmy Kimmel Reveals Details of His Son's Birth & Heart Disease." *YouTube* video, 2:05, posted by Jimmy Kimmel Live on May 1, 2017, www.youtube.com/watch?v=MmWWoMcGmo0.
94 Itzkoff, Dave. "Jimmy Kimmel on Health Care, National Tragedies and Twitter Feuds." *The New York Times*, October 15, 2017, www.nytimes.com/2017/10/15/arts/television/jimmy-kimmel-politics.html.

95 Rutenberg, Jim. "Colbert, Kimmel and the Politics of Late Night." *The New York Times*, September 24, 2017, www.nytimes.com/2017/09/24/business/colbert-kimmel-and-the-politics-of-late-night.html.
96 Ibid.
97 Framke, Caroline. "How Late Night with Seth Meyers Became the Calm in a Political Comedy Storm." *Vox*, August 25, 2017, www.vox.com/culture/2017/8/25/16189952/seth-meyers-interview-trump-2017.
98 Carter, Graydon. "The Trump Presidency Is Already a Joke." *Vanity Fair*, March 22, 2017, www.vanityfair.com/news/2017/03/graydon-carter-trump-presidency-is-already-a-joke.
99 "Trump Hits Back at Late Night Shows Critical of Republicans." New York Public Radio, *The PBS NewsHour*, October 7, 2017, www.wnyc.org/story/trump-hits-back-at-late-night-shows-critical-of-republicans/.
100 Kimmel, Jimmy. "Excellent Point Mr. President! You Should Quit that Boring Job—I'll Let You Have My Show All to Yourself #MAGA." *Twitter*, October 7, 2017, 7:41 a.m., https://twitter.com/jimmykimmel/status/916674867734355968?lang=en.

3
IT'S HARD TO MAKE A JOKE OUT OF A JOKE

The story of Seth Meyers and Donald Trump pales in comparison to that of Alec Baldwin and Trump. If there was speculation about the degree to which Meyers got under Trump's skin, there is no doubt whatsoever that Baldwin's impersonations of Trump for *Saturday Night Live* (*SNL*) sent him into a frenzy. We know this because Trump had a habit of watching the show when Baldwin was on and then tweeting insults during or after the show. It was not the first time that a comedian had bothered a politician, but it certainly was the first time that a candidate for president chose to publicly and immediately whine about the comedian's bit to the entire world via *Twitter*. Unlike Meyers, Baldwin is not principally known as a political satirist or even as a comedian. Nor is he especially noteworthy as an impersonator. But, when Baldwin decided to impersonate candidate Trump for *SNL*, his performance immediately became the stuff of legend.

Baldwin first impersonated Trump on October 1, 2016, for *SNL* on the premiere of its 42nd season, replacing Darrell Hammond who had impersonated candidate Trump for *SNL* earlier in the campaign.[1] Hammond's Trump was essentially a bombastic buffoon; Baldwin's Trump was an entirely different creature. The new *SNL* version of Trump was mean, racist, sexist, narcissistic, toxic, and disgusting. In his initial appearance, parodying the first debate between Trump and Hillary Clinton, Baldwin's Trump lobbed insults at everyone around him. He referred to moderator Lester Holt (played by *SNL* regular Michael Che) as "Coltrane" and "jazzman"; he accused Clinton and Barack Obama of taking his microphone "to Kenya" and breaking it, then he demeaned Monica Lewinsky, calling her "very heavy."[2] As *The Atlantic* pointed out in a piece following Baldwin's debut as Trump, this new version of the candidate painted him "as a sneering racist, rather than a harmless blowhard."[3] More importantly, Baldwin's Trump only slightly exaggerated Trump's own words. "The thing about the blacks is that they're killing each other,"

Baldwin barked in the sketch.[4] "All the blacks live on one street in Chicago . . . it's called Hell Street, and they're on Hell Street, and they're all just killing each other, just like I am killing this debate."[5]

SNL already had a long history of mocking Trump, as explained in the previous chapter, and it also had allowed Trump to host the show twice. Trump appeared as host once in 2004 during his stint as host of *The Apprentice*, and again in November 2015 in an episode that led to significant controversy as viewers urged SNL to dump Trump, fearing that allowing him to host would legitimize his candidacy. Nevertheless, SNL, which has tended to frame itself as nonpartisan, went ahead with Trump as host, even though no other candidate had been offered such a chance. In the opening monologue, Trump mocked his own ego: "It's wonderful to be here. I will tell you this is going to be something special. Many of the greats have hosted, as you know, this show, like me in 2004."[6] He also announced, "Part of the reason I'm here is that I know how to take a joke. They've done so much to ridicule me over the years. This show has been a disaster for me."[7] As his response to the Baldwin impersonations would later show, though, Trump clearly could not take a joke, and SNL was about to elevate its ridicule of him to a new level. If he thought of the show as a disaster for him in 2015, after he won the election, it got a whole lot worse.

Before Baldwin's appearance as Trump, it was comedians like Stephen Colbert who offered the public the sort of Trump impersonation designed to have political impact. When Trump announced his run for office, Colbert was off air, having stepped down as host of Comedy Central's *The Colbert Report* to prepare to take over as the new host of *The Late Show* for CBS. His new show wasn't set to debut until September 8 of 2015, but Colbert seized the opportunity and released a YouTube video spoofing Trump, "Announcing an Announcement," which posted on the same day (June 16, 2015) that Trump announced his candidacy.[8] Channeling his persona at the White House Correspondents' Association Dinner when he roasted President George W. Bush, Colbert managed to mock not just Trump's behavior but also his political platform: "Ladies and gentleman, I'm pleased to announce that I have an announcement to make: Donald Trump has announced he is running for President of the United States."[9] And, in exactly the same fashion as his WHCAD performance, the humor was both flat and eviscerating. "I agree with Donald that America is dead—buried in a coffin, in salted earth with our enemies pissing on it and laughing," he said.[10] "And Donald Trump is the only man who can—excuse me, I'm just moved—I'm physically moved by the knowledge that Donald Trump is the only man who can dig up the corpse of that nation and marry it."[11] The brilliance lay in the way in which Colbert channeled Trump's crazy, nonsensical, overblown, egomaniacal blather while being Trump and adoring Trump at the same time. Colbert went on for six minutes and managed to highlight many bizarre Trump idiosyncrasies. In one moment, he literally foamed at the mouth.

The other comedian to take an early stab at a politically hard-hitting Trump impersonation was Anthony Atamaniuk, who first appeared as Trump in

August 2015 on various improv shows. In October 2015, he appeared alongside James Adomian, who impersonated Bernie Sanders, for a fake debate.[12] The success of that pairing led to a "Trump vs. Bernie" tour that eventually grew to about 40 cities and some international destinations like Amsterdam, Dublin, and London. They then took their act to Comedy Central's @midnight, billing the encounter as "the socialist vs. the sociopath." Both Atamaniuk and Adomian were openly anti-Trump, and there was little doubt that the object of their satirical comedy was to help audiences see the difference between Sanders' socialist populism and Trump's narcissistic, faux populism. Atamaniuk would appear as Trump with characteristic bronzer on his face and a Make America Great Again baseball hat on his head and say things like, "I'm killing everyone in the polls—and if I'm elected president, I'll kill everyone. I promise you that."[13]

The success of Atamaniuk's impersonation led to *The President Show* on Comedy Central which aired April–November 2017.[14]

"Laughing at the President is a proud American tradition and we hope not to disappoint anyone in that department," Atamaniuk said as the show was being announced.[15] "But our political system is too broken for us to be content joking about one man, even though he is a disastrous silly little toddler boy."[16] The show format had Atamaniuk as Trump attempting to bypass the "crooked media" by hosting his own TV news program from the Oval Office. He appeared alongside Peter Grosz in character as Vice President Mike Pence. After an opener and a pretaped piece, the show had Atamaniuk conduct an interview in character with a guest. Keith Olbermann appeared on the premiere. While the show didn't have quite the same degree of public impact—Trump didn't tweet about it, it wasn't the

FIGURE 3.1 Atamaniuk as Trump on *The President Show*.

Source: *The President Show*, Comedy Central, https://www.cc.com/shows/the-president-show. License free image.

topic of mainstream news coverage, and it had a far smaller viewership than *SNL*, rarely topping a half million viewers—it did offer the public a valuable take on Trump. As *The Atlantic* put it, Atamanuik's Trump did an excellent job of tapping into Trump as a "self-promoter with the energy of a carnival barker and a deep well of insecurity."[17]

How Baldwin Got (and Got to) Trump

Colbert's Trump bit and Atamaniuk's ongoing impersonation offered some of the most politically incisive renditions of candidate Trump—that is, up until Baldwin stepped in and made impersonation history. Once Baldwin took up the mantle of Trump, his impersonations immediately influenced public opinion, affecting those both for and against Trump.[18] But where Baldwin really made history, as will be discussed later, was in the way in which his performance affected Trump directly, leading Trump to complain via *Twitter*. Trump's *Twitter* rants then offered the public a chance to directly engage the candidate and interact with the comedy. The first time in U.S. history that we had an *SNL* impersonation of a candidate shape an election outcome was when Tina Fey impersonated Sarah Palin during the 2008 election. Research has concluded that Fey's version of Palin had devastating consequences for the McCain-Palin ticket.[19] In contrast, Baldwin's impersonations did not keep Trump out of office, but there is little doubt that Baldwin's version of Trump had a substantial impact on public perception of the candidate.

Baldwin impersonated Trump five separate times between October 1 and Election Day 2016, appearing in all but one of the pre-election episodes of *SNL*'s 42nd season. The impersonations not only invigorated *SNL*'s ratings but also finally offered *SNL* viewers an edgy, gloves-off version of Trump. Unlike the sillier version offered by Hammond, Baldwin's Trump was frightening. Hammond had played Trump for *SNL* largely according to the persona he had developed when Trump starred on *The Apprentice*. The result was tepid comedy at best. Hammond's candidate Trump was smug and clueless, a toothless rendition considering that the real Donald Trump he was mimicking was calling Mexican immigrants rapists and criminals at the time. Hammond's lame Trump joined other bland impersonations like Jimmy Fallon's innocuous mirroring of Trump.[20]

Baldwin's Trump came far closer to Colbert's than to Hammond's. In the five times he portrayed Trump in the lead-up to the election, he showed Trump to be paranoid, sexist, racist, aggressive, and frighteningly stupid.

Baldwin's Trump only went slightly beyond the original. Similar to the way in which Fey impersonated Palin, much of Baldwin's impersonation was often a copy of what Trump had already done. The power of this sort of impersonation is that when we see absurd behavior mimicked by another person, the obvious farce and extreme stupidity are easier to notice. In one example, Baldwin loomed over Kate McKinnon's Clinton in the sketch after the second debate in much the same way that Trump actually seemed to stalk Clinton in the original event, except on *SNL* the stalking happened to the music of *Jaws*.[21] That performance marked the first

56 It's Hard to Make a Joke Out of a Joke

Baldwin as Candidate Trump
The actor's five impersonations on SNL before the 2016 election

10/1/16- Baldwin debuts Trump impersonation during his cold open of the Season 42 premiere. The skit satirizes the 2016 Presidential Election debate between Trump and Hillary Clinton. Baldwin's over-the-top and braggadocious depiction of the Republican nominee earns immediate praise.

10/08/16- A spoof of the previous week's Vice Presidential Debate between Tim Kaine and Mike Pence is interrupted by breaking news– the release of the *Access Hollywood* tape. Baldwin's Trump doubles-down in the aftermath on CNN.

10/15/16- SNL's take on the second presidential debate parodies Trump's stalking of Clinton around the informal town hall setting with the *Jaws* theme music in the background. Baldwin's Trump espouses racist and sexist views throughout the debate.

10/22/16- In the third and final presidential debate parody on SNL, Baldwin's Trump and McKinnon's Clinton exchange jabs just weeks before the election. Trump is defensive against sexual assault allegations and refuses to say if he'll accept the results of the election– largely mirroring direct quotes from the real-life Trump that week.

11/05/16- In their final appearance before the election, SNL's Trump and Clinton make their final appeals on *Out Front with Erin Burnett,* before breaking the 4th wall and wandering arm-in-arm with one another into Times Square, where they reluctantly embrace one another's supporters.

FIGURE 3.2 Baldwin as candidate Trump.

Source: *Saturday Night Live,* NBC, https://www.youtube.com/user/saturdaynightlive. License free image.

time that Trump would directly tweet about Baldwin on *SNL*.[22] "Watched Saturday Night Live hit job on me. Time to retire the boring and unfunny show. Alec Baldwin portrayal stinks. Media rigging election!"[23]

The tweet is a perfect example of the cognitive dissonance that Trump likes to use when going after critics. He first insults the critic as terrible at what they do; then he

FIGURE 3.3 The first time Trump tweets an attack on *SNL* and Alec Baldwin.
Source: @realdonaldtrump, *Twitter*.; *Saturday Night Live*, NBC.

suggests that they have immense power over him and it isn't fair. How can the show be boring and unfunny, but also capable of rigging the election? Even more importantly, as I'll explain in the next chapter, the tweet also showed that, for Trump, *SNL* was as likely to influence voters as mainstream news outlets like CNN. From his view, the news media and the comedic satire media were all the same thing.

In Baldwin's third debate sketch, Trump whines about the media again. Tom Hanks plays Chris Wallace and asks Trump to explain why he thinks the media isn't fair to him. Baldwin's Trump begins by saying that the media is making "him look so bad."[24] "And how are we doing that?" asks Hanks' Wallace.[25] "By taking all of the things I say and all of the things I do and putting them on TV," Trump answers.[26] In that bit, Baldwin emulated Trump's odd sniffling during the actual debate, while also uttering incomprehensible gibberish about foreign policy. Meanwhile, McKinnon's Clinton looked alternately bored, irritated, and smug.

A major feature of the Baldwin impersonations was Trump's toxic masculinity. By playing Trump as a sexual predator who imagined that he was constantly desirable, Baldwin was able to call out the specific ways in which Trump tied his misogyny in with his political persona. In the impersonation of the first debate, Baldwin's Trump made multiple sexual references, such as "I am going to be so calm and so presidential that all of you watching are going to cream your jeans."[27] The next week, when Baldwin played Trump in the sketch that addressed the leaked tape in which Trump admitted "grabbing women by the pussy," not only was Baldwin's Trump incapable of apologizing, but he was also incapable of adjusting his behavior: "Women, if you give me a chance, I promise, I can do a whole lot more than just grab it—I can bop it, twist it."[28] Baldwin's just a bit more over-the-top version of Trump caused women (and men) across the country to cringe in disgust.

Impersonating an Impersonation of a President

Looking back on these first five Baldwin impersonations, one thing remains clear: both the comedians and the audience expected Trump to lose. If anything, in hindsight, McKinnon's Clinton seems painfully glib about a likely win. This would all change in the next iteration of the Baldwin impersonations: the ones with president-elect Trump. Given the centrality of Baldwin's candidate Trump impersonations, it was no surprise that, after the election, his version of Trump dominated the scene. Suddenly, Baldwin's Trump was no longer a joke about a joke; now it was a joke about a serious joke. In the first post-election episode of *SNL*, Baldwin made no appearance, but the central theme of the show was Trump's victory. McKinnon gave a heart-wrenching rendition of recently deceased Leonard Cohen's "Hallelujah," and the mood was fairly somber.[29]

After the election, Baldwin's Trump now joined the long history of presidential impersonations—a comedic habit in this country since the John Kennedy era, when comedians first started emulating and embellishing the personality traits of presidents to great comedic effect.[30] After the Watergate scandal, comedian David Frye mocked Richard Nixon's paranoia and insecurity. And who could forget Chevy Chase's bumbling, clumsy Gerald Ford? Yet, what makes the Baldwin impersonation unique thus far in the history of presidential impersonations is that it went far beyond an effort to emulate a president's mannerisms and habits of speech. Baldwin's Trump didn't just act and speak like Trump; his performance revealed a raw and disturbing view of the man. Yet, beyond wanting to expose the "real" Donald Trump to the public, Baldwin had a particular challenge in his post-election Trump persona. And that was the fact that Trump himself often seemed to be impersonating a politician. Again and again in his public appearances, Trump had already seemed like an impersonation of a presidential candidate on the campaign trail. He appeared bewildered as he meandered off topic in the middle of sentences. His speech patterns were laughable and incoherent. His hand gestures, staging, and props added to the sense that he was just pretending. His childish insults and adolescent defensiveness already sounded ridiculous. It's not just that he didn't seem serious; it's also that he seemed to so openly be playacting. The performative quality to Trump's public persona presented a unique challenge to comedians who impersonated him: it's hard to mock a mockery.

Impersonations depend on the art of parody—on not being the person you are being. The gap between a serious original and a comedic imitation is where much of the comedy lies. Presidential impersonations typically depend on a few key features: the audacity of mimicking one of the most powerful people on the planet, the ability to emulate and exaggerate key features of a "unique" personality, and the ability to poke through the public veneer of a world leader and reveal a private, vulnerable, average person. But most important is that the impersonation is typically expected to exaggerate, to take characteristics of the original person and embellish and enhance them. It's generally all in the name of good fun—an example of mostly goofy humor that serves to deflate the aura of a public figure for a moment.

Impersonations are not always comedic, of course. In fact, impersonations have two main registers: entertainment or fraud. One is an example of identity theft; the other is an example of silly mockery. And that of course is why impersonating President Trump was such a tricky art. Trump already seemed to be impersonating a president—faking it and offering the U.S. public the fraudulent posturing of a man who is pretending to be president. While impersonations are often a form of flattery—calling attention in the end to the power of the individual rather than really undercutting that power in any significant way—some impersonations can and do serve to reframe how the public thinks about the person being parodied. Baldwin's impersonations went a long way to unmasking Trump and making it difficult for the audience to lose sight of his belligerent and bigoted demeanor. There is also little doubt that one of the prime sources of powerful impersonations in U.S. politics has been *SNL*, a show that has repeatedly created parodic images of presidents and politicians that have literally shaped public perceptions of the individuals.[31] Yet Baldwin's *SNL* impersonations were unlike any that the show had ever aired because they went far beyond mocking physicality and habits; they worked to present Trump as a toxic male and an incompetent politician. That is why Baldwin's impersonations were such a refreshing and powerful alternative to the fluff offered by comedians like Hammond and Fallon. Baldwin's impersonations laid bare the bombastic and performative qualities of Trump's persona, and they highlighted the specific aspects of his political platform that were blatantly antidemocratic.

While the idea of impersonating an impersonation was funny during the campaign, it took on a new urgency after the election. In the post-election *SNL* sketch that aired in November, Baldwin portrayed Trump as entirely confused about what it meant that he had actually won.[32] As Outi J. Hakola points out, Baldwin's post-election Trump "still used the pursed lips, but instead of signaling aggressiveness, these now expressed inexperience with an almost child-like pout and insecure look."[33] Once again Baldwin was accompanied by McKinnon, this time appearing as a fatigued and overwhelmed Kellyanne Conway.[34] In the sketch, Baldwin's Trump begins to greet high-ranking guests, but then it hits him: this is no longer just a performance, and his words are no longer just empty campaign slogans.[35] People may actually expect him to follow through on the things he has promised. Rather than imagine that he might consult with actual experts, his response is to ask Siri for help: "Siri, how do we kill ISIS?"[36] The scene is brilliant satirical comedy. While this moment is totally fabricated, the public could actually believe that Trump might ask Siri rather than a qualified advisor. He already had a history of going on *Twitter* rants in the early hours of the morning, refusing to answer substantive policy questions, and surrounding himself with sycophants and extremists. Unlike any president before him, he seemed entirely unwilling to consult advisors with expertise on any subject.

In another post-election *SNL* sketch, Trump can't stop retweeting during a security briefing.[37] The retweets highlighted in the sketch were actual events: Trump had, in fact, done that—but the brilliance of the sketch was the way in which viewers had to come to grips with the potential reality of when and where

ALEC BALDWIN'S TOP TEN TRUMP IMPERSONATIONS ON SATURDAY NIGHT LIVE

POST-2016 PRESIDENTIAL ELECTION TO 2018 MIDTERM ELECTIONS

1 PRESIDENT-ELECT TRUMP - 11/19/16
In his first appearance since the 2016 election, Baldwin's Trump - now president-elect - meets with advisers and worries about keeping his promises, asking Siri how to defeat ISIS at one point.

2 TRUMP AND KANYE IN THE OVAL - 10/13/18
In a parody of Kanye West's bizarre rant the week prior, Trump finds himself unable to focus before finally realizing West is just "black me."

3 TRUMP CALLS WORLD LEADERS - 02/04/17
In his first appearance since being sworn into office, Baldwin's Trump, joined by a Grim Reaper depicted by Steve Bannon, places troubling calls to leaders around the world.

4 TRUMP JOINS *THE O'REILLY FACTOR* - 04/08/17
Trump is a guest on Bill O'Reilly's show, where he attempts to defend the host against sexual assault and harrassment allegations. Baldwin plays both characters.

5 TRUMP IN *PEOPLE'S COURT* - 02/11/17
Trump faces off against judges from the Ninth Circuit Court in a parody of the popular court drama as they face-off over the travel ban.

6 TRUMP AND THE CHRISTMAS "GHOSTS" - 12/02/17
Baldwin's Trump is visited by three Christmas ghosts - Michael Flynn, Billy Bush, and Vladimir Putin - before finally coming face-to-face with Hillary Clinton.

7 TRUMP, COHEN, & STORMY DANIELS - 05/08/18
Donald Trump's personal attorney Michael Cohen (played by Ben Stiller) uses one of his many phones to call porn star Stormy Daniels (playing herself), who Trump can't resist talking to.

8 SEAN SPICER CONFRONTS TRUMP - 05/13/17
Press Secretary Sean Spicer (played by Melissa McCarthy) presses Trump about rumors that he will be replaced by Sarah Huckabee Sanders.

9 TRUMP CAN'T STOP TWEETING - 12/03/16
In his second appearance as president-elect, Baldwin's Trump keeps interrupting his security briefing in order to retweet followers praising him on Twitter.

10 TRUMP CALLS INTO *FOX AND FRIENDS* - 02/03/18
The President calls into his favorite morning show to brag about his first year in office and complain about the media.

FIGURE 3.4   Alec Baldwin's Top Ten impersonations of Trump on *SNL*.

those retweets happened. The audience knew that the idea of the president-elect retweeting a high school kid was absurd, but to have that take place in the context of a security briefing was comedic genius. By then, the public had already learned that Trump was skipping these meetings and denigrating their value to him, yet when the audience had to grasp the reality that Trump considered a retweet of a high school kid more urgent than the acquisition of knowledge about global affairs, it drove home the idea that he was impersonating a president more than being one.

Besides having heightened the presidential impersonation to a new art form, Baldwin managed to repeatedly get under Trump's thin skin. As *The Daily Beast* reported, "Trump has tweeted against *SNL* and Baldwin after nearly every single episode in which the actor has appeared, but as the inauguration approaches, it has become increasingly more unnerving and desperate."[38] Even more hilarious was the fact that while the episode that mocked Trump's tweets was still on air, Trump took to *Twitter* to attack Baldwin. "Just tried watching Saturday Night Live—unwatchable! Totally biased, not funny and the Baldwin impersonation just can't get any worse. Sad."[39] With his moody response, Trump didn't just prove the point of the sketch; he actually added to the satirical effect of the impersonation. Rather than act like a grown-up—or a president for that matter—Trump performed the role of a petulant child. This reaction makes the actor performing the role of an adult acting like a petulant child look like the mature one—a reality that should feel uncanny because a comedian should not seem more mature than the president. Yet it has been consistently true that comedians have seemed more mature and reasoned than President Trump was. Then, after the hilarious sketch in which Baldwin impersonated Trump at his press conference, Trump huffed out this response: "@NBCNews is bad but Saturday Night Live is the worst of NBC. Not funny, cast is terrible, always a complete hit job. Really bad television!"[40] The deep irony of the tweet was that it reinforced Trump's complete inability to handle a free press and his continued confused habit of lumping news together with a comedy show. But the real reason why the Trump *Twitter* replies to Baldwin's sketches are a sign of how the impersonations had impact is the way in which they then gave the public a chance to engage with Trump and call out his foolishness.

Each time Trump went to *Twitter* to have a hissy fit, the public responded. Their comments showed an engaged and critical citizenry who had been emboldened by Baldwin's sketches to call out the absurdity of Trump's behavior. For instance, after the sketch that showed Trump panicking as he realized he had work to do, Trump tweeted, "I watched parts of @nbcsnl Saturday Night Live last night. It is a totally one-sided, biased show—nothing funny at all. Equal time for us?"[41] This gave Baldwin a chance to directly reply to Trump: "@realDonaldTrump Equal time? Election is over. There is no more equal time. Now u try 2 b Pres + ppl respond. That's pretty much it."[42] Baldwin wasn't just schooling Trump on election media law; he was also reminding him to do his job. Even better, though, were the replies of average citizens to this exchange, like this example: "I can't believe the f*&#ing president is engaged in a Twitter war with an actor who portrays him on SNL."[43] Or this one: "The man who says that he'll defeat daesh in 2 months gets owned by an actor in 4 tweets . . . Priceless!!"[44] Because Trump would take to *Twitter* to respond to Baldwin's act, he opened up a space for public critique of his presidency. And these sorts of interventions are one of the key ways in which citizens were able to resist allowing Trump and his team to control the public narrative.

From the time that Trump announced his campaign to the midterm elections of 2018, Baldwin appeared on *SNL* 38 times impersonating him. While *SNL* had a history of doing numerous presidential impersonations, the frequency of the

Baldwin appearances as Trump was novel. He appeared 20 times during the 42nd season, ten times during the 43rd season, and eight times during season 44. Baldwin also won an Emmy in 2017 for his role on the show. But even more interestingly, Baldwin spilled his Trump persona beyond *SNL*, publishing a spoof parody memoir co-authored with *Spy Magazine* founder Kurt Anderson titled *You Can't Spell America Without Me*. He also blended his performance with political activism.[45] He joined Michael Moore, Al Sharpton, Mark Ruffalo, Robert De Niro, and other celebrities to lead a pre-inauguration protest in downtown Manhattan.[46] During that event, Baldwin brought out his impersonation to humor the crowd, but he also showed that his criticism of Trump was dead serious: "Donald Trump and Steve Bannon and Mike Pence and all these people that are part of the Trump administration think that you are going to lay down. Are you going to lay down?" he asked.[47] These public interventions were also a first for *SNL*. Baldwin went after Trump not just on *Twitter* but also in public rallies, media appearances, and interviews.

It's important to point out that the Baldwin impersonations did not stand alone. Not only was Baldwin always accompanied by a cast offering brilliant impersonations of other public figures, McKinnon as Clinton, Jeff Sessions, and Conway, for example, but there was also a series of sketches in which Baldwin did not appear that depicted key Trump staffers. Perhaps the most significant example was Melissa McCarthy, who impersonated Sean Spicer four separate times before he was eventually fired. McCarthy's Spicer was immediately legendary and earned her an Emmy. Especially noteworthy was the speculation that it was McCarthy's impersonation that may have gotten Spicer fired. As *Vanity Fair* reported (emphasis in original),

> Washington insiders believe that Melissa McCarthy's popular impression of Sean Spicer was at least *partially* responsible for the former press secretary losing his position at the White House. "Trump doesn't like his people to look weak," a source told Politico of the President's reaction to McCarthy's wicked, incisive performance.[48]

Spicer was Trump's first press secretary, and he literally embodied Trump's hostile attitude toward a free press and his penchant for alternative facts. During Spicer's six-month tenure as press secretary for Trump, he defended the size of the inauguration crowd as the largest ever (it wasn't),[49] claimed Hitler didn't use gas on his own people,[50] and memorably hid in the dark behind White House bushes.[51] McCarthy's Spicer chewed gum violently, hurled insults at the press, and engaged in physical comedy that made a complete mockery of Spicer's bombastic style.

After Spicer was fired, McCarthy retired her impersonation, but *SNL* kept lining up sketches that offered viewers sharp and incisive comedic interventions of the Trump team. One extraordinary example was Matt Damon's impersonation of Supreme Court nominee Brett Kavanaugh's testimony at the Senate Judiciary hearing.[52]

It's Hard to Make a Joke Out of a Joke 63

FIGURE 3.5 Matt Damon as Brett Kavanaugh for an *SNL* Cold Open.

Source: "Kavanaugh Hearing Cold Open," *Saturday Night Live*, NBC, https://www.youtube.com/watch?v=VRJecfRxbr8. License free image.

The clip immediately went viral and again worked as a framing device that only slightly exaggerated Kavanaugh's exact words. It also, like Baldwin's Trump, simply took the impersonated behavior up a notch from the original. Damon's Kavanaugh yelled at the committee, "Just wait until I get on that Supreme Court, 'cause then you're all going to pay,"[53] a sentiment that seemed entirely in keeping with Kavanaugh's attitude but was one of the few things he had not specifically uttered. Once Damon said it, though, the public couldn't easily forget it. The impersonation was taken so seriously that it was even cited by a senior contributor to *Forbes*, who called Damon's satire of Kavanaugh's performance an accurate depiction of appalling behavior.[54]

Representing (Almost) Everything Trump Hated

As explained earlier in this chapter, one of the most challenging components of the Trump presidency for comedians was the way in which he already seemed like an impersonation. Trump's performative style, braggadocio, and basic lack of understanding of the workings of the U.S. government presented aesthetic challenges to comedians who wanted to impersonate him. Trump's uncanny persona required comedians to go beyond simply emulating his speech patterns and physical habits, which was why Jimmy Fallon's impersonation of Trump fell flat.[55] Fallon did the standard move of offering an exaggerated physical rendition of Trump, but that was boring because it captured neither Trump's bluster, nor his dangerous ineptitude, nor his bigoted, sexist, selfish nature.

It's not just that Fallon's Trump fell flat; it was also that the aesthetic space within which he presented his version of Trump, as a celebrity, white, hetero male on a late-night network comedy show, was ill-equipped to offer the sort of

FIGURE 3.6 Jimmy Fallon's Trump impersonation falls flat.

Source: "Donald Trump," *The Tonight Show with Jimmy Fallon*, NBC, https://www.youtube.com/watch?v=N30zt9mRi_k. License free image.

creative dissonance that would offer high representational impact. Even though Alec Baldwin's version of Trump on *SNL* was a powerful satirical intervention, largely due to the fact that Trump was so regularly bothered by it that it offered a spectacle of his insecurities, some of the best Trump mockery came from outside of the professional celebrity class. The musical parodies of Trump posted by Randy Rainbow on *YouTube*, for instance, regularly attacked Trump's character in a tone that was both disturbed and admonishing.[56] An openly gay performer mockingly chiding Trump through show tunes on such a popular site offered novel representational aesthetics that were able to expose the dangerous, delusional realities of Trump. Even more importantly, a lesser-known performer like Rainbow skewering a powerful figure like Trump was inherently ironic in ways that celebrity impersonations like those of Baldwin or Fallon could never be.

Sarah Cooper's impersonations of Trump enjoyed a similar innovative creative space within which to make fun of Trump in a critically productive way. Cooper, though, used an even more creative platform than *YouTube* because her work first appeared via *TikTok*, the platform for user postings of short videos.[57] *TikTok* was known as a space that bypassed traditional celebrity venues, offering creators of all types a chance to be seen.

Cooper's *TikTok* videos stood out as remarkable for their understated, yet complex renditions of Trump.[58] Cooper simply lip-synced Trump. Viewers would hear his voice, yet see her saying his words. Occasionally she appeared in split screen—as one image of her mouthed Trump's words another reacted to them—a tactic that offered a complex layering, with Cooper both embodying and observing her own embodiment of Trump. Yet, even when the image was singular, just her mouthing Trump's words and her facial expressions offered layers of meaning. Typically, she seemed to be both reacting to his words and offering her interpretation of his inner

It's Hard to Make a Joke Out of a Joke 65

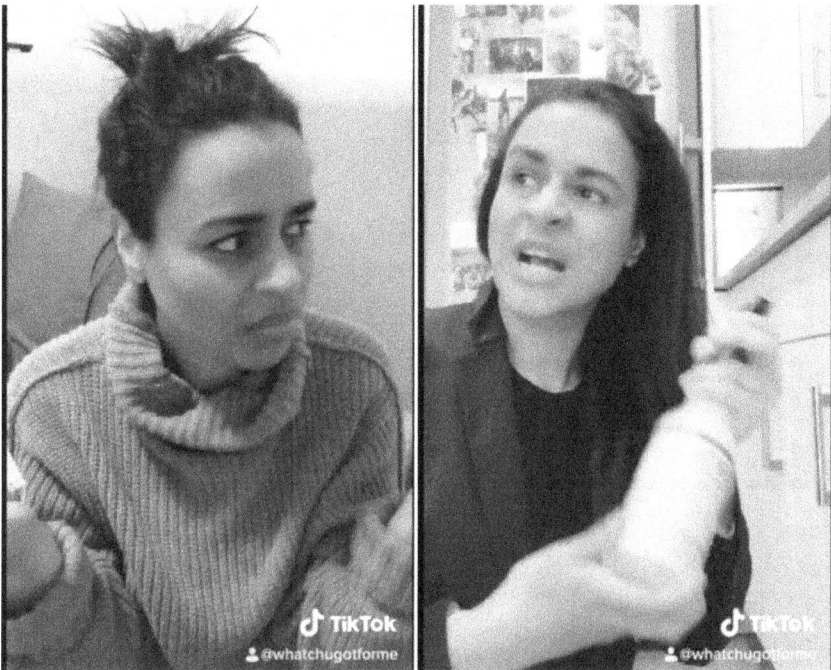

FIGURE 3.7 Sarah Cooper's impersonations offered both her own reaction to Trump's words as well as her rendition of his facial expressions.

Source: Sarah Cooper, *TikTok* @whatchugotforme, License free image.

thoughts. Her performance was doubly layered, signaling both astonishment and concern as Trump's observer, while simultaneously displaying the same bullying, narcissistic stupidity as Trump did.

The fact that Cooper did this performance as a female, Jamaican-American comedian, cleverly passing judgment on a callous moron, added an incisive layer to her impersonations that was aesthetically innovative. Cooper literally represented (almost) everything Trump hated—as a female immigrant of color—which added even greater representational force to her work. As she described it, she wasn't trying to do an impersonation or an impression, she was "interpreting" Trump for the "emotionally blind."[59] Her re-embodiment of Trump with actual sound bites of him talking had a deliberate communicative purpose. The idea was to create sufficient representational space to make it easier to truly see Trump. By only reprising his words, devoid of his precise choreographed physicality, Cooper aimed to make it easier to return representational gravitas to the Trump spectacle. Removing his physicality by disembodying his voice was an effort to make him more real. As she described it in an interview with Stephen Colbert, if you couldn't see Trump's BS when you watched him speak, then watching her say it would work to expose his BS.[60]

It wasn't just that Cooper disconnected Trump physically from his words; it was also that she embodied him as a woman. Prior to Trump, it was uncommon to see female comedians, especially women of color, impersonate (white) male

FIGURE 3.8 Melissa McCarthy as Sean Spicer on *SNL*.

Source: "Sean Spicer Press Conference," *Saturday Night Live*, NBC, https://www.youtube.com/watch?v=UWuc18xISwI. License free image.

politicians, particularly presidents. In fact, male comedians often embody women, but the reverse is rare.[61]

This lack of reciprocity explains, in part, why Kate McKinnon's Jeff Sessions and Melissa McCarthy's Sean Spicer impersonations[62] were such powerful elements of Trump-era *SNL*.[63] For, in yet another novel development for satire during the Trump years, suddenly there was a wave of female comedians effectively impersonating powerful men, a shift that was brought on, at least in part, by the mainstreamed celebration of toxic masculinity that defined Trumpism. But there was more to the novelty of Cooper's impersonation. Typically, the impersonator gains representational power from their own gravitas as a performer, supplementing the aura of the celebrity with their own creative aura. This, of course, was at least part of the reason why Baldwin's Trump drew such attention and why McCarthy's Sean Spicer was so epic.

Cooper, however, was relatively unknown when she started lip-syncing to Trump, and was even reportedly considering quitting comedy before her Trump impersonations went viral.[64] With Cooper, it was exactly her capacity to upend Trump's celebrity so effectively as an unknown performer that then translated into her own celebrity. Cooper's impersonation was especially noteworthy for how it inverted the traditional power dynamics of impersonations and for the uncanny way in which she embodied a fearful, blustery, incoherent Trump alongside her rendition of a concerned citizen.

Lip-syncing could seem like a simple gag, yet with Cooper it became high art, a fact that Cooper proved when she took her work to Netflix in 2020 for a special called *Everything's Fine*.[65] In a brilliant display of how a different platform could offer her work new possibilities, she shot a scene with Helen Mirren in which the two recreated the 2005 audio of Trump boasting about sexually assaulting women to *Access Hollywood*'s Billy Bush.[66] Mirren portrays Bush and Cooper does Trump.

Having the two women reenact a deeply misogynistic scene is yet another example of the representational potential offered by the disembodied re-embodiment of toxic males by women. It has to be noted, as well, that Mirren's own stature as a graceful, yet strong, female celebrity added considerable irony to her crass rendition of Bush. The dynamics between the two women as they stripped down the misogynistic performativity of "locker room" masculinity drive home the ironic aesthetic of Trump-era satire: they show how truly disturbing and strangely bizarre these men are, rendering them visible and absurd at the same time.

That Cooper started her satire of Trump on *TikTok* is noteworthy. Trump was the first U.S. president to personally manage his own social media image, largely through *Twitter* and, to a lesser extent, *Facebook*. He also regularly knew how to navigate and control his representation on cable television, most specifically on Fox News. What's interesting, as highlighted in Trump's meltdowns over *SNL*, is that Trump tended to take the position that he was being discriminated against by the media either by liberal-leaning negative representations of him or by exclusion.

His stance on how the media were mean to him makes his reaction to *TikTok* even more interesting. While Trump tended to argue that he was being censored and treated unfairly in spaces like *Twitter*, with *TikTok*, he simply wanted it banned. The front-facing argument by the Trump team was that *TikTok* represented a Chinese threat to national security. For those familiar with Trump's efforts to control

FIGURE 3.9 Helen Mirren and Sarah Cooper re-enact the 2005 *Access Hollywood* tape.

Source: "The Tape," *Sarah Cooper: Everything's Fine*, Netflix is a Joke, https://www.youtube.com/watch?v=QRu-QUeqoMs. License free image.

his media image, that argument fell flat. Rather, what seemed more likely was that Trump wanted to ban *TikTok* because the platform represented a social media outlet that was totally out of his control. *TikTok* had been used, for example, to successfully ruin a major Trump rally that had been scheduled in Tulsa, Oklahoma, in June 2020.[67] TikTokers, along with other online users, coordinated a campaign to register for tickets to the event and never show up.

While *TikTok* has a complicated connection to political activism, and while there is significant evidence that its content is controlled, there seems little doubt that the platform was an effective space for anti-Trump advocacy. The reality that *TikTok* was a space that offered average people, both in the United States and abroad, a venue within which to not just mock the President but also to truly affect his image, made the *TikTok* interventions of Cooper even more significant as a satirical innovation. Cooper's satirical art was defined by the way that she ironically exaggerated an exaggeration in order to reveal the absurd truth.

Satire Versus the Bully

Trump's performative bluster posed a unique challenge for his impersonators, but he also threw a wrench into the tool kit used by satirists in general. Even before he won the election, comedians were harping about how Trump had changed the art of their mockery. As *New Yorker* satirist Andy Borowitz explained it, the trouble with Trump satire was that comedians could no longer rely on exaggeration or hyperbole to make their point:

> One thing about satire: you're trying to portray a kind of heightened version of reality, to perhaps point out the absurdity of reality. With Trump, you can't go beyond who he actually is. I did a discussion on *The New Yorker* radio show with [editor] David [Remnick] and I said once millions of Americans decided to give a game show host nuclear weapons, that really defied satire.[68]

Trey Parker, co-creator of *South Park*, echoed Borowitz's sentiments: "It's really tricky now as satire has become reality."[69] Yet, they still did a satirical cartoon that presented the Trump-Clinton contest as a choice between the "giant douche or the turd sandwich."[70] *The Onion* had the same problem. One of their Trump-era headlines read, "Eric Trump Scolds Father That He Mustn't Inquire About the Businesses, For He's Sworn Not to Tell," a fairly accurate description of the so-called firewall between the 45th president and his family enterprise.[71]

As *The Economist* pointed out, the reality in the Trump era is that straight headlines are often bizarrely close to ones that are *Onion*-esque.[72] They remind us that Trump spokeswoman Conway was briefly barred by CNN for using alternative facts, stating that her references to a fictitious jihadist atrocity, which Conway called the "Bowling Green Massacre," were the last straw. They also recall when Trump's wife, Melania, sued a newspaper for reporting lurid untruths about her on the basis that this cost her the "once-in-a-lifetime opportunity" of making millions as "one of the most photographed women in the world." "No satirist could do better," they write.[73]

There was another unique challenge posed by Trump for satirists: that he was a bully. If it is hard to mock someone who is already an exaggerated hyperbole of a man, then it is even harder to do it when that hyperbolic person is also a bully. The trouble is that the bully has a lot in common with the satirist—both use sarcasm, mockery, invective, caricature. The difference between the bully and the satirist is their goal in using these extreme modes of communication. As Robert Harris has aptly explained, riffing off the insight of British satirist Jonathan Swift,

> The best satire does not seek to do harm or damage by its ridicule . . . but rather it seeks to create a shock of recognition and to make vice repulsive so that the vice will be expunged from the person or society intended to benefit by the attack. Whenever possible, this shock of recognition is to be conveyed through laughter or wit.[74]

While Trump acted like a bully, regularly mocking any- and everyone he pleased—even a disabled reporter—it posed some real challenges for those comedians who wanted to use satirical irony to expose his flaws and call out his vice.[75]

The extremes of Trump led to extremes in the comedy used to mock him. In one example, Colbert, who generally avoids the most invective forms of irony, went after Trump in May 2017, shortly after Trump had insulted CBS newsman John Dickerson during an interview on *Face the Nation*.[76] Colbert began by defending his CBS colleague, then he unleashed a tirade aimed at Trump that was by turns intrinsically witty and outright offensive:

> Mr. President, you're not the POTUS, you're the "gloat-us." You're the glutton with the button. You're a regular "Gorge Washington." You're the "presidunce," but you're turning into a real "prick-tator."

FIGURE 3.10 Trump mocks a disabled reporter.

Source: "Trump mocks reporter with disability," CNN, https://www.youtube.com/watch?v=PX9reO3QnUA. License free image.

Colbert said:

> Sir, you attract more skinheads than free Rogaine. You have more people marching against you than cancer. You talk like a sign-language gorilla that got hit in the head. In fact, the only thing your mouth is good for is being Vladimir Putin's cock holster.[77]

The outburst led to an FCC investigation to determine whether Colbert should be fined—and it also led to significant outrage among Colbert viewers who found the monologue to be excessively vulgar and also homophobic.[78] While the FCC decided there was no line crossed by the obscenities, the real takeaway to the story was that those mocking Trump were finding it harder and harder to know where to draw the line. And one of the critical consequences of these extremes is that Trump redefined what it means to be an ironic president. How exactly can you use irony to mock someone who is already ironic?

The Bitter Irony of Donald Trump

There is a famous literary analysis quote that says, "irony trumps everything," because it "provides additional richness to the literary dish" and it "keeps us readers on our toes, inviting us, compelling us, to dig through layers of possible meaning and competing signification."[79] But after the 2016 election, it became clear that Trump "ironied" everything, except his version of adding irony didn't make anything richer—except maybe satire because satire had to develop new, creative strategies to make irony an effective foil to folly and vice.

Shortly after the 2017 inauguration, James Strick wrote in a letter to the editor of *The Washington Post*, "I cannot believe I live in a country that made President Obama show his birth certificate but won't make President Trump show his tax returns."[80] He titled his letter, "A Bitter Irony."[81]

While the concept of irony is the sort of thing that scholars can spend their lives studying, it's not as tricky a concept as it might seem. As explained in the introduction to this book, there are basically two core types of irony—rhetorical (in which words are used in ways that are different from their literal meaning) and situational (in which you expect an outcome, but the opposite happens). Rhetorical (or creative) irony is saying that you are really happy that the tax bill passed, when you really are *not* happy at all. Situational irony is having a president who doesn't "believe in" science being in charge of the response to a pandemic.

Creative, rhetorical irony tends to be exceptionally successful at provoking reflection and exposing social crises. And it is an essential element of satirical comedy. Satire uses irony to expose abuses of power, lapses in reason, hubris, and manipulation. Rather than directly describe the problem, the satirist uses creative irony to get the audience to infer it. The art lies in the gap between what is meant and what is said. For example, almost all of the headlines from Borowitz's satirical pieces for the *New Yorker* offer valuable training in the art of irony: "Trump

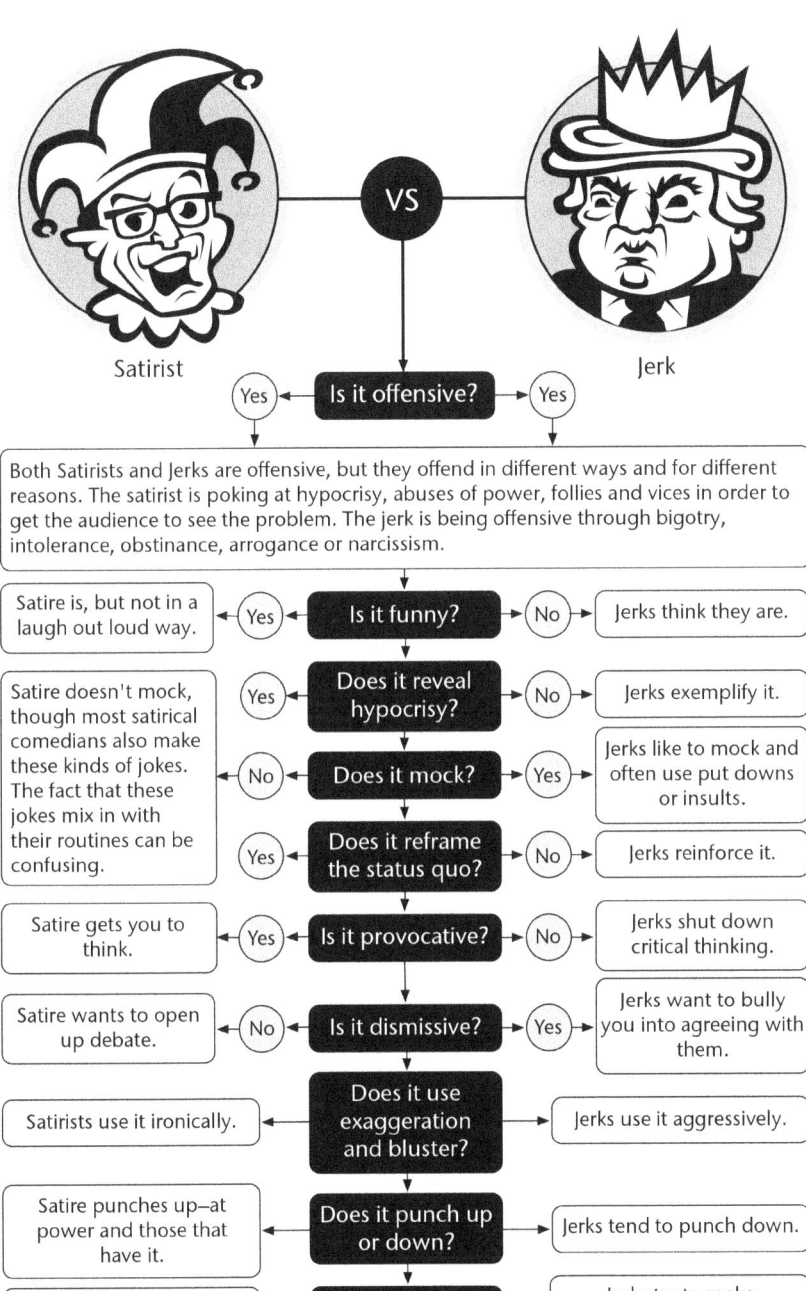

FIGURE 3.11 How to tell the difference between a satirist and a jerk.

Design credit: Tamara Knoss.

voters celebrate massive tax cut for everyone but;"[82] "Nazis feeling neglected after Republicans embrace child molesters;"[83] "Cheney receives heart transplant; Bush still on waiting list for brain."[84]

These headlines may not make it obvious that irony in the Trump era is entering a new phase. The George W. Bush era joke seems similar enough. But there is much about Trump irony that is vastly different from its earlier incarnations. One of the core differences is that, after 9/11, as Bush sent the United States to war in Afghanistan and Iraq, irony was considered a brave way to poke at the status quo, whereas now irony is literally everywhere. A study found that Trump was the most mocked president in U.S. history.[85] But, as I've explained, some of those jokes are simply crude insults about an orange-faced, small-handed troll; they don't depend on irony for their comedic punch, and they can be just as mean as Trump is when he mocks people he doesn't like.

Politically productive satire has to move beyond name-calling, humiliating, and demeaning humor; it has to require the audience to use analytical skills to make sense of the irony. What we found a lot of, though, in the Trump era, was a blend of the two forms—similar to the example of Colbert's Trump tirade mentioned earlier. Another excellent example comes from Samantha Bee's "Not the White House Correspondents' Dinner" roast of President Trump, in which she artfully blended both types of mockery—aggressive insults and insightful ironic wit—often in the same joke.[86] She said that Trump had run away from Vietnam, and he had run away from the White House Correspondents' Association Dinner.[87] She then mentioned that the reason he wore baggy golf pants was so that you couldn't see him constantly shitting himself.[88] And, in her best example, she sassed: "Donald Trump proved that pussies can get elected as long as he doesn't have one."[89] Bee came under fire for her "full frontal" language when she went on a rant in June 2018 as the Trump administration was separating immigrant children from their parents. Over the weekend, as news was breaking of the suffering of immigrant families, Trump's daughter Ivanka posted a picture of her with her child in a move many saw as completely tone deaf to the immigrant families in crisis. Bee went after her:

> You know, Ivanka, that's a beautiful photo of you and your child, but let me just say, one mother to another. Do something about your dad's immigration practices, you feckless cunt! He listens to you! Put on something tight and low-cut and tell your father to fucking stop it.[90]

Bee eventually apologized amid significant backlash for using the "c word." But what's really interesting about her rant is that this time there was no satire to her comments at all, just rage.[91]

These types of cracks were simply never lobbed at George W. Bush in any sort of mainstream comedy during his tenure as president. After 9/11, *Vanity Fair* editor Graydon Carter declared that the terrorist attacks would signal "the end of the age of irony."[92] There were multiple articles in those grim days that suggested that irony

FIGURE 3.12 Samantha Bee goes after Ivanka.

Source: Maura Dowling, "Samantha Bee calls Ivanka a 'feckless c***'", https://www.youtube.com/watch?v=_k2GQDhLZQw. License free image.

was dead or dying. The basic idea at the time was that irony is too irreverent, too closely connected to comedy, and too highbrow to be of use in a crisis. And when good and evil really do seem easy to define, as was the case for many post-9/11, irony doesn't work. The satirists, irony masters, fell silent in those early days. Jon Stewart cried on air.

And yet, as Zoe Williams pointed out in a 2003 piece for *The Guardian*, "Naturally, irony was back within a few days, not least because of the myriad ironies contained within the attack itself (America having funded al-Qaida is ironic; America raining bombs and peanut butter on Afghanistan is ironic)."[93] Irony may fall silent in the face of a fresh tragedy, but it will always come back, and this is because irony is a prime weapon against disinformation, lies, abuses of power, and emotive hysteria. Because rhetorical irony depends on the use of words in ways different from their literal meaning, it is able to especially sting in times of deception and crisis. When Colbert stood next to Bush and roasted him at the 2006 White House Correspondents' Association Dinner, he said,

> I stand by this man. I stand by this man, because he stands for things. Not only for things, he stands on things, things like aircraft carriers and rubble and recently flooded city squares. And that sends a strong message, that no matter what happens to America, she will always rebound with the most powerfully staged photo-ops in the world.[94]

Colbert used irony to help make sense of the hubris of the Bush presidency, and he used it to cut through the ways in which the Bush administration manipulated its image for the media. It's valuable to remember the way in which irony helped us to make sense of the post-9/11 context, because Bush and Vice President Dick Cheney may have been masters at lying, but they were anything but ironic. And that is why Trump messed with irony so badly. Trump himself embodied irony, and that is why it is both so easy and so hard to make fun of him.

Trump is a performance, maybe even a meme, but certainly not a statesman.[95] As I've explained, mockery of an impersonation makes it hard enough for irony to take hold, but it's even worse because Trump himself regularly uses a belligerent, jeering tone that comes awfully close to ironic jabs. His use of "scare quotes"—as in his famous quote about being wiretapped—is an excellent example of Trump seeming to use language ironically.[96]

When Trump made a big deal to Tucker Carlson that he had used quotes around the word wiretap, meaning he wasn't being literal, it led Moises Velazquez-Manoff to suggest that Trump had "ruined irony, too."[97] As Michael Hirschorn puts it, "When facts are made stupid things and there is no coherent center to mediate truth, most irony starts falling on deaf ears because there is no lingua franca."[98] This is why the ironic satire of the Trump era depends less on hyperbole and exaggeration and more on irony to encourage the audience to think critically, use logic, and engage in rational thought.

Another critical problem for irony in the Trump age is the fact that Trump never seems to be using words in any of their intended ways. He redefined basic words like "great" and "fake." He made things up. He speaks in incoherent babbles. He rants and raves. This challenges the satirist, who depends on puns, wordplay, and other creative misuse of language to draw attention to lapses in judgment, deception, and deliberate misinformation. Yet, it is exactly satirical wordplay that helps to expose Trump-style abuses of language. In one excellent example, we can note that a lot of Trump protest signs now revolve around ironic puns and wordplay. Take this protester's sign, for example: "I've seen smarter cabinets at IKEA."[99]

Another challenge for satirists is the fact that Trump lies all the time, brazenly and unabashedly. Trump was the "lyingest" president ever. In his first seven months in office, Trump lied over 1,000 times, an average of five times a day.[100] But the key challenge for ironic comedy was the fact that Trump's lies were significantly different from the Bush-Cheney lies, because Trump's were accompanied by sarcastic barbs, bullying epithets, and a constant tone of mockery. The Bush administration

Terrible! Just found out that Obama had my "wires tapped" in Trump Tower just before the victory. Nothing found. This is McCarthyism!

FIGURE 3.13 Trump tweets nonsense about wiretapping.

Source: @realDonaldTrump, *Twitter*, https://www.bbc.com/news/world-us-canada-39283054. License free image.

FIGURE 3.14 Just one example of the many ways that protest signs use ironic wordplay to mock Trump.

Source: Phil Venditti, "I've seen smarter cabinets at Ikea," *Flickr*, https://www.flickr.com/photos/venditti_min_min-venditti/37193822855. Used with permission.

lied with gravitas; Trump's lied with mocking bluster. And it wasn't just Trump; White House Press Secretaries Sean Spicer and Sarah Huckabee Sanders displayed a constant attitude of annoyance and disdain. This is all to say that the Trump era made irony harder, but that is exactly why it was the best defense against him.

There are two uses of language that purposefully separate words from truth: lies and irony. As I've explained it, Trump's lies often seem ironic because they are performed in a bloviating way. Even when Trump seems most sincere, he also seems like a joke, making it hard to take his invective seriously. How else to process his tendency to use belittling barbs in tweets about national security?

Take, for example, the text of this tweet: "The Chinese Envoy, who just returned from North Korea, seems to have had no impact on Little Rocket Man. Hard to believe his people, and the military, put up with living in such horrible conditions. Russia and China condemned the launch."[101] In it, Trump belittles a foreign leader and threatens national security via social media. It's a truly unique spectacle of poor leadership. The only way to challenge a leader who is both a caricature and a dangerous liar is with the sort of irony that rescues reason. And the only way to resist bullying mockery meant to put others down is with smart irony meant to encourage an audience to engage in critical reflection. This means that, even though Trump made it difficult for political comedy to effectively satirize him, those who used satire to mock Trump offered one of the most effective means for exposing his combination of bullying, lies, bigotry, and bluster.

This, of course, leads to one of the most surprising consequences of Trump-era satire: the odd way in which Trump led satirists to play "conservative" and "straight" to him. While satire has long been a champion of reason over folly, analysis over accolades, and critique over crisis, it has also generally been seen as a way to disrupt the status quo and to question social structures that are intrinsically oligarchic, repressive, and manipulative. Satire, by nature, is radical and revolutionary, designed to spur audiences to call into question accepted beliefs. But some of that spirit shifted after Trump, because he and his supporters seemed to have so little respect for or even understanding of any of our democratic institutions. Trump supporters would regularly wear shirts saying they supported Russia more than Democrats. The Trump team seemed interested, at times, in burning every U.S. institution into the ground. From public schools to the judicial system, many of the social structures we had assumed were a common part of U.S. life seemed to be under threat, and that led many comedians to play it straight to Trump's irreverence and extremism. Suddenly, it was satirists who were defending the Constitution rather than urging audiences to burn the flag.

While many comedians like Lee Camp, who regularly targets corporate America, remained laser focused on calling out systemic abuses of power, there was an odd turn in U.S. satire in which comedians were working hard to defend institutions rather than to dismantle them. Sure, they remained critical of each and every institution, as usual, yet there was a decided urgency then to defend democracy rather than simply critique it. Recall that George Carlin once did a famous riff on why he didn't vote because, he argued, voting meant you didn't have a right to complain.[102] That sort of sarcastic rant that suggested it was no use to bother with everyday politics rarely ever happened under Trump.

I'll focus on this issue more closely in Chapter 5 when I discuss how satirists gave Trump a civics lesson. But let's consider, for example, the effect that Trump had on the comedy of Jimmy Kimmel, who was perhaps the most successful frat-boy comedian of his time prior to the rise of Trump as a politician. Kimmel had never been a political comedian, but Trump changed that. Kimmel first became outspoken politically in the wake of the birth of his son, who had needed special medical attention, leading Kimmel to fight for better healthcare for all children. Then, after the 2018 massacre at Marjory Stoneman High School in Parkland, FL, Kimmel went after Trump's refusal to tackle gun violence:

> You've literally done nothing. Actually, you've done worse than nothing. You like to say this is a mental health issue, but one of your very first acts as president, Mr. Trump, was to actually roll back the regulations that were designed to keep firearms out of the hands of the mentally ill. You did that. Your party voted to repeal the mandates on coverage for mental health. So I agree, this is a mental illness issue. Because if you don't think we need to do something about it, you're obviously mentally ill.[103]

Sure, there was a joke in there, but really this was Kimmel playing it straight.

Another example of a comedian increasing the use of political satire in their work is the case of Trevor Noah, who originally took over for Jon Stewart as host of *The Daily Show* and was expected to pivot away from the political work that had defined the show under Stewart's reign. In early interviews, South Africa–born Noah spoke about how he was going to move away from the type of satire Stewart did and toward something less overtly political and less specifically targeted at the Fox News mentality. This meant that, as Noah launched his career as host and the U.S. became immersed in a new election cycle, *The Daily Show* became less relevant as a source of political comedy. As Hot Air reported, there was a real decline in the social significance of *The Daily Show* in the early part of the 2016 election. Folks simply didn't share clips from the show the way they used to: "First of all, the zingers aren't really as *zing worthy* as they once were. And perhaps more to the point, they probably don't hurt as much because there just aren't that many people watching."[104]

That would all change as the election loomed near. By September 2016, Noah was fully committed to using his comedy to dismantle Trump's positions. Noah became especially interested in targeting Trump's anti-immigrant policies as well as his not-so-subtle racism. As Trump continued to attack immigrants and people of color in his rallies and speeches, Noah delivered a smackdown of Trump's views of immigrants and minorities in a video posted online: "The greatest country in the world is the country that accepts people who come in from everywhere in the world, Mr. Donald Trump," Noah said.[105]

> And I know you think that half the country is a basket of deportables. Yeah, I said it, "deportables," not "deplorables." But the good people of America know the greatest country in the world is the country where you can come in and create anything.[106]

Mentioning that Steve Jobs was the son of an immigrant, he went on:

> You know what came from Syria? The iPhone came from Syria, Donald Trump. The same iPhone you tweet shit about the refugees on. Every time you tweet with those fat, little fingers of yours, you should be saying thank you to them for giving you that same phone.[107]

Noah's gloves had come off, and he was delivering a joke-free, angry, insult-laden rant—a move he never had expected to be making when he originally took over for Stewart. While this rant was just sharp and angry, Noah's comedy after the election became one of the best examples of political satire. Working with a team of strong comedians, *The Daily Show* returned to its former spot as one of the nation's most important critical sources of political comedy.

Offering a different twist on Trump's effect on comedy, Michael Moore found himself less and less inclined to go for a gag as Trump and his team got closer and closer to power. Moore was the only political comedian—and arguably the only major voice of the left—who saw Trump coming. He urged his fans to take Trump seriously while many comedians were still chortling at the possibility of a Trump presidency. In July of 2016, Moore posted a piece on *Alternet* and on his own website that listed five reasons why he thought Trump would win.

> I am sorry to be the bearer of bad news, but I gave it to you straight last summer when I told you that Donald Trump would be the Republican nominee for president. And now I have even more awful, depressing news for you: Donald J. Trump is going to win in November. This wretched, ignorant, dangerous part-time clown and full-time sociopath is going to be our next president. President Trump. Go ahead and say the words, 'cause you'll be saying them for the next four years: "PRESIDENT TRUMP."[108]

While the post had some sharp wit and lots of sass, it also proved to be one of the most cogent analyses of the political landscape offered by anyone in the media. It certainly showed that Moore needed to be taken seriously as a source of political insight—even if much of his insight was often wrapped in his trademark style of witty satire. In one of his best gags, Moore penned a satirical letter to Ivanka Trump telling her that it was time for her to stage an "intervention" and get her dad out of the race—because he simply wasn't well.[109] The letter was classic Moore—sassy, smart, silly, and serious. As the election drew near, Moore became more and more committed to trying to mobilize voters to support Clinton, releasing a film of his performance, *Michael Moore in TrumpLand*. Rather than viciously attacking Trump and praising Clinton, the film takes an entirely different tack: it begins by showing respect for Trump supporters, by understanding their rage, and by acknowledging their views—including their hatred of Hillary Clinton.[110] The key to the film isn't just that Moore finds much to value in Clinton's record; it is that he finds a way to push past the sense of political polarization that has shaped our voting blocs into hostile territories. In the film, Moore stages a conversation that can serve as a model for democratic deliberation—where, even if we disagree, we don't have to lose a sense of our common humanity.[111] After the election, Moore didn't let up. In post-election rallies, he called for an army of comedy to come after Trump, he staged a highly successful Broadway show that often ended up on the street in front of the Trump Tower in protest, and he released his most powerful –and least funny –film yet *Fahrenheit 11/9*, which asks his audience to take seriously Trump's threats to democracy and to mobilize a midterm vote. In one of the most disturbing scenes, Moore shows a clip of Hitler but superimposes Trump's voice.[112] The message was far from subtle.

These are only a few examples of how the Trump era changed the way in which satirists worked, increased the politicization of comedians, and ramped up their activism. There are countless other examples. Chelsea Handler, who had a Netflix show, ended her second season in 2017, saying she was devoting herself to activism in the wake of the Trump win. Even the goofball comedy of Fallon developed an edge as he decided to define himself as clearly anti-Trump. The list goes on. Across the board, as Trump went from joke candidate to serious-yet-still-a-joke president, it was noteworthy that more and more comedians were becoming political, and more and more often they were delivering rants to their audiences that offered more rage than punchlines. Thus, in one of the most ironic consequences of the Trump era, the more of a joke his administration became, the more the comedians got serious.

Notes

1. "Donald Trump vs. Hillary Clinton Debate Cold Open – SNL." *YouTube* video, 9:45, posted by *Saturday Night Live* on October 1, 2016, www.youtube.com/watch?v=-nQGBZQrtT0.=
2. Ibid.
3. Sims, David. "Alec Baldwin's Scarier, Nastier Donald Trump." *The Atlantic*, October 3, 2016, www.theatlantic.com/entertainment/archive/2016/10/alec-baldwin-donald-trump-snl/502610/.
4. "Donald Trump vs. Hillary Clinton Debate Cold Open – SNL." *YouTube* video, 9:45, posted by *Saturday Night Live* on October 1, 2016, www.youtube.com/watch?v=-nQGBZQrtT0.
5. Ibid.
6. "Saturday Night Live." Season 41, Episode 4, NBC, November 7, 2015.
7. Ibid.
8. "Announcing: An Announcement." *YouTube* video, 6:32, posted by *The Late Show with Stephen Colbert* on June 16, 2015, www.youtube.com/watch?v=OFVC3qYGYiE.
9. Ibid.
10. Ibid.
11. Ibid.
12. "Trump vs. Bernie." *Wikipedia*, June 15, 2019, https://en.wikipedia.org/wiki/Trump_vs._Bernie.
13. Rottenberg, Josh. "Anthony Atamanuik and James Adomian Have Turned 'Trump vs Bernie' into a Comedy Hit." *Los Angeles Times*, April 29, 2016, www.latimes.com/entertainment/tv/la-ca-st-trump-sanders-show-20160501-story.html.
14. Wilstein, Matt. "Why 'The President Show' Star Can't Go Out in Public as Trump Anymore." *Daily Beast*, July 10, 2022, www.thedailybeast.com/why-the-president-show-star-cant-go-out-in-public-as-trump-anymore.
15. Strause, Jackie. "Comedy Central Launches Weekly Trump-Aimed Late-Night Show." *The Hollywood Reporter*, April 3, 2017, www.hollywoodreporter.com/live-feed/president-show-comedy-central-launches-weekly-trump-aimed-late-night-show-990727.
16. Ibid.
17. Sims, David. "Why Comedy Central's 'The President Show' Might Just Work." *The Atlantic*, April 28, 2017, www.theatlantic.com/entertainment/archive/2017/04/why-the-president-show-might-just-work/524757/.
18. For more on this, see Hakola, Outi J. "Political Impersonations on *Saturday Night Live* During the 2016 U.S. Presidential Election." *European Journal of American Studies*, vol. 12, no. 2, 2017, document 7, Online since 10 August 2017, connection on July 26, 2022, http://journals.openedition.org/ejas/12153.
19. Baumgartner, Jody C., Jonathan S. Morris and Natasha L. Walth. "The Fey Effect: Young Adults, Political Humor, and Perceptions of Sarah Palin in the 2008 Presidential Election Campaign." *Public Opinion Quarterly*, vol. 76, no. 1, 2012, pp. 95–104, https://academic.oup.com/poq/article-abstract/76/1/95/1894315.
20. "Donald Trump Interviews Himself in the Mirror." *YouTube* video, 5:48, posted by *The Tonight Show Starring Jimmy Fallon* on September 11, 2015, www.youtube.com/watch?v=c2DgwPG7mAA.
21. "Donald Trump vs. Hillary Clinton Town Hall Debate Cold Open – SNL." *YouTube* video, 8:27, posted by *Saturday Night Live* on October 16, 2016, www.youtube.com/watch?v=qVMW_1aZXRk.

22 Trump, Donald J. "Watched Saturday Night Live Hit Job on Me: Time to Retire the Boring and Unfunny Show. Alec Baldwin Portrayal Stinks. Media Rigging Election!" *Twitter*, October 16, 2016, 4:14 a.m., https://twitter.com/realdonaldtrump/status/787612552654155776.
23 Ibid.
24 "Donald Trump vs. Hillary Clinton Third Debate Cold Open – SNL." *YouTube* video, 1:20, posted by *Saturday Night Live* on October 16, 2016, www.youtube.com/watch?v=-kjyltrKZSY.
25 Ibid.
26 Ibid.
27 "Saturday Night Live." Season 42, Episode 1, NBC, October 1, 2016.
28 "Saturday Night Live." Season 42, Episode 2, NBC, October 8, 2016.
29 "Election Week Cold Open." *YouTube* video, 0:25, posted by *Saturday Night Live* on November 13, 2016, www.youtube.com/watch?v=BG-_ZDrypec.
30 Wan, William. "The Surprisingly Dark, Twisted History of Presidential Impersonators in America." *The Washington Post*, June 27, 2016, www.washingtonpost.com/news/post-nation/wp/2016/06/27/the-surprisingly-dark-twisted-history-of-presidential-impersonators-in-america/?utm_term=.35a2894a71a7.
31 Howard, Adam. "How 'Saturday Night Live' Has Shaped Our Politics." *NBCNews.com*, September 30, 2016, www.nbcnews.com/pop-culture/tv/how-saturday-night-live-has-shaped-american-politics-n656716.
32 "Donald Trump Prepares Cold Open." *NBC, SNL*, November 19, 2016, www.nbc.com/saturday-night-live/video/donald-trump-prepares-cold-open/3428575.
33 Hakola, Outi J. "Political Impersonations on Saturday Night Live During the 2016 U.S. Presidential Election." *European Journal of American Studies*, July 31, 2017, https://journals.openedition.org/ejas/12153.
34 "Donald Trump Prepares Cold Open." *NBC, SNL*, November 19, 2016, www.nbc.com/saturday-night-live/video/donald-trump-prepares-cold-open/3428575.
35 Ibid.
36 Ibid.
37 "Classroom Cold Open." *NBC, SNL*, March 12, 2016, www.nbc.com/saturday-night-live/video/classroom-cold-open/3435356?snl=1.
38 Wilstein, Matt. "Alec Baldwin Goes High as Donald Trump Goes Low in SNL Twitter Battle." *Daily Beast*, January 15, 2017, www.thedailybeast.com/alec-baldwin-goes-high-as-donald-trump-goes-low-in-snl-twitter-battle.
39 Trump, Donald J. "Just Tried Watching Saturday Night Live—Unwatchable! Totally Biased, Not Funny and the Baldwin Impersonation Just Can't Get Any Worse. Sad." *Twitter*, December 3, 2016, 9:13 p.m., https://twitter.com/realdonaldtrump/status/805278955150471168?lang=en.
40 Trump, Donald J. "@NBCNews Is Bad but Saturday Night Live Is the Worst of NBC. Not Funny, Cast Is Terrible, Always a Complete Hit Job. Really Bad Television!" *Twitter*, January 15, 2017, 2:46 p.m., https://twitter.com/realdonaldtrump/status/820764134857969666?lang=en.
41 Trump, Donald J. "I Watched Parts of @nbcsnl Saturday Night Live Last Night. It Is a Totally One-Sided, Biased Show—Nothing Funny at all. Equal Time for Us?" *Twitter*, November 20, 2016, 5:26 a.m., https://twitter.com/realdonaldtrump/status/800329364986626048?lang=en.
42 HABFoundation. "@realDonaldTrump Equal Time? Election Is Over. There Is No More Equal Time. Now U Try 2 b Pres + ppl Respond. That's Pretty Much it." *Twitter*, November 20, 2016, 5:56 a.m., https://twitter.com/abfalecbaldwin/status/800337003426484224?lang=en.
43 DesPeaux, Cliff. "I Can't Believe the f*&#ing President Is Engaged in a Twitter War with an Actor Who Portrays him on SNL." *Twitter*, November 20, 2016, 9:09 a.m., https://twitter.com/despeaux/status/800385515513991168?ref_src=twsrc%5Etf

w%7Ctwcamp%5Etweetembed%7Ctwterm%5E800385515513991168&ref_url= https%3A%2F%2Fwww.salon.com%2F2017%2F01%2F21%2Falec-baldwins-donald-trump-tightrope-brilliantly-impersonating-a-president-whos-already-impersonating-a-president%2F.

44 Drako, Paulo. "The Man Who Says That He'll Defeat Daesh in 2 Months Gets Owned by an Actor in 4 Tweets . . . Priceless!!" *Twitter*, November 23, 2016, 3:46 p.m., https://twitter.com/X7Drako/status/801572699873087488.

45 Baldwin, Alec and Kurt Anderson. *You Can't Spell America Without Me*. Penguin Books, 2017.

46 Winfrey, Graham. "Michael Moore, Robert De Niro, Alec Baldwin and More Lead Anti-Trump Rally in NYC." *IndieWire*, January 19, 2017, www.indiewire.com/2017/01/michael-moore-robert-de-niro-alec-baldwin-anti-trump-rally-1201770862/.

47 Ibid.

48 Robinson, Joanna. "S.N.L.: Could Matt Damon's Crazed Impression Hurt Brett Kavanaugh?" *Vanity Fair*, September 30, 2018, www.vanityfair.com/hollywood/2018/09/snl-matt-damon-brett-kavanaugh-impression-trump.

49 Slobin, Sarah. "The Truth About the Crowd at Trump's Inauguration, in One Photo." *Quartz*, January 22, 2017, https://qz.com/891784/the-truth-about-the-crowd-at-trumps-inauguration-in-one-photo/.

50 De Haldevang, Max. "Sean Spicer Just Claimed That Hitler 'Was Not Using Gas on His Own People'." *Quartz*, April 11, 2017, https://qz.com/955858/sean-spicer-donald-trumps-press-chief-claimed-that-hitler-was-not-using-gas-on-his-own-people/.

51 Simon, Johnny. "'Turn the Lights Off': How the White House Hides from a Crisis, in Photos." *Quartz*, May 10, 2017, https://qz.com/980272/after-trump-fires-fbi-director-comey-photos-of-sean-spicer-hiding-in-the-shadows/.

52 "Kavanaugh Hearing Cold Open-SNL." *YouTube* video posted by *Saturday Night Live* on September 30, 2018, www.youtube.com/watch?v=VRJecfRxbr8.

53 Ibid.

54 Denning, Steve. "Chief Justice Roberts Requests Tenth Circuit to Investigate Kavanaugh Ethics Questions." *Forbes*, October 13, 2018, www.forbes.com/sites/stevedenning/2018/10/11/chief-justice-roberts-requests-tenth-circuit-to-investigate-kavanaugh-ethics-questions/#126491a01877.

55 "Donald Trump: 'First Is the Worst, Second Is the Best (Jimmy Fallon).'" *YouTube* video posted by *The Tonight Show Starring Jimmy Fallon* on February 4, 2016, www.youtube.com/watch?v=N30zt9mRi_k.

56 "Randy Rainbow." *YouTube* channel, www.youtube.com/channel/UC07F26kHKkpW_qqvXzEGALA.

57 Byrne, Deirdre. "Sarah Cooper, That Woman from TikTok Lip-syncing to Trump, Grew Up in Rockville." *MyMCM*, July 16, 2020, www.mymcmedia.org/sarah-cooper-that-woman-from-tiktok-lip-syncing-to-trump-grew-up-in-rockville/.

58 "Sarah Cooper." *TikTok* profile, www.tiktok.com/@whatchugotforme?lang=en.

59 "Sarah Cooper's Viral Trump Lip Sync Videos Act as an Interpreter for the Emotionally Blind." *YouTube* video posted by *The Late Show with Stephen Colbert* on October 28, 2020, www.youtube.com/watch?v=bKr8i23RwiU.

60 Ibid.

61 For a fun take on this point, see Delmacy, Nick. "Why Do so Many Men Imitate Women for Comedy but Not the Other Way Around?" *Cypher Avenue*, 2014, https://cypheravenue.com/why-do-so-many-men-imitate-women-for-comedy-but-not-the-other-way-around/.

62 "Sean Spicer Press Conference (Melissa McCarthy) – SNL." *YouTube* video, posted by *Saturday Night Live*, on February 5, 2017, www.youtube.com/watch?v=UWuc18xISwI.

63 Littleton, Cynthia. "Melissa McCarthy Returns to 'SNL' as a 'Calm' White House Press Secretary Sean Spicer." *Business Insider*, February 12, 2017, www.businessinsider.com/snl-melissa-mccarthy-donald-trump-white-house-press-secretary-sean-spicer-2017-2.

64 Marks, Andrea. "'I Have to Pinch Myself': Sarah Cooper's Rapid Rise from Trump TikToker to Netflix Star." *Rolling Stone*, October 27, 2020, www.rollingstone.com/tv/tv-features/sarah-cooper-interview-everythings-fine-1081258/.
65 Lyonne, Natasha. *Sarah Cooper Everything's Fine*. Netflix, 2020, www.netflix.com/title/81314070.
66 "The Tape Sarah Cooper: Everything's Fine Netflix Is a Joke." *YouTube* video, posted by *Netflix Is a Joke* on October 29, 2020, www.youtube.com/watch?v=QRu-QUeqoMs.
67 Lorenz, Taylor, Kellen Browning and Sheera Frenkel. "TikTok Teens and K-Pop Stans Say They Sank Trump Rally." *The New York Times*, June 21, 2020, www.nytimes.com/2020/06/21/style/tiktok-trump-rally-tulsa.html.
68 Warren, James. "Satirist Andy Borowitz Explains the Fine Art of Lampooning Trump." *Poynter*, October 31, 2017, www.poynter.org/news/satirist-andy-borowitz-explains-fine-art-lampooning-trump.
69 Guardian Staff. "South Park Creators to Back Off Trump Jokes: 'Satire Has Become Reality'." *The Guardian*, February 2, 2017, www.theguardian.com/tv-and-radio/2017/feb/02/south-park-donald-trump-mr-garrison.
70 "President Trump Is Making Satire Great Again." *The Economist*, February 11, 2017, www.economist.com/united-states/2017/02/11/president-trump-is-making-satire-great-again.
71 "Eric Trump Scolds Father That He Mustn't Inquire About the Businesses, for He's Sworn Not to Tell." *The Onion*, February 3, 2017, www.theonion.com/eric-trump-scolds-father-that-he-mustn-t-inquire-about-1819579588.
72 "President Trump Is Making Satire Great Again." *The Economist*, February 11, 2017, www.economist.com/united-states/2017/02/11/president-trump-is-making-satire-great-again.
73 Ibid.
74 Harris, Robert. "The Purpose and Method of Satire." *VirtualSalt*, November 22, 2018, www.virtualsalt.com/satire.htm.
75 Second Nexus Staff. "We Need to Talk About How Donald Trump's Policies Are Harming Disabled Americans." *Second Nexus*, January 16, 2018, https://secondnexus.com/news/politics/trump-policies-harm-disabled/.
76 "This Monologue Goes Out to You, Mr. President." *YouTube* video, 11:13, posted by *The Late Show with Stephen Colbert* on May 2, 2017, www.youtube.com/watch?v=HaHwlSTqA7s.
77 Ibid.
78 De Moraes, Lisa. "No FCC Fine for Stephen Colbert's Late-Night Donald Trump C★★★ Holster Crack." *Deadline*, May 23, 2017, https://deadline.com/2017/05/stephen-colbert-donald-trump-fcc-no-fine-mouth-cock-holster-monologue-1202101084/.
79 Foster, Thomas. *How to Read Literature like a Professor: A Lively and Entertaining Guide to Reading Between the Lines*. Harper, 2017, p. 261.
80 Strick, James. "A Bitter Irony." *The Washington Post*, January 23, 2017, www.washingtonpost.com/opinions/a-bitter-irony/2017/01/22/1117c8fe-df43-11e6-8902-610fe486791c_story.html?utm_term=.1cea79d7782b.
81 Ibid.
82 Borowitz, Andy. "Trump Voters Celebrate Massive Tax Cut for Everyone but Them." *The New Yorker*, November 16, 2017, www.newyorker.com/humor/borowitz-report/trump-voters-celebrate-massive-tax-cut-for-everyone-but-them.
83 Borowitz, Andy. "Nazis Feeling Neglected After Republicans' Embrace of Child Molesters." *The New Yorker*, December 5, 2017, www.newyorker.com/humor/borowitz-report/nazis-feeling-neglected-after-republicans-embrace-of-child-molesters.
84 Borowitz, Andy. "Cheney Receives Heart Transplant; Bush Still on Waiting List for Brain." *The New Yorker*, June 15, 2012, www.newyorker.com/humor/borowitz-report/cheney-receives-heart-transplant-bush-still-on-waiting-list-for-brain.

85 Associated Press. "Trump Likely to Be Most Mocked President by Late Night, Study Finds." *The Hollywood Reporter*, May 5, 2017, www.hollywoodreporter.com/news/trump-be-mocked-president-by-late-night-study-finds-1000499.
86 "Not the White House Correspondents' Dinner: Samantha Bee Roasts Donald Trump | TBS." *YouTube* video, 1:11, posted by *Full Frontal with Samantha Bee* on April 28, 2019, www.youtube.com/watch?v=xqT4A250CuM.
87 Ibid.
88 Ibid.
89 Berry, Lorraine. "The 10 Best Jokes from Sam Bee's Not the White House Correspondents' Dinner." *Pastemagazine.com*, April 30, 2017, www.pastemagazine.com/articles/2017/04/the-10-best-jokes-from-sam-bees-not-the-white-hous.html.
90 Bradley, Laura. "Samantha Bee Apologizes One Last Time for Ivanka Trump Comment-but with a Catch." *Vanity Fair*, June 7, 2018, www.vanityfair.com/hollywood/2018/06/samantha-bee-ivanka-trump-apology-full-frontal.
91 "Samantha Bee calls Ivanka a 'feckless c***' but Don't Forgive Roseanne!" *YouTube* video, posted by Maura Dowling on May 31, 2018, www.youtube.com/watch?v=_k2GQDhLZQw.
92 Randall, Eric. "The 'Death of Irony', and Its Many Reincarnations." *The Atlantic*, September 9, 2011, www.theatlantic.com/national/archive/2011/09/death-irony-and-its-many-reincarnations/338114/.
93 "The Final Irony." *The Guardian*, June 28, 2003, www.theguardian.com/theguardian/2003/jun/28/weekend7.weekend2.
94 "Stephen Colbert: The White House Correspondents' Dinner Speech." *The Guardian*, May 2, 2006, www.theguardian.com/world/2006/may/02/usa.georgebush.
95 "MEME Theory: How Donald Trump Used Memes to Become President." *YouTube* video, 35:04, posted by EmpLemon on November 8, 2017, www.youtube.com/watch?v=r8Y-P0v2Hh0.
96 Trump, Donald J. "Terrible! Just Found Out That Obama Had My 'Wires Tapped' in Trump Tower Just Before the Victory. Nothing Found. This Is McCarthyism!" *Twitter*, March 4, 2017, 3:35 a.m., https://twitter.com/realDonaldTrump/status/837989835818287106?ref_src=twsrc%5Etfw&ref_url=https%3A%2F%2Fwww.nytimes.com%2F2017%2F03%2F20%2Fopinion%2Ftrump-ruins-irony-too.html.
97 Velasquez-Manoff, Moises. "Trump Ruins Irony, too." *The New York Times*, March 20, 2017, www.nytimes.com/2017/03/20/opinion/trump-ruins-irony-too.html.
98 Hirschorn, Michael. "The End of Irony—9/11 Encyclopedia—September 10th Anniversary." *New York Magazine*, August 27, 2011, http://nymag.com/news/9-11/10th-anniversary/irony/.
99 Venditti, Phil. "I've Seen Smarter Cabinets at IKEA." *Flickr*, September 12, 2017, www.flickr.com/photos/venditti_min_min-venditti/37193822855.
100 Lewis, Charles. "Truth and Lies in the Trump Era." *The Nation*, October 13, 2017, www.thenation.com/article/truth-and-lies-in-the-trump-era/.
101 Trump, Donald J. "The Chinese Envoy, Who Just Returned from North Korea, Seems to Have Had No Impact on Little Rocket Man. Hard to Believe his People, and the Military, Put Up with Living in Such Horrible Conditions. Russia and China Condemned the Launch." *Twitter*, October 30, 2017, 4:25 a.m., https://twitter.com/realDonaldTrump/status/936209447747190784?ref_src=twsrc%5Etfw&ref_url=http%3A%2F%2Ftime.com%2F5042837%2Fdonald-trump-north-korea-twitter-china%2F.
102 "George Carlin: Why Voting Is Meaningless – 'If You Vote, You Have No Right to Complain'." *Sheepheads*, December 14, 2015, https://sheepheads.wordpress.com/2015/12/14/george-carlin-why-voting-is-meaningless-if-you-vote-you-have-no-right-to-complain/.
103 Yahr, Emily. "Read Jimmy Kimmel's Emotional Monologue That Begs Trump to Address Gun Control." *The Washington Post*, February 16, 2018, www.washingtonpost.com/

news/arts-and-entertainment/wp/2018/02/16/read-jimmy-kimmels-emotional-monologue-that-begs-trump-to-address-gun-control/?noredirect=on&utm_term=.dd84d1b27d3c.
104 Shaw, Jazz. "Even John Kasich Has Noticed That *The Daily Show with Trevor Noah* Is Tanking." *Hot Air*, March 31, 2016, https://hotair.com/archives/2016/03/31/even-john-kasich-has-noticed-that-the-daily-show-with-trevor-noah-is-tanking/.
105 Nededog, Jethro. "Trevor Noah Rips Apart Donald Trump's Anti-immigration Views in Profanity-filled Rant." *Business Insider*, September 15, 2016, www.businessinsider.com/trevor-noah-donald-trump-immigration-rant-2016-9.
106 Ibid.
107 Ibid.
108 Moore, Michael. "5 Reasons Why Trump Will Win." *Michaelmoore.com*, https://michaelmoore.com/trumpwillwin/.
109 Moore, Michael. "An Open Letter to Ivanka Trump from Michael Moore: 'Your Dad's Not Well'." https://michaelmoore.com/DearIvanka/.
110 Moore, Michael. "Michael Moore in Trumpland." 2016, www.imdb.com/title/tt6163356/.
111 Ibid.
112 Moore, Michael. "Fahrenheit 11/9." 2018, https://fahrenheit119.com/.

4
THE FIRST MEDIA-CREATED PRESIDENT

There is perhaps no better example of the absurd and disturbing relationship Donald Trump has had to the media than the "covfefe" story. On day 132 of his presidency, just after midnight, Trump tweeted, "Despite the constant negative press covfefe."[1]

By the next day, the tweet was gone, replaced by, "Who can figure out the true meaning of 'covfefe'??? Enjoy!"[2]

But in the early hours of the day between the two tweets, a literal *Twitter* army rose up to mock the concept of "covfefe."[3]

Even Merriam Webster got in on it.[4]

And, of course, comedians couldn't resist the chance to mock the tweeted typo. Jimmy Kimmel emphasized the fact that Trump kept upstaging the comedians by being ridiculous himself: "What makes me saddest is that I know I'll never write anything funnier than #covfefe."[5]

The key to the "covfefe" story was that, in the first of the two tweets, Trump was attacking the press with no context of any kind. And perhaps even more importantly, despite the absurdity of the tweet, the press covered it the next day almost as though it were as important as the latest budget bill. Thus, the "covfefe" story is as much a story about a president who takes to *Twitter* late at night to blurt out inanities as it is about news media obsessed with him.

The mainstream news media literally covered each and every trivial, idiotic thing Trump did from the start of his campaign. As Justin Charity explained it,

> It's as if Trump does in fact realize that he is nothing if not a content opportunity, a chance for the news media to exercise only its most overeager, embarrassing judgment, which maybe explains how a nation that is now under the spell of a former TV game-show host came to take journalism for granted.[6]

DOI: 10.4324/9781003294177-4

FIGURE 4.1 Trump tweets about "covfefe."

Source: @realDonaldTrump, *Twitter* 31 May 2017, https://twitter.com/realDonaldTrump/status/869766994899468288. License free image.

FIGURE 4.2 Trump notes the power of his tweet.

Source: @realDonaldTrump, *Twitter* 31 May 2017, https://twitter.com/realdonaldtrump/status/869858333477523458. License free image.

The story of the tweets epitomizes Trump's strange relationship with the media and the odd way that making fun of him helped to unite his critics. The "covfefe" tweet made no sense, was easy to mock, illustrated the public's concern that their president was firing off loony tweets at midnight, and exposed the way in which the media often let Trump set the terms of his press coverage.

But the media story about Trump is a bit more complicated than the story of "covfefe." It was, after all, Trump's celebrity media status that helped catapult him to the center of the 2016 GOP primary in the first place. The press already had a long history of offering free airtime to Trump and his latest stunt. And well before Trump became a political candidate, the news media had been gravitating more and more toward a tabloid, sensationalist style with an endless array of "breaking" stories and hyped-up taglines. The media's obsession with Trump, though, is

The First Media-Created President 87

FIGURE 4.3 One of many tweets that mocked the president's tweet.

Source: @Phil_Lewis, *Twitter* 31 May 2017, https://twitter.com/Phil_Lewis_/status/869797513427116033. License free image.

FIGURE 4.4 Merriam-Webster piles on the Trump tweet.

Source: @MerriamWebster, *Twitter* 31 May 2017, https://twitter.com/MerriamWebster/status/869782666572443648. License free image.

FIGURE 4.5 Jimmy Kimmel adds to the mocking of Trump's typo.

Source: @jimmykimmel, *Twitter* 31 May 2017, https://twitter.com/jimmykimmel/status/869799353724026880. License free image.

actually part of a longer story, one in which the news media have gravitated more and more toward stories that are sensational. To make sense of the way in which the traditional news media covered Trump, this chapter documents how the news media changed since the Walter Cronkite era of straight news journalism. From the advent of cable news to the complexities of social media, news media coverage has undergone a series of shifts that coalesced together to make Trump a news sensation. In fact, the story of the Trump presidency is as much a story about our changing media landscape as it is a story about a shift in politics.

Even more interesting is the fact that the story about the connections between Trump and the media is as silly as it is serious. Each day of his presidency was filled with a combination of absurd, ridiculous moments and disturbing, even ominous, ones. I've described the combination as tragicomedy—an unsettling blend of tragedy and comedy at the same time. Covering these sorts of twists and turns was especially challenging for the mainstream news media, but satire turned out to be exceptionally good at pointing out these extremes. As Jon Stewart once remarked while hosting *The Daily Show*, sometimes it is hard to determine whether absurd behavior is a consequence of stupidity or evil. On an episode in 2010, he decided to illustrate this point by calling in two of his correspondents, John Oliver and Wyatt Cenac, to discuss a Fox News gaffe where the conservative news channel was hyping hysteria over a so-called Ground Zero mosque that had actually been funded by one of Fox News' owners. Oliver makes the argument that Fox News is stupid; Cenac that it is evil.[7] But, of course, the answer is that it is a bit of both.

These sorts of contrasts were taken to an entirely new level by the Trump administration. It was often difficult to decide whether to laugh at the sheer stupidity of Trump and his *kakistocracy*[8] or to cry in horror at their pure evil. But that's the catch. We tended to focus on Trump as a reality TV president living in a Fox News–fueled alternate universe, and that caused us to miss the tragicomic style of his theatrics. When we focus on Trump as a reality TV president, we miss the fact that he was more than just a mesmerizing, debased, media spectacle. In a *Time* magazine article on Trump as a reality TV president, Jeff Nesbitt speculated that the Trump presidency would feel like "a political reality TV show played out on a grand stage, with producers scripting the biggest fights behind the scenes while

FIGURE 4.6 Image from the August 23, 2010, debate on *The Daily Show* between John Oliver and Wyatt Cenac.

Source: "The Parent Company Trap," *The Daily Show with Jon Stewart*, Comedy Central, 23 August, 2010, https://www.cc.com/video/nka3cd/the-daily-show-with-jon-stewart-the-parent-company-trap. License free image.

leaving plenty of room for unrehearsed, populist public drama."[9] All of this came true, but that wasn't the whole story. *Time* called Trump the "first truly made-for-television president," and yet it would be more accurate to say that he was the first made-by-television president. It was the media that catapulted him to fame by endlessly offering Trump a platform through which to hawk his brand. The critical issue, though, is that the brand itself was filled with contradictions and complexities, an odd combination of hubris, malice, and farce, that the traditional news media had a particularly hard time processing.

Perhaps, most importantly, Trump's brand artfully combined the absurd with the devastating. As Bernard Shaw puts it, tragicomedy makes "the spectator laugh with one side of his mouth and cry with the other."[10] Trump critics thus found themselves alternately amused and shocked. The art of the spectacle of tragicomedy is that it never gives the spectator a break, and it constantly alters their emotional state. It produces a never-ending extreme of emotional responses and a mind-numbing set of incompatible realities. It wears us out. Trump, though, took the tragicomic form to new levels. One of the special elements of Trumpian tragicomedy was its endless loop. Just as a tragicomic cycle begins to fade out, another pops up in its place. It's like tragicomic Whack-a-Mole. The stupid and the evil just keep popping up out of nowhere, and the news media can't take their eyes off the show.

What would have happened, for instance, if the news media had chosen to ignore a stupid late-night tweet with a typo? Might the news have covered something else more important? And what if the "news" was not always about Trump? But that's not what happened, and it is not what continued to happen, even once it was clear that he had lost the 2020 election. For the most part, the news media are reactive, allowing their focus to disproportionately cover Trump's every move.

New York Times science editor Michael Roston made the point when he tweeted, "President Trump, America's assignment editor."[11]

Trump didn't just control his news media coverage; he was also obsessed with consuming it himself. Reports suggest that Trump consumed more news media, mostly from Fox News, than previous presidents since the advent of 24/7 news broadcasting on cable. His aides reported that he woke up each day and nervously flipped through TV channels and read tweets.[12] He was a media junkie in a way the nation hadn't seen before in a sitting president.

Adding yet another twist to the story is the reaction of the public to Trump's media coverage, a reaction that highlights the rising political polarization that increasingly defines our nation's political attitudes. Despite the fact that Trump came under constant criticism in the news media, especially, for example, when he refused to concede an election he had obviously lost, his supporters remained loyal. As Matt Taibbi documents in *Hate, Inc.*, their lack of interest in objective news media coverage of Trump is largely due to a radical shift in the sources of news that different constituencies consumed before the 2016 election and after.[13] While it has always been true that the left has gravitated to certain news outlets and the right to others, the polarization of news media consumption was exceptionally stark in 2016, and it only got worse in 2020. What's more, the registers through which voters consumed media were polarized. As Dannagal Young explains in *Irony and Outrage*, it wasn't just the outlets that were different; it was the tone and tenor of them that were radically opposed as well, with Republicans leaning more toward outrage and Democrats toward irony.[14] In the 2016 election, there was virtually no news outlet that appealed to both Democrats and Republicans. Not one overlapping news source crossed party lines. To make it more complicated, 47 percent of consistent conservatives gravitated to only one news source, Fox News, while consistent liberals trusted 24 out of 36 news sources in a 2014 poll conducted by the Pew Research Center. For liberals, the top news sources were BBC, NPR, and PBS.[15]

This division was then exacerbated by the rise of "fake" news—a term that resonates on at least five levels, which I'll analyze more later, the most important of which is the weaponized use of misleading information to influence political behavior.[16] Fake news stories got to almost everyone in 2016, but they were considerably more successful with conservatives, another factor that further divided the electorate. Rumors, conspiracy theories, and hype are nothing new for an election, but what was new in 2016 was the fact that, in the days leading to the election, fake news stories were shared at a higher rate than legitimate ones and more often by those who later voted for Trump.[17] The speed and reach of these stories further created a dilemma for credible news sources, especially in a landscape in which audiences exhibited great distrust in the news and often gravitated toward alternative outlets. How could the news media capture public attention without themselves emulating the sensationalism of many fake news sites?

If one were to sum up the connection between the Trump era and news media, the common thread would be that the story is a case of extremes. To understand the complexities of the way in which Trump was covered in the news requires one to pay attention to a lot of seemingly contradictory information, such as the fact that it became the satirical comedians who were often informing the public more than the mainstream news. Or the fact that Trump both easily manipulated the news media and also paid high sums of money to keep potentially damaging stories out of it. Or the fact that, as the 2016 election neared, fake news was shared more frequently than traditional news on *Facebook*. To make it even more complicated, most of the news media practices we witnessed during the Trump era were not actually unique to Trump but had been a long time in the making. While it would be appealing to suggest that it was the Trump era that ushered in a decline in quality news coverage, the truth is that much of the news media were already doing a pretty lousy job of covering critical political issues well before Trump decided to run.[18] The election of Trump, therefore, made a series of shifts in the news media system even more obvious than they were before.

The Media's Trump Obsession

While it would be convenient to begin describing the connection between the Trump presidency and the news by analyzing the impact of Trump's tweets, his denigration of the news media, and the ways in which this behavior contributed to public distrust of the news, that's not really where this all started. It started with the news media's very own Trump obsession—an obsession that may well be responsible for Trump winning the 2016 election. It's difficult to fully outline the degree to which the media were already obsessed with Trump well before he even announced his candidacy. As I showed in the second chapter of this book, we had already had three decades of Trump jokes before Seth Meyers roasted him in 2011. In *Fahrenheit 11/9*, Michael Moore revisits the time that he appeared alongside Trump on the Roseanne Barr show back in the 1990s. The point is that Trump rose to prominence as a candidate at least in part because he was already a very well-known figure in the media.

As many jumped to understand how it was that Trump could become a front-runner in the 2016 GOP primary, others were quick to note that he would never have been able to advance as a candidate without his legacy as host of *The Apprentice*. As Emily Nussbaum wrote for *The New Yorker*, "[I]f 'The Apprentice' didn't get Trump elected, it is surely what made him electable."[19] Before *The Apprentice* launched in 2004, Trump's career seemed to have tanked. His bankruptcies, scandals in Atlantic City, and difficulty raising capital all signaled that he was losing his edge. Then, producer Mark Burnett approached him in 2002 about launching a reality show that would redefine the Trump image. Before the U.S. public knew what had happened, a disgraced businessman was being touted as a "titan of industry."[20] Critical to the story of the rise of reality TV Trump was the role of Jeff Zucker, then head of TV programming for NBC, who saw in the Trump TV show a way to rescue NBC.

Think what you want about the Trump brand of swashbuckling, but none of his celebrity swagger would have been possible if TV execs hadn't already launched the reality TV era and given Trump a platform to attract national attention. Burnett, who was responsible for Trump's offer to host a show for NBC, is known as the father of reality TV. He produced *Survivor* for CBS, initiating a new genre of TV that offered viewers raw, emotive aesthetics at a low production cost. What Burnett loved in Trump was his penchant for saying "whatever he wants"—a habit destined to keep viewers glued to the TV to watch Trump's next outrageous outburst.[21] In a panel discussion about *The Apprentice* in 2004, Burnett described what it was about Trump that made him perfect for reality TV:

> If you're Donald's friend, he'll defend you all day long. If you're not, he's going to kill you. And that's very American. He's like the guys who built the West. America is the one country that supports the entire world—because of guys like Donald, who create jobs and a tax base that can support the entire planet.[22]

Burnett then went on to say that *The Apprentice* was "a love letter from me to America, and to New York City, because we chose New York City, about what makes America great." This was Burnett in 2004, literally handing Trump his 2016 campaign slogan.

The Apprentice would hit ratings snags almost immediately after the first season, and there were various efforts to ramp up interest in the show. It was canceled, then revived as *Celebrity Apprentice*. By 2015, NBC fired Trump. He had already been an Obama-baiting birther for four years by then, but his comments about Mexican rapists when he launched his presidential campaign were too much for the network. Even though he would spend most of his campaign complaining that the media had treated him unfairly, it was clear that without their obsession with him, he would have never built up the necessary celebrity cache to enter the national spotlight as a presidential candidate with no prior military or government experience.

Trump, though, wasn't a common celebrity; he was a celebrity who already had a history of playing the media to his benefit. Perhaps one of the most notorious examples of this was the accusation that Trump pretended to be his own spokesman in interviews with reporters in the 1990s. In May of 2016, *The Washington Post* acquired audio of an interview between a *People* magazine reporter and a so-called Trump spokesman, who is clearly just Trump himself.[23] In it, his Queens accent is unmistakable. The *Post* reported that Trump later admitted to the impersonation in another *People* magazine article, but during the 2016 election, he denied the charade.

This game pales, though, in connection to Trump's major media stunt: his birther mania, where he publicly called on Barack Obama to prove he was a U.S. citizen in 2012. Everything about Trump's birtherism was designed to give him a stream of free press. In a video made in Trump Tower, Trump stated,

> If Barack Obama opens up and gives his college records and applications, and if he gives his passport applications and records, I will give, to a charity

of his choice—inner city children in Chicago, American Cancer Society, AIDS research, anything he wants—a check, immediately, for $5 million. The check will be given within one hour after he released all of the records, so stated.[24]

At the time, Obama had already released his long-form birth certificate, but Trump decided to claim that was insufficient proof. It was a perfect example of how Trump could create a media sensation out of thin air. Trump was able to create a spectacle where there shouldn't have been one. And, even more importantly, he was able to set the terms. Rather than cover the story as the delusions of a megalomaniac, the media allowed the Trump offer to draw attention. All eyes were on Trump, not on Obama, and not on any other major news story. Trump had literally created a media spectacle out of nothing but bluster and swagger.

But there's more. Two years later, in a speech at the National Press Club, Trump would recount the story and suggest that, despite giving him a fairly endless stream of media coverage over his ridiculous stunt, the media had gotten it wrong. In his 2014 speech, Trump said that, at the last minute, he had actually upped his offer to $50 million:

> Now then, what wasn't reported by the press is, sometime just prior to the expiration date of that offer, I raised the offer to $50 million. $50 million! For charity. Pick your charity, for $50 million, and let me see your records! And I never heard from him.[25]

What astonishes about this later moment is that (1) Trump was an invited speaker at the National Press Club, a fact that reveals a lot about how the press was already fascinated by him, and (2) he used that moment to criticize his press coverage while being honored by the press itself. It was a perfect demonstration of the bizarre ways in which Trump would force the press to cover him bashing it once he became a politician. Even weirder, the press seemed to love him anyway because, despite his blustering comments, he drew a sell-out crowd. In the opening remarks by then–National Press Club President Myron Belkind, Belkind gushed over the way that Trump had been able to build and manage his brand, suggesting it was time for journalists to follow Trump's lead.

Processing this moment is critical to understanding the media's relationship to Trump. Well before he had announced his campaign, Trump was treated in the media as a celebrity regularly involved in scandals and other ridiculous behavior, as a pundit who had opinions that were worth discussing, as a source of knowledge and advice about success, and as an orange-faced buffoon. One of the reasons it became so hard for the media to address the policy implications of a Trump presidency was because he had already built a relationship with them—one in which he was always both absurd and fascinating. Most of the early coverage of the Trump campaign –and much of the news coverage of his presidency—followed these same patterns of laughing at him, being in awe of him, and obsessing over him at the same time.

But wait, you may be thinking, we can't just lump all of "the media" together. Surely there is a difference between the broadcast news, morning talk shows, print news, and reality TV. Those divisions should be there, but the Trump era exposed how the lines between different types of media had already begun to blur significantly. Then Trump simply blew those divisions right apart. When we talk about Trump, it is extremely hard to create a dividing line between the ways in which he is covered in the straight news press and in the media at large. Because Trump has always used both entertainment media and news media to help produce his brand, defining his media persona as largely crafted by the press is not just impossible but actually incorrect. And, to make it more complicated, if it had at one time been possible to separate a comedian like Johnny Carson from a journalist like Walter Cronkite, by the time of the Trump campaign, those lines were far less clear. What, for instance, do we do with a show like *Fox and Friends*? Or how do we make sense of the shouting match panels on CNN? And how do we account for the fact that an appearance on Stephen Colbert's *The Late Show* can have a measurable impact on a politician's polling? As explained by Jeffrey Jones in his 2010 book *Entertaining Politics*, news media had already adopted many entertaining features well before the Trump campaign.[26] To make matters even more messy, Trump, for his part, didn't make much of a distinction across types of media. For him, the division was whether he was being treated well or critiqued. In his view, there was no real difference between a sketch from *Saturday Night Live* (*SNL*), a daytime talk show, or a report by Anderson Cooper.

Again, the story here is that Trump was the symptom, but not the cause. In fact, if we want to blame anyone for really helping to blur the lines between the press and entertainment, it would be Jeff Zucker, who started his tenure as head of CNN stating that he wanted to "broaden the definition of news."[27] It was Zucker, after all, who gave Trump his show on NBC, only to then leave NBC to take over CNN. Zucker was the one who directed CNN to cover the Trump campaign endlessly, often airing nothing but an empty podium as Trump showed up late for a rally. As *The New York Times* put it, Zucker decided to use the Trump campaign to turn CNN into a new version of "must-see TV." Trump was well aware of the extent to which he was being given extra airtime by CNN, and apparently, according to MSNBC host Joe Scarborough, Trump used to refer to Zucker as his "personal booker." To further complicate things, each time Trump attacked CNN, its ratings went up. In 2016, CNN's average daytime audience was up over 50 percent, and its prime-time audience popped 70 percent. That year the network earned nearly $1 billion, making it the most profitable year in CNN's history.[28] Its 2018 numbers, thanks to the fact that it framed the midterm elections as a referendum on Trump, only went up.

There is another side to the story of Trump and the media that is unique in the history of political coverage: Trump had already weathered endless scandal coverage well before he was a candidate, and none of it had hurt his image in any significant way. In fact, documentation of the history of Trump's scandals and the media coverage of them would take its own book. Dating back to the 1970s, Trump had been involved in sex scandals, with a long list of women attempting to sue him for unwanted advances or worse.[29] His connections to beauty pageants, first as an attendee and later as an owner, were rife with stories of Trump's creepy behavior and sexual harassment. In one story, Trump reportedly joined one model in bed, uninvited. Even his former wife Ivana accused him of marital rape, though she later recanted. While Trump has, thus far, avoided any convictions, there is actual tape of him admitting to sexual assault. The 2005 *Access Hollywood* tape, on which Trump brags about being able to "grab them by the pussy," clearly supports many of the women who have accused him of attacking them.[30]

While we don't want to lose sight of the credible array of victims who have accused Trump of assault, it is critical to process the fact that when these stories broke in the news media, they did not hurt the Trump brand in any measurable way. This all points to the fact that, for Trump, scandals not only had no impact but were possibly only helpful to him, allowing him to build his image as tough, independent, and outside of the reach of social norms. Trump was well aware of his special scandal status, which is why he was brash enough to say during a January 2016 rally that he could "stand in the middle of 5th Avenue and shoot somebody" and not lose any voters.[31] While this was as much a statement about his supporters as it was about his image, it also spoke volumes about Trump's boast that the news media were completely incapable of covering him in a way that might have any negative impact on his campaign. Recall, as a point of comparison, that when Democrat Gary Hart was running in the 1988 primary, his candidacy was destroyed by a sex scandal including Donna Rice.[32] At the time, Hart was by far the strongest contender for the Democratic nomination, with a double-digit lead. Polls showed that Hart would beat George Bush by 13 points. All of that would end when news broke of an alleged affair with Rice.

The story about Hart's fall, though, is again as much a story about the news media as it is about a politician's ethics. Prior to the Hart scandal, the news media had learned to follow the lead of Bob Woodward and Carl Bernstein, the two *Washington Post* reporters who had successfully brought down Richard Nixon with their reporting on Watergate. While for some their fame was tied to their dogged search for the truth, the reality is that their legacy also left reporters with a heightened taste for scandal. As Matt Bai explains it in the *New York Times Magazine*, after Watergate, journalists became obsessed with uncovering any and all scandals, whether significant or not.[33] This remains true today. What has changed, though, is the fact that, in the era of Gary Hart, a scandal could destroy a politician's career. Not so with Trump.

Trump had already had a tremendous amount of scandal coverage before he announced his run. Beyond the sex scandals, there were stories of the use of undocumented labor (including models), racial housing discrimination, four bankruptcies, mafia ties, tenant intimidation, a fake university, antitrust violations, refusal to pay workers and contractors, violation of self-dealing rules with the Trump Foundation, and more.[34] Throughout all of these scandals, Trump had learned to treat the news media with bluster, bullying, and contempt. He had sued lawyers and threatened libel suits. And he had cozied up to media moguls like David Pecker, chairman of American Media, which publishes *The National Enquirer*. Pecker would later admit to paying off Trump accusers and burying negative stories on the candidate's behalf during the 2016 campaign. Michael Cohen, Trump's lawyer before and during the campaign, would admit to paying off women who had scandalous stories to tell. Cohen also played point when Trump was negotiating interview appearances. Seth Meyers explains that Cohen attempted to broker an interview between Meyers and Trump, essentially sending a list of questions Trump would agree to and a list of topics that were off-limits.[35] Meyers, of course, declined the charade, but the story reveals yet another facet to the dynamics between Trump and the media. Trump both bullied and feared the media. On the one hand, he seemed unconcerned that there could be any story that would affect his image. On the other hand, there was proof that he had tried to suppress negative stories, even at the risk of engaging in criminal behavior. This contradiction again is critical to understand. Trump was equally dismissive of the press and scared of it.

All media coverage of Trump wasn't about scandals, though. There was plenty of brand-building coverage as well. Take, for example, the 1989 *Time* magazine cover that features Trump with the line, "This man may make turn you green with envy—or just turn you off. Flaunting it is the fame, and TRUMP is the name."[36] The cover featured a photo of Trump holding the ace of diamonds, wearing a red tie, and looking smug. While the media loved to poke at Trump, there is little question that they also loved to cover his brash style.

Trump played up his swagger for the media, and they lapped it up. And when they didn't, he just pretended they did anyway. In one especially odd example of Trump simulating his own media coverage, he apparently put framed fake *Time* magazine covers in at least five of his clubs. As *The Washington Post* reported, a framed fake cover of a May 2009 *Time* magazine featuring Trump on the cover was hung in at least five of Trump's clubs, from South Florida to Scotland. "Donald Trump: The 'Apprentice' is a television smash!" the headline read, and above the *Time* nameplate there was another headline in all caps: "TRUMP IS HITTING ON ALL FRONTS . . . EVEN TV!" As the *Post* notes, one of the obvious tells that the cover is a fake is the fact that an exclamation point appears after both headlines: "Time headlines don't yell."[37]

Well before he announced his run, Trump knew he could play the media, and he knew that when they didn't cover him the way he wanted, he could attack them and create his own media scandal. Trump likes to boast that the news media love him because he boosts ratings, and there is no doubt that he is right. In 2017, for example, MSNBC had its best year yet, increasing its prime time viewing by 550,000 viewers compared with 2016.[38] Ratings were up across the board, suggesting that the news media had little incentive to dial back their coverage of him.

Trump's unusual relationship with the news media explains why coverage of his candidacy was so radically disproportionate to that of other candidates in the 2016 race. There are data on the degree of coverage each candidate received in the 2016 race, and those figures point directly to a highly unusual media obsession with Trump throughout his campaign. Without question, from the moment that Trump announced his candidacy, he was the center of press attention. In fact, he was the

FIGURE 4.7 The fake *Time* Donald Trump cover.

Source: David A. Fahrenthold, "A Time magazine with Trump on the cover hangs in his golf clubs. It's fake," *The Washington Post*, 27 June 2017, https://www.washingtonpost.com/politics/a-time-magazine-with-trump-on-the-cover-hangs-in-his-golf-clubs-its-fake/2017/06/27/0adf96de-5850-11e7-ba90-f5875b7d1876_story.html?utm_term=.0ed208c038e7. License free image.

most heavily covered candidate each month. As Thomas Patterson of Harvard's Shorenstein Center documents, the difference in the coverage of Trump wasn't even close. In the early months, Trump had 63 percent of coverage compared to 37 percent for his most heavily covered rival.[39]

From the very start it became clear that the media could not resist giving Trump free coverage. It is critical to remember that, when Trump ran his campaign, he didn't have a super PAC raising funds to help promote him. By all accounts, he also skimped on spending money for on-the-ground organizing and field offices. Even more significant, he spent less than his rivals on television advertising. To illustrate the gap, by February of 2016, he had spent about $10 million on television ads, compared to $82 million spent by the Jeb Bush campaign. Trump didn't spend nearly as much as his competition, but he was on air far more. The gap is described as paid versus earned media.[40] While earned media typically outweigh paid media in an election cycle, the Trump campaign set new standards for the gap. As *The*

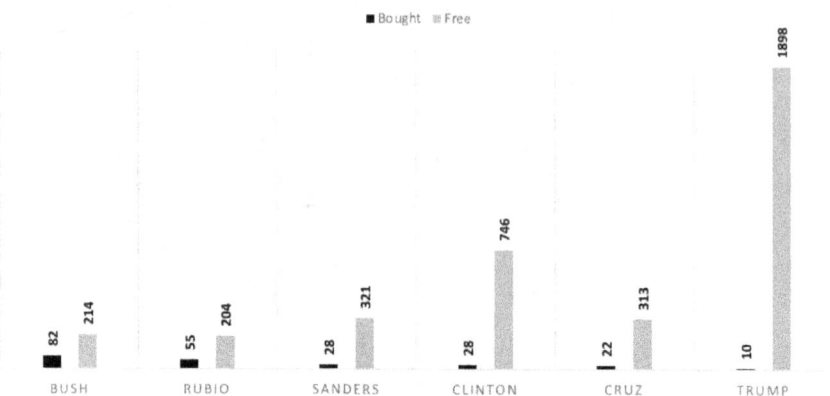

FIGURE 4.8 This graph illustrates the huge gap between Trump's paid versus earned media in comparison with other candidates.

New York Times reported, "The big difference between Mr. Trump and other candidates is that he is far better than any other candidate—maybe than any candidate ever—at earning media."[41]

By February of 2016, Trump had earned nearly $2 billion in free media coverage—an amount that exceeded the combined numbers for both Ted Cruz and Hillary Clinton in the same time frame.

Patterson explains that during the general election period, the pattern of overcovering Trump continued. Each week, Trump got more press attention than Clinton did. In the end, Trump received 15 percent more coverage than Clinton in the general race. But even more noteworthy was the fact that Trump was regularly able to set the terms, define the stakes, and get airtime, even when the story was about Clinton. Patterson notes that when a candidate was seen in the news talking about Clinton, the voice heard was typically Trump's and not hers. Yet when the talk was about Trump, he was also more likely to be the voice behind the message. "Lock her up" and "Make America great again" were heard more often than "He's unqualified" and "Stronger together."[42]

Patterson attributes the news media's fascination with Trump to the fact that he offered them a candidate "ideally suited to journalists' story needs;" he was new and different, and—even better—he offered an endless stream of outrage and conflict. Both Clinton and Trump, for example, tweeted throughout the campaign. But there was virtually no coverage of Clinton's tweets. In contrast, as I've explained already, Trump's tweets became an ongoing source of news coverage, even when they weren't filled with typos. Both candidates also gave speeches regularly, yet because Clinton's were not filled with bullying and aggression, from the candidate as well as from the audience, they received far less media attention than Trump's did. As Patterson describes it, Trump appealed to journalists as no other presidential nominee had in modern times.

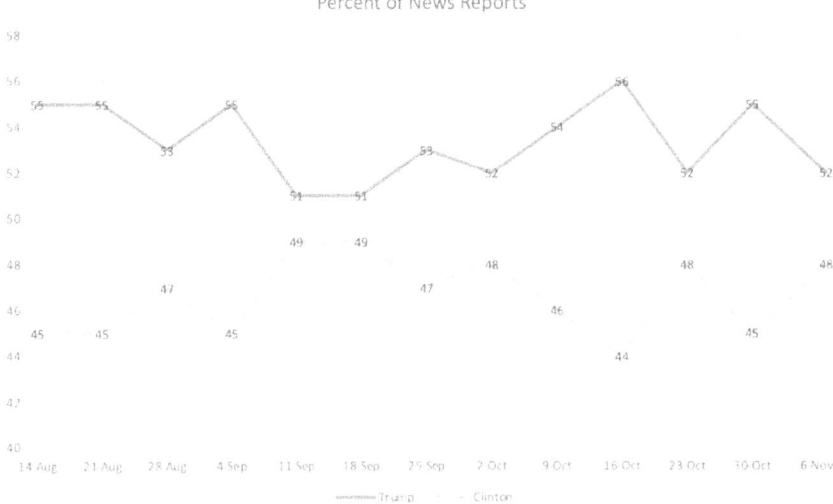

FIGURE 4.9 Breakdown of percentage of news reports about each candidate.

Source: Thomas Patterson, "News Coverage of Donald Trump's First 100 Days", Harvard Kennedy School Shorenstein Center on Media, Politics, and Public Policy, May 18, 2017, https://shorensteincenter. org/news-coverage-donald-trumps-first-100-days/. License free image.

The obsession with Trump didn't end after the election. Harvard's Shorenstein Center on Media, Politics and Public Policy analyzed news coverage of Trump's first 100 days in office.[43] It gathered data on news reports in the print editions of *The New York Times*, *The Wall Street Journal*, and *The Washington Post*, the main newscasts of CBS, CNN, Fox News, and NBC, and three European news outlets (the UK's *Financial Times* and BBC and Germany's ARD), and what it found was astonishing. After the inauguration, Trump was the topic of 41 percent of all news stories. As a point of comparison, he received three times the amount of coverage given to previous presidents. Even more importantly, he was also the featured speaker in nearly two-thirds of his coverage. Despite the fact that almost all of the topics covered were negative stories about Trump, the Shorenstein study further found that Republican voices accounted for 80 percent of what newsmakers said about the Trump presidency, compared to only 6 percent for Democrats and 3 percent for those involved in anti-Trump protests. So, again, despite most stories having a negative slant, the coverage itself gave far more airtime to Republican voices than to Democratic ones.

When Trump wanted media attention, he got it. Consider this comparison. When President Obama wanted to directly address the nation to discuss a policy change for Dreamers—immigrants brought to the United States as children—the networks refused to cover it. In contrast, when Trump wanted to directly address the nation to make a case for his border wall, each network covered it, despite the fact that overwhelming evidence suggested that a border wall costing over $5 billion was not in the nation's best interest.[44] While there was some early debate

> Matthew Chapman
> @fawfulfan
>
> Obama: I need airtime to discuss a policy change to give work permits to Dreamers.
>
> ABC/CBS/NBC: No, that's too partisan.
>
> Trump: I manufactured a fake border crisis and shut down the govt over it and I want airtime to issue threats to Democrats.
>
> ABC/CBS/NBC: Of course, sir!
>
> 6:57 AM · Jan 8, 2019 · Twitter for iPhone

FIGURE 4.10 This tweet by reporter Matthew Chapman illustrates the double standard of the news media's treatment of Obama versus Trump.

Source: @fawfulfan, *Twitter* 8 January 2019, https://twitter.com/fawfulfan/status/1082607143239540737. License free image.

about whether to air the address, in the end, Trump's speech aired on 11 networks and was seen by 43.3 million viewers. In contrast, when Obama addressed the nation in 2014 about fighting ISIS, his address was seen by 34 million people.[45]

Trump's outrageous amount of free coverage, the disproportionate time given to his voice and those of other Republicans, and the fact that the news media cover everything he does, even his stupid tweets, all point to a media obsession with Trump unlike any we have seen in the history of U.S. political news media. While it is difficult to assess the ability of the news to shape public opinion, one thing is clear: the news media's obsession with Trump suggested that he was news. As political scientist Bernard Cohen explains it, the press "may not be successful much of the time in telling people what to think, but it is stunningly successful in telling them what to think about."[46]

Will the Real Fake News Please Stand Up?

Clearly one part of the story about Trump and the media is that fact that the mainstream press coverage showed an intense fascination with Trump, one that may well have affected voters. Another is the fact that, for the first time in U.S. history, there was a measurable incursion of propagandistic fake news that was specifically geared to supporting Trump's campaign.

The term "fake news" was deployed so regularly throughout the 2016 campaign to mean different things that it often lost any clear meaning. At one level, as I've already outlined, there was a legitimate claim that the "real" news was falling down on the job. As I'll explain in greater detail to follow, for decades the news media in the United States have gravitated toward a sensationalist, tabloid format that favors ratings over reality. But the news media's absolutely outrageous obsession with Trump's every move was only part of the problem. There had also been a measurable rise in punditry and opinion reporting over Walter Cronkite–style, "and that's the way it is" reporting. Added to that were stories of journalists lacking integrity. In one especially disturbing example, there was the case of Brian Williams, who had fabricated stories of his own journalistic heroism. In 2015, he recanted a story of his experiences covering the Iraq War in which he claimed that he had been on a helicopter that was forced down after being shot with an RPG. As punishment, he had to take a leave of absence from NBC for six months.[47] Then there were the rash of sexual misconduct claims lodged against a series of media superstars, including Charlie Rose, Matt Lauer, Glenn Thrush, Bill O'Reilly, Roger Ailes, and Les Moonves—to name only some of them. As Michael Moore makes clear in his film *Fahrenheit 11/9*, there is significant evidence to suggest that Hillary Clinton was not given a fair shake by the media in the 2016 campaign, given the overwhelming power wielded at the time by men who had a history of sexually harassing women.[48]

After Trump was elected, the "real" cable news shows had a habit of inviting a Trump spokesperson or apologist to join a panel to debate an issue. This practice was especially common on CNN. There was no measurable news value to what tended to devolve into shouting matches. In the early days, Trump representatives often found themselves able to go on air and say anything they wanted with almost no resistance of any kind. It was CNN's Jake Tapper who first started to push back, but even when he did question Trump spokesperson Kellyanne Conway, she was given quite a bit of time to repeat her outrageous claims.

Take, for example, the moment after the 2018 State of the Union Address when Tapper said he would like Trump to stop lying.[49] In that exchange, Conway appeared, yet again, with Tapper as a guest. As they discussed the speech, Tapper told Conway he was tired of the president lying and wished he would stop. But Conway got the best of Tapper. She first disputed the claim that Trump lied, and then she turned the conversation around by claiming that Tapper had only said that because he wanted "to go viral" by mentioning Trump and lies. The video did go viral, and while it brought attention to Tapper, it inadvertently reinforced Conway's claim and made her case for her. Score: Conway 1; Tapper 0. The point is that even when the mainstream news was trying to resist the Trump administration's manipulation of the truth, they often seemed to be just another act in the circus.

These were only some of the reasons why public trust in the news media was in severe decline as Trump took over the White House. After the 2016 election, public trust was the lowest Gallup had ever recorded. Overall, 32 percent of the U.S. public expressed "a great deal" or "a fair amount" of trust in the mass news media, but the real news was the stark division across parties. Only 14 percent of Republicans believed that the news media got the facts straight.[50]

The public's declining trust in the mainstream news media was a key factor in the rise of propagandistic fake news during the 2016 election. It was partly because

FIGURE 4.11 Jake Tapper with Kellyanne Conway in what appears to be yet another publicity stunt of feigned outrage.

Source: "Tapper to Conway: 'I'd Like Trump to Stop Lying'", CNN, May 6, 2018, https://www.cnn.com/videos/politics/2018/05/06/tapper-presses-kellyanne-conway-trump-truths-lies-sot-sotu.cnn. License free image.

Americans Who Believe the News Media Get the Facts Straight

Republicans	14%
Democrats	62%

FIGURE 4.12 Gallup finds a stark political divide on trust in the news media.

Source: Art Swift, "Americans' Trust in Mass Media Sinks to New Low", Gallup, September 14, 2016, https://news.gallup.com/poll/195542/americans-trust-mass-media-sinks-new-low.aspx. License free image.

the public already thought of the news media as "fake" that the actual fake news was able to spread.

There are essentially five meanings for the phrase "fake news": the first is fake news as propaganda. There is now considerable evidence that before, during, and after the 2016 election there was a substantial amount of propagandistic fake news aimed at sowing division across parties and raising support for Trump. Research shows that the bulk of these efforts stemmed from within Russia. Totals released from social media companies and the congressional committees investigating the Russian efforts to influence the 2016 presidential election through social media show that 80,000 Russia-linked stories reached over 126 million adult American *Facebook* users. In addition, *Twitter* has suspended approximately 2,700 accounts since the election and identified nearly 36,000 Russian "bot" accounts.[51] In a 37-page indictment of 13 Russians from Special Counsel Robert Mueller in February 2018, it appeared that the Internet Research Agency, linked to the Russian government, spent approximately $1.25 million on fake ads on social media in the lead-up to the 2016 election. From mid-2015 to mid-2017, Russian ads totaled about 37 million impressions, but some estimates posit that as many as one-third of the country could have been exposed to Russian ads and fake news during this period.[52]

Even more disturbing was the handful of fake news stories that were able to gain enough attention from the larger public that they were later repeated in the mainstream media. Among these were conspiracy theories related to Hillary Clinton and those closely associated with her campaign about the death of Democratic National Committee (DNC) staffer Seth Rich. The second high-traction, fabricated, anti-Clinton story involved a child sex-trafficking ring being run out of a pizza restaurant in Washington D.C. Both of these stories were covered in the mainstream media—on cable news and in print—for several days, even though both were littered with unsubstantiated claims and were directly linked to anonymous commenters on *4Chan* and *Reddit*. The fact that a propaganda story started on a comment-thread website like *Reddit* and then migrated into the mainstream news further underscores the blurring of media lines that we saw during the election. These shifts proved that the notion that "news" starts with accredited journalists was clearly history.

Added to the well-documented efforts to influence voters by using fake news propaganda was the fact that the 2016 election was marked by the rise of for-profit fake news, some of which considered itself hoax news. This was a different, yet no less pernicious, form of fake news. One example of the spread of this sort of fake news was the story of Macedonian teenagers who made up fake news stories for clicks and money.[53] The Macedonian millennials weren't specifically attempting to influence the election or analyze U.S. politics. Their goal was to attract U.S. visitors through *Facebook* and make money off of the sales of display ads on their bootleg politics sites.[54] The core idea behind these fake articles was that it was easy to make things up that would be shared by ideologues. One sample headline read, "Hillary Clinton in 2013: 'I Would Like to See People Like Donald Trump Run for Office; They're Honest and Can't Be Bought.'"[55] While the article was entirely made up, the for-profit fake news peddlers knew that such a headline would get traction, so they kept producing stories like it.

Perhaps the most infamous purveyor of fake news in 2016 was Paul Horner, who was reported to have died mysteriously shortly after the election. Horner, who was 38 in 2016, managed to get Trump's son Eric and his campaign manager, Corey Lewandowsky, to tweet links to his fake news stories, a practice that guaranteed Horner a nice take in click revenue. He even managed to hoax sites like *Google* into including his pieces in trending news. Horner wrote pieces with titles like, "The Amish in America Commit Their Vote to Donald Trump; Guaranteeing Him a Presidential Victory" and "Donald Trump Protester Speaks Out: 'I was Paid $3,500 to Protest.'"[56] Horner imagined his work as parody, but really it was a hoax, designed to deliberately dupe users. When asked later about his influence on the election, Horner stated, "My sites were picked up by Trump supporters all the time. I think Trump is in the White House because of me. His followers don't fact-check anything—they'll post everything, believe anything."[57]

While researchers are still trying to analyze the full impact of propagandistic and for-profit fake news, we now know that thousands of such stories circulated.[58] The effects of these stories, though, went well beyond the issue of news credibility. Research shows that both Democrats and Republicans were susceptible to ideologically slanted news that was in line with their personal views and were thus 15 percent more likely to believe fake news stories with which they agreed. Data show a marked partisan breakdown, though, in the extent to which fake news was believed and shared. Republicans were far more likely to fall for fake news—they viewed more fake news and shared it more often.[59] We also know that the spread of fake news skewed by age, with older *Facebook* users, especially those over 65, far more likely to fall for fake news than younger users.[60] Yet, one of the thorny questions that remains is whether there is evidence that any of this fake news swayed voters. Given that almost all of the stories viewed and shared simply confirmed existing voter sentiments, it is hard to determine whether the circulation of these stories affected the overall outcome of the election. While one set of researchers believes there is evidence that these stories might have caused enough voters to defect from Clinton and move to Trump, as of yet, the data are not conclusive.[61]

But there is one way in which this fake news does seem to have affected voters: it increased social divisions and sowed even more partisan discord. In fact, a review of fake stories showed that they were less about misinforming the public and more about being inflammatory. Perhaps the best example of this is the story referenced earlier, which came to be known as Pizzagate. The rumor was that Clinton and her team ran a child sex-trafficking ring out of a D.C.-based pizza parlor. The pizza parlor, which had no connection to the story whatsoever, was subsequently picketed. Then, in December 2016, nearly a month after the election, Edgar Maddison Welch entered the pizza parlor and fired three gunshots with an AR-15-style rifle, claiming that he was there to save the kids. To underscore the tenacity of the fake news mindset, after Welch was arrested, some conspiracy theorists claimed the shooting was a staged effort to discredit their legitimate concerns.[62]

And that leads us to yet another version of fake news: alt-right, pro-Trump news. In the midst of the growing circulation of propagandistic and for-profit fake news was a whole new level of openly partisan, alt-right "news" hawked by conspiracy theory types like Alex Jones and the fringe right "news" found on Breitbart. Again, this is a story with a far longer history than that of the political career of Donald Trump. As I'll show in the following, the real pivot point is 1987 when the Fairness Doctrine was abolished, allowing for the rise of openly partisan talk radio shows. Suddenly, a personality like Rush Limbaugh could fill hours and hours of airtime with unsubstantiated political rants. While alt-right media in this country started on radio, they quickly moved on to other formats: Fox News for cable, Breitbart on line, and Alex Jones on *YouTube*, just to offer a sample.

To understand the series of key moments that contributed to the way in which the media covered Trump, check out this brief list of pre-2016 highlights:[63,64,65,66,67]

TIMELINE OF PRE-2016 KEY MEDIA MOMENTS

1969: Presidential candidate Richard Nixon speaks of the "silent majority" that is unrepresented, and vice presidential candidate Spiro Agnew speaks of liberal "media bias." Together these concepts shape many conservative attitudes about the news media going forward and foment an attitude of distrusting news media among conservative voters.

1976: Basic cable television launches and forces prime time newscasts to compete with a wide range of entertainment programming, eventually offering viewers the choice of watching the news or shows like *Baywatch*. Thus begins a visible difference in the ways in which news media broadcasts attempt to use flash and flare to keep viewers tuned in.

1987: FCC abolishes the Fairness Doctrine, which required the holders of broadcast licenses both to present controversial issues of public importance and to do so in a manner that was—in the FCC's view—honest, equitable, and balanced. The abolishment of the Fairness Doctrine leads to the rise of figures like Rush Limbaugh and other examples of alt-right news radio hosts who are able to fill hours of airtime with partisan rants.

1988: CNN is founded as the first 24/7 news channel. Because there isn't an endless cycle of news to cover, news shifts from reports to pundit and panel shows, on which viewers are given a couple of minutes of content and then asked to watch panelists fight about it. The structure leads to a real decline in viewer knowledge of facts and an increase in fear-based reporting.

1995: Matt Drudge launches "The Drudge Report," a right-leaning, email-based newsletter that eventually becomes a website. "The Drudge Report" influences news media not only by favoring right-wing views but also by favoring "the most salacious aspects of American politics." Drudge, along with his website, is labeled one of the "Top 10 anti–Barack Obama conservatives" in 2009. Many argue that he played a major role in disrupting the Obama administration's messaging.

1996: The Telecommunications Act deregulates the news media industry and unleashes a wave of consolidations. This shift then paves the way for right-wing Sinclair Media to take over a number of local television stations. These stations are required to air "must-run" segments, most of which echo right-wing views. By 2020, Sinclair Media–owned local television reaches 40 percent of all U.S. households.

1996: Launch of Fox News, the first openly partisan, 24-hour cable news station. Fox causes a shift to the left for MSNBC, which had previously hosted shows with conservatives like Ann Coulter and Laura Ingraham. The launch of Fox News also leads to a rise in the political polarization of news viewers.

1999: Alex Jones launches *InfoWars*, a conspiracy theory and fake news website that regularly has over 10 million monthly visits. The site uses hype and fear to suggest that there is a war over our minds.

1999: Jon Stewart takes over as host of *The Daily Show* on Comedy Central. He pivots the show to a more biting satire of news and politics. His viewers will eventually score higher than those of any cable news network in their knowledge of current events.

9/11/2001: The attacks on the United States lead to a dramatic shift in cable news reporting, including, among other things, the use of the bottom ticker to keep a running set of headlines during broadcasts. Information is more fragmented, and almost all major news stories have a hyped-up title and introductory graphic. The warmongering of TV and print news after the attacks sows distrust in the American public.

2004: *Facebook* launches and allows users to share news items, many of which may not be from reputable sources. Sixty-seven percent of Americans report that they get some of their news from social media.

2005: *Reddit* launches. While not openly partisan, *Reddit*'s comment-driven, user-moderated format makes it especially susceptible to alt-right, conspiracy theory hype. The subreddit /r/The_Donald has nearly a half-million users in the summer of 2017 when one of its users posts a doctored video that has Trump symbolically beating up CNN. Trump later shares the video on his *Twitter* feed.

2005: *The Colbert Report*, with Stephen Colbert in character as a right-wing pundit, premieres. Colbert coins the term "truthiness" on his first episode. He later launches a super PAC and runs for president twice.

2006: *Twitter* launches. It allows sharing similar to *Facebook*, but it also makes it easy for users to speak directly to politicians and celebrities. The traditional hierarchy of communication breaks down, allowing average users to go "viral" with just one tweet.

2007: Breitbart launches an on-line site for reporting a far-right spin on the news. It is framed as "*The Huffington Post* of the right."

2008: A study shows that George W. Bush made 935 false statements in the two years leading up to the Iraq War. These findings simply underscore Stephen Colbert's description of the Bush administration's connection to truth as "truthiness," things that feel true but aren't true. Some argue that the Bush era of lying paved the way for the "alternative facts" of the Trump administration.

2009: Jon Stewart is voted the most trusted newscaster, winning 44 percent of a nationwide poll conducted by *Time Magazine* shortly after Walter Cronkite died. NBC's Brian Williams comes in second place with 29 percent.

2014: *Last Week Tonight*, with host John Oliver, premieres on HBO. The show focuses on long-form satire that allows Oliver and his team to do deep research on a subject. A number of episodes, such as the one on net neutrality, have direct and immediate public impact.

The relationship between alt-right extremism and the rise of Trump has been well documented.[68] In fact, it seems quite clear that, without the support of alt-right media, Trump would never have had a chance at winning. Throughout the 2016 campaign, Trump maintained close ties to the powerful media figures of the right, including Alex Jones, Bill O'Reilly, Sean Hannity, and Rush Limbaugh, but it would be his decision to work with Steve Bannon that would make Trump's full embrace of alt-right media most visible. Bannon, who was a founding member of the alt-right, on-line "news" source Breitbart, was appointed chief executive of Trump's campaign in August of 2016, replacing Paul Manafort. After the election, he was named "chief strategist" for the transition team, and he accompanied Trump into the White House holding this newly created title.

Bannon's presence as part of the executive team caused ripples of concern, not only because he was deeply tied to the incendiary rhetoric of the alt-right media but also because of his less-than-subtle white nationalist tendencies. But the critical part of the story from the perspective of the media and their ties to Trump was the way in which Bannon repeatedly claimed that the news media were the enemy. Shortly after the inauguration, Bannon publicly described the news media as "the opposition party."[69] "The media should be embarrassed and humiliated and keep its mouth shut and just listen for a while," Bannon said in a post-inauguration interview.[70] "I want you to quote this," Bannon added. "The media here is the opposition party. They don't understand this country. They still do not understand why Donald Trump is the President of the United States."[71]

It was thanks to Bannon's hostile attitude toward the news media that it became easy for Trump to call any unfavorable news "fake." So that, too, is another register of the meaning of fake news. And it is a register that Trump was able to employ to great effect. This was so in large part because, since the 1969 Nixon-Agnew campaign, the right had long attempted to sow distrust in the press among Republican voters. Spiro Agnew told audiences that the media were biased against the right and run by liberal coastal elites, a claim that, while overblown, was not entirely false on its face. Almost 50 years later, the right had long been conditioned to think that the major news outlets skewed liberal and disparaged its worldview.

What perhaps was most amazing about Bannon's statement that the press was the opposition party was the fact that it emerged in the wake of Press Secretary Sean Spicer's false claims about attendance numbers at the Trump inauguration. In one of the first ways that the Trump administration made it clear that it would operate differently from former administrations regarding the press, Press Secretary Sean Spicer came out to the podium on his first day swinging. In his first appearance, Spicer reiterated Trump's claim that he had had the highest number of attendees at his inauguration in history. At the time, there were no official numbers, but public transit and aerial photos clearly disputed those claims. Spicer, however, simply parroted his boss' lies. And to make it worse, he blamed the press for purposefully misleading the public on the numbers. Then he refused to take questions. Former press secretaries, including Ari Fleischer, who served in the administration of President George W. Bush, expressed alarm at the hostile attitude Spicer had toward the notion of a free press. After Spicer's performance, Fleischer tweeted that he was "uncomfortable and concerned."[72]

As Fleischer predicted, the news media were destined to want to hold Spicer accountable for his lies. But rather than admit to the falsehood, the Trump team sent out Bannon, who responded to the situation by calling the media the enemy of the people. It also sent out Kellyanne Conway, who described Spicer's statement as "alternative facts" during an interview with Chuck Todd for NBC. Todd had asked Conway to explain why Spicer would even bother to lie about something that could easily be disproved. When Conway retorted with her alternative facts claim, Todd replied, "Look, alternative facts are not facts. They're falsehoods."[73] Conway would later defend her choice of words, defining "alternative facts" as "additional facts and alternative information," an equally unsettling turn of phrase that rightly had critics describing the Trump administration as Orwellian.[74]

Two years into the Trump administration these sorts of antics had become commonplace, but in the early days of the new changing of the guard, the public and the press were noticeably shaken. Dan Rather responded to the series of events saying,

> These are not normal times. These are extraordinary times. And extraordinary times call for extraordinary measures. When you have a spokesperson for the President of the United States wrap up a lie in the Orwellian phrase "alternative facts".... When you have a press secretary in his first appearance before the White House reporters threaten, bully, lie, and then walk out of the briefing room without the *cojones* to answer a single question.... Facts and the truth are not partisan. They are the bedrock of our democracy. And you are either with them, with us, with our Constitution, our history, and the future of our nation, or you are against it. Everyone must answer that question.[75]

While Rather was right to worry whether the truth would survive the Trump presidency, there was one other big lesson learned by the alternative fact inauguration fiasco. Anytime the Trump administration would be questioned over anything, it would offer a two-pronged response: it would bully and spin. In this case, Bannon was the bully. He refused to even entertain questions about Spicer's lies and instead used interviews as an opportunity to bash the press and further discredit the news media in the eyes of Trump supporters. Conway, alternatively, refused to acknowledge that the lies were lies, offering up a version of information and reality that was rightly compared to Orwellian "newspeak." That dual action of responding to a legitimate query with belligerence and gaslighting would confound the mainstream news, which simply had no script for handling such tactics.

And that's where the satirists came in. Because satire naturally goes after BS and has no commitment to so-called balance, it became much easier for the satirists to cover the absurdity of the Trump administration than the mainstream news.

Satirists had no need to have panels representing diverse views when one of those "diverse" views consisted of outright lies. And even though many TV satirists did need to maintain good contacts to help with future bookings, they had far less political cronyism than the news networks. They certainly were not in the business of paying Trump supporters to hawk his position, as happened on the networks with figures like Jeffrey Lord, who was eventually fired from CNN after he tweeted "Sieg Heil" at a liberal activist.[76]

Why Satirical "Fake" News Is Some of the Best News We've Got

The last meaning of the term "fake news" is that of satirical news. Recall that, before the 2016 election, the most common use of the term "fake news" was in reference to satire news. Back when Jon Stewart was host of *The Daily Show*, he was regularly referred to as a fake newsman. And, more importantly, at the time the moniker wasn't negative.

There are basically two types of fake satirical news. One is more aptly called satire news. This type of comedic fake news doesn't twist the actual facts of the story but, rather, gives a satirical, snarky, sarcastic spin to the news. This was the style of Stewart and Colbert when they worked for Comedy Central, and it has only grown in popularity since with Trevor Noah, Hasan Minhaj, John Oliver, Samantha Bee, Lee Camp, Seth Meyers, and others, all offering a version of it on their cable TV shows. Colbert and Stewart, though, arguably defined or redefined the genre for the American public when they hosted shows back-to-back on Comedy Central.

Stewart was host of *The Daily Show* from 1999 to 2015, and, during that time, he transitioned the show into one of the nation's most important sources of news information, especially for younger viewers. Stewart's brand of sarcastic, yet sincere, disbelief allowed him to skewer politicians and the media alike. Colbert, who had been a correspondent on *The Daily Show*, launched his own show, *The Colbert Report*, in 2005. He stepped down as host in 2014 to prepare to take over for David Letterman on CBS's *The Late Show*. Colbert's Comedy Central show was a perfect complement to Stewart's. Performing in-character satire, Colbert parodied right-wing pundit shows by playing an overblown version of a Bill O'Reilly-esque gasbag. Even though Colbert's satire was in character as a delusional pundit, he also managed to use his show to inform the public on a number of critical issues. Taken together, the two comedians became a go-to source for political news, even though they regularly insisted that their primary goal was to entertain their audiences.

Stewart and Colbert often joked that they distilled the news and repackaged it, but they didn't make up facts and present them as true. Instead, their satirical take on the news often offered viewers an excellent way to reflect on the issues without the sanctimonious or sensationalist spin often found on cable news. Often, too, the satire news of Stewart and Colbert was actually a takedown of the flaws in the traditional news itself. In one particularly funny bit from 2014, Stewart mocked

FIGURE 4.13 This cartoon by Pulitzer Prize–winning cartoonist Joel Pett shows how satire used puns to help make sense of Trump's version of fake news.

Source: Joel Pett. Used with Permission.

CNN for obsessing over a missing Malaysian Airlines plane and covering the story incessantly, even though there was no news to report.[77]

The second type of fake satirical news is the sort that makes up ridiculous headlines and outlandish stories as a parody of the news. This sort of satirical fake news is the style of Andy Borowitz' columns for *The New Yorker* or the posts on *The Onion*. While, at times, these headlines can read awfully close to a legitimate headline, they are purposeful manipulations of the truth designed to get readers to

FIGURE 4.14 Jon Stewart makes fun of Wolf Blitzer's coverage of the missing Malaysian Airlines flight.

Source: "The Curious Case of Flight 370", *The Daily Show with Jon Stewart*, March 24, 2014, http://www.cc.com/video-clips/6lqtfn/the-daily-show-with-jon-stewart-the-curious-case-of-flight-370. License free image.

laugh while critically processing an absurd feature of society. In one example from January 2019, when the government was shut down over the Trump border wall standoff, Borowitz jokingly wrote a headline that Supreme Court Justice Brett Kavanaugh had offered "to pay for [the] wall by recycling his empties."[78] Most readers would immediately know that the headline was false. But the joke, which underscores the depravity of those affiliated with the Trump administration and its border wall desires, would be clear.

The Onion sarcastically describes itself as "America's finest news source." In its first issue after the attacks of 9/11/2001, *The Onion* mocked the U.S. response to the attacks. Headlines read, "U.S. Vows to Defeat Whoever it is We're at War With" and "American Life Turns into Bad Jerry Bruckheimer Movie." A photo caption read, "Holy Fucking Shit: Attack on America."[79] The headlines were both tongue-in-cheek and spot-on in their ability to characterize the hyperbolic speech of those days. While some thought it was too soon to make light of the events of 9/11 when the issue first came out, the goal of the satire was to mock the sense of panic that was overtaking political discourse and media coverage at the time.

The examples from *The Borowitz Report* and *The Onion* also point to another major difference between satire news and satirical fake news: the first educates the public about an issue; the second expects the public to know the basic gist of the story and parodies it. Satire news needs to be consumed in full, whereas satirical fake news can be appreciated by reading the headline only. In fact, Borowitz has joked that his job mainly consists of writing joke headlines, because it is via only the headline that much of his work is shared.

While the Borowitz/*Onion* approach to satirical fake news is fun and engages critical thinking, it is the first type—satire news—that has become increasingly important in the current news media landscape. In fact, beginning in the post-9/11 era, as the satire news of Jon Stewart and Stephen Colbert really took off, there was a shift in the relationship between satire news and mainstream news in our country that persists today. For the first time in U.S. history, audiences were getting their news first from satire news, and then looking into details of the story later from traditional sources. And, despite all the seemingly logical reasons why that inverted flow of information would cause concern, it turns out that the satire news, overall, often did a better job of informing the public on facts than the straight news did.

There was a series of studies done to test viewer knowledge of current events, and in each case, satire news viewers scored astonishingly high. In 2007, Pew

Knowledge Levels by News Source

	Knowledge level		
	High %	Mod %	Low %
Nationwide	35	31	34=100
Among the regular audience of...			
Daily Show/Colbert Report	54	25	21=100
Major newspaper websites	54	26	20=100
NewsHour with Jim Lehrer	53	19	28=100
O'Reilly Factor	51	32	17=100
National Public Radio	51	27	22=100
Rush Limbaugh's radio show	50	29	21=100
News magazines	48	27	25=100
TV news websites	44	33	23=100
Daily newspaper	43	31	26=100
CNN	41	30	29=100
News from Google, Yahoo, etc.	41	35	24=100
Network evening news	38	33	29=100
Online news discussion blogs	37	26	37=100
Local TV news	35	33	32=100
Fox News Channel	35	30	35=100
Network morning shows	34	36	30=100

How to read this table:
Nationwide, 35% of Americans score in the high knowledge category (answering at least 15 of 23 questions correctly.) Among regular viewers of the Daily Show and Colbert Report, 54% scored in the high knowledge category.

FIGURE 4.15 Pew showed that viewers of *The Daily Show* and *The Colbert Report* score higher on knowledge of the news than viewers of most traditional news outlets.

Source: "Public Knowledge of Current Affairs Little Changed by News and Information Revolutions", Pew Research Center, April 15, 2017, http://www.people-press.org/2007/04/15/public-knowledge-of-current-affairs-little-changed-by-news-and-information-revolutions/. License free image.

Research did a study of viewer knowledge level by news source and found that viewers of *The Daily Show* and *The Colbert Report* scored among the highest in knowledge level of any of the news sources tested. Meanwhile, Fox News viewers scored nearly dead last.[80]

Another study conducted by Fairleigh Dickinson University in 2012 tested viewers' knowledge of current issues based on news consumption and, again, found that viewers of *The Daily Show* scored high. The study found that the largest effect was that of Fox News: "[A]ll else being equal, someone who watched only Fox News would be expected to answer just 1.04 domestic questions correctly—a figure which is significantly worse than if they had reported watching no media at all."[81]

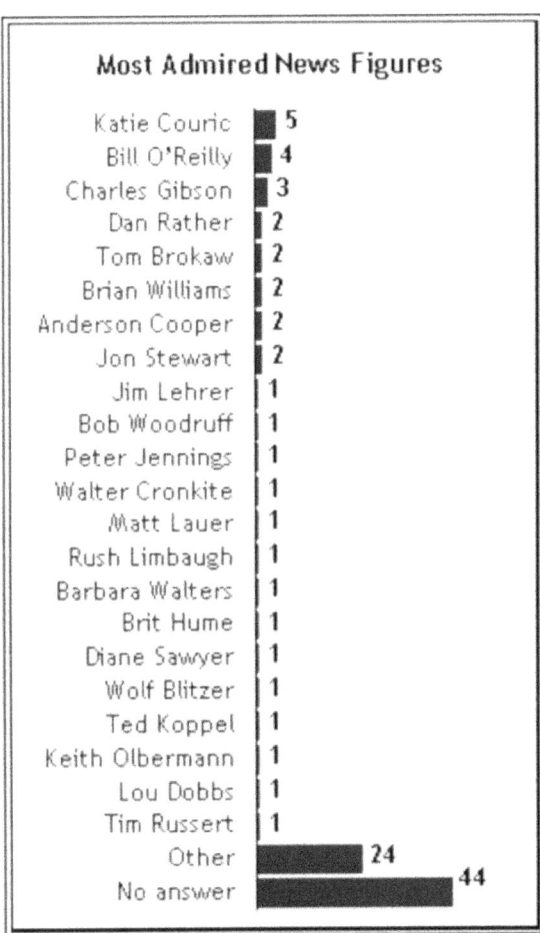

FIGURE 4.16 Pew found greater fragmentation among most admired news figures; Jon Stewart placed surprisingly high on the list.

Source: "Today's Journalists Less Prominent", Pew Research Center, March 8, 2007, http://www.people-press.org/2007/03/08/todays-journalists-less-prominent/. License free image.

For these reasons and more, viewers also trusted Stewart and Colbert more than regular newscasters and reporters. A 2007 Pew study found that Jon Stewart tied with Dan Rather, Tom Brokaw, and Brian Williams for most admired news figure.[82] The fact that he was even included in the list at all should come as a surprise, let alone the finding that he ranked among some of the nation's top news anchors.

Then, shortly after iconic newsman Walter Cronkite died in 2009, *Time* conducted a poll to determine who the most trusted newsman was at the time.

THE DAILY SHOW WITH JON STEWART TOP TEN

1 INDECISION 2000
As George W. Bush claimed victory over Al Gore through a lengthy recount and a controversial Supreme Court verdict, *The Daily Show*'s "Indecision 2000" was virtually the only cable show to express outrage. The election coverage earned *The Daily Show* a permanent place as a serious (but entertaining) source of American political coverage.

2 POST-9/11 REFLECTION
On his first show after the September 11 attacks, a visibly upset Stewart took a somber tone and showed his audience his heartfelt concern for his nation. "I'm sorry to do this to you," he said. "It's another entertainment show beginning with an overwrought speech of a shaken host, and television is nothing if not redundant. So, I apologize for that. It's something that unfortunately we do for ourselves so that we can drain whatever abscess is in our hearts and move on to the business of making you laugh — which we haven't been able to do very effectively lately."

3 FROM SCREEN TO PAGE
Stewart and his Daily Show cohorts took their satire to the reading masses with *America (The Book): A Citizen's Guide to Democracy Inaction* in 2004. A parody of a high school textbook--including activities and discussion questions--the book reminded the nation that we were all in dire need of civics education. Tom Carson, reviewing the book in the New York Times, wrote it was "not only more informative about how American government and culture work than the textbooks it burlesques, but gives us a keener sense of having a stake in both." And it features naked Supreme Court Justices. Publisher's Weekly named it "Book of the Year."

4 CROSSFIRE UNDER FIRE
In October 2004, Stewart appeared as a guest on CNN's debate show *Crossfire* hosted by Tucker Carlson and Paul Begala and expressed his concerns about the program. When asked to "be funny" he responded that he wasn't there to perform. "It's not so much that it's bad as it's hurting America . . . Stop hurting America," Stewart said in reference to the "partisan hackery" that he critiqued *Crossfire* for perpetuating. In January 2005, CNN canceled *Crossfire* and most credit Stewart's shaming of the hosts for the decision.

5 STEWART OUT-BECKS BECK
In March 2009, Stewart dedicates almost half of an entire show to parodying alt-right personality Glenn Beck's pundit performances. Beck always tried to show how his views were logical and true, often using a black board and suggesting he was "teaching" his audience. Stewart mocked this and exposed the faulty logic and hyperbole at the center of Beck's attacks on the "secular progressive agenda."

6 A REAL HEALTHCARE DEBATE
In 2009, as most mainstream media allowed conservatives to frame the narrative over healthcare, Stewart confronted anti-health-reform activist Betsy McCaughey and exposed the basic fallacies in her anti-health care spin. Revealing his inner geek, Stewart referred to life-expectancy statistics, Medicare reimbursement policies, physician incentives and average health-insurance costs to refute McCaughey's claims about the health-reform bill. Stewart called her "dangerous" and said, "I like you, but I don't understand how your brain works." More of the same hard-hitting counters to Republican fear-mongering over health care would appear after the passage of the Affordable Care Act.

FIGURE 4.17A,B The Stewart Top Ten.

7 **STEWART VS. CRAMER**
In the wake of the 2008-09 Wall Street meltdown and the lack of useful coverage of those events, Stewart and his staff did a number of pieces exposing the truth behind the economic meltdown. The most visible confrontation took place between Stewart and Jim Cramer of CNBC's *Mad Money* on March 12, 2009 on *The Daily Show*. Stewart quickly exposed the hypocrisy behind many of Cramer's claims and chastised him for encouraging viewers to stay in the market when he knew it was risky. The interview was the second most-viewed episode in the show's history with 2.3 million viewers.

8 **STEWART CHAMPIONS CARE FOR FIRST RESPONDERS**
The first responders on 9/11 quickly had a series of health concerns that required special medical attention, but they weren't getting it. In 2010, as support for a bill to provide them with care was stalling, Stewart dedicated half of his show to their story. Lawmakers and journalists would later credit Stewart with helping to pass the bill and *The New York Times* referred to him as the "modern-day equivalent of Edward. R. Murrow."

9 **STEWART VS. O'REILLY**
Both O'Reilly and Stewart faced off on each other's shows dating back to 2001. Each time the encounter was highly provocative, but it was the debate they held in 2012 in the midst of the presidential election debates--"The Rumble in the Air Conditioned Auditorium"--that best epitomized their showdown. Eclipsing the presidential candidates, the two went head-to-head on some of the most significant policy issues facing the nation, from health care to foreign policy to entitlements--and they did so with the goal of educating and entertaining their audience.

10 **STEWART STANDS UP FOR VETERANS' RIGHTS**
Stewart has been a staunch advocate for veterans' rights, and in 2013 he zeroed in on their health care needs. Coverage of problems with attending to veterans' claims began in April with a piece called "The Red Tape Diaries." Then in May, *The Daily Show* decided to call attention to the massive backlog of veterans' health claims with a bit called "Zero Dark 900,000." That piece was followed in September 2013 with one called "Ignoring Private Ryan." Together they offered the public the best coverage of this massive failure to protect the health and welfare of veterans. Could there be anything more patriotic?

FIGURE 4.17A,B (Continued)

Jon Stewart shocked everyone by being voted number one, beating out Charlie Gibson, Brian Williams, and Katie Couric, and leading many to wonder how a "fake" newsman beat out the "real" deal.[83] The answer was that, by that point in Stewart's career, viewers saw the comedian as an advocate for the U.S. public, who were hungry for facts and disgusted by the sensationalism of the mainstream news and the doublespeak of politicians. Stewart, despite his sarcasm and irony, seemed sincere to viewers. While he clearly was a comedian first, Stewart's show had also been used regularly to raise issues of critical interest to the public. At times, he simply offered an ironic take on a ridiculous issue. At other times, as in his infamous takedown of CNN's *Crossfire* in which he asked Tucker Carlson to "stop hurting America," he questioned the status quo in ways that were immediately gratifying to the public. He even debated Bill O'Reilly in order to make some of his political points to a broader public.[84] He also used his comedy to advocate for issues, like healthcare for the 9/11 responders, a move that bolstered his integrity but also shamed the mainstream news networks that weren't covering the story at all. Figure 4.17 is a snapshot of ten moments when the comedy of Stewart made a difference.[85]

116 The First Media-Created President

FIGURE 4.18   Stewart and O'Reilly go head-to-head at their debate.

Source: "Jon Stewart Crushes Bill O'Reilly in Debate," YouTube, 6:25, posted by The Young Turks from John Stewart on October 9, 2012, http://www.youtube.com/watch?v=CK03KI6WMz4. License free image.

While Stewart often played the role of a sincere, yet bewildered comedian who simply wanted politicians and the press to do their jobs and serve the U.S. public, Colbert's Comedy Central show offered a different take. Because he played the role of a conservative pundit, he could embody and mock from within the pundit persona. That character also allowed him to play with the egocentric nature of most punditry. He then used his own satirical, ego-driven character to mobilize "the Colbert nation" to engage in a number of stunts, including supporting him in a fake run for president. Figure 4.19 is a snapshot of ten key moments from his show.[86,87]

Colbert announced he was leaving his Comedy Central show in 2014. Then Stewart announced his departure in 2015. This meant that, as the U.S. headed into the 2016 election, the nation lost two of the most important satirical news sources in our history. What's more, we were losing these two voices at exactly the same time that one of the most, if not the most, ridiculous political figure to run for president was taking the stage. At the time that Stewart and Colbert announced their departures from Comedy Central, it was a real cause for concern, because the two of them had worked together in measurable ways to advance democratic discourse. They were more trusted than the regular news media, they informed their viewers better, and they had had significant success in calling attention to issues of national concern that were being ignored in the mainstream media. What's more, they often became the news themselves: they regularly covered stories that would then get picked up on cable news the next day. In fact, by the time of their departures, their public impact had been documented by a series of studies that showed that they had influence over shaping public opinion, motivating civic action, and framing debates over major issues.[88]

If we stop to consider the role that the press should play in a democracy, we can note that Stewart and Colbert performed all of those tasks, even if they were primarily interested in entertaining their audiences. The press has been referred to as "the fourth estate"—a play on the European notion of three estates: the clergy, the nobility, and the commoners. Under that logic, the press operates as a fourth form

THE COLBERT REPORT TOP TEN

1 TRUTHINESS
On his first episode of *The Colbert Report*, Colbert launched a recurring segment entitled "The Wørd." "Truthiness" was The Word that launched that first show, and it became an overnight sensation, becoming the "word of the year" for Merriam-Webster and the American Dialect Society in 2006. It encapsulated the post-9/11 turn away from facts--especially in the rhetoric of George W. Bush, who often spoke of making decisions based on his "gut." And it epitomized Colbert's ability to satirically play with words in a way that made the public recognize the lack of rational decision-making that had come to dominate national politics.

2 THE BUSH ROAST
Colbert performed at the 2006 White House Correspondents' Association Dinner, roasting President Bush, literally, to his face. The performance went viral as fans found great pleasure in seeing Colbert speak "truthiness to power." Stewart would later refer to the performance as "ballsalicious." The performance catapulted Colbert into international fame as a satirist to watch.

3 BETTER KNOW A DISTRICT
One of the most famous recurring segments of *The Colbert Report* became a victim of its own success. Colbert would interview members of Congress, often exposing their limited intellectual abilities. Famous examples were when he interviewed Georgia Rep. Lynn Westmoreland who had sponsored a bill to publicly display the Ten Commandments but could only name three of them himself, and when New York Rep. Yvette Clark claimed that the Dutch had slaves in 1898. Colbert's interview with Robert Wexler, who was running unopposed in Florida, went viral when he convinced Wexler to say something that would surely ruin his election if he had an opponent. The silly statement then was aired as serious on mainstream news--setting off a feud with Colbert and leading politicians, like Nancy Pelosi, to suggest to House members that they avoid the show.

4 COLBERT FOR PRESIDENT
On October 16, 2007, Colbert announced on his show that he would run for President of the United States. Originally the plan was to run for both the Republican and the Democratic nomination in his home state of South Carolina. But when he learned the filing fee for the Republicans would be $35,000, he opted to run only on the Democratic ticket, but was eventually denied a place on the ballot. His Facebook page for the campaign had more than 1,000,000 likes within one week and polls had him as high as 13% against Rudy Giuliani and Hillary Clinton. He resumed his bid in 2011, asking voters to vote for him as President of South Carolina, using the ballot spot slotted to Herman Cain (who had dropped out of the race by then) as a vote for him.

5 COLBERT GOES TO IRAQ
For one week in June of 2009 Colbert shot his show from Iraq as a way to raise support for the troops. Riffing on comedian Bob Hope's visits to the front, Colbert engaged in a variety of theatrics meant to entertain the troops and help connect their experiences to the U.S. public. He also used the shows to help raise funds for the Yellow Ribbon Fund that assists injured veterans.

6 COLBERT EDITS *NEWSWEEK*
The same month he went to Iraq, he guest-edited an issue of Newsweek. Colbert used the issue to shame the media and the administration over the Iraq War. "I know what you're thinking: 'Isn't the Iraq War over?' That's what I thought, too," he wrote in his editor's introduction. "We stopped seeing much coverage of the Iraq War back in September once the economy tanked, and I just figured the insurgents were wiped out because they were heavily invested in Lehman Brothers." The issue was mixed with serious pieces on the war and some fun Colbert contributions.

FIGURE 4.19A,B The Colbert Top Ten.

118 The First Media-Created President

7 COLBERT AND CAMPAIGN FINANCE
Outraged by the effects of the Supreme Court's Citizens United decision, which allowed corporations to give unlimited and anonymous amounts to campaigns, Colbert decided to start his own Super PAC so that he could teach his audience how the scam worked. Operating from June 2011-November 2012, the Super PAC inspired citizen-activists to start their own Super PACs, and Colbert used his own to finance a series of ads and teach the public about the effects of big money on campaigns.

8 COLBERT SHOWS US HOW TO GIVE
Beginning with a broken wrist on the show in 2007, Colbert used his persona and power to get his fans to raise money for causes. Some were silly--like the wrist strong effort--but many were serious. Colbert led a major effort to raise money for tsunami victims, used his Super PAC money to help victims of Hurricane Sandy, and got fans to contribute to DonorsChoose.org, which supports teachers across the nation.

9 COLBERT GOES TO CONGRESS
After participating in the "Take Our Jobs" program meant to help the public understand the plight of undocumented workers, Colbert appeared before Congress to talk about immigration reform. He began in-character, but then he broke character to make a heartfelt plea on their behalf "I like talking about people who don't have any power," he said, the bravado gone from his voice as he worked his way to a downer of a punchline. "It seems like the least powerful people in the United States are migrant workers who come here . . . . And at the same time, we invite them here and ask them to leave . . . . I don't want to take anyone's hardship away from them [but] migrant workers suffer and have no rights."

10 COLBERT TWEETS
Colbert is active on *Twitter* and often uses it to move his comedy outside of the confines of his TV show. In 2010 he won the "Golden Tweet" for the most retweeted tweet. Then in 2011 he responded to claims made by representatives of AZ Senator Jon Kyl that the senator's fabrications about Planned Parenthood were "not intended to be factual statements." Hearing that the senator's staff thought such a response made sense, Colbert decided to invent the hashtag "#notintendedtobeafactualstatement" and encouraged his audience to tweet round-the-clock non-facts about the senator. That first night there were more than a million tweets per hour using that hashtag. Then Colbert staffers created a twitter bot with the handle @RealHumanPraise in response to news that Fox News encourages staffers to prop up fake online accounts to anonymously combat negative stories about the channel. The automated, nonsensical tweets appear with the hashtag #PraiseFox.

FIGURE 4.19A,B   (Continued)

FIGURE 4.20   Colbert announces the launch of @RealHumanPraise on *Twitter*.

Source: "David Folkenflik," Colbert Nation, November 4, 2013, http://www.colbertnation.com/the-colbert-report-videos/430203/november-04-2013/david-folkenflik. License free image.

of power that can influence society. The core idea is that the press not only influences society but also acts as a watchdog on power. But, as I've explained, by the time that Stewart and Colbert emerged on the scene, public trust in the press had significantly waned, opening the door for a new type of news—satire news—to rise in prominence as a source of both news and fun, critical commentary on society. Comedians like Stewart and Colbert became the watchdogs of the watchdogs. Some referred to them as "the fifth estate."[89]

It was reasonable to worry that, as Colbert and Stewart left their posts on Comedy Central, the nation would lose a significant source of critical information, but well before they announced their departures, there were signs that the satire news era in our nation was flourishing. As I'll describe in the next chapter, the departure of Stewart and Colbert from their back-to-back Comedy Central slots only opened the door for a broader and more varied array of satire news sources to emerge in force, ready to take on the Trump candidacy with a potent blend of irony, sass, and hyperbole. When Colbert debuted in his new role as host of *The Late Show* in September 2015, he went right after the mainstream news' obsession with Trump, likening its nonstop coverage of him to binging on Oreos.

Samantha Bee, Trevor Noah, John Oliver, Seth Meyers, and Jimmy Kimmel, among many, many others, quickly stepped in to point out the absurdity of Trump and his team. In fact, the satire news was actually in a much better position to "cover" Trump than the mainstream news itself for a variety of reasons. First, satire news, given its grounding in comedy, has no commitment to "balance" viewpoints and doesn't need to offer "all sides" of a situation that is ridiculous. This meant that when Trump did something absurd, the comedians could just point it out and make fun of it, whereas the mainstream news often felt obligated to have someone on air to defend Trump. Also, even though satire may seem partisan, it is committed to calling out BS, questioning the status quo, and pointing out abuses of power. This meant that as the mainstream press was letting Trump set the terms of his coverage, the satire news refused to let him call the shots.

But, perhaps, the biggest advantage that satire news had over straight news in covering Trump was that he was a joke. He was over-the-top, bombastic, hyperbolic, and a bully. He was absurd and already looked like a caricature. He could barely speak English, and his statements were filled with logical inconsistencies and lapses of reason. While the mainstream news scrambled to present itself as impartial, to offer multiple views on an issue, and to try to take Trump seriously, the comedians saw no need to do that whatsoever.

While we might want to make fun of Trump for the ways that he let comedians get to him, there was one way in which he had a point. When the comedians made fun of him, they were influencing public opinion, and they were shaping the national conversation about him.[90] And, at times, they were offering more incisive coverage than that found in the mainstream news. This was why Trump would repeatedly attack comedy shows like *SNL*, explaining that its "coverage" of him was biased and unfair.[91]

While we could detour into a conversation about how Trump doesn't understand the free speech laws in this country, or we could be distracted by his thin skin, the

120 The First Media-Created President

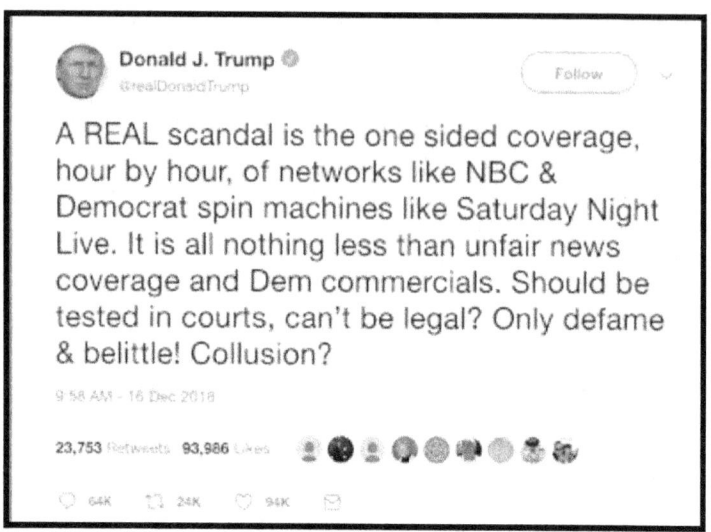

FIGURE 4.21 One of the many times that Trump attacked *SNL* as though it were a news media outlet.

Source: @realDonaldTrump, *Twitter* December 16, 2018, https://twitter.com/realDonaldTrump/status/1074302851906707457. License free image.

real takeaway here is that he did have a point that certain types of satire were as effective at covering him as the news was. Turns out that comedians get jokes in ways that journalists might not.

This doesn't mean, however, that the comedians didn't see the serious consequences of a Trump presidency; it just means that they were uniquely positioned to deal with the exaggerated, ridiculous ways that Trump and his team communicated to the public. As I explained earlier, the Trump team had a two-pronged response to its inauguration coverage: bully and spin. While the mainstream media struggled to find their footing, the satirists were able to go after both the bullying and the spin effectively, in part because invective and exaggeration are two of the most common tools in satire. The difference, though, is that satirists use their tools to spark critical reflection, not shut down debate. Perhaps more importantly, satire doesn't have to take itself seriously. It can have fun, be silly, and mock—all moves that were hard for the mainstream press to do while maintaining an expected level of gravitas.

That balance between playfulness and insightful critique serves satire well as a counter to Trumpian discourse. In fact, as coverage of Trump has shown, it has been difficult for the press to maintain a degree of seriousness when covering Trump stories that are simply absurd. For example, CNN's Don Lemon couldn't help but burst out laughing after CNN aired a series of Paul Manafort clips in which Manafort insisted that Trump had no business dealings with Russian oligarchs.[92] While viewers can appreciate why Lemon laughs, it is still unsettling to see a news anchor giggling over a potential political scandal. In comparison, though, when Trevor Noah covered the story for *The Daily Show*, he showed the same clip, smiled, and mocked Manafort.[93] The difference is that we expect Noah to do it, but it is odd to see a CNN anchor break out laughing. This explains yet another advantage satire has for covering Trump over the straight news: when the satirists laugh at what is absurd, they are just doing their job as expected. When the journalists do it, it's unsettling, even if it is understandable. In fact, it was extremely difficult for the straight news to find the right emotional response to Trump. Even when it projected outrage or shock at Trump behavior, it often rang hollow.

This is all to say that the satire news was a perfect foil for Trump because it could cover Trump in ways that the mainstream press couldn't. Each time Trump and his team came out with yet another outrageous statement, the press had a difficult time figuring out how best to cover it. Should it be outraged? Concerned? Shocked? Serious? Balanced? Meanwhile, the satirists could simply point out that the claim was outrageous, unfounded, idiotic, and disturbing. This is why Melissa McCarthy's impersonation of Sean Spicer for *SNL* was more effective than the straight news at pointing out how troubling Spicer's post-inauguration press conference was. She embodied his bullying absurdity and put it on display, while the mainstream press had panels on to debate whether the crowd was or wasn't the biggest in U.S. history and whether Spicer was or wasn't serving the public. In the Spicer example, it's not hard to see which form of "covering" Trump worked better.

In fact, we can now note that, from the 2016 primaries to the 2018 midterms to the 2020 election, the mainstream press itself increasingly began to adopt some satire news tricks. In yet another consequence of Trump's strange relationship with the news media, more and more straight news figures like Jake Tapper, Rachel Maddow, and Anderson Cooper began to turn to irony and sarcastic sass in their own coverage. Think, for example, of Cooper's recurring segment "The Ridiculist," which predated the Trump era, but became even more powerful during it, often setting a tone that Cooper would use in other segments of his show.[94] However, as the next chapter will show, even though the mainstream news media got better at covering Trump over time, it is still the case that the satirists have been the best at speaking truth to power in the Trump era. The next chapter digs into the various ways in which satirists worked to show that the emperor was in fact naked. Or, as John Oliver put it, satirists were exceptionally good at making "Donald Drumpf again."

Notes

1 Trump, Donald J. "Despite the Constant Negative Press Covfefe." *Twitter*, May 30, 2017, 12:06 a.m., Archived from the original on January 1, 2022, https://web.archive.org/web/20170531054122/; https://twitter.com/realDonaldTrump/status/869766994899468288.
2 "Who Can Figure Out the True Meaning of 'Covfefe'??? Enjoy!" *Twitter*, May 31, 2017, 11:09 a.m., Archived from the original on December 15, 2020.
3 Lewis, Philip. "Y'all Are so Quick #covfefe." *Twitter*, May 31, 2017, 8:07 a.m., https://twitter.com/Phil_Lewis_/status/869797513427116033.

4 Merriam Webster. "Wakes Up: Checks Twitter. Uh ... Lookups fo ... Regrets Checking Twitter. Goes Back to Bed." *Twitter*, May 31, 2017, https://twitter.com/Merriam Webster/status/869782666572443648?ref_src=twsrc%5Etfw%7Ctwcamp%5 Etweetembed%7Ctwterm%5E869782666572443648%7Ctwgr%5E%7Ctwcon% 5Es1_&ref_url=https%3A%2F%2Ftime.com%2F4799171%2Fmerriam-webster-donald-trump-covfefe%2F.
5 Kimmel, Jimmy. "What Makes Me Saddest Is That I Know I'll Never Write Anything Funnier than #covfefe." *Twitter*, May 31, 2017, 2:15 a.m., https://twitter.com/jimmykimmel/status/869799353724026880.
6 Charity, Justin. "Here's a Smart Blog About 'Covfefe,' Which Is Dumb." *The Ringer*, May 2017, www.theringer.com/2017/5/31/16043182/donald-trump-twitter-covfefe-memes-media-292870104291.
7 "The Parent Company Trap." *The Daily Show* with Jon Stewart. Season 15. *Comedy Central*, August 23, 2010, www.cc.com/video/nka3cd/the-daily-show-with-jon-stewart-the-parent-company-trap.
8 McClennen, Sophia A. "Degeneration Nation: It Takes a Village of Idiots to Raise a Kakistocracy Like Donald Trump's." *Salon*, May 30, 2017, https://twitter.com/Phil_Lewis_/status/869797513427116033.
9 Nesbit, Jeff. "Donald Trump Is the First True Reality TV President." *Time*, December 9, 2016, http://time.com/4596770/donald-trump-reality-tv/.
10 Dukore, Bernard Frank. *Where Laughter Stops: Pinter's Tragicomedy*. University of Missouri Press, 1976.
11 Rosten, Michael. "Donald Trump, America's Assignment Editor." *Twitter*, January 24, 2016, 6:51 p.m., https://twitter.com/michaelroston/status/824087325500211200.
12 Rozsa, Matthew. "Donald Trump's Watching a Lot of Television and It's Worrying His Aides: Reports." *Salon*, January 25, 2017, www.salon.com/control/2017/01/24/donald-trump-is-addicted-to-the-media-and-its-worrying-his-aides/.
13 Taibbi, Matt. *Hate Inc: Why Today's Media Makes Us Despise One Another*. OR Books, 2020.
14 Young, Dannagal G. *Irony and Outrage: The Polarized Landscape of Rage, Fear, and Laughter in the United States*. Oxford University Press, 2020.
15 Mitchell, Amy, et al. "Political Polarization and Media Habits." *Pew Research Center*, October 21, 2014, www.journalism.org/2014/10/21/political-polarization-media-habits/.
16 The five types of fake news are the following: fake news as propaganda designed to persuade politically, fake news for profit and/or hoax designed to dupe, alt-right fake news as misinformation designed to mislead and rile audiences up, fake news as sensationalist news designed to captivate the audience, and fake news as satire news designed to educate the audience using irony. More analysis on these types of fake news can be found later in this chapter.
17 Silverman, Craig. "This Analysis Shows How Viral Fake Election News Stories Outperformed Real News on Facebook." *Buzzfeed News*, November 16, 2016, www.buzzfeednews.com/article/craigsilverman/viral-fake-election-news-outperformed-real-news-on-facebook#.emA15rzd0.
18 For more on the decline of the news media in terms of objective reporting, see Geoffrey Baym's *From Cronkite to Colbert*. Paradigm, 2010; Jeffrey Jones's *Entertaining Politics: Satiric Television and Political Engagement*. Rowman & Littlefield, 2010.
19 Nussbaum, Emily. "The TV That Created Donald Trump." *New Yorker*, July 24, 2017, www.newyorker.com/magazine/2017/07/31/the-tv-that-created-donald-trump.
20 Ibid.
21 Ibid.
22 Ibid.
23 Fisher, Marc and Will Hobson. "Donald Trump Masqueraded as a Publicist to Brag About Himself." *The Washington Post*, May 3, 2016, www.washingtonpost.com/

politics/donald-trump-alter-ego-barron/2016/05/12/02ac99ec-16fe-11e6-aa55-670cabef46e0_story.html.
24. Fahrenthold, David. "Trump Said He'd Give Away $5 Million- or Maybe $50 Million- for Proof Obama Was Born in the U.S. Will He Pay It?" *The Washington Post*, September 16, 2016, www.washingtonpost.com/news/post-politics/wp/2016/09/16/trump-said-hed-give-away-5-million-or-maybe-50-million-for-proof-obama-was-born-in-the-u-s-will-he-pay-it/?utm_term=.f24d5301afa4.
25. "Building the Trump Brand." *National Press Club Luncheon* with Donald Trump, 15, May 27, 2014, www.press.org/sites/default/files/20140527_trump.pdf.
26. Jones, Jeffrey P. *Entertaining Politics: Satiric Television and Political Engagement*. Rowman & Littlefield, 2010.
27. Mahler, Jonathan. "CNN Had a Problem: Donald Trump Fixed It." *The New York Times*, April 4, 2017, www.nytimes.com/2017/04/04/magazine/cnn-had-a-problem-donald-trump-solved-it.html.
28. Ibid.
29. Graham, David. "The Many Scandals of Donald Trump, a Cheat Sheet." *The Atlantic*, January 23, 2017, www.theatlantic.com/politics/archive/2017/01/donald-trump-scandals/474726/.
30. "Trump's Uncensored Lewd Comments About Women from 2005." *YouTube* video, 0:35, posted by CNN on October 7, 2016, www.youtube.com/watch?v=FSC8Q-kR44o.
31. Lacapria, Kim. "Donald Trump 'Fifth Avenue' Comment." *Snopes*, January 24, 2016, www.snopes.com/fact-check/donald-trump-fifth-avenue-comment/.
32. Little, Becky. "How Gary Hart's Sex Scandal Betrayed His Character." *History, A&E Television Network*, November 7, 2018, www.history.com/news/gary-hart-scandal-front-runner.
33. Bai, Matt. "How Gary Hart's Downfall Forever Changed American Politics." *The New York Times*, September 18, 2014, www.nytimes.com/2014/09/21/magazine/how-gary-harts-downfall-forever-changed-american-politics.html.
34. Graham, David. "The Many Scandals of Donald Trump, a Cheat Sheet." *The Atlantic*, January 23, 2017, www.theatlantic.com/politics/archive/2017/01/donald-trump-scandals/474726/.
35. Isaac-Dovere, Edward. "Meyers: 'Trump Wanted Me to Apologize On-Air for Making Fun of Him.'" *Politico* Magazine, May 8, 2018, www.politico.com/magazine/story/2018/05/08/seth-meyers-trump-whcd-jokes-apologize-218323.
36. Pine, D. W. "The Stories Behind Donald Trump's TIME Covers." *Time*, January 19, 2021, https://time.com/5928282/donald-trump-time-covers/.
37. Fahrenthold, David. "A Time Magazine with Trump of the Cover Hangs in His Golf Clubs: It's Fake." *The Washington Post*, June 27, 2017, www.washingtonpost.com/politics/a-time-magazine-with-trump-on-the-cover-hangs-in-his-golf-clubs-its-fake/2017/06/27/0adf96de-5850-11e7-ba90-f5875b7d1876_story.html?utm_term=.0ed208c038e7.
38. Adgate, Brad. "The Ratings Bump of Donald Trump." *Forbes*, April 18, 2018, www.forbes.com/sites/bradadgate/2018/04/18/the-ratings-bump-of-donald-trump/#7cf77d937ec1.
39. Patterson, Thomas. "News Coverage of the 2016 General Election: How the Press Failed the Voters." *Harvard Kennedy School Shorenstein Center on Media, Politics, and Public Policy*, December 7, 2016, https://shorensteincenter.org/news-coverage-2016-general-election/.
40. Ibid.
41. Confessore, Nicholas and Karen Yourish. "$2 Billion Worth in Free Media for Donald Trump." *The New York Times*, March 15, 2016, www.nytimes.com/2016/03/16/upshot/measuring-donald-trumps-mammoth-advantage-in-free-media.html.
42. Patterson, Thomas. "News Coverage of the 2016 General Election: How the Press Failed the Voters." *Harvard Kennedy School Shorenstein Center on Media, Politics, and

Public Policy, December 7, 2016, https://shorensteincenter.org/news-coverage-2016-general-election/.
43. Patterson, Thomas. "News Coverage of Donald Trump's First 100 Days." *Harvard Kennedy School Shorenstein Center on Media, Politics, and Public Policy*, May 18, 2017, https://shorensteincenter.org/news-coverage-donald-trumps-first-100-days/.
44. Chapman, Matthew. "Obama: I Need Airtime to Discuss a Policy Change to Give Work Permits to Dreamers. BAC/CBS/NBC: No, That's Too Partisan. Trump: I Manufactured a Fake Border Crisis and Shut Down the Govt Over It and I Want Airtime to Issue Threats to Democrats. ABC/CBS/NBC: Of Course, Sir!" *Twitter*, January 8, 2019, 12:57 p.m., https://twitter.com/fawfulfan/status/1082607143239540737.
45. "Remarks by President Obama in Address to the United Nations General Assembly." *National Archives and Records Administration, National Archives and Records Administration*, September 24, 2014, https://obamawhitehouse.archives.gov/the-press-office/2014/09/24/remarks-president-obama-address-united-nations-general-assembly.
46. Cohen, Bernard C. *The Press and Foreign Policy*. Princeton University Press, 1963, p. 13.
47. "Brian Williams." *Wikipedia*, 2019, https://en.wikipedia.org/wiki/Brian_Williams.
48. Moore, Michael. "Fahrenheit 11/9." 2018, https://fahrenheit119.com/.
49. "Tapper to Conway: 'I'd Like Trump to Stop Lying'." *CNN*, 2018, www.cnn.com/videos/politics/2018/05/06/tapper-presses-kellyanne-conway-trump-truths-lies-sotsotu.cnn.
50. Swift, Art. "Americans' Trust in Mass Media Sinks to New Low." *Gallup*, September 14, 2016, https://news.gallup.com/poll/195542/americans-trust-mass-media-sinks-new-low.aspx.
51. Hart, Kim. "Here Are the Election Facebook Ads Russia Bought." *Axios*, November 1, 2017, www.axios.com/dems-release-russia-bought-facebook-ads-2505026286.html.
52. "Russia Spent $1.25 Million Per Month on Ads, Acted Like an Ad Agency: Muller." *AdAge*, February 16, 2018, https://adage.com/article/digital/russia-spent-1-25m-ads-acted-agency-mueller/312424/.
53. Read, Max. "Can Facebook Solve Its Macedonian Fake-News Problem?" *New York Magazine*, November 4, 2016, http://nymag.com/intelligencer/2016/11/can-facebook-solve-its-macedonian-fake-news-problem.html.
54. Ibid.
55. "Fact Check: Fabricated Quote by Hillary Clinton About Trump Running for Office." *Reuters*, July 27, 2020, www.reuters.com/article/uk-factcheck-hillary-clinton-trump-quote/fact-check-fabricated-quote-by-hillary-clinton-about-trump-running-for-office-idUSKCN24S1TC.
56. Dewey, Caitlin. "Facebook Fake-News Writer: 'I Think Donald Trump Is in the White House Because of Me'." *The Washington Post*, November 17, 2016, www.washingtonpost.com/news/the-intersect/wp/2016/11/17/facebook-fake-news-writer-i-think-donald-trump-is-in-the-white-house-because-of-me/?noredirect=on&utm_term=.d6f54bff1cbd.
57. Ibid.
58. In a set of studies, Matthew Gentzkow and Hunt Allcott show that the public had considerable exposure to fake news; what they don't conclude is whether that exposure affected election outcomes.
59. Allcott, Hunt and Matthew Gentzkow. "Social Media and Fake News in the 2016 Election." *Journal of Economic Perspectives*, 2017, https://web.stanford.edu/~gentzkow/research/fakenews.pdf.
60. Emerson, Sarah. "Boomers Share the Most Fake News on Facebook, Study Finds." *Vice*, January 9, 2019, https://motherboard.vice.com/en_us/article/439z8g/boomers-share-the-most-fake-news-on-facebook-study-finds?utm_source=vicefbus&fbclid=IwAR0q4IioJlQrXn3ik4CK9TeTtd670UFq4ZJY4bi1pVWzss7vdCDC41sOjEA.

61 Gunther, Richard, et al. "Trump May Owe His 2016 Victory to 'Fake News', Study Suggests." *The Conversation*, February 15, 2018, https://theconversation.com/trump-may-owe-his-2016-victory-to-fake-news-new-study-suggests-91538.
62 Menegus, Brian. "Pizzagaters Aren't Giving This Shit Up." *Gizmodo*, December 5, 2016, https://gizmodo.com/pizzagaters-arent-giving-this-shit-up-1789692422.
63 "Drudge Report." *Wikipedia*, September 15, 2019, https://en.wikipedia.org/wiki/Drudge_Report#cite_note-abctone-57.
64 Ridley, Matt. "It's Time for a Bonfire of the Regulatory Quangos That Are Destroying Our Democracy." *The Telegraph*, September 16, 2019, www.telegraph.co.uk/opinion/.
65 McClennen, Sophia A. "Forget Fake News – Alt-Right Memes Could Do More Damage to Democracy." *Salon*, July 8, 2017, www.salon.com/2017/07/08/forget-fake-news-alt-right-memes-could-do-more-damage-to-democracy/.
66 "Study: Bush, Aides Make Up 935 False Statements in Run-Up to War." *CNN*, 2008, www.cnn.com/2008/POLITICS/01/23/bush.iraq/.
67 El-Ghobashy, Tamer. "Jon Stewart Is This Generation's Cronkite: Poll." *NBC*, July 27, 2009, www.nbcnewyork.com/news/archive/NATLJon-Stewart-is-The-Most-Trusted-Name-in-News-Poll.html.
68 Lowndes, Joseph. "Far-Right Extremism Dominates the GOP. It Didn't Start–and End–with Trump." *The Washington Post*, November 8, 2021, www.washingtonpost.com/outlook/2021/11/08/far-right-extremism-dominates-gop-it-didnt-start-wont-end-with-trump/.
69 Grimbaum, Michael. "Trump Strategist Stephen Bannon Says Media Should 'Keep Its Mouth Shut'." *The New York Times*, January 26, 2017, www.nytimes.com/2017/01/26/business/media/stephen-bannon-trump-news-media.html.
70 Ibid.
71 Ibid.
72 Martin, Michel. "Former White House Press Secretary Uncomfortable with Spicer's First Briefing." *NPR*, January 22, 2017, www.npr.org/2017/01/22/511103584/former-white-house-press-secretary-uncomfortable-with-spicers-first-briefing.
73 "Alternative Facts." *Wikipedia*, 2019, https://en.wikipedia.org/wiki/Alternative_facts.
74 Nuzzi, Olivia. "Kellyanne Conway Is a Star." *New York Magazine*, March 18, 2017, http://nymag.com/intelligencer/2017/03/kellyanne-conway-trumps-first-lady.html?gtm=bottom&gtm=bottom.
75 Rather, Dan. "Facebook." January 22, 2017, https://m.facebook.com/story.php?story_fbid=10158087282405716&id=24085780715&__tn__=*s.
76 Stelter, Brian. "CNN Severs Ties with Jeffrey Lord." *CNN Business*, August 10, 2017, https://money.cnn.com/2017/08/10/media/jeffrey-lord-cnn-ties/index.html.
77 Stewart, Jon. "The Curious Case of Flight 370." *The Daily Show with Jon Stewart*, March 24, 2014, www.cc.com/video-clips/6lqtfn/the-daily-show-with-jon-stewart-the-curious-case-of-flight-370.
78 Borowitz, Andy. "Kavanaugh Offers to Pay for Wall by Recycling his Empties." *The New Yorker*, January 10, 2019, www.newyorker.com/humor/borowitz-report/kavanaugh-offers-to-pay-for-wall-by-recycling-his-empties.
79 The Onion. "From the Archives: The September 11th Issue." *Twitter*, September 11, 2020, https://twitter.com/TheOnion/status/1304481100316672001/photo/1.
80 "Public Knowledge of Current Affairs Little Changed by News and Information Revolutions." *Pew Research Center*, April 15, 2017, www.people-press.org/2007/04/15/public-knowledge-of-current-affairs-little-changed-by-news-and-information-revolutions/.
81 Cassino, Dan, et al. "What You Know Depends on What You Watch." *Public Mind Poll*, Fairleigh Dickinson University, May 3, 2012, http://publicmind.fdu.edu/2012/confirmed/.
82 "Today's Journalists Less Prominent." *Pew Research Center*, March 8, 2007, www.people-press.org/2007/03/08/todays-journalists-less-prominent/.

83 Riggio, Ronald. "Why Jon Stewart Is the Most Trusted Man in America." *Psychology Today*, July 24, 2009, www.psychologytoday.com/us/blog/cutting-edge-leadership/200907/why-jon-stewart-is-the-most-trusted-man-in-america.
84 "Jon Stewart Crushes Bill O'Reilly in Debate." *YouTube* video, 6:25, posted by The Young Turks from John Stewart on October 9, 2012, www.youtube.com/watch?v=CK03KI6WMz4.
85 These highlights appeared first in McClennen, Sophia A. and Remy M. Maisel. *Is Satire Saving Our Nation?: Mockery and American Politics*. Palgrave Macmillan, 2014.
86 Ibid.
87 "David Folkenflik." *The Colbert Report*, November 4, 2013, www.colbertnation.com/the-colbert-report-videos/430203/november-04-2013/david-folkenflik.
88 For details on the various ways in which Stewart and Colbert affected civic action, see McClennen, Sophia A. and Remy M. Maisel. *Is Satire Saving Our Nation?: Mockery and American Politics*. Palgrave Macmillan, 2014.
89 Ibid.
90 For more on the specific ways that political comedy shapes public opinions, see Lichter, Robert, Jody C. Baumgartner and Jonathan S. Morris. *Politics Is a Joke: How TV Comedians Are Remaking Political Life*. Routledge, 2018.
91 Trump, Donald J. "A Real Scandal Is the One-Sided Coverage, Hour by Hour, of Networks Like NBC & Democrat Spin Machines Like Saturday Night Live: It Is All Nothing Less Than Unfair News Coverage and Dem Commercials. Should Be Tested in Courts, Can't Be Legal? Only Defame & Belittle! Collusion?" *Twitter*, December 16, 2018, 5:58 a.m., https://twitter.com/realDonaldTrump/status/1074302851906707457.
92 Mazza, Ed. "Don Lemon Can't Stop Laughing as Old Paul Manafort Clip Comes Back to Haunt Trump." *Huffington Post*, November 30, 2018, www.huffingtonpost.com/entry/don-lemon-laughing-paul-manafort-donald-trump_us_5c00ed2ee4b0249dce737c53.
93 Noah, Trevor. "Paul Manafort's Double Flip, Trump's Climate Change Gibberish & Ivanka's Email Snafu." *The Daily Show with Trevor Noah*, 2018, www.cc.com/video-clips/8hsdrs/the-daily-show-with-trevor-noah-paul-manafort-s-double-flip-trump-s-climate-change-gibberish-ivanka-s-email-snafu.
94 "Anderson Cooper 360°." *Wikipedia*, April 24, 2022, https://en.wikipedia.org/wiki/Anderson_Cooper_360%C2%B0.

5
"LET'S MAKE DONALD DRUMPF AGAIN"

In February of 2016, shortly before the Super Tuesday primaries, which Donald Trump looked poised to win, John Oliver, host of *Last Week Tonight* on HBO, decided it was time to go after the bombastic candidate.[1] "Donald Trump is America's back mole," Oliver said. "It may have seemed harmless a year ago, but now that it has gotten frighteningly bigger it is no longer wise to ignore it."[2] Oliver, in contrast to fellow comedians like Stephen Colbert, had largely avoided focusing on the Trump meltdown of the week, instead using his long-form satire show to cover other issues. But by February of 2016, Oliver and his team decided that the growing successes of Trump deserved a satirical reality check.

Oliver nailed Trump's appeal, noting that a big part of Trump's draw was the fact that he was "unpredictable and entertaining."[3] Oliver also acknowledged that he might seem like a "protest candidate who says it like it is," but insisted that the reality of Trump's endlessly equivocating statements meant that the real Trump didn't match the impression. Oliver's critical point was that, "Donald Trump can seem appealing until you take a closer look. Much like the lunch buffet at a strip club."[4] He then went on to deconstruct each and every thing that Trump supporters said they liked about him.

Oliver started with the impression that many Trump supporters had that their candidate was straightforward and honest. Dissecting that view, Oliver pointed out that Trump had even blatantly lied about Oliver's own show. In 2015, Trump appeared in interviews suggesting that *Last Week Tonight* had asked him to appear as a guest on the show four or five times. Oliver then explained to viewers that Trump was so confident in his lie that even Oliver himself had to check with his staff to see whether it was true. An incredulous Oliver drove home the idea that Trump doesn't just lie; he lies with such considerable arrogance that it is hard not to believe him.

DOI: 10.4324/9781003294177-5

128 "Let's Make Donald Drumpf Again"

Next, Oliver reminded his audience of a *Twitter* exchange in which Trump suggested that he had turned down an invitation to be on Oliver's boring show, to which Oliver responded that yes, the show was boring, but no Trump had never been invited on.[5]

The tweets reinforced the idea that it was the satirists who had to reclaim the truth from the bluster and bully of Trump, and they showed how the satirists were able to do that with a dry, sharp sense of humor.

FIGURE 5.1 John Oliver reminds viewers of a previous *Twitter* exchange with Donald Trump.

Source: "Donald Trump: Last Week Tonight with John Oliver (HBO)", YouTube video, posted by Last Week Tonight on February 28, 2016, 21:53, https://www.youtube.com/watch?v=DnpO_RTSNmQ&t=2s. License free image.

FIGURE 5.2 John Oliver compares Trump's regard for the truth to a lemur's interest in the Supreme Court vacancy.

Source: "Donald Trump: Last Week Tonight with John Oliver (HBO)", YouTube video, posted by Last Week Tonight on February 28, 2016, 21:53, https://www.youtube.com/watch?v=DnpO_RTSNmQ&t=2s. License free image.

The overall gist of Oliver's Trump roast was the deep disregard Trump has for the truth: "I think he just doesn't care about what the truth is," Oliver said. "Donald Trump views the truth like [a] lemur views the Supreme Court vacancy," he went on. "I don't care about that in any way, please fuck off, I have a banana."[6]

Oliver then unpacked other Trump boasts, including the idea that Trump wasn't beholden to anyone and wasn't taking corporate money for his campaign. Next, he went after Trump's claim that he is a tough guy, using the story of how Trump regularly sends photos of his hands to former *Spy Magazine* editor Graydon Carter, who'd called Trump a "short fingered vulgarian" back in 1988.[7] Last, he went after Trump's constant brag that he is a huge success, referring to his bankruptcies, his wildly fluctuating account of his net worth, his tendency to value his "brand" at $3 billion, and the fact that almost everything with his name on it has been a tremendous failure.

But the most important lesson in Oliver's show was the message that Trump had built an image of himself that didn't line up with the truth. Given the way that Trump seemed to be able to control his public persona, Oliver urged voters to look behind the Trump brand and focus on Trump's true character. "If he is actually going to be the Republican nominee," Oliver cautioned, "it is time to stop looking at the mascot and start looking at the man."[8]

To illustrate the fact that most of the Trump brand is artifice, Oliver pointed out that, a few branches back in his family tree, Trump's last name was actually Drumpf. And, quoting Trump himself, who had previously mocked Jon Stewart for changing his name, Oliver explained that Trump should be "proud of his heritage." "Drumpf is much more reflective of who he actually is," Oliver explained.[9] He then asked viewers who were thinking of voting for Trump how they'd feel if they had just met a guy named Donald Drumpf, "a litigious, serial liar with a string of broken business ventures and the support of a former Klan leader he can't decide whether or not to condemn."[10] Oliver then implored, "Would you think that HE would make a good president, or is the spell somewhat broken?" In his final move, Oliver asked America to "Make Donald Drumpf again."[11]

To help "make Donald Drumpf again," Oliver told his audience he had purchased DonaldJDrumpf.com[12] and was selling hats at cost with the new slogan. When he appeared three weeks after the episode as a guest on *The Late Show with Stephen Colbert*, Oliver announced that they had already sold 35,000 hats.[13] He also told Colbert that Jay Z had called HBO asking to have a hat of his own.

The episode was hilarious, but, even more importantly, it was both entertaining and informative. Oliver artfully educated the audience on the various ways in which the Trump brand was smoke and mirrors. The analysis was sharp, witty, and memorable and was taken up by various Trump critics across social media, in particular the hugely funny *Twitter* @RealDonalDrumpf parody account.[14] While many commentators on traditional news networks had unpacked features of Trump's bluster, there was little doubt that Oliver's creative and insightful and sarcastic take on Trump was arguably more effective at outlining the flaws in his persona than anything the public had yet seen.

As if that wasn't enough proof that satire during the 2016 election was offering a vital service to voters, Oliver didn't just succinctly summarize all that was wrong with Trump; he offered information the public hadn't yet heard on any news network ever: Trump's family name had formerly been Drumpf. It is critical to pause and reflect on the fact that it was Oliver and his team who broke the story of the Trump family's true name. Think about it: by that time in the race, Trump had already engaged in months of bullying, racist invective and disturbing white nationalism. The press had covered his anti-immigrant stand, had pointed out Trump's own immigrant history, and had reminded audiences of the fact that Trump's wife and many of his employees were immigrants. But, somehow, the press had missed the fact that his family name was not originally Trump. It was a staggering oversight, made even more noteworthy by the fact that a comedian on HBO was the one to reveal Trump's inconvenient truth.

Oliver didn't just cover the hypocrisy of the Trump campaign with more journalistic insight than that found on many news outlets; he did it in a way that was intelligent, sassy, sarcastic, and sharp. While Trump still went on to win, it remains true that Oliver's satire resonated with a substantial segment of the U.S. public and that his framing of Trump's flaws helped to provide a public narrative accessible to Trump critics. As *Time* reports, the episode set a record for HBO. There were a total of 85 million video views and another 6 million television views.[15] There were over 35 million *YouTube* views. Oliver's episode, website, and hats also offered his audiences ways to spread the message on their own as active agents, sharing and engaging—via comments, clips, and other forms of interaction—the story of Drumpf. Oliver didn't just reframe the conversation; he unmasked Trump himself, literally showing the public that the emperor was, in fact, naked. It wasn't his fault that some Americans still wanted to see Trump as an emperor despite having been shown the naked truth.

The "Satire League" to the Rescue

Oliver wasn't alone. In fact, there was a whole team of satirists ready and able to take on the hypocrisies, hubris, and hate speech of the Trump era. Again and again, these comedians went after the extreme right-wing views of Trump and his allies, attempting to protect our nation from their culture of lies, fear, hatred, irrationality, and incompetence. While making Trump jokes was often easy and fun for comedians, the satirists I'll highlight here did much more than make jokes about an outrageous public figure. In fact, Trump wasn't even the sole focus of their jokes—even if he was a common target. At the heart of much of this critique was the fact that Trump represented an extreme version of the overall mindset of the right. For decades, but especially in the wake of the Tea Party movement, right-wing politics had grown increasingly caustic, fact averse, and irrational. Recall, for example, that in the post-9/11 years, it was common for anyone who criticized the Bush administration's decision to go to war in Iraq to be branded a traitor who didn't love their country.

The sort of logic that suggested that only the right knew what it meant to uphold national values laid the groundwork for the sort of flawed thinking that buttressed the Trump administration. By the time that Trump was elected, the right had convinced itself that it was under constant attack from lefty liberals who wanted to destroy the country. For decades, the right had touted conservative "values" and claimed that the left's only agenda was negative and destructive.

Geoffrey Nunberg documents these efforts in his book *Talking Right: How Conservatives Turned Liberalism into a Tax-Raising, Latte-Drinking, Sushi-Eating, Volvo-Driving, New York Times-Reading, Body-Piercing, Hollywood-Loving, Left-Wing Freak Show*.[16] What he shows is that, well before the rise of Trump, conservatives had learned to set the narrative and control the conversation, forcing the left into a constantly defensive position. Following the logic of Richard Nixon, conservatives argued that they represented the true mainstream of the country and that liberals were elitists and out of touch. Rejecting these claims, Nunberg argues, is not enough. And that is where satire comes in. It turns out that as conservatives tried to corner the idea of true American patriotism, satirists offered their audiences a different type of patriotism—one that depended on sharp, critical thinking and a defense of democratic institutions. The patriotic satirist is clever, sarcastic, sincerely dedicated to democracy, and committed to calling out manipulations of the truth and, thus, was well positioned to counter the version of America offered by the right as Trump rose in power.

While the satirical comedians who took on right-wing politics in the Trump era largely worked alone, and there was no truly coordinated "Satire League," to think of the cohort of public figures who used political comedy to counter Trumpian logic as a "Satire League" offers an effective metaphor for the way in which this group came together to make a difference. There regularly was a heroic, patriotic nature to the satirical interventions against Trump-inspired politics. Satirists, both professional and amateur, championed justice, rallied the public, fought for reason, and vanquished stupidity, and they worked to restore faith that Trumpism hadn't overtaken all of the nation.

To this point, shortly after Trump was elected, Michael Moore appeared at a rally in New York alongside figures like Cher and Alec Baldwin. In his speech, Moore encouraged the audience to "form an army of comedy" to challenge the soon to be inaugurated Trump administration. "He's affected by comedy!" Moore said.

> If you make fun of him, if you ridicule him, or if you just show that he's not popular . . . I'm telling you, my friends, this is how he'll implode. This is his Achilles' heel . . . everyone here has a sense of humor. Use it. Participate in the ridicule and the satire for the emperor who has no clothes. Let's form an army of comedy, and we will bring him down.[17]

Moore had a few reasons to call for the spread of satire: (1) there was already considerable proof that satirical jabs really got under Trump's skin; (2) those

FIGURE 5.3 The "Satire League" to the rescue.[18]

Design Credit: Tamara Knoss.

engaged in satirical resistance reduce their feelings of fear and are often invigorated by the comedy to keep active; and (3) Moore knew, from his own work, that satirical comedy offers an excellent way to speak truth to power and to reframe the dominant narrative, and it is a highly successful tactic to foster political participation and protest. Also, as I mentioned in the previous chapter, it turns out that satirical comedy has a track record in our nation of doing a strong job of informing the public and keeping it politically engaged. To add to that, as I'll explain in more detail in the last chapter, we also have proof that those who consume and produce satire are smarter on issues and better at problem-solving. So, the formation of an army of comedy or a "Satire League" to fight for justice was not such a bad idea. And, given the already existing ways that the Trump team was a joke, it made sense to use humor to describe it.

But wait, you may be thinking, if satire was so powerful, then how did Trump go on to crush Super Tuesday 2016? Or even better, how was it that, despite mounting evidence against him, and despite two impeachments, he wasn't convicted? And why was it that his supporters never really wavered even after he lost in 2020? And why did the caustic, divisive rhetoric of the right only increase in the Trump years? These, of course, are important questions. But they take a zero-sum view of the pros and cons of political satire, and that approach misses the reality of how satire works. While there are times when it is possible to point to a specific satirical intervention and document in detail its immediate impact, that is less commonly possible. Satire does not operate with obvious winners and losers, because its primary goal is to elevate critical thinking, rational discourse, and reason. Satire doesn't tell us what to think; it asks us to think, to question, and to resist prevailing opinions that have no basis in reality. But, perhaps even more importantly, satire doesn't speak to everyone, because not everyone likes it or is receptive to it. Not everyone can process irony. In fact, research shows that those who identify as conservative or right wing are far less able or inclined to process irony.[19] And only a very few of us, regardless of party affiliation, are open to hearing mockery aimed at something we support.

So, the notion that satire was going to sway the Republican mindset is ludicrous on its face. We know for certain that Oliver's Drumpf and all the other political jokes aimed at Trump didn't affect those who were already poised to vote for the candidate. In fact, two years into his scandal-ridden, policy-challenged presidency, polls showed that support for Trump hadn't changed, even after the 2019 government shutdown.[20] The facts about the administration weren't influencing his supporters any more than the satirical jokes about it. But here's the thing that must be kept in mind: anti-Trump satire wasn't aimed at the Trump supporter. So, there's no reason to be surprised that political satire didn't change the minds of Trump's base. This should seem obvious, but it bears repeating: *satire is not appreciated by all people in the same way*. Whether one finds the joke entertaining or persuasive is directly tied to the connection one has to both the comedian and the target of the comedian's joke. As I'll explain in more detail in the next chapter, satire is not ever likely to convince an ally of a person being mocked to change their mind. Despite Oliver hopefully wondering whether knowing that Trump's original family name was Drumpf would change the views of those inclined to vote for him, Trump supporters never were the intended recipients of any of these jokes.

Yet, as this chapter will show, both during the election and after, satire did make a difference, and that is because satire has a number of critical ways in which it sustains democracy: it informs the public in a fun and critically engaged way; it offers news information, insights, and commentary that sometimes are absent from traditional news outlets; it shapes public narrative by offering framing ideas, images, and words that help to provide citizens with a collective vocabulary; it builds a community of "it getters" who are in on the joke; it offers citizens ways to speak truth to power; it invigorates and energizes political activists; it primes audiences to seek more information on an issue; it uses humor to lower audience barriers to thinking about difficult or unpleasant issues; and it creates opportunities for public action and engagement.

As I mentioned in the previous chapter on the news media and Trump, satire in America has increasingly performed a watchdog function on both the news and our politicians. It has also had a larger and larger role in shaping public opinion on major social issues. No longer just a distraction, satirical comedy shows have become more and more central in shaping political debates. Consider the fact that before Bill Clinton decided to appear on Arsenio Hall's show in 1992 and play the sax, political candidates avoided shows that did not seem serious. Today, in contrast, almost all presidential primary candidates will appear on a range of entertaining nightly shows, many of which will be hosted by satirical comedians. Even more noteworthy, it will be the comedians who will ask them tough questions—sometimes tougher ones than they get from traditional venues.

But there's more. We have mounting evidence of the impact that these shows have on mobilizing voters. When Stephen Colbert hosted *The Colbert Report*, studies showed that the so-called "Colbert Bump" could be noted for politicians who appeared on the show as guests.[21] There was a general trend of increased political donations for candidate guests—measurable regardless of party, even if Democratic candidates tended to see more of a "bump."[22] And this is but one example of the ways that we can note a correlation between satire and political action. Research by Mark Bourkes has further shown that "political satire can set the public agenda as well as the political agenda."[23] One excellent example of this, which will be mentioned in more detail to follow, was the way in which John Oliver covered the net neutrality debate, encouraging viewers to comment on the FCC website, a request that got such a vigorous response that it eventually led to a system slowdown.[24] In a further example, Lauren Feldman and Caty Borum Chattoo argue in *A Comedian and an Activist Walk into a Bar* that, while a lot of scholarship focuses on the ways in which satire can increase political polarization, the reality is that satire is actually quite effective at community building.[25]

A Ministry of Satire?

Political satire has always held a powerful role in shaping public opinion, especially during moments of crisis, catastrophe, and repression. Yet, as I've explained throughout this book, Trump-era satire developed unique traits due to the complexities of making jokes about a joke, impersonating an impersonation, and parodying a parody. One of the unexpected consequences of the Trump administration was the fact that satirists often found themselves in the unusual position of defending democratic institutions, acting, if you will, as the conservators, eerily conjuring the image of conservatives, who had to keep everything together.

Now, it is generally the case that the satirist champions truth over lies, democracy over tyranny, integrity over corruption. Some satirists may seem to have a radically nihilistic, cynical, or pessimistic bent, but, in general, satirists hold to a fairly high ethical code and are optimistic that humanity can and should be better. This is why the satirist pokes fun at power, mocks oligarchy, and questions the status quo. By mocking an existing flaw in society, the satirist hopes to provoke the audience to see the flaw and do something about it.

Despite these general tendencies, it is usually the case that the satirist is the outsider—critical of the system, not defending it. Weirdly, though, the Trump effect on satire caused a bit of an inversion. Again and again, in the face of an administration that often seemed to not even know how government works, and in reaction to a set of supporting politicians who seemed hellbent on serving their own interests more than those of the citizenry, the satirists found themselves in the role of defending civic institutions. And while these trends were visible during the post-9/11 years, when Jon Stewart and Stephen Colbert fashioned themselves as the true patriots in contrast to the Bush administration, the combination of incompetence, hubris, and disrespect for democratic institutions of the Trump presidency took these practices to a whole new level.

The second chapter of this book describes the events of the 2011 White House Correspondents' Association Dinner (WHCAD) and addresses the question of whether Seth Meyers could be blamed for prompting Trump to run. Without question, that event was a significant one for the story of the connections between

FIGURE 5.4 Satirical cartoonist Matt Wuerker suggests that Trump will destroy centuries-old institutions in this cartoon that came out shortly after the fire at Notre Dame.[26]

Source: Matt Wuerker. Used with permission.

satire and Trump. At that time, Trump was just a celebrity businessman who had gotten considerable media attention for demanding that President Obama produce his birth certificate. As I explained, it is highly unlikely that the roast did, in fact, prompt Trump to run. But it is likely that his experience of being roasted by Meyers in 2011 later led Trump to boycott the dinner. In fact, the first WHCAD after Trump was inaugurated in 2016 illustrates how the Trump era led to some significant shifts in the interaction between the White House and satirical comedy.

For the 2017 WHCAD, then–*Daily Show* correspondent Hasan Minhaj hosted the event and made history. It was the first time that a sitting president had decided to skip the dinner for no good reason, and it was the first time that the comedic monologue at that dinner was delivered by a Muslim American comedian. Coincidence? Nope. In fact, it was easy to predict that Trump was not going to show up and listen to Minhaj roast him to his face.

One of the special features of the event is the way that it celebrates a free press and the First Amendment. Historically, the president delivers a comical speech, followed by a comedian who roasts the president. Now, it is not unusual for the comedian host to talk about the values of the First Amendment, especially because celebration of the liberties of free speech is such a major part of the event. But the key is that they are doing so with the president sitting right there in the room, and they are usually doing that while mocking the president—a liberty afforded only in societies that have a broad definition of free speech.

Trump would turn all of that on its head. Well before he took the oath of office, it was clear he didn't much appreciate free speech values. His long history of threatening and suing the media and comedians already documented that. But Trump surprised many when he decided to simply skip the event. Instead, he held a rally in Pennsylvania, during which he engaged in his characteristic habits of making up stories about his successes, bashing the press, and taking potshots at his critics while his supporters cheered. But more disturbingly, as Michael Gerson points out, Trump devoted "about half his speech to the dehumanization of migrants and refugees as criminals, infiltrators and terrorists."[27]

It's important to remember that, at the time, Trump was focused on building support for what was commonly called a "Muslim ban." After only days in office, Trump signed an executive order blocking refugees from Syria from entering the United States indefinitely, barring all refugees from resettlement for 120 days, and prohibiting nationals of seven predominantly Muslim countries from entering the United States for 90 days.[28] The original effort was thwarted, but, after three iterations, eventually the Supreme Court upheld a version of it. So, just as Trump was holding a speech to gather support for an openly Islamophobic policy, Minhaj, the first Muslim American to host the WHCAD, was offering a comedy routine that defended the values of the Constitution. The situational irony couldn't have been starker. The comedian was upholding the Constitution, while the president was insulting it.

The WHCAD has been running since 1921. It is an event that honors the reporters who cover the White House and helps to promote their association, which offers several scholarships and grants to students interested in journalism. But more importantly, it is an event that celebrates our nation's commitment to a free press and to free speech. The role of comedy at the event is key because it reminds us that we are not only a nation that supports critical reporting on our government but also a nation that supports making jokes about it.

When Stephen Colbert spoke at the dinner in 2006, the event was epic as well.[29] While Colbert performed for a less-than-thrilled George W. Bush, U.S. citizens witnessed the first time Bush had been called out on the war in Iraq to his face while in public. Colbert went after the faulty logic used by the Bush administration to justify the war, but he also went after the news media that had been Bush's accomplice. In one of his most noteworthy moments, he mocked the news media for simply accepting the Bush administration's version of events. He told the reporters in the room to "write that novel you got kicking around in your head. You know, the one about the intrepid Washington reporter with the courage to stand up to the administration? You know, fiction!"[30]

Minhaj, in contrast, did not go after the press for simply accepting the Trump administration's version of events. Instead, he went after the press' problem of trust. He pointed out that, "[W]e are living in the golden age of lying. Now's the time to be a liar, and Donald Trump is liar-in-chief."[31] He then explains that what is astonishing is that Trump is constantly called out on his lies, and it simply doesn't matter. It doesn't affect his supporters at all. That leads Minhaj to wonder whether "maybe it's because we're living in this strange time where trust is more important than truth."[32] Minhaj cleverly notes that Trump has managed to totally redefine trust. There is nothing trustworthy about Trump. He not only lies openly; he also reneges on his promises daily. And yet his followers still trust him. So, just as Colbert went after Bush's truthiness, Minhaj went after Trump's trustiness.

Minhaj explained that even if the news media tell the truth, the public doesn't believe it because it doesn't trust the press. And he acknowledged that the public has a point—the press has been far from perfect. Calling out CNN and MSNBC, he mocked them for their silly and sensationalist coverage. He also spared no words for Fox News reporters, whom he suggested should simply be too embarrassed to even show up at the dinner. He jabbed at them for their network's payout to Bill O'Reilly, who had been paid to leave his post at Fox News after he was accused of sexual harassment. But he also went after their open Islamophobia. "As a Muslim, I like to watch Fox News for the same reason I like to play 'Call of Duty.' Sometimes, I like to turn my brain off and watch strangers insult my family and my heritage," he quipped.[33] Throughout his speech, Minhaj reminded his audience that he was speaking as a Muslim American. "I would say it is an honor to be here, but that would be an alternative fact," he joked. "No one wanted to do this. So of course, it landed in the hands of an immigrant."[34]

One of the most brilliant elements of Minhaj's speech was the creative and compelling way that he combined the defense of a free press with the defense of free speech and of a plural society:

> [T]his event is about celebrating the First Amendment and free speech. Free speech is the foundation of an open and liberal democracy. From college campuses to the White House, only in America can a first-generation, Indian American Muslim kid get on this stage and make fun of the president. The orange man behind the Muslim ban.[35]

And yet, as Minhaj was defending the First Amendment, he pointed out that Trump was openly hostile to it: "Donald Trump doesn't care about free speech. The man who tweets everything that enters his head refuses to acknowledge the amendment that allows him to do it."[36] There is a certain poetic justice to the fact that the first Muslim American comedian to host the WHCAD used the occasion to school an Islamophobic, free-press-hating, libel-threatening president on the meaning of the First Amendment.

And yet, as Minhaj made clear in his speech, Muslim Americans had something in common with the media: they were both under attack by the Trump White House. Minhaj opened his speech by joking about how fragile his very own free speech rights felt under Trump: "My name is Hasan Minhaj, or as I'll be known in a few weeks, no. 830-287."[37] It was a joke that was funny and serious at the same time. And it was a brilliant reminder that comedians are one of the first targets of authoritarian regimes. Once in office, Trump didn't want to ban only Muslims; he repeatedly hinted at wanting to ban jokes about him as well. He even called for an FCC investigation into *Saturday Night Live* (*SNL*) for making jokes about him.[38]

The Minhaj example is only one in a long list of moments when satirists schooled Trump on the Constitution, the branches of government, what it means to be presidential, and more. In one particularly important instance of this pattern, Seth Meyers did an exceptionally strong takedown of Trump after the tragic attacks on protesters in Charlottesville, VA, during the "Unite the Right" rally in August 2017. After the attacks, Trump came out to criticize the "violence on many sides," a statement that infuriated those who thought that there was an obvious difference between the protesters and the neo-Nazi, alt-right.[39] After Trump's remarks, a series of comedians went after him, including John Oliver, Jimmy Fallon, Stephen Colbert, and Jimmy Kimmel. But it was Meyers who really stood out in his condemnation of the attacks.

"'On many sides'," Meyers echoed in disbelief on *Late Night*.

> If that choice of words made you feel sick to your stomach, the good news is you're a normal and decent person. The jury is still out on the president, as he initially refused to condemn the white supremacists in this country.[40]

Meyers may have started by going after Trump's character in general, but he quickly turned his comments to the specific ways that his administration was openly racist. "Some ignored it or played it down when Donald Trump claimed our first black president wasn't born in this country," Meyers said.[41]

> It was racist and insane, but he was written off as a clown—a bitter little man who didn't know an American could have a name like "Barack Obama." And then he called Mexicans rapists during the speech announcing his candidacy; he called Elizabeth Warren Pocahontas. Then he brought Steve Bannon into the White House with him, worked to take away voting rights from black people, and hammered away at the idea that Chicago was a wasteland because of the violent black people living there. And now white supremacists and American Nazis are visible, and energetic, and demonstrative in a way that we have not seen in our lifetimes.[42]

What's fascinating in this monologue isn't just the sharp and poignant way that Meyers is outlining the evidence of Trump's racism; it is the fact that it really has no jokes of any kind. It is just a straight critique. But the real kicker was when Meyers shifted gears into schooling Trump on what the job of president entails:

The leader of our country is called a "president" because he's supposed to *preside* over our society. His job is to lead, to cajole, to scold, to correct our path, to lift up what is good about us and to absolutely and unequivocally and immediately condemn what is evil in us. And if he does not do that—if he does not preside over our society—then he is not a president. You can stand for a nation, or you can stand for a hateful movement. You can't do both. And if you don't make the right choice, I am confident that the American voter will.[43]

It was a bold and powerful statement, but, even more interestingly, it was a bit out of character for the traditional satirist who might assume, for example, that anyone in a position of power was likely to be self-aggrandizing or who might take a relatively dim view of institutions themselves. While Jon Stewart had earlier championed the persona of the sincere satirist, whose goal was to rescue the best of American traditions from those who were corrupt and unethical, these moments from Minhaj and Meyers represent a larger sea change in U.S. political satire. Under Trump, it regularly became the norm for satirists to lecture the Trump administration, his political allies, and his supporters on what a democracy actually looks like, how it functions, and what it values. It was almost like the Trump era necessitated the creation of a figurative "Ministry of Satire" whose members were dedicated to using mockery, parody, and political jokes in order to sustain our democratic institutions.

Card-Carrying Satirists

Of course, one other metaphor we might entertain for the satirists is that of the card-carrying satirist—a riff on the "card-carrying communist." That idea plays up the notion of the U.S. citizen engaged in actions that might be deemed treasonous by some but that were self-fashioned as a dedicated revolutionary movement designed to move the country forward. Certainly, there was an element of rebellion and resistance and a desire for revolt among some of the political comedy that emerged in the Trump era. In fact, Michael Moore's call for an army of comedy is a pretty good example of that impulse. As we will see in more detail to follow, every single anti-Trump protest or march had a healthy dose of satirical signs and slogans. In fact, satirical jabs were a consistent feature of almost all forms of political action. Satire became a central element of protest, both on the streets and on screen.

Whether we imagine them as superheroes, government workers, a subversive insurgency, or some combination thereof, there were a wide range of highly visible satirists who regularly and effectively engaged in using satire to mock the president while also defending democracy. So, how did the satirists get at the truth of Trump? How did they use Trump jokes to illuminate flaws in the right-wing mindset? In what ways did comedians differ from each other? How did they complement and sometimes do the work of the news media? How did they engage and spur the public to action? The following sections break down some of the top Trump-era satirists to highlight their best moments, explain their unique style, and analyze why their work helped to make Donald Drumpf again.

FIGURE 5.5 "Ministry of Satire" ID card for John Oliver.

Design credit: Eric Spielvogel.

John Oliver deserves a special spot in the rundown of top Trump satire, because, as mentioned at the start of this chapter, he made a concerted effort to not allow satire about Trump to dominate his work. But when Oliver did go after Trump, his satirical jabs were some of the sharpest of all. Despite his own protests to the contrary, John Oliver arguably takes the lead when it comes to televised satire designed to have impact.

Oliver made his name as a political satirist in the United States while serving as a correspondent for *The Daily Show with Jon Stewart*. Over the years that he worked alongside Stewart, he appeared in a number of well-known skits, but it was his run as a short-term host of the show in the summer of 2013 when Stewart was on leave directing *Rosewater* that led many to wonder when he'd land his own show. Not long after, Oliver was offered the chance to host a show for HBO and granted significant creative control with considerable resources, including a team of researchers. The show premiered in April of 2014 and has been a notable and significant part of the satire scene ever since.

From the start, the show has had its own special style. It dives deep into topics, taking full advantage of its ad-free formatting on HBO. Its weekly airing allows it to avoid the immediate news cycle, and its team of researchers helps to provide original information for Oliver to cover. In addition, the central topic of the show often gets an uninterrupted 15-minute run, a significantly longer amount of airtime than most televised satirists can manage. Moreover, it tends to choose subjects that are largely off the radar of other political comedians and the mainstream press.

The format of the show is typically recap, rant, crescendo: the recap runs down current events, the rant centers in on a topic, and the crescendo builds to Oliver's call for audience engagement.[44]

Oliver, who is originally from the United Kingdom, illustrated early on that his show would have more of a global angle, and he dove into this decision bravely by using his first show to cover the elections in India. His second episode focused on the death penalty. Both pieces, though, had something in common: they each

OLIVER'S TRUMP HIGHLIGHTS 2015 - 2018

1 TELEVANGELISTS - AUGUST 15, 2015
In a sharp rebuke of TV pastors and megachurches, Oliver creates his own fake church, raises $70,000, and donates it to Doctors Without Borders.

2 VOTING - FEBRUARY 14, 2016
Oliver harshly criticizes voter I.D. laws and other measures that states have taken to suppress the vote ahead of the 2020 Presidential election.

3 MAKE DONALD DRUMPF AGAIN!
Oliver presents a scathing takedown of the Republican nominee, highlighting his business failures, revealing his real name to be "Drumpf," and asking why he won't accept it.

4 PRESIDENT-ELECT TRUMP - NOVEMBER 13, 2016
In a somber tone, Oliver paints a picture of the future with President Donald Trump. He critiques the media and their culpability in Trump's rise.

5 GERRYMANDERING - APRIL 9, 2017
Oliver offers up a balanced and informative assessment of partisan gerrymandering and the threat it poses to democracy in America.

6 NET NEUTRALITY II - MAY 7, 2017
Oliver takes on the FCC over Net Neutrality - in the days following the piece, the FCC website for public comment crashes.

7 COAL - JUNE 18, 2017
Despite a warning to cease and desist from a corrupt, Trump-supporting coal magnate not to air a story about him, Oliver tears him apart. The coal magnate later sues, but it's thrown out of court.

8 VARIOUS EPISODES
In a popular recurring bit during the Trump-era, Oliver "catches" the President in a lie and excitedly announces "We Got Him!" only to find out it doesn't matter and he is still president.

9 MIKE PENCE - MARCH 18, 2018
After Vice President Mike Pence's wife and daughter released a children's book about their family rabbit, Oliver parodied the short story with a gay rabbit in order to protest Pence's stance on gay rights.

10 FAMILY SEPARATION - NOVEMBER 4, 2018
The comedian takes a hard swipe at the Trump administration and its harsh immigration policies, specifically family separation at the border.

FIGURE 5.6   Oliver's Trump-era highlights.

showed that Oliver planned to offer viewers a highly sophisticated take on a topic mixed with silly comedy on the order of dick jokes, a style that might be best described as satire for goofball wonks. One of the centerpieces of Oliver's style is the way in which he will engage with an issue using a level of logic more erudite than that commonly found among his contemporaries, but, in order to keep the audience entertained and to give it a break from what can be very heavy topics, he will go on a smart, critical rant only to then cleverly pull back into a joke that often is far sillier and more banal than those normally found on similar shows. His signature style, then, is an artful balance between super smart jokes and super silly ones.

There is one other element that really distinguishes the show. It goes deeper on a topic, but it doesn't stop there. It then has a habit of encouraging viewer activism at a level even higher than Stephen Colbert did on *The Colbert Report*. Colbert was very active in encouraging his viewers to raise attention to issues. He regularly created *Twitter* hashtags that he asked the "Colbert nation" to use. He even once got his viewers to crash a *Wikipedia* entry on elephants. Then later he ran for president—twice—a stunt that allowed him to educate viewers about election finance. Oliver, for his part, has carried on some of the same tactics Colbert used on Comedy Central, for instance, getting viewers to crash the FCC website on the issue of net neutrality. Several critics, though, see in Oliver a satirist that has more of an edge and a bite than either Stewart or Colbert. A few months after the debut of the show, Daniel Kenny suggested that Oliver "found his voice and his place in political commentary, separate from Stewart and—in several respects—better."[45] As *The Atlantic* explained it, from day one Oliver's enemy has been "apathy." His goal has been to cover topics in ways that get his audience to do something about them.[46]

Oliver has covered such varied issues as human rights in Tibet—a segment that included an interview with the Dalai Lama, the Scottish independence referendum, the status of Puerto Rico, and legal guardianship in elder care. In fact, he regularly seems to go after the least "sexy" topic he can—as though part of the show's art is trying to see if he can make an extremely dull topic not just interesting, but truly engaging. Oliver's comedy is regularly described as "eviscerating," and the post-show headlines often suggest that he "destroyed" a person or policy. In fact, he has also been called the "chief comedy news influencer."[47]

Evidence of his impact can be seen in the way that his style is now emulated across other satire news shows. From Seth Meyers' "A Closer Look" segments to the longer, wonkier bits that aired on Samantha Bee's *Full Frontal* to Hasan Minhaj's *Patriot Act*, which focused on one topic for its half-hour on Netflix when it aired from 2018 to 2020, there is evidence that Oliver's style of offering deep analysis and thorough research alongside satirical comedy has become increasingly popular.

As Alissa Wilkinson points out for *Vox*, there is an interesting takeaway to the popularity of Oliver's style of political comedy: while it might seem counterintuitive in an era in which meme culture is on the rise, and we are constantly warned of short attention spans, there is evidence that insightful, long-form satire is a very popular genre. That popularity stems directly from the fact that it digs deep on issues, offers original research, and prides itself on extensive fact-checking. In fact, such long-form, in-depth pieces are largely missing from most televised news. As Wilkinson puts it, "[A] thorough investigation that takes the audience's intelligence seriously and lasts more than a few minutes is increasingly rare."[48] Instead, she notes that, "[A] lot of the deeper analysis has increasingly fallen to comedy shows."[49] What Oliver and his fellow political comedians have mastered is the ability to make the news entertaining and illuminating. But, in contrast with the straight news, the catch is that the satirists are not expected to educate their audiences on an issue. They are expected to be funny. And when asked, they will insist, again and again, that they are comedians through and through, with no larger social mission than to amuse.

Oliver repeatedly has maintained that he is a comedian and not a journalist nor an activist, yet in the Trump era, he often found himself crossing that line. In the first episode after Trump was elected, Oliver made it clear that he hoped his audience would push back. "We need to stay here and fight," he said.[50] He then went on:

> For the last eight years, we've had a president we could assume would generally stand up for the rights of all Americans. But that is going to change now. So, we're going to have to actively stand up for one another. And it can't just be sounding off on the internet or sharing think pieces or videos like this one that echo around your bubble. I'm talking about actual sacrifice to support people who are now under threat.[51]

There were no jokes and no gags, just impassioned words to his audience to stay strong and think collectively about how to resist the coming Trump policy. He then went on to be clear about ways people could help, including offering a list of organizations that would need donations. As *The Atlantic* explained it, Oliver's post-election rant made it very difficult to tell where, precisely, the "comedian" ends and the "activist" begins.[52]

But, as I've explained, Trump simply ramped the activist angle to Oliver's comedy up a notch. Even before Trump seemed to make comedic interventions so much more serious, Oliver had already explained that the creative process to the show often led him and his staff to feel a real journalistic commitment to the topic they were covering. As he explained their creative process, he described a transition:

> You see something that's a little bit weird, you start looking into it and then three days in we have the same meeting, which is basically going, "Holy s—t, this is a lot worse than we thought it was going to be."[53]

And while Oliver is quick to applaud the in-depth journalism found on sites like *Frontline* and *ProPublica*, he notes that, "The problem is the loudest journalism in America is generally saying the least."[54]

In contrast, Oliver's satirical interventions are both loud and informative. The fact that HBO allows clips to circulate easily on *YouTube* greatly increases the reach of his work. As you can see in the chart highlighting Oliver's Trump-era moments, I've included two early examples of his sharpest activist satire, because the episodes on net neutrality and the financial shenanigans of megachurches helped to pave the way for some of the significant Trump-era episodes. Early in the election cycle, Oliver continued to try to keep his comedy sharp and meaningful, avoiding, for the most part, digs into the politicians. One of his noteworthy episodes looked at the way in which voter ID laws had been used to suppress the vote. Next came his epic episode designed to "Make Donald Drumpf Again," which I analyzed at the start of this chapter. After the election, Oliver offered his somber take on the ways that his audience needed to steel itself for the coming years and prepare to do more than just share clips to protect our democracy.

One of the cleverest recurring Trump-focused bits on *Last Week Tonight* was a segment called "We Got Him," in which Oliver shared with the audience a new piece of information that under any other circumstance would end a politician's career. Not so with Trump. The bit offered an excellent spin on how Trump constantly avoids being held accountable, and, even better, it highlighted the emotional roller coaster we all felt as we learned a damning piece of information, got excited that it would make a difference, and then watched as it fizzled out and did nothing. To watch as a dejected Oliver is shamed by a mascot makes these pieces even more hilarious and biting.

Oliver covered a number of Trump-era policies, especially its harsh immigration policies, but perhaps one of the most interesting segments was the one in which he went after the coal industry.[55] It's important to remember that, when running for office in 2016, Trump repeatedly discussed how he was going to reinvigorate the coal industry. Oliver, though, in his piece, decided not to focus on Trump, but rather on coal magnate Bob Murray, who owns Cleveland-based Murray Energy Corp. Dubbing Murray "a geriatric Dr. Evil," Oliver dug deep into his past and highlighted a bizarre news conference he held after a 2007 coal mine collapse that killed six miners. Oliver skewered Murray's practices and the industry overall, only to then cede the spotlight to a man in a squirrel costume, affectionately referred to as "Mr. Nutterbutter," a joke on Murray who apparently claimed that a squirrel had told him to go into the coal business.

The squirrel then proceeded to insult Murray, who had earlier sent the show a cease-and-desist letter, not dissimilar from the types of harassment Trump himself famously sent to media he worried were coming after him. "Hey, Bob," the man in the squirrel costume said to the camera. "Just wanted to say: If you're planning on suing, I do not have a billion dollars. But I do have a check for three acorns and 18 cents." Mr. Nutterbutter then flipped a giant whiteboard to reveal a fake check made out to "Eat Shit, Bob!" Beneath it, the check's memo line read, "Kiss my ass!"[56]

Oliver then went on: "Bob Murray, I didn't really plan for so much of this piece to be about you, but you kind of forced my hand on that one," he said. "And

FIGURE 5.7   Mr. Nutterbutter tells Bob Murray to "eat shit," highlighting the way that Oliver blends satirical punch with all-out silliness.

Source: John Oliver, "Last Week Tonight", HBO, "Coal," June 19, 2017, https://www.youtube.com/watch?v=aw6RsUhw1Q8. License free image.

I know you're probably going to sue me over this. But, you know what? I stand by everything I said."[57]

Murray did, of course, sue. And the case was eventually dropped. But what was perhaps the funniest outcome of the exchange was the fact that an ACLU amicus brief on the case mirrored Oliver's satirical sass when it argued against Murray's claim. "It is apt that one of Plaintiff's objections to the [John Oliver] show is about a human-sized squirrel named Mr. Nutterbutter, because this case is nuts," the ACLU-WV wrote.[58] The brief was filled with sarcastic and satirical jabs like this: "Plaintiff's Requested Injunction is Clearly Unconstitutional. You Can't Get a Court Order Telling the Press How to Cover Stories, Bob." And this: "Anyone Can Legally Say 'Eat Shit, Bob!'"[59]

Again and again, Oliver's work has aimed to rescue the truth and logic from situations that are absurd. Even in his Trump-era work, he avoided focusing on the personality features of the man himself in favor of looking at the serious flaws in his policies, his habit of gaslighting, his disregard for our democratic traditions, and his incessant lying.

If John Oliver was the satirist who largely tried to avoid allowing Trump to become the center of his work, Stephen Colbert was the opposite. As host of *The Late Show*, which airs on late-night TV Monday through Friday for CBS, Colbert was the one comedian sure to regularly skewer the latest Trump inanity. In fact, as you'll note in the chart of Colbert's top Trump moments, there are literally a ton of choices to sort through, making it virtually impossible to offer a simple list of his best ones.

But it wasn't always this way. In April of 2014, David Letterman announced his plans to retire as host of *The Late Show*. One week later, Colbert was announced as his

FIGURE 5.8 "Ministry of Satire" ID card for Stephen Colbert.
Design credit: Eric Spielvogel.

replacement. At the time, Colbert had his own show for Comedy Central, *The Colbert Report*, in which he performed in-character satire, embodying a right-wing, bloviating, yet charismatic pundit. Colbert's character was, without question, one of the most significant contributions to U.S. satire in history. He coined words like "truthiness" that shaped public discourse, he engaged his audiences in novel ways, encouraging them to tweet using hashtags or to start their own super PACs, and he asked them to support his run for president. He testified before Congress on the rights of migrant workers, and he worked with Jon Stewart to stage a major rally on the National Mall as a lead-in to the 2010 midterm elections. Working in tandem with the satirical comedy of Stewart, Colbert had been a central part of the major transformation of the public role of satire in the United States. His viewers were both more knowledgeable and more engaged. And his comedy didn't just comment on the news; it made it.[60]

Colbert's in-character performance was such a significant part of the satire landscape in 2014 that there were reasonable concerns that, with his announcement to step down, the nation would lose a major critical voice. But it got worse. On February 10, 2015, Stewart also announced he was stepping down from his role as host of *The Daily Show*. Taken together, Stewart and Colbert had redefined the role of political satire in this nation, making it not just a comment on the issues but a defining factor in them. Their comedy worked in a productive synergy, appearing back-to-back nightly, with Stewart offering a moral compass while deconstructing the latest absurdity, and Colbert performing the absurdity in an exaggerated way for all to see. The two comedians had become national icons, often more trusted than journalists or politicians. It was difficult not to speculate that the nation would be heading for some dark times without their satire to comment on the next election cycle.

Not long after Colbert announced he would take over for Letterman, he appeared in character on *The Daily Show* to gloat that he could leave his post because he had "won television," and, arguably, he had a point. The announcement came on the heels of news that Colbert would be retiring his much-loved pundit persona and doing the CBS show as the real Stephen Colbert. But who was the real Colbert and would he still be funny? Would his comedy still have a political bite? It was easy to see that he would be a great entertainer. Even while hosting for Comedy Central, he had shown that he had considerable talents, singing and dancing, for instance, that far exceeded his role of sitting behind a desk and conducting sharp interviews. But would he still offer viewers the satirical wit and clever logic that had defined his earlier work?

Early on, the signs suggested that he would flounder a bit on this question. In the months he spent preparing for his new host role on CBS, Colbert wavered between offering fans Jimmy Fallon–style goofball comedy, connected, for example, to the beard he grew while on hiatus, and sharp political satire. Colbert repeated in pre-premiere interviews that he definitely planned to continue to offer a full slate of Trump jokes. At a press conference, Colbert explained, "I'm not going to name any names, but let's just say I want to do jokes on Donald Trump so badly and I have no venue, so right now I'm just dry-Trumping."[61] He then went on to live tweet and create the then-popular hashtag #drytrumping.[62] But again, the question wasn't whether he would mock Trump; it was whether that mockery would have the same satirical bite as his earlier work.

In those early days, the answer was that some of his work would have an edge, and some would just be goofy mockery. One of his most noteworthy pre–*Late Show* moments was when he impersonated Donald Trump shortly after Trump announced his campaign. In a short *YouTube* video titled "Announcing an Announcement," Colbert parodied Trump's campaign announcement, offering viewers an only slightly exaggerated version of the bombastic speech itself.[63] Then, on his very first show for CBS, he did a bit that likened doing Trump jokes to binging on Oreos.

When Colbert debuted for CBS on September 8, 2015, Trump was far from the GOP frontrunner, but by then Colbert was already able to detect a critical problem in the media coverage of Trump: like bystanders to a car wreck, they couldn't take their eyes off him. His opening bit was called, "All You Can Trump Buffet," and it allowed Colbert to make Trump jokes by way of mocking the media's obsession with him: "I promise you, just like the rest of the media, I will be covering all of the presidential candidates—who are Donald Trump."[64] Riffing off of Trump's claim that he would no longer eat Oreos because Nabisco had moved its plant to Mexico, Colbert alternated between watching media coverage of Trump and pigging out on Oreos. "One is enough. That is the only Trump story I'll be treating myself to tonight," Colbert said, hiding the Oreos under his desk.[65] "Well, maybe just one more," Colbert went on as he ate another Oreo and showed a clip of Trump and Fusion host Jorge Ramos.[66] Eventually, he gave in and poured the whole bag of Oreos over his face while clips of Trump played on. Colbert told viewers he knew that binging on Trump was bad for him, but he couldn't resist. Of course, later, data would show that Colbert's opening night skit was prescient, because, as argued in the previous chapter, Harvard's Shorenstein Center verified in a post-election study that the media had given Trump far more attention than his primary race warranted given his early polling numbers.[67] "Trump is arguably the first bona fide media-created presidential nominee," it claimed.[68]

While Trump jokes did appear in a central way after Colbert launched his new show, overall, the tone of the coverage was far more centrist, more aimed at silly than satirical. Despite his high debut night numbers, early on Colbert slipped behind both Jimmy Fallon and Jimmy Kimmel in ratings for the same time slot. He still had strong moments, but, in general, he had a hard time attempting to shape his comedy in a more middle-of-the-road, less politically edgy way. Perhaps the best example of this wavering came when he had two consecutive shows with key interviews in late September of 2015.[69] First came his interview with Ted Cruz, who Colbert literally eviscerated, blowing up the logic of Cruz's arguments in one of the most incisive exchanges the candidate encountered on the campaign trail. The next night he interviewed Trump, something few late-night comedians were able to land. And, while the interview would not get booed the same way that Jimmy Fallon's hair tousling interview did, most agreed that Trump bested Colbert in the exchange. Each time Colbert tried to zing Trump more softly, Trump outdid him. Colbert offered Trump an apology for earlier negative things he'd said about him and then asked whether Trump had any apologizing to do, but Trump refused and made Colbert look silly. Later, when Colbert asked Trump to listen to statements and determine whether he had said them or Colbert's Comedy Central character had, Trump got each one right.

But perhaps one of the most interesting features of Colbert's evolution as a Trump jokester on his CBS show comes not from the degree of his Trump jokes but rather from their tenor. Early on, few comedians or journalists or other politicians took Trump seriously (except Michael Moore, whose unique take will be described to follow). Sure, comedians like Colbert could not resist an obsession with Trump, but back in 2015 few really thought it would be possible that Trump could win. This meant that the jokes about Trump's absurdity were all falling within a realm in which he was still seen as a sideshow and not the circus headliner.

One of the best examples of this style of Trump joke was a bit that aired on *The Late Show* in March 2016 after the first GOP debate when Trump had decided to make hay over whether he had small hands and, by association, a small penis. During the debate, Trump went after Marco Rubio, saying that Rubio had insulted the size of his hands. "Look at those hands, are they small hands?" said the then-frontrunner of the GOP primary. "And, he referred to my hands—'if they're small, something else must be small.' I guarantee you there's no problem. I guarantee," Trump went on.[70] The comments reeled throughout the media, with headlines from outlets like CNN reading "Donald Trump Defends Size of Penis."[71]

COLBERT'S TRUMP HIGHLIGHTS 2015 - 2019

1 ANNOUNCING AN ANNOUNCEMENT - JUNE 16, 2015
A day after Trump announces he's running for president, Colbert does his best impersonation of Trump- mirroring the incoherence of the so-called billionaire's statements.

2 ALL-TRUMP DEBATE - JANUARY 29, 2016
Colbert moderates a "debate" between Trump- highlighting his tendency to flip-flop and offer-up competing narratives.

3 PENIS JOKE - MARCH 8, 2016
After Trump defends his penis size, Colbert asks, "Why would a guy with a small penis put his name in giant letters on the top of a skyscraper?"

4 TRUMP AND NAZIS - JUNE 15, 2016
Colbert, using a blackboard and chalk, connects a series of words and ideas related to Donald Trump's statements until it draws a perfect swastika, implying his racist and anti-Semitic tendencies.

5 TRUMPINESS - JULY 18, 2016
Colbert returns to his conservative character and presents a Colbert-Report-style segment of The Word on "Trumpiness" - which doubles-down on Truthiness and ignores all facts and truth.

6 GOODBYE TO BILL O'REILLY - APRIL 20, 2017
Colbert pays "tribute" to Fox News host Bill O'Reilly after he is fired for sexual harrassment, returning to his former *Colbert Report* character and saying goodbye to his self-described hero.

7 COCK HOLSTER - MAY 2, 2017
After Trump disrespects CBS's John Dickerson during an interview, Colbert says the only thing Trump's mouth is good for is being Vladimir Putin's "cock holster."

8 TRUMP'S COLORS - JANUARY 16, 2018
Colbert hammers Trump's immigration policies and, after learning that Trump only likes certain Starburst flavors, declares, "So Trump likes some colors more than others, just like his immigration policy."

9 TRUMP STOLE FROM ME - NOVEMBER 28, 2018
After Trump says he trusts his gut more than others' brains, Colbert points back to the first episode of his first show where he said the same thing and announces he'll sue Trump.

10 POST-MUELLER REPORT - MARCH 26, 2019
After Trump claims vindication from the collusion investigation, Colbert pulls out a "Reasons Trump is a Bad President" board to display all of his other problems and erases just one small line.

FIGURE 5.9 Colbert's Trump-era highlights.

Of course, comedians like Colbert couldn't resist. In his satirical spoof of the moment, Colbert began the bit saying, "speaking of incredibly rich people we like to watch and don't know why, Donald Trump."[72] He then showed the clip of Trump guaranteeing there was "no problem" only to come back with, "If Trump is elected, he will make sure that the Republicans are the party of the big tent"—a line he could barely utter without cracking up. He then said the "people have the right to know the size of your executive branch."[73] Colbert next went on to discuss how utterly bizarre it was to have a frontrunner talking about the size of his penis in a presidential debate. He next dove into the absurdity of the moment by noting with amazement, "I can't believe these are absolutely legitimate jokes to be making about a presidential debate right now."[74] He went on somberly, "[N]ow for those of you who have been following American democracy for the last 240 years, we have officially hit a new low in American political discourse."[75] So, despite having his own fun with Trump dick jokes, at the heart of Colbert's bit was a deeper take on the way that political discourse had so badly devolved.

Watching Colbert make dick jokes about Trump in early 2016 is eerie, because, even though he was clearly trying to use his satirical wit to get at Trump, it is also clear that he really saw Trump more as a joke and still couldn't imagine he could actually become president. At the time, in the news media and on comedy shows, Trump was still impossible to take seriously. Sure, his rampant racism and disregard for democratic traditions and the rule of law caused concern, but virtually no one imagined he would be elected president. But, if Colbert, along with much of the U.S. public, loved mocking Trump while avoiding the real threat he posed, that would soon change. Just as many in the American public had to adjust to a new reality after the election, so too did Colbert.

Trump was still a joke after he won, but he was a serious joke, and Colbert was arguably one of the best comedians at highlighting the difference. There was a marked shift in Colbert's Trump jokes after the election, one that quickly catapulted him to the top ratings for his time slot. Within weeks of the election, Colbert had thoroughly shifted gears and taken off the gloves, a move that rather than alienate viewers, drew them to him. While the post-election Colbert still peppered many of his Trump jokes with outright mockery of Trump's ridiculous hair or gross body, he could now be counted on to use his opening monologue to take on the latest Trump crisis, which meant going after a whole host of right-wing politicians and pundits. Because Colbert is on five nights a week—in total contrast to a show like John Oliver's—his jokes are highly topical and timely. They offer nightly zingers in direct response to the news of the day, and they thrive at unpacking the BS of the moment. Also, in contrast to Oliver's and other satire news shows, Colbert's format is late-night comedy—an hour-long show that begins with a stand-up monologue, moves to a behind-the-desk sequence, and includes music, interviews, and other possibly silly skits. This means that, even on nights when he is offering his best satirical wit, the show overall includes a good bit of variety entertainment. To Colbert's credit, he has revised the standard format for the one-hour late-night show, and the two opening sequences typically do include a substantial amount of satire. He has also changed the game with his interviews, which regularly include many more politicians, intellectuals, and influencers than his competitors, who still largely interview celebrities.

Colbert was at his most powerful as a Trump-era comedian when he focused on the way that the Trump team and its allies practiced faulty logic, twisted the truth, and BSed the American people.[76] One stellar example was when Colbert asked a team of experts to design a border wall. Explaining that Trump hadn't offered many details pertaining to his vision other than the idea that the wall was

FIGURE 5.10 Colbert delivers yet another monologue critiquing Trump.

Source: "Colbert Mini-Monologue: Trump's Incoherent NYT Interview," The Late Show with Stephen Colbert, CBS, February 1, 2019, https://www.youtube.com/watch?v=aw6RsUhw1Q8. License free image.

going to be "so big and so strong and so strong," "impenetrable," and "beautiful," Colbert consulted a contractor, an architect, an engineer, an interior designer, and a "concrete" guy to see whether the idea was feasible.[77] As they hash through their options, the tab for Trump's wall quickly climbs to $1 trillion, leading Colbert and his experts to suggest that it is best to construct a 2,000-mile highway alongside the wall: "Because what is a highway if not a wall on its side?" Colbert pointed out.[78] By then, numerous news reports had covered the fact that the wall project was untenable, but Colbert's sketch was able to use absurdity to highlight the folly of Trump's vision. It was a perfect example of how the exaggerated ridiculousness of satire is well suited as a foil to ridiculous ideas.

Colbert's most infamous Trump put-down prior to the 2018 midterms was more of a story of simple mockery than biting satire. On May 1, 2017, Colbert's monologue focused on a recent interview Trump had done with John Dickerson for CBS's *Face the Nation*, which focused on his first 100 days in office.[79] In the interview, Trump had insulted Dickerson, calling his show "fake news" and telling him he frequently referred to the news show as "Deface the Nation." In response, Colbert opened his rant saying, "John Dickerson has way too much dignity to trade insults with the President of the United States to his face. But I sir, am no John Dickerson."[80] He then went on a total tirade against the president, hurling a series of insults at him that included lines like he attracts more "skinheads than free Rogaine" and that the only thing his mouth is good for is "being Vladimir Putin's cock holster."[81] Colbert then recreated Dickerson's interview, this time making himself the interviewer and editing in far more satisfying Trump replies. The recreated interview was classic satire, ironically exposing the absurdity of Trump by editing replies to Colbert's questions that felt like honest answers rather than the typical Trump bluster. In his final question, Colbert asks Trump, "How would you sum up your first hundred days?" To which the edited Trump answers, "It's hurting the country."[82]

This part of Colbert's bit, though, would get lost. Instead, his line about Trump's mouth only being good as "Vladimir Putin's cock holster" immediately created a buzz, including accusations that Colbert had been homophobic. The hashtag #FireColbert circulated, and the FCC investigated whether the episode crossed the line for profanity. In the end, it stated that the line had been properly censored, and Colbert apologized for using words that were cruder than necessary. But the story is a good example of how Colbert's comedy for CBS regularly included a good dose of simple mockery, designed to put down the president and offer the public a collective sense of relief that someone was bitingly saying the things on their mind. What's interesting to note is that, in the Trump era, Colbert offered an interesting balance between exaggerated insults and smart, ironic satire.

Perhaps one of Colbert's most lasting interventions in the Trump era took place when he coined the term "Trumpiness" as a corollary to his Bush era neologism "truthiness." On Colbert's first episode of *The Colbert Report* on October 17, 2005, he introduced what would become a recurring segment, "The Word." That night's "word" was "truthiness," a term he coined only moments before the show's taping, replacing "truth" because it was not "absolutely ridiculous enough."[83] He then went on to define truthiness saying,

> Now I'm sure some of the "word police," the "wordinistas" over at Webster's are gonna say, "Hey, that's not a word." Well, anybody who knows me knows I'm no fan of dictionaries or reference books. They're elitist. Constantly telling us what is or isn't true. Or what did or didn't happen.[84]

As Colbert would later explain it, the idea behind truthiness was to offer a public vocabulary for a condition that had become all too common. "We're not talking about truth, we're talking about something that seems like truth—the truth we want to exist," he explained.[85]

At the time, the Bush administration had led the United States into an unnecessary war in Iraq and had also dragged the U.S. into Afghanistan, even though not one of the 9/11 hijackers was Afghan. Justifications were made at the time for these wars, but these were largely all lies, misstatements, or flat out BS. Research would later show that the Bush administration lied 935 times as it made its case for war.[86] At the time that Colbert came out with the word truthiness, it was still largely true that the mainstream news media weren't holding the administration accountable for these lies. Instead, back then, it would be the satirical comedians like Stewart and Colbert who often offered the most cutting critiques of the Bush team.

When Colbert coined truthiness, it was still possible to contrast truthiness with the truth. Not so with Trump, who regularly just made up things without any sense whatsoever of the truth behind his bombastic assertions. And this is why Colbert nailed it with "Trumpiness," which he defined as something that does not even have to feel true, much less be true.[87] Of course, when Colbert came up with the word, Trump had yet to be elected. Colbert's use of "Trumpiness" also predated Kellyanne Conway's use of the term "alternative facts," but it captured its essence. In fact, "Trumpiness" was by no means limited to the words of Trump himself; it was more a commentary on an era of public discourse in which the far right regularly made things up and then defended its alternative facts viciously.

Colbert's prescient use of the term "Trumpiness" was made all the funnier, uncanny, and insightful when, shortly after the 2016 election, he did a monologue for *The Late Show* in which he explained that he planned to sue Trump for stealing his bit. Colbert then highlighted a quote from a Trump interview with the *Washington Post* in which Trump said, "I have a gut, and my gut tells me more sometimes than anybody else's brain can ever tell me."[88] Referring back to the time Colbert introduced the word "truthiness" to the American public, he replayed almost the exact same words from his 2005 show. "Trump stole my bit!" Colbert exclaimed. "That is clear copyright infringement. He is stealing my anti-intellectual property! So tonight, I am officially announcing that I am suing Donald J. Trump for stealing my old character. It's official!" he announced.[89]

Of course, Colbert wasn't serious about suing. What was serious, though, was the takeaway that the newly elected president was a far less charismatic, far more insidious version of Colbert's old character. In contrast, as Colbert hosted out of character on his new show, viewers could see that the real Colbert was as dedicated as ever to using his comedy not just to entertain but also to hold those with power accountable.

FIGURE 5.11 "Ministry of Satire" ID card for Samantha Bee.
Design credit: Eric Spielvogel.

Before Colbert decided to sharpen his teeth on *The Late Show*, Samantha Bee was giving the public the sort of sharp, edgy, political satire it was craving. At the time that her show *Full Frontal* launched on TBS in February of 2016, it still wasn't clear what role televised political satire would play during the 2016 election in the absence of Colbert and Stewart from Comedy Central, but it was obvious that her show was going to matter. And matter it did, up and until it was canceled by TBS in 2022.

While Bee's new show premiered alongside the excellent satirical work of Oliver and other political comedians like Lee Camp (who will be discussed later) and Larry Wilmore (whose show was eventually canceled), there was little doubt when Bee's show was first released that her specific version of edgy, angry, smart satire was the perfect foil to the 2016 election. Bee's comedy focuses on a sharp use of language and a refusal to let the prevailing mainstream narratives hold sway. Bee's comedy uses irony like a dagger, and she aims it at mindsets she considers to be truly hostile to a dignified life. Her signature style is to be righteously angry over things that should really piss us off.

On her first show, she began, "People, I have to be honest with you. We wrote like two hours of jokes about Democrats, but we had to throw them all out because then the Republicans laid out a banquet of all-you-can-eat crazy."[90] Jumping right into the question of whether it was "fair" to focus so much political comedy on the right, Bee didn't just make jokes about the right wing, she pointed out exactly why she needed to.

That first episode aired shortly after the 2016 Iowa caucus, which allowed Bee to go after the candidates while demonstrating that she was running a show on which a caustic, callous form of humor would be the norm. The show screened a sound bite from GOP primary candidate Ted Cruz's victory speech on February 1 in Iowa, and then the camera cut to Bee tying a noose. Yes, that's right, a noose. That moment was an early indication of the gloves-off form of comedy Bee envisioned for her show. In comparison, Colbert loves to play with props, but it's unlikely he would make that sort of sinister move. Viewers couldn't tell whether Bee was preparing the noose to kill herself or Cruz, but, either way, the idea that 2016 was an election cycle that might lead to suicide or homicide was a point viewers would not see from the likes of Colbert, Stewart, or Oliver. The best part of the bit was when her anger overcame her, and she dropped the noose to harangue Iowa Republicans for selecting "fish-faced, horseshit salesman Ted Cruz as their new prized heifer."[91] She then went on to blast both Hillary Clinton and Bernie Sanders. On that same episode, she also turned her attention to the pro-life insanity of candidates like Ted Cruz and Marco Rubio, referring to Rubio's stance on abortion as "literally the stupidest thing I've ever heard" and backed by a "cabal of fetus fanatics." As *Rolling Stone* described it, Bee's comedy was "quite literally outraged."[92]

Bee became the first female correspondent to work with Jon Stewart on *The Daily Show*, joining the team in 2003. One of her special skills was her ability to conduct interviews in which she was able to encourage people to expose their deepest absurdities—a talent that Colbert would hone as a correspondent on the show as well. Many wondered whether she would be named as Stewart's successor when he stepped down, but instead it was soon announced that she would be hosting her own show, once a week on TBS.

Much attention to her new show focused on the fact that Bee broke into the boys' club as the first female comedian to host a late-night comedy show.[93] There is little question that her success as a female comedian is significant. But the real reason Bee's show became so important was because of her mode of humor, not her gender. Her show had a healthy dose of feminist comedy, but, arguably, she didn't have to be a woman to offer that. Instead, Bee's feminist interventions were important because they were the perfect balance of angry, ironic, and smart. Focusing less on the hypocrisy and "bullshit" that were often the target of Stewart, Bee zeroed in on how hypocrisy is used to cover up injustice. In so doing, she took the characteristic WTF of Stewart's comedy to a whole new level.

With the title of her show—*Full Frontal*—Bee played with the double meaning of the term, swapping the vulnerability and sexual objectification of full-frontal nudity with a full-frontal assault. As the 2016 election increasingly veered toward a Donald Trump win, Bee's satire-as-attack offered a valuable counterpoint to the bully and bluster of Trump and his team.

On her second show, she highlighted the fallout after the unexpected death of Supreme Court Justice Scalia. Puzzling over the idea that Republicans would ignore the Constitution so that they could block a new nominee, Bee exclaimed that Mitch McConnell wanted to "have a Supreme Court vacancy for a year because some chinless dildo wants a justice who will use his gavel to plug up your abortion hole."[94] Again, the power of Bee's takedown of the GOP stance is the fact that, even though her metaphors were graphic, she was exactly on point. McConnell did get his way, and it did constitute a threat to women's reproductive health.

While Bee joins the ranks of a growing number of high-profile female comedians, apart from Tina Fey's brilliant impersonation of Sarah Palin and Michelle Wolf's short-lived run on Netflix, Bee is most noteworthy for being a strong female comedian who works in political satire. In fact, even when we factor in the work of comedians like Chelsea Handler or Sarah Silverman, Samantha Bee was the only major female political satirist hosting her own show when Trump was elected in 2016. In September 2020, Amber Ruffin, who has worked with Seth Meyers, began to host her own show for NBC's *Peacock*, offering valuable diversity for female political satirists on late night. But until she launched her show, Bee was the only female satirist covering politics on her own late-night show.

One key feature of Bee's comedy is her vulgar language, a fact that has consistently outraged her right-wing critics.[95] But what really makes her use of language so sharp is her flat-out refusal to sugarcoat what she is saying. Yet, as might be expected, her crass words often serve to distract from her larger point. This was especially true on an episode in which she went after Ivanka Trump and called her "a feckless c@#t," a move that created a fury of criticism similar to that which followed Colbert's "cock holster" jibe.[96] The context for the Bee episode was the Trump administration's separation of migrant families at the U.S. border. In the

BEE'S TRUMP HIGHLIGHTS 2016 - 2019

1 TRUMP VOTERS - MARCH 14, 2016
Bee sits down with a group of young, educated Trump voters to dig into their support of the former reality TV show host. Later, she hosts a reception for them where her hired fact-checker has a breakdown.

2 GETTING SERIOUS ON GUN CONTROL - FEBRUARY 14, 2016
After the Pulse Nightclub shooting, a visibly emotional Bee asks the crowd, "Hey, is it okay if instead of making jokes, I just scream into the camera for seven minutes?"

3 "PEOPLE ARE SAYING TRUMP CAN'T READ?"- OCTOBER 31, 2016
Bee turns a Trump tactic around on him, conspiratorially suggesting that he can't read, but then backing that up with clips that make it actually seem true.

4 GREAT FEMINISTS IN FEMINISM HISTORY - JANURARY 18, 2017
During one popular recurring segment, Bee "thanks" Kellyanne Conway for pushing the feminism movement forward but actually criticizes her for her work that hurts women's issues.

5 NOT THE WHITE HOUSE CORRESPONDENTS DINNER - APRIL 29, 2017
In lieu of the Trump-less WHCD, Bee hosted her own event that raised $200,000 to protect free speech and featured Will Ferrell reprising his impersonation of George W. Bush.

6 COVFEFE - MAY 31, 2017
After Trump's infamous late-night tweet that ended in the word "covfefe," Bee announces that the President has finally followed through on a campaign promise, as the tweet and subsequent public response actually Made America Great Again.

7 PUERTO RICO - MARCH 28, 2018
Bee travels to Puerto Rico in order to dedicate an entire episode to learning more about the U.S. territory in the aftermath of Hurricane Maria and following Trump's botched recovery efforts.

8 ICE MISPLACES 1,500 MIGRANT CHILDREN - MAY 30, 2018
At the height of the family separation saga, Bee harshly criticizes the Trump administration and, specifically, Ivanka Trump who she tells to do something and not be a "feckless cunt."

9 MIGRANT KIDS UPDATE: TRUMP BROKE IT - JUNE 20, 2018
After Trump ends his family separation policy and claims he inherited it from the Obama administration, Bee details the role Trump and others had in creating the separation crisis and other immigration issues.

10 COLLUSION CONCLUSION - MARCH 27, 2019
Following the culmination of the Mueller investigation, which did not bring charges against Trump for collusion or obstruction of justice, Bee reminds viewers that's actually a good thing and that "you don't need the Mueller report to tell you that Donald Trump is a bad, corrupt man."

FIGURE 5.12 Bee's Trump-era highlights.

midst of the horror of babies separated from mothers, Ivanka Trump tweeted a photo of herself with one of her children. Bee went after her tone-deaf post, calling her out for her complicity with an administration that was actively harming the lives of young children. The important part of her rant against Ivanka was her use of the word "feckless." It was literally the perfect word to describe Ivanka's milquetoast inaction in the face of her father's brutal policies. Yet, the use of the "c-word," given its association with misogyny, was a major distraction, one that even led some to call for the show to be canceled. Unsurprisingly, even President

FIGURE 5.13   Samantha Bee calls Ivanka Trump a "feckless c@#t" for not intervening in her father's politics concerning migrant families.

Source: "Samantha Bee calls Ivanka Trump a 'feckless c***'", Full Frontal With Samantha Bee, TBS, May 31, 2018, https://www.youtube.com/watch?v=k4QgdZ3eIis&t=15s. License free image.

Trump suggested she be taken off the air. The uproar was so loud that eventually Bee apologized.

After apologizing for crossing the line and using a word in a way that might cause distress to some, Bee went on:

> We spent the day wrestling with the repercussions of one bad word, when we all should have spent the day incensed that as a nation, we are wrenching children from their parents and treating people legally seeking asylum as criminals. If we are okay with that then, really, who are we?[97]

Bee reminded her audience and her critics that the brouhaha over a callous word only served to underscore the larger problem of callous behavior. How could we care more about a word said on air than the lives of children?

Of course, in the Trump era, every reaction to his antics seemed to be questioned endlessly. After Bee apologized, some critics suggested she had caved to pressure from the right to do so. Bee responded, "The apology was not offered to the right," she said. "It was not offered as a concession to their demands, at all. . . . There is literally nothing that I can do to please loud voices on the right, and I don't expect to try anytime soon."[98] In fact, Bee basically irritated and annoyed the right from the time her show first launched and until it was eventually cancelled in 2022. The right-wing *Newsbusters* had a meltdown practically every time she aired. It referred to her as "vile," missing the point that what she was mocking was vile.[99] Her constant trolling from the right got so severe that she used it as a source of comedy. Her staff set up 1-844-4-TROLLZ with a voicemail that said, "Hello, you have reached the Samantha Bee rape-threat line. No one is here to take your call, but your offer of nonconsensual sex is important to us." Later, a menacing voicemail left on the line was featured in a *Full Frontal* online video to cheers and popped champagne.[100]

The fact that her comedy had such bite and came from a female unafraid to question patriarchal structures regularly incited the right into a frenzy. Each week, with each new episode, her segments drew the ire and condemnation of conservative outlets. Breitbart called one segment from her premiere an "all-out assault against Republicans."[101] The piece went on to complain that Bee "manipulated a number of clips aimed at making Republican presidential candidates appear reckless and unintelligent." *Newsbusters* described her as a witch who was bewitching liberals.[102]

Following the legacy of Jon Stewart, whom Bee credits as one of her greatest influences, *Full Frontal* didn't just offer us the sort of snarky comedy we needed to make sense of ridiculous times; it also provided a helpful corrective to the news media circus. Her viewers were not just entertained; they were informed. One excellent example of this was one of her best Trump-era pieces, in which she sat down with college-educated Trump supporters in March of 2016 in order to try to understand how anyone with any intelligence could back the bigoted gasbag.[103] At the time that she did the piece, it was regularly the case that Trump supporters were depicted as fringe personalities—marginalized, racist, and uneducated. Bee refused to buy that stereotype and decided to interview a range of college-educated Trump supporters. The piece was brilliant, not only because it showed her audience that they had underestimated the reach and scope of Trump's appeal but also because it revealed the depth of fact-averse thinking among even the most educated Americans. After a group interview, Bee and her Trump-supporting interviewees broke for a party, which she had promised to them as payback for agreeing to let her ask them questions. Then, accompanied by a fact checker, she walked around and spoke to them individually. She was especially curious about her African American Trump supporter. When she specifically asked him about how he handled Trump's racist rhetoric, the supporter downplayed Trump's racism and offered the excuse that Trump "speaks in an old way." Then when the supporter walked away, Bee said, "Watching someone choke down a piece of their soul just to belong broke my fact-checker."[104]

The episode was brilliant, but it was also telling. Why exactly had the mainstream media missed this cohort of Trump supporters? Bee made a point of treating her interviewees with respect, even if she couldn't help looking askance at some of their statements. Yet what remains most astonishing about the bit was the fact that Bee was literally the only major media figure—whether comedian or journalist—to even consider doing a story like that.

After the election, Bee steadied herself and ran a show that consistently went after the hubris, malice, and immorality of the Trump administration, right-wing politicians, and extremist pundits. Much of her focus was on the fact that the government was being run by selfish, sexist, unethical bigots. Her consistent message pointed to the basic immorality of the right-wing power elite. Usually, this feature of satire is harder to notice because mockery is not obviously a source of introspection and reflection. It is weird to think that comedians who crack jokes about dicks might also be offering their audiences guidance toward a better moral compass. But at its heart, satire is always about asking the audience to challenge corruption, to fight abuses of power, and to reject a culture of lies, manipulation, and dishonesty. That is why shows like Samantha Bee's *Full Frontal* didn't just cover Trump's "evil" agenda; they actively worked to encourage their audiences to thwart it. In response to the events in Charlottesville, the show's website featured a piece on "Life After Hate," a group that helps to bring people out of the white supremacist movement.[105] "Life After Hate" unsurprisingly had its budget cut by the Trump administration, so *Full Frontal* supported the group's crowdfunding efforts and encouraged its audience to donate to the group.[106]

Samantha Bee's show had a "full frontal" way of addressing stupidity, hubris, and faulty logic that was creative and provocative. One of the ways in which Bee's show was unique in the satire landscape was that her anger served as a strong counterpoint to the sort of belligerent bullying common among the right and central to Trump's persona. Bee's show demonstrated the difference between righteous anger and aggressive, selfish, abusive anger.

FIGURE 5.14 "Ministry of Satire" ID card for Seth Meyers.

Design credit: Eric Spielvogel.

Seth Meyers enjoys a special spot in the Trump-era political comedy lineup. As detailed in the second chapter of this book, he is often credited for spurring Trump to run. The idea, which I argue is largely disputed by the facts, is that Meyers roasted him so severely at the 2011 White House Correspondents' Association Dinner that Trump decided to run in retaliation. Either way, though, there is little question that Meyers and Trump enjoy a "special relationship" buttressed, at least in part, by the experience of 2011.

In the fallout from 2011, Meyers was also able to recount the conditions Trump's lawyer, Michael Cohen, attempted to impose on him should Trump agree to appear on *Late Night* to be interviewed. Apparently, the only way that Trump would appear was if Meyers agreed to apologize to him for the jokes he had made to his face back in 2011. Meyers, unsurprisingly, decided not to do it.[107] Thus, the story of Meyers and Trump is a long and interesting one. In fact, Meyers first encountered Trump well before he was host of his own show. Meyers joined the cast of *SNL* in 2001, and by 2006 Tina Fey and he were head writers for the show. At that time, Meyers also did the "Weekend Update" segment, and from 2008 to 2013 Meyers became its sole anchor.

Meyers had his first encounter with Trump in 2004 when the future president hosted *SNL* in order to promote his show *The Apprentice*. Meyers appeared in one sketch with Trump in which he played Trump's son on a public-access show called "Fathers and Sons."[108] That experience taught him something crucial about Trump: he really doesn't understand comedy. Instead, he sees everything from the point of view of his ego. "He did not strike me as somebody who had ever even processed if something was funny or not," Meyers explained. "If the joke was about him being handsome or rich, he liked it. If the premise was based on his looks or his success, he would say, 'Oh, I like that.' But he wouldn't laugh or smile."[109] Thus, Meyers had had ample time to observe Trump and the way he reacted to jokes well before the 2011 roast.

It is also worth recalling that Meyers famously wrote one of *SNL*'s most influential contemporary skits: Tina Fey's return to *SNL* as a guest star to impersonate 2008 Republican vice presidential candidate Sarah Palin. Meyers coined the now-famous line, "I can see Russia from my house," which was uttered by Fey's Palin character, not the real Alaska governor herself—but, to this day, many Americans are still unaware that it was a made-up line on the show.[110]

This all serves as a reminder that, well before he hosted his own show, Meyers had been playing a significant role in political comedy. Meyers began his new post as host of *Late Night* on NBC in February of 2014, taking over for Jimmy Fallon who moved to the earlier NBC slot.

As Meyers recast the show to his skills, he eventually abandoned the common stand-up monologue to instead start off behind his desk delivering a monologue that could be accompanied by images in a similar fashion to "Weekend Update." The style of *Late Night* falls between what is found today on *The Late Show with Stephen Colbert* and the sort of satire news found on *The Daily Show with Trevor Noah*. Because Meyers' show is still more late-night comedy than satire news, it is accompanied by a house band, celebrity interviews, and silly skits that often have

MEYERS' TRUMP HIGHLIGHTS 2016 - 2018

1 POST-ELECTION MONOLOGUE - NOVEMBER 9, 2016
With a somber tone, Meyers says he's been wrong at every turn in the last few years, so if that's the case, he concludes Trump will probably be "a great fucking president!"

2 TRUMP'S LONG LIST OF TWEET TOPICS - FEBRUARY 9, 2017
After a mosque shooting in Canada, Meyers criticizes Trump for not tweeting in support of the victims, pointing out that he had time to tweet about 28 other unrelated topics instead and rolls the list as he sits back with a drink.

3 TRUMP'S FIRST SOLO PRESS CONFERENCE - FEBRUARY 16, 2017
Meyers skewers Trump for his crazy first press conference, in which he yells at the media and says, "What president hasn't had to say I'm not ranting and raving? Who could forget Lincoln's tirade at Gettysburg? Or FDR's fireside meltdowns?"

4 TRUMP ON PROTESTS - SEPTEMBER 25, 2017
Trump calls for NFL players to be fired for protesting and says ratings are down because people want to see him. Meyers quips that no one is tuning in to watch Trump shuffle around like an old man.

5 MEYERS HOSTS THE GOLDEN GLOBES - JANUARY 7, 2018
Speculating that his previous jokes may have made Trump run for president, he tries his hand at it again, telling Oprah that "You will never be president! You do not have what it takes!"

6 TRUMP DOESN'T RUN - FEBRUARY 26, 2018
Meyers criticizes Trump after he says he would've run into the school to stop the Parkland shooter, saying he doesn't believe he'd run at all and won't even walk down stairs, pointing at his famous escalator ride.

7 TRUMP IS A WEIRDO - JULY 26, 2018
Following another series of Trump attacks on the media, Meyers tells the audience, "Trump is a classic New York weirdo. If he weren't president, he'd be the dude in Central Park feeding pigeons and naming them after the 1986 New York Mets."

8 BREAKING DOWN TRUMP'S TARIFFS - JULY 26, 2018
When Trump threatens to levy further tariffs on Chinese goods, Meyers warns of price increases on many favorite products- Trump ties, Trump hats, Trump flags, Trump socks, and more.

9 TRUMP AND LEBRON JAMES - AUGUST 2018
Trump attacks LeBron James after the basketball star says he would never sit across from the President. Meyers adds, "Trump isn't an at-risk youth, but LeBron just took him to school."

10 THE UN LAUGHS AT TRUMP - SEPTEMBER 28, 2018
After Trump gets laughed at during a UN speech, Meyers says, "See, he fixed it, now instead of laughing behind his back, they laugh right in his face."

FIGURE 5.15   Meyers' Trump-era highlights.

nothing to do with politics or the news. Yet, what has made the show most noteworthy and newsworthy is its increasingly sharp political comedy. In fact, Meyers typically pulls the highest number of viewers for his time slot across the three basic cable networks.

The show has several recurring segments, but the one that has really popped the show and that has the most political content is "A Closer Look." Similar to the long-form segment of John Oliver's *Last Week Tonight*, "A Closer Look," while funny, tends to be more serious and issue focused. Credit for the more serious news angle of the segment comes at least in part from the head writer for the segment, Sal Gentile, who was a political journalist before turning his attention to comedy. Another critical aspect of the segment is the fact that it is long—much longer than traditional comedy bits. In a panel discussion on the show, Meyers described how "A Closer Look" went against conventional wisdom by running longer and more in-depth than pieces on similar shows. Meyers explained that the "conventional wisdom" when his show began in 2014 was that viewers would prefer "short, poppy, punchy" online segments. But rather than follow that trend, Meyers and his writers went another way only to find that "A Closer Look" segments have "more traction" online. Meyers explains that, "[A]nything that has caloric value as far as the news works better for us online."[111]

Meyers also stands out in the field of basic cable for the simple fact that he had turned his focus to political comedy well before any of his peers and, early on, he was regularly targeting Trump. Meyers and *Late Night* initially struggled to attract an audience and suffered poor reviews, but most commentators and viewers alike have attributed the strategic move toward overtly political content with bringing new life into a show that regularly draws 1.5 million viewers and also maintains a significant day-after following on social media (*YouTube, Twitter, Facebook*). "A Closer Look" segments regularly pull over 5 million views on *YouTube*.

Meyers isn't unique only for doing long-form political comedy on basic cable during a late-night comedy show; his work is also noteworthy for his signature style. Meyers, like Colbert, is highly charismatic, but, in contrast to Colbert, Meyers tends to be far more smiley and far less edgy in his political comedy. Instead, his signature style is to be genuine and warm. When he sharpens his teeth and goes after hubris, stupidity, or abuse, there is rarely a sense of malice or anger. In that sense, his style is almost the total opposite of that of Samantha Bee. In terms of content, Meyers also consistently takes the position that his job is to remind politicians, and his viewers, of what a real leader is supposed to be like. For example, after Trump's first press conference as president, Meyers schooled Trump on the way he had congratulated himself for not melting down:

> What president hasn't had to say I'm not ranting and raving? Who could forget Lincoln's tirade at Gettysburg? Or FDR's fireside meltdowns? And, of course, Ronald Reagan's famously saying, "Mr. Gorbachev, if you don't tear down this [bleep] wall, I'm going to lose my [shit]!"[112]

Meyers, as explained earlier, was also at the forefront of schooling Trump and his allies on basic civics. Similar to the style of Jon Stewart, Meyers takes a sincere view that it is his duty to use his bully pulpit to foster a strong democracy. That sense of commitment often leads him to defend U.S. institutions and to use his comedy to point out hypocrisy, corruption, faulty logic, and abuses of power. That doesn't mean, though, that he didn't go for silly jokes that used comedy to make it clear that the administration was unhinged. In one excellent example, Meyers pointed out the hypocrisy of the spin that came out of the Trump White House. After CNN asked Trump adviser Kellyanne Conway why the president hadn't condemned the shooting of Muslims in Canada by a right-wing fanatic, she responded by saying, "[H]e doesn't tweet about everything."[113] This might have been a good point, if it had any merit. But rather than lambaste Conway for another falsehood, Meyers just pulled out a flask and had a drink while a ticker rolled across the screen listing the many absurd, trivial, and random things Trump had tweeted about:

> Meryl Streep, Arnold Schwarzenegger, The Ratings for the All-New Celebrity Apprentice, The Musical "Hamilton," Gary Busey's Mechanical Dog, Robert Pattinson and Kristen Stewart's Relationship, People who drink Diet Coke, Katy Perry and Russell Brand's relationship, Wind turbines in Scotland, "My many enemies," Himself eating a taco bowl, SNL, Himself eating KFC, Samuel L. Jackson, Penn Jillette, Macy's, Vanity Fair, Major League Baseball, Megyn Kelly, Low Energy Jeb Bush, The Super Bowl, Joy Behar, T-Mobile Service, The Song "Rockin in the Free World," "Sleepy Eyes" Chuck Todd, Ronda Rousey, The Microphone at the First Debate, and "Haters and Losers."[114]

It was a brilliant piece of satire because it was both funny and smart and left the viewer with a strong and unforgettable impression.[115] Even more to the point, it was again a comedian who literally shut down Conway's lie, a move that eventually happened with greater frequency on the news networks, but still only paled in comparison to the regular takedowns of administration hubris and hypocrisy coming from comedians. It was repeatedly the comedians who were the ones calling out the BS and lies at a pace that far exceeded that found on traditional news outlets.

FIGURE 5.16   Meyers goes after Trump's tweets on another segment, which lists one weekend of topics.

Source: "Trump Melts Down on Twitter, Defends Fox News Hosts: A Closer Look," Late Night with Seth Meyers, NBC, March 18, 2019, https://www.youtube.com/watch?v=AKdNko2cUp0&feature=emb_imp_woyt. License free image.

One of the absolute highlights of Meyers' Trump-era comedy was his brutal, and largely joke-free, evisceration of the president after the Charlottesville attacks. As described earlier, that segment also highlighted a special role that the Trump era offered political comedians: they were increasingly occupying the role as guardians of institutions rather than as critics of them. Meyers is likely the one political comedian hosting a show on cable who most embodies the sincere satirist who hopes to save our democracy so that he can go back to doing silly jokes and grinning.

FIGURE 5.17 "Ministry of Satire" ID card for Jimmy Kimmel.
Design credit: Eric Spielvogel.

If there was one way to prove that the presidency of Donald Trump changed comedy in the United States, it would be the transformation of Jimmy Kimmel from a frat-boy jokester into a seriously ironic comedian. Let's be clear, Kimmel still offers a heaping dose of frat-boy, bro humor. He was, of course, once a co-host of *The Man Show*. One of his most famous bits involves a long-standing feud with Matt Damon, as well as a video with a series of stars titled, "I'm fucking Ben Affleck." But Trump brought on a new sincerity to Kimmel's comedy, one that, while likely spurred on by his own family context, was certainly enabled by the 2016 election.

In January 2003, Kimmel left his post on *The Man Show* to launch his new show for ABC, *Jimmy Kimmel Live!* When his show first premiered, Kimmel's comedy largely was a form of dude jokes, influenced, at least in part, by his admiration of the work of Howard Stern. He also relied heavily on pop culture commentary and viral gimmicks (like Mean Tweets and telling your kids you ate their Halloween candy). His humor tended toward observational comedy, black comedy, and insult comedy, often delivered in a deadpan way. For these reasons, Kimmel had built up a specific fan base that enjoyed that type of humor, a fact that would make his Trump-era transformation highly significant.

The shift started with the birth of his son Billy in April of 2017. Billy was born with a rare heart defect and required emergency surgery. When Kimmel returned to the air afterward, he was a changed man, and he was prepared to let his audience see it.[116] That night, as he showed himself to be vulnerable and sensitive and capable of connecting a highly personal event to a political landscape, was a sea change for Kimmel. Over the course of the 13-minute segment, Kimmel cried, made a few standard self-deprecating jokes, and then he deliberately shifted into a different gear.[117] He purposefully linked Billy's personal health challenges with the Trump administration's efforts to cut the National Institutes of Health. He was clear about two things: that his son had been born with significant privilege, which meant that Kimmel didn't have to worry about hospital bills. The experience, however, had made him deeply aware of the struggles facing many families who didn't have his means but also needed major medical care for their children. And he became highly aware of the fact that medical research is a public good that requires investment and commitment from political leaders. After that night, Kimmel's transformation was being discussed everywhere. As longtime friend Ellen DeGeneres put it,

> You can't *not* remember that night. The fact that you're seeing a really strong, smart, funny man cry is beautiful. He's not trying to be tough. He's not trying to pretend. He's not trying to act like a talk-show host. And it wasn't salacious. It wasn't to get ratings. It was just raw, and you don't see that on television that much.[118]

Up until that moment, Kimmel had made the conscious decision to avoid politics in his jokes. With David Letterman as one of his biggest influences, Kimmel wanted to follow in his footsteps and never let his audience in on his own political views. But then Donald Trump won the presidency, and, as Kimmel puts it, "This sounds romantic, but I've never felt this way about a president before."[119] Later, when Kimmel chastised Trump for not supporting gun control legislation after the shooting at Marjory Stoneman Douglas High School in Parkland, FL, he stated, "If you don't think we need to do something about it, you're obviously mentally ill."[120]

Since his shift in April of 2017, Kimmel hasn't looked back. His show still includes goofy jokes that often make fun of the misfortunes of others, but he has become a regular ironic critic of Trump and his allies. In one especially funny exchange from October 2017, Kimmel got into a *Twitter* feud with Donald Trump, Jr., only to then describe the exchange on his show.[121] He started by saying that he had had a perfectly normal weekend: "Went to a wedding. Got a flu shot. Wound up in a fight with the President's son on *Twitter*."[122] The feud started when Trump decided to go after late-night comedians in a tweet that read, "Late Night host [sic] are dealing with the Democrats for their very 'unfunny' & repetitive material, always anti-Trump! Should we get Equal Time?"[123]

166 "Let's Make Donald Drumpf Again"

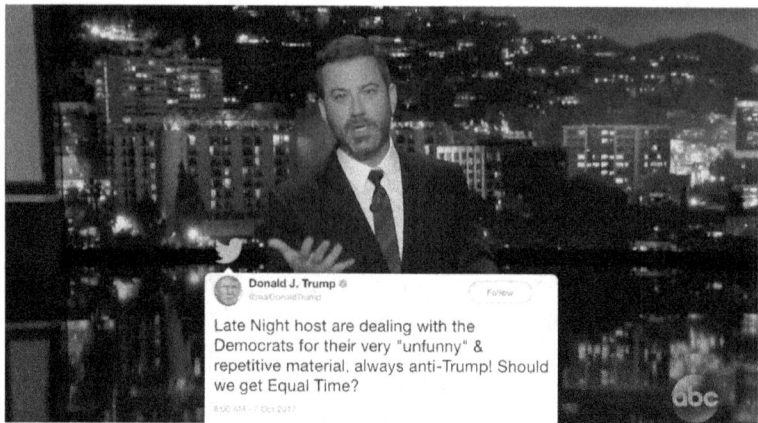

FIGURE 5.18 Kimmel describes how he got into a *Twitter* feud with the president's son.

Source: "Jimmy Kimmel on Twitter Fight with Donald Trump Jr.," *Jimmy Kimmel Live*, ABC, October 10, 2017, https://www.facebook.com/watch/?v=10155734294473374. License free image.

Kimmel shared the tweet with his audience and then replied, "Which is an interesting question, especially because the President tweeted this demand for equal time after watching *Fox and Friends* breathlessly drool about how great he is for three hours straight," Kimmel said, adding, "He took the time with his little thumbs to put the word 'unfunny' in quotes, which means we have a president who doesn't know how air quotes work. We basically have Joey from 'Friends' running this country."[124]

So, Kimmel explains, he decided he had to respond to the president's tweet and sent off this reply to Trump: "Excellent point Mr. President! You should quit that boring job—I'll let you have my show ALL to yourself #MAGA."[125] In response, the president's son Donald Trump, Jr., shot a tweet back to Kimmel: "Thoughts on Harvey Weinstein? #askingforafriend."[126] This leads Kimmel to offer a backstory. In the wake of the exposé of Harvey Weinstein as a sexual predator, it was insinuated that Weinstein was not being joked about on late-night comedy shows because he was a liberal who had contributed to Hillary Clinton's campaign. In the following exchange between Kimmel and Donald Jr., Kimmel promises to make jokes about Weinstein but, before signing off, sends a tweet telling Donald Jr. to watch the *YouTube* video that reveals Donald Trump's infamous *Access Hollywood* "pussy grab" comment. "So anyway, note to DJTJ," Kimmel concluded. "Next time you're defending your father and you think it's a good idea to draw a parallel between him and a freshly accused sexual predator? Don't. It doesn't help. It really doesn't."[127]

Since Kimmel's turn toward the political, he has gone after healthcare reform, gun control, and immigration policy. But Kimmel's most significant Trump intervention, as evidenced in the exchange with Trump's son discussed earlier, took place when Kimmel went after Trump's right-wing toxic masculinity, outsized

KIMMEL'S TRUMP HIGHLIGHTS 2017 - 2019

1 GETTING SERIOUS ON HEALTHCARE - MAY 1, 2017
In the aftermath of a serious health scare involving his newborn son, Kimmel takes the time to rail on Republican lawmakers and Trump who were trying to rip away healthcare for millions at that very time.

2 GUN CONTROL AFTER VEGAS SHOOTING - OCTOBER 2, 2017
Kimmel, originally from Las Vegas, goes after senators who continue to support gun rights and receive money from the NRA following the massacre in Las Vegas, posting each of their pictures.

3 SHITHOLE COUNTRIES - JANUARY 12, 2018
After leaks from the White House indicate Trump called African countries and Haiti "shithole countries," Kimmel can't believe that the *actual* President of the *actual* United States would say this.

4 "STOP BEING TERRIBLE" - MARCH 13, 2018
Referencing a recent tweet from Trump that criticized the comedian's targeting of him, Kimmel responds and tells Trump to "stop being terrible" and we'll stop making the jokes.

5 INTERVIEWING KANYE WEST - AUGUST 9, 2018
Kimmel interviews Trump-supporter Kanye West and presses him on the Trump administration's family separation policies at the border, asking if they can be defended, after which the rapper goes silent.

6 WHY DID DONALD TRUMP CROSS THE ROAD - AUGUST 16, 2018
On International Tell A Joke Day, Kimmel asks, "Why did Donald Trump cross the road?" and, in Trump style, says he didn't because that's fake news and then rails off ten reasons why he would have if he really wanted to.

7 MAGA SANTA - DECEMBER 17, 2018
Kimmel presents a Trump-supporting Santa, who demands viewers say Merry Christmas and debuts his own "Make Christmas Great Again!" hats.

8 BORDER "CRISIS" - JANUARY 9, 2019
The comedian goes after Trump for what he sees as a manufactured crisis at the southern border, steeped in racism and xenophobia.

9 TRUMP HALFTIME SHOW - JANUARY 21, 2019
At precisely the halfway point of Trump's first term, Kimmel commemorates the occasion with a "halftime" show dedicated to the "best" of the President over the last two years.

10 WHAT NATIONAL EMERGENCY? - FEBRUARY 1, 2019
Kimmel slams the President for his plan to declare a national emergency to build the wall and criticizes him for taking money away from "real emergencies like floods and hurricanes."

FIGURE 5.19 Kimmel's Trump-era highlights.

male ego, and dangerous megalomania. Given Kimmel's own macho bravado, his critique of the right-wing male ego is an especially powerful and much-needed addition to the menu of satirical Trump-era takedowns. For example, in January of 2018, Kimmel did a piece in which he went after Trump's particularly batshit week, which included, among other things, the actual president of the actual United States referring to Haiti and African nations as "shithole" countries.[128] To have Kimmel school the president on what it means to be an overly callous, stupid man was especially striking given Kimmel's own history of making jokes that trade on locker room humor, frat boy jokes, and a general bro sensibility. The point is that it was deeply ironic to have a comedian like Kimmel suddenly become a model for masculine leadership.

If Jimmy Fallon's Trump impersonation fell flat due to the fact that it came from a white, celebrity, hetero male on a late-night network comedy show, that exact same representational space afforded Kimmel significant cache as he went after Trump. What's more, Kimmel's Trump jokes were often made on *Twitter*, a platform that Trump himself used to increase his political presence (at least until he was banned from the platform). In fact, it was on *Twitter* where it was possible to really see how Kimmel was serious about taking ironic jabs at Trump. On February 26, 2017, for example, Kimmel tweeted at Trump, "Hey @realDonaldTrump u up?"[129] He often sent out memes as well like one from December 11, 2020, that posted as Trump was contesting the election results, in which Kimmel photoshopped a crying baby Trump onto a *Time* cover that featured Joe Biden and Kamala Harris as "Person of the Year."[130]

Even better, use of the platform of *Twitter* to ironically mock Trump opened satirical critique to the public. Each time Kimmel mocked Trump, a host of average *Twitter* users piled on in the comments to offer their own satirical jabs, some of which were even funnier and more pointed than the original Kimmel joke. On *Twitter*, Kimmel created a public sphere of ironic mocking that continuously put Trump's hollow, yet toxic, masculinity fully on display.

This was why Kimmel became an especially important part of the satirical humor lineup for comedy in the Trump era. The power of Kimmel's ironic and impassioned interventions came from the very fact that comedy in the interest of the public good had not previously been one of his interests. In contrast to the work of Oliver or Colbert, the innovative element of Kimmel's satire mode comes from the irony of him doing these sorts of interventions in the first place. The irony of Kimmel's sincerity, as a comedian with his own history of shallow jokes, positioned him to be a productive foil to expose the shallow, yet dangerous, reality of Trump. The absurdity of Kimmel as a figure dedicated to defending the nation, therefore, offered the representational force needed to expose Trump's own destructive tendencies. As *GQ* put it in a piece describing the shift in his comedy, the new Kimmel should have a tombstone that reads, "For someone who did nothing but fuck around, he didn't fuck around."[131]

One of the biggest stories to break in the narrative of satire and the Trump era was the announcement in February 2015 that Jon Stewart would step down as host of *The Daily Show*, leaving his show potentially rudderless in an election cycle. For many, the idea of going through an election without the voice and vision of Stewart was unthinkable, given the centralized role his show and his comedy had played in shaping public perspectives on politics. Even more significantly, Stewart stepped down with a measurable record of impact, having regularly been considered more trustworthy than journalists and having been proven to educate his viewers more than many news shows did. If Seth Meyers might be credited with prompting

FIGURE 5.20 Kimmel taunts Trump with a meme mocking his childish refusal to accept the election results.

Source: @jimmykimmel, *Twitter* 11 December 2020, https://twitter.com/jimmykimmel/status/1337552201397366786. License free image.

Trump to run because of his jabs and jokes during the 2011 White House Correspondents' Association Dinner, some worried that the absence of Stewart's critical voice might contribute to a Trump win.

As folks were concerned about *The Daily Show* without Jon Stewart, it soon got worse. Within hours of the announcement that the next host of *The Daily Show*

FIGURE 5.21 "Ministry of Satire" ID card for Trevor Noah.
Design credit: Eric Spielvogel.

would be South African comedian Trevor Noah, many worried he was not the right choice to take over for Stewart. After the announcement, fans were reassured that the show would continue in the fake satire news tradition, but it would offer a younger, more global take on issues. Yet the choice of Noah was somewhat perplexing. He did not have a strong record as a satirical comedian, and, even worse, his own *Twitter* feed offered a few examples of some questionable jokes that seemed infantile, if not outright bigoted and sexist.[132]

The choice of Noah to host *The Daily Show* came after news broke of a series of comedians turning down the job, and that led to further speculation that Comedy Central may have made a mistake in its choice. In my early assessment of the decision to hire Noah, I cautioned that there were two key ways in which his comedy might not be a good fit to continue the hard-hitting satire that Stewart had made legendary during his 16 years as host of the show. The first concern was that Noah's jokes would land from the perspective of an outsider, making it difficult for him to offer productive satire of U.S. politics. Sure, neither Bee nor Oliver was born in the United States, but each of them had years of working and living in the United States, and, more importantly, their comedy came from a position in which they had a stake in the issues they were raising.

Satire is a form of comedy that depends on building a community between the jokester and the audience. The audience is "in" on the joke. And the abuse of power, hypocrisy, and folly is the butt of the joke. Stephen Colbert on *The Colbert Report* referred to his viewers as "it getters." In order for Noah to be able to productively satirize issues taking place within the United States, he would need to create a bond with his viewers so that it did not feel that he was just making fun of their country. When Noah was announced, there was little evidence he could pull that off. He had almost no experience as a comedian working in the United States, other than the three times he had appeared as a correspondent on *The Daily Show* when Jon Stewart was hosting. And in those appearances, his comedy came from an outsider perspective bewildered at the incongruities and follies of U.S. society. That sort of comedy could only go so far.

My other cause for concern was Noah's own comedic style, which *The Guardian* described as "a mix of observational comedy and knowing jabs at racial stereotypes."[133] That style, while potentially funny, has little to do with effective political satire. When Noah first assumed his spot behind *The Daily Show* desk, many initial worries were compounded. Ratings dropped, he seemed to regularly flub lines, and, overall, the comedy felt tepid.[134] Critics felt that the show had lost its impact, and Noah came under almost constant fire. Maureen Ryan of *Variety* went after Noah's lack of edge: "[It's] as if our reliable attack dog had suddenly lost its teeth and self-medicated with Xanax."[135] Willa Paskin described Noah's *The Daily Show* as flat and insignificant in an election cycle that screamed for edgy, satirical evisceration:

> He's out to neutralize, not to awaken. How did the program devoted to scaling bullshit mountain in all its incarnations, the program that once had a gospel choir sing "Go fuck yourself" to a Fox News correspondent, come to feel so beside the point?[136]

Added to that were Noah's own interviews in which he insisted that he was not interested in the same topics that Stewart had been and that he did not plan to simply take over for the former host. As he explained to *The Guardian*, "I'm trying to build something from the ground up." In the early months, though, the show faltered a bit as it found its footing.[137] Jabs at politicians seemed more like caricatures than ironic satire. An early example of this was the time that Noah mocked Trump by comparing him to African presidents.[138] The bit served to reinforce stereotypes about Africa's political problems, while making fun of Trump's hubris. While the clip became one of his early hits as a host, it did little to use humor and irony to stimulate critical thinking.

In fact, in his early phase as host, it seemed clear that Noah's comedy would be a radical departure from that of Stewart. Satire geeks divide political comedy into two camps.[139] One, associated with the Roman satirist Horace, is gentle, mild mockery that points out our foibles and follies. The other, associated with the Roman satirist Juvenal, has a sharp edge that aims to expose social failures and incite change. Horatian satire laughs at hypocrisy; Juvenalian uses passionate sarcasm to expose evil. Horatian satire is light. Juvenalian is serious. They both use irony, puns, and parody to entertain their audience—but only one type of satire has any real social significance. In contrast to Stewart's Juvenalian style, early on Noah offered his audience the lighter Horatian version of satire. It is easy to make

172 "Let's Make Donald Drumpf Again"

THE DAILY SHOW'S TRUMP HIGHLIGHTS 2015 - 2019

1. ARE ALL COPS RACIST? - OCTOBER 1, 2015
During a period of heightened police violence tensions, correspondents Roy Wood Jr. and Jordan Klepper ride along with police to learn about bias training.

2. TRUMP IS AN AFRICAN DICTATOR - OCTOBER 2, 2015
Trevor Noah digs into Trump and concludes that he has all of the signs of an African dictator, with his flashy appearance and ignorance of democratic values and norms.

3. THE WHITE ISIS - DECEMBER 23, 2015
Correspondent Hasan Minhaj determines that Donald Trump is an extremist leader who attracts followers with propaganda and promotes a war between the West and Islam- and concludes that he is White ISIS.

4. DONALD J. TRUMP PRESIDENTIAL TWITTER LIBRARY
In order to preserve the musings of Donald Trump on his favorite social media platform, Noah and the show created their own library to house his tweets for eternity.

5. TRUMP IDEOLOGY TEST - AUGUST 19, 2016
Klepper goes out and meets with Trump supporters and discovers that most of his supporters can't even marry their own views with what Trump has previously said.

6. NOAH AND TOMI LAHREN - DECEMBER 1, 2016
Noah sits across from one of Trump's biggest supporters- firebrand Tomi Lahren- and takes down her major talking points and positions, dealing her a serious blow in credibility like no one had previously.

7. MASTER RACE NEEDS TO PLAY IT COOL - AUGUST 21, 2017
After the protests and violence in Charlottesville, Noah and Roy Wood Jr. wonder about the legitimacy of white supremacy and Wood asks, "If you're really the master race, how are you so dumb?"

8. THE CELEBRITY PRESIDENT - 2017-2020
After Trump came into office, the show kept track of the particularly high turnover in the administration among senior officials- maintaining their own *Apprentice*-like tally.

9. WHERE IS THE CIVILITY? - JUNE 26, 2018
Noah blasts conservatives for their continued calls for "civility" in the political process again- pointing out that it clearly went out the door with Trump and "tolerance got grabbed by the pussy."

10. POLICY VS. PRIVILEGE - APRIL 24, 2019
As the 2020 Democratic primary heated up, Noah criticizes Pete Buttigieg for failing to have policy ideas under his belt and "winging it" while Elizabeth Warren and Kamala Harris are serious and ready.

FIGURE 5.22 *The Daily Show with Trevor Noah's* Trump-era highlights.

someone in power look like an idiot, and it can be very funny. And Noah showed early on that he was good at that.

There is a major difference, though, between mockery, which can lead to apathy, and satire, which encourages critical thinking and active engagement. While these forms of comedy intersect and overlap, there is a key distinction. One leads voters to laugh at the circus; the other encourages them to kick the circus out of town.

In the first year of the show under Noah's leadership, it looked like all the political edge of *The Daily Show* was lost. Then the team went to cover the Republican National Convention in July of 2016, and everything started to shift. As Noah explains it, the convention in Cleveland was the first time that the team had gone on location. And it was the first time that a Trump presidency started to seem quite viable.

> It was the first time we had gotten out of the building and the show was in an unfamiliar space. Because of that, we were now engaged in this completely different thing, and we were all learning together. It was also when Donald Trump became real. Up to that moment, every fantasy of him being somewhat denounced by the Republicans was still lingering in people's minds. Cleveland is when it all became real.[140]

After that there was no turning back. With each episode, Noah grew more and more confident and more and more engaged in the political issues his comedy targeted. The tenor of the show began to shift. The bland interviews he did early on, like the softball one he did with Republican Primary candidate Rand Paul, changed. Bolstered by an extraordinary team of correspondents, Noah finally came into his own. He began to offer his own unique style, one that combined his global perspective and mixed-race heritage with a younger, more millennial comedic tilt. Noah remained as smiley as he had been from the start of the show, but now his gentle and congenial demeanor was combined with a sense of political commitment to issues of social justice.

To give a sense of this shift, in December of 2016 Noah interviewed alt-right celebrity and commentator for *The Blaze* Tomi Lahren. The interview went viral, not only because Noah treated her with respect but also because he deflated her arguments. But it got better, because, later, when Lahren referred to the survivors of the Parkland High School shooting as crisis actors, Noah and his team went after her, describing Lahren as the real crisis actor. They released a short video that stated, "Right now, a mainstream media organization is paying a young person to pose as a victim on TV. In reality, this 'victim' is being coached to recite highly scripted talking points."[141] Next, they screened clips of Lahren complaining about the oppression of gun owners, Christians, and conservatives. Then, an on-screen text called on viewers to "Tweet #TammyMustGo @FoxNews and DEMAND that they pull this CRISIS ACTOR off the air."[142]

As this exchange shows, by late 2016 Noah and his team had come a long way. Yes, they still took a global, multicultural perspective, but now the show had teeth and now it cared about impact. Urging viewers to tweet to get Lahren fired was a sign of how it was moving beyond distracting jokes toward politically productive comedy. Within this mix, Noah often relied heavily on his correspondents, many of whom are truly excellent political comedians. Jordan Klepper and Hasan Minhaj were early standouts, both of whom later went on to host their own politically edgy shows. In addition, Roy Wood and Desi Lydic consistently offered excellent pieces. In a highlight from Lydic, she went after the cable news reliance on pundit panels in a clip called "Cable News Panels Are Sh★itshows," in which she outlined how "panel debates on cable news have devolved into chaotic and incoherent shout-fests."[143] In one from Roy Wood, "The Master Race Needs to Play It Cool," he lectures racist groups on how they need to be "more low-key during the Trump administration."[144]

But perhaps more important for the themes of this book are the specific ways in which Noah positioned himself as a critic of Trump. As evidenced early on, Noah's take on Trump was often to be slightly less surprised by Trump's bombastic narcissism than other comedians given his own familiarity with demagogues from Africa. This angle, of course, was the focus of his viral Trump is an African president piece. But later, as he became more seasoned, Noah did an excellent job of suggesting that he had firsthand experience with authoritarianism and megalomania, which gave him a special edge in diagnosing those tendencies in Trump. This also allowed Noah to temper his outrage, often offering a subtler irony that had less of the sharp edge found on Colbert and Bee. Another critical feature of Noah's Trump-era style was his warm sincerity. While he was still capable of being a goofball, and often laughed at his own jokes, he increasingly took on a gentle gravitas during his pieces that investigated evidence of social injustice in the United States. These were some of his more powerful moments.

One perfect example of this was his excellent takedown of the calls for civility in the wake of reports that White House Press Secretary Sarah Huckabee Sanders had been turned away from a restaurant. Going after the way that the right whined about how it wasn't "civil" to do that to Sanders, Noah analyzed the inherent bias in calls for civility. As he put it, "Conservatives demand 'civility' in an attempt to silence critics of the Trump administration," leading him to point out that "calls for civility tend to come from people in positions of privilege."[145]

One of the best highlights of *The Daily Show* from the Trump era was the creation of the "Donald J. Trump Twitter Library," a traveling exhibit that was part 3D satire, part pop-up museum, marshaling a millennial vibe. The show allowed visitors to sit on a golden toilet and write tweets while appreciating framed iconic tweets from the president. "Every president since Franklin D. Roosevelt has been honored with a meticulously curated memorial library commemorating the documents of historical value crafted during his time as leader of the free world," read a release about the show.[146]

> Continuing this hallowed tradition and seeing no need to wait for him to leave office, *The Daily Show* will once again honor our current president with this library, showcasing our Commander in Chief's preferred vessel for communicating with the public, his Twitter feed.[147]

Among the exhibits were a video of people, places, and things that the President called "sad!"; a series of testimonials from high-profile victims as they recounted the trauma of being attacked by Trump on *Twitter*, and a comprehensive timeline

FIGURE 5.23 Trevor Noah eviscerates the civility argument.

Source: "Trevor Noah EVISCERATES the Civility Argument," YouTube, *The Daily Show with Trevor Noah*, June 26, 2018, https://www.youtube.com/watch?v=qljfObaUG2s. License free image.

from the former *Apprentice* star's very first tweet about his appearance on Letterman in May 2009.[148]

The Twitter library also resulted in a book that documents the exhibit. In the introduction to the book, Noah writes,

> When Donald J. Trump launched his campaign for president in 2015, I laughed at the idea. If there's one thing I knew about Americans, it's that they wanted their presidents to be dignified, intelligent, and black. Trump had none of these qualities. Even worse, Trump had tweets![149]

He then later muses that, in the end, he and his team acknowledged that these tweets were, in fact, history. The book—and the exhibit upon which it is based—let Trump's own inanity speak ironically for itself. Also, it did an excellent job of questioning the role that social media played in the Trump era, because Trump himself clearly was a master at using social media to speak directly to his supporters. Trump makes this point clear:

> The tweeting, I thought I'd do less of it, but I'm covered so dishonestly by the press—so dishonestly—that I can put out Twitter—and it's not 140, it's now 140, 280—I can—you know, I go bing, bing, bing and I just keep it going and they put it on as soon as I tweet it out—this morning on television, Fox—[mocks reporter] "Donald Trump, we have breaking news." I put out a thing.[150]

Trump may have had quite the *Twitter* presence, but so, too, did Noah. In fact, one of the key ways Noah popped the reach and impact of *The Daily Show* was through the ways that he and his team used social media. The younger, more social media savvy vibe also meant that the show picked up more of the much-coveted younger demographic. According to *The Wrap*, shortly after his debut, the viewership of *The Daily Show with Trevor Noah* was up 20 percent in the 18- to 24-year-old demographic, and his on-demand streams were up 44 percent.[151] He also was an early hit on *Twitter*, doubling Stewart's mentions and launching the show to third place in the Twitterverse behind *The Tonight Show* and *@midnight*.

Noah also was a central satirist to offer ironic insight into U.S. racism, and this was especially important in the lead-up to the 2020 elections when the nation responded not only to Trump's inept handling of the COVID-19 crisis but also to his racist response to the murder of George Floyd. As the Black Lives Matter movement grew in power and support, Noah's satire was an important voice. During those days, well-known comedian Dave Chappelle released *8:46*, a stand-up show recorded in the wake of Floyd's death. The special went viral. It wasn't just the sharp, moving, and insightful way that Chappelle described the death of George Floyd as both inconceivable and predictable; it was the basic outrage that Chappelle channeled in solidarity with protesters. Perhaps more importantly, the special stood out for the way that it did not use the signature, deadpan irony Chappelle famously tends to use when discussing race and racism. Noting the shift in his own tone, at one moment Chappelle stated, "This is not funny at all."[152]

Noah had covered the racism of Trump supporters from early on in his run as host, but his interventions took on greater and greater sharpness as he honed his skills as a political comedian. Since his viral interview with white nationalist Tomi Lahren, Noah has amassed a long list of similar interventions, all of which have in common the fact that he questions the premises and the core assumptions that ground most white supremacist ideology. It is a brilliant reminder of the special comedic charge of satire, which, in this case, is not after laughs but rather uses wit and reason to expose the faulty logic, BS, and irrationality of those defending police violence.

One of the signature elements of *The Daily Show with Trevor Noah*'s coverage of the Trump presidency was the way that it combined smart, politically incisive humor with a less catastrophic view of the Trump era. During tapings, Noah recorded segments aimed at his global audience, "Come to *The Daily Show* because you want to remember it's not the end of the world," he'd say.

> Come to *The Daily Show* because we're not alarmists. Come to *The Daily Show* because we're going to laugh. When you search for the joke, you search for the truth, because the best comedy is based on truth. We're going to laugh all the way because if you're not laughing, you're afraid.[153]

Noah is at his best when he fights fear with his own signature style of warm, insightful, satirical sass.

FIGURE 5.24 "Ministry of Satire" ID card for Hasan Minhaj.
Design credit: Eric Spielvogel.

Hasan Minhaj began his career in stand-up and joined *The Daily Show with Jon Stewart* as a "Senior Political Correspondent" in 2014. Early on in his career at *The Daily Show*, Minhaj stood out for his sharp delivery and incisive wit. He then transitioned to working alongside Trevor Noah when he took over as host. Both during his time with Stewart and then later with Noah, Minhaj became noteworthy for pieces in which he used his own identity as a Muslim American to critique Islamophobia and combat racist stereotypes.

One of his highlights working with Noah was a piece that aired in December of 2015 as the Trump campaign was gathering steam. In a piece titled "Donald Trump: The White Isis," Minhaj started off by saying he agreed with Trump that it wasn't safe for Muslims to enter the country.[154] When Noah asked him if he meant that "Muslims were a danger," Minhaj qualified that what he meant was that "Muslims *are* in danger. One third of members of a party are supporting a racist maniac. And that is why Muslims shouldn't enter the country until we figure out what is going on."[155] He then offered Noah a theory:

> Donald Trump is an extremist leader who came out of nowhere. He's self-financed, recruits through social media, attracts his followers with a radical ideology to take over the world, and is actively trying to promote a war between Islam and the West.

To which Noah replied, "Oh my god, Hasan. He is White ISIS."[156]

But then it got even better. After Minhaj pointed to some extremely obvious pattern matches between Trump and ISIS, he then talked about what needed to happen next. "Where are all the moderate white conservatives?" he exclaimed. "They've got a responsibility to step up and speak out against WHISIS."[157] In response, Noah aired a bunch of clips of leading conservatives critiquing Trump's proposed Muslim ban. Yet, Minhaj countered that "it was just easier on my brain to be irrationally afraid of an entire group of people."[158] The bit did an excellent job of using satire and ironic wit to invert a common pattern of blaming Muslim moderates for extremism. The inversion of those dynamics, so that it was the white moderates who were to blame, helped to make it clear that the common trope of calling on the Muslim community to police extremists was a totally absurd notion.

In June of 2016, Minhaj was tapped to host the Radio & Television Correspondents' Association Dinner, and he used the opportunity to openly criticize members of Congress for their failure to act on gun control legislation in the wake of several mass shootings that had directly preceded his speech. After a series of jokes, including one suggesting that, if Trump won, all brown people would need to flee the country, Minhaj focused in on his central point:

> Whether you like it or not we all have to step up and fight for each other, otherwise the whole thing is a sham. And until we do that, hijabis are going to get harassed in the streets, members from the trans community are going to be demonized for using the bathroom, and my brothers and sisters in the African-American community—their spines are going to continue to get shattered in the back of paddy wagons until we stand up and say something.[159]

It was a clear sign that Minhaj was committed to using his comedy to advocate for social justice, and it was a good example of the ways in which he uses satire to demonstrate the common experiences of marginalized communities. But his real targets were the members of Congress, whom he shamed for taking NRA money while sending thoughts and prayers to those victimized by gun violence.

Minhaj then went on to release a one-hour Netflix comedy special, *Hasan Minhaj: Homecoming King*, which won him a Peabody Award. Minhaj's real breakout moment as a satirist came when, as discussed previously, he hosted the first White House Correspondents' Association Dinner in April 2017 after Trump was elected. Trump opted to skip the event, instead holding a rally in Pennsylvania during which he bashed the press and stoked more bigotry among his supporters. Meanwhile, it was Minhaj who used the occasion to speak in defense of the First Amendment, highlighting the fact that only in America could a Muslim American comedian speak at a public event in front of government officials about the flaws in the president. Minhaj's speech also showcased his penchant for sharp puns and clever turns of phrase. In one moment, he said he does "not see, Steve Bannon."[160] Bannon, an openly white nationalist, remained employed at the time by the White House, a fact that was outrageous on its face. Yet, rather than making a detailed joke about Bannon's racism, Minhaj simply kept repeating "not see Steve Bannon" enough times that "not see" morphed into "Nazi." It was a brilliant example of the comedian's artful use of language.

In March of 2018, Netflix announced it was going to produce a series with Minhaj as host, and, in October of 2018, the first episode of *Patriot Act* premiered. Promotions for the show stated that Minhaj would "explore the modern cultural and political landscape 'with depth and sincerity.'"[161] Minhaj was the first Indian American to host a weekly comedy show, and he and his team sought to refresh what they described in an interview with *Vulture* as the stale atmosphere of late-night comedy.[162] In comparison with most satirical comedians who often downplay their role as a provider of news to their audience, Minhaj and his team openly acknowledged that one of their goals was to break stories of interest and importance to the public.

MINHAJ'S TRUMP HIGHLIGHTS 2015 - 2019

1 THE WHITE ISIS - DECEMBER 23, 2015
While Minhaj was still a correspondent on *The Daily Show*, he dives into Trump's campaign rhetoric and declares that he is a radical trying to spread an extremist ideology and can be declared White ISIS.

2 WHITE HOUSE CORRESPONDENTS' DINNER - APRIL 29, 2017
In the first WHCD of the Trump presidency, which the President refused to attend, Minhaj slams Trump for his prejudice against Muslims and commends the valuable work of journalists.

3 SHOPPING WITH TAN FRANCE - OCTOBER 25, 2018
In the lead-up to his new show on Netflix, Minhaj goes shopping for new attire with fellow South Asian Netflix star Tan France, where they talk about their experiences as children of immigrants.

4 SAUDI ARABIA - OCTOBER 28, 2018
After the murder of Jamal Khashoggi, Minhaj dives into the controversies of the Islamic kingdom and oil empire on the first episode of his new show *Patriot Act*, highlighting Trump and co.'s support of their vile actions.

5 AMAZON HOLIDAY COMMERCIAL - NOVEMBER 4, 2018
In a sweeping analysis of Amazon, Minhaj criticizes many of their business practices and creates a new holiday commercial for the company which highlights many of the sketchiest practices.

6 MINHAJ WON'T SAY TRUMP'S NAME - NOVEMBER 7, 2018
As a guest on *Late Night with Stephen Colbert*, Minhaj says he doesn't talk much about Trump during his show, saying the President doesn't deserve it and likens him to Voldemort in Harry Potter.

7 TAKING DOWN SUPREME - NOVEMBER 18, 2018
On *Patriot Act*, Minhaj harshly criticizes the uber-valuable street wear brand and slams the company for their oft-copyright infringement and ties to the Carlyle Group.

8 IMMIGRATION ENFORCEMENT - NOVEMBER 25, 2018
In the first episode of *Patriot Act* dedicated to Trump, Minhaj focuses on recent immigration policies in the U.S., ICE, and the family separation at the southern border.

9 CIVIL RIGHTS AND TRUMP - MARCH 3, 2019
Minhaj goes after the Trump administration's crackdown on civil rights, including widespread housing and legal discrimination being led by Cabinet secretaries and senior leadership.

10 TIME 100 GALA - APRIL 23, 2019
During a toast at the Time 100 Gala, Minhaj, an honoree, blasted fellow honoree Jared Kushner for his close relationship to the Saudi Crown Prince and his failure to fight for human rights.

FIGURE 5.25 Minhaj's Trump-era highlights.

From the start, the show was hailed as a refreshing addition to the satire menu, with Minhaj lauded for his energy, wit, and smart use of irony. Minhaj wasn't preachy, but he was fired up. He was exceptionally good at making silly jokes that had a deep and insightful edge, as in this example: "Saudi Arabia was basically the boy band manager of 9/11. They didn't write the songs, but they helped get the group together."[163] The show's goal was to be "timely and timeless," and, as Minhaj explained, one element of his style was to demonstrate that he sincerely cared about the topic he was covering.[164] He also tried to go after topics that had been largely ignored by others because they seemed too controversial. This was why he dedicated an episode to affirmative action in which he specifically asked the Indian American community to think about its role in the story. "I really wanted to look at the white space that exists in the medium," he explained, "these sorts of topics that are kind of radioactive for a lot of other hosts to touch."[165] Early on, fans began to notice that, with Minhaj, they were getting a fearless comedian who wasn't afraid to take on topics others considered taboo.

One of the most noteworthy episodes from *Patriot Act* focused on the United States' odd connection to Saudi Arabia.[166] In October 2018, in the wake of the murder of *Washington Post* journalist Jamal Khashoggi at the Saudi Arabian embassy in Turkey, Minhaj focused his show on the relationship the United States has to the kingdom. When few journalists wanted to fully investigate the real backstory to the Khashoggi incident, Minhaj decided to confront the story head-on—a move that he admits created fear for him and his team. The Saudis were claiming that the murder was carried out by rogue elements, allowing them to shield Mohammed bin Salman (MBS) from guilt. But Minhaj wasn't buying it: "MBS is not modernizing Saudi Arabia, the only thing he's modernizing is Saudi dictatorship," he added.[167] Pulling no punches, Minhaj openly called the Saudi government's behavior a cover-up. But the real focus of the episode went deeper into the various ways that the kingdom violates human rights. He also highlighted the "deep financial and political ties between the United States and Saudi Arabia, the country's involvement in Yemen and crackdowns on women's rights advocates."[168] The episode was so sharp in its attack that the Saudis had Netflix remove the show from the air in its country (though it still was watchable there on *YouTube*.)

The Saudi episode showed that Minhaj was willing to take on tough, controversial topics that many journalists wouldn't tackle. It also showed that his satirical focus was far wider than the Trump meltdown of the day. In fact, in an interview with Stephen Colbert on *The Late Show* on November 2018, he refused to utter Trump's name as a way to reinforce the idea that he didn't think the controversial president deserved to be the center of so much attention.

That said, Minhaj did two important episodes between launching his show in 2018 and ending it in 2020 that focused on the damage caused by the Trump administration. Each focused on the far wider, systemic fallout from Trumpism, rather than the Trump persona itself. In "Immigration Enforcement," Minhaj analyzed Trump's immigration policy, especially the separation of families at the border.[169] The show offered Minhaj's signature style of a barrage of facts combined with sharp wit. The episode was also noteworthy for the fact that his team was able to dig up old high school footage of Steve Miller, who served as a senior advisor to Trump and who is credited as being the white supremacist mastermind behind Trump's immigration policies. Miller was the architect of the travel ban and was the key driver in the move to separate families. Minhaj underscored the creepy quality to Miller by screening old footage his team found of Miller, including a clip from when Miller appeared on *Fox and Friends* to promote his pet endeavor, the "Terrorism Awareness Project."[170] They even found a clip from a high school campaign in which Miller said, "Every candidate that's ever been elected has failed to do one important thing. I will say and I will do things that no one in their right mind would say or do."[171]

The best episode that documented the ills of the Trump era, though, was the one on "Civil Rights and Trump."[172] In it, Minhaj went after Trump's cabinet and documented a shared strategy that ran across the leaders Trump chose to head key government departments. In similar fashion to John Oliver, Minhaj aptly diagnosed the problem and presented it to his audience in a way that was sharp and funny. Minhaj explained that across the Trump team there was a common pattern of (1) not doing shit (i.e. not enforcing existing policies in the public interest); (2) undoing shit (i.e. rolling back significant legislation that helped safeguard the public); and (3) doing awful shit (i.e. passing laws that were truly horrifying in their callousness).[173] Not only was the episode smart and insightful, it also offered a larger context for the long-term impact the nation faced after the Trump team left office.

The rhythm of *Patriot Act* was fast, and the graphics, which appeared around him and on the stage, offered critical counterpoints to Minhaj's quick wit. As *Paste Magazine* put it, Minhaj had "a distinctly youthful TED Talk energy which he puts to work getting the audience riled up."[174] After his first 13 episodes, Minhaj announced

FIGURE 5.26 Minhaj is amazed by a high school Steve Miller.

Source: "Immigration Enforcement," Patriot Act with Hasan Minhaj, Netflix, November 25, 2018, https://www.youtube.com/watch?v=H1g3P3g_Css. License free image.

that the show would turn to even more investigative reporting. "Going forward," he explained, "we're gonna start breaking long-lead investigative reports that we're providing all the footage and sources for. I'm really excited to do that."[175] Minhaj also made it clear that he would continue to throw "truth bombs" and "poke both corporate and international bears that are sometimes dictators."[176] In contrast with many other political comedians, Minhaj made it clear that covering important stories with integrity and wit was his main goal, and that is why his show offered a significant contribution to the range of political satire projects available to the public. Unfortunately, in August 2020, Netflix announced it was canceling the show, but there seems little doubt that Minhaj will eventually find a new venue for his work.

FIGURE 5.27 "Ministry of Satire" ID card for Lee Camp.

Design credit: Eric Spielvogel.

Lee Camp's unique contribution to the Trump-era satire scene was his unflinching interest in highlighting U.S. oligarchy, elitism, and systemic abuses of power through a fierce blend of satire and activism. In 2014, Camp launched his own satirical news show *Redacted Tonight*, which aired on RT America and was billed as "your antidote to the propaganda of corporate media."[177] Camp—described by *Salon* as "Jon Stewart with sharper teeth"—appealed to an audience that had become increasingly dissatisfied with mainstream news.[178] Taking advantage of the fact that RT America had no advertising, Camp went after any and all corporate and political malfeasance he could uncover. Caitlin Johnstone described him as "one of America's handful of surviving comics still using humor to punch up at real power."[179] And he made his audience laugh while doing it.

While Camp has been critiqued repeatedly for working for a network funded by the Russian government, he explained that his interest in highlighting corporate abuses in the United States made the venue of RT America a good fit, because on RT America his show didn't have corporate sponsors. Camp said he was drawn to RT in the first place precisely because of the editorial freedom. He knew he wouldn't have to worry about pressure from advertisers. As he explained in the opening of one episode: "People [ask] me why Redacted Tonight is on RT and not another network . . . I'll tell you why. My anti-consumerism, anti-two-party-corporate-totalitarianism isn't exactly welcomed with open arms on networks showing 24/7 Wal-Mart ads."[180]

CAMP'S TRUMP HIGHLIGHTS 2015 - 2019

1 MEDIA IS LYING ABOUT HILLARY'S CAMPAIGN - OCTOBER 24, 2015
Camp dives into the 2016 election early on, harshly criticizing the media's willingness to defend Hillary Clinton and to widely claim that she dominated the early Democratic primary debates against Bernie Sanders.

2 ELECTION FRAUD SPECIAL REPORT - APRIL 29, 2016
After the conclusion of the 2016 primary elections, Camp dedicated an entire episode to the concerns over election security and legitimacy after election observers express worry.

3 THE REAL REASON THE U.S. WANTS WAR WITH IRAN - FEBRUARY 10, 2017
Camp asserts that the Trump administration may pursue a conflict with Iran in order to stop the country from dropping the U.S. dollar as the "petro dollar" and traces how similar processes played out prior to the invasion of Iraq and NATO action in Libya.

4 RIGGED 2018 MIDTERMS? - MARCH 14, 2018
Following a "train wreck" 2016 election, Camp speculates that the 2018 midterms will be no improvement, as election integrity continues to flounder in the face of special interests.

5 EIGHT GREAT MYTHS OF AMERICA - JUNE 29, 2018
Camp ticks through many "myths" that exist in the United States, including "We have democracy," "We have an independent judiciary," and "You are free," offering up a detailed explanation of why they aren't true due to elite and corporate interests.

6 TRUMP'S HILARIOUS SPEECH TO THE UN - OCTOBER 1, 2018
After Trump delivers his second address to the UN General Assembly, in which those in attendance laughed during the speech, Camp calls out his hypocrisy on Saudi Arabia and the U.S. failure to support the UN framework.

7 SOCIAL MEDIA'S LIES - NOVEMBER 16, 2018
In the midst of a number of serious events, namely widespread forest fires in California and potential foreign influence in the midterm elections, Camp slams the mainstream media for failing to give viewers the full truth and calling out what is actually taking place.

8 THE MOST CENSORED STORIES OF 2018 - JANUARY 4, 2019
During his first show of 2019, Camp ticks through some of the censored stories of 2018, including the $21 trillion in unaccounted government spending and the root causes of the opioid crisis.

9 TRUMP ADMIN ADMITS THEY WANT VENEZUELA'S OIL - FEBRUARY 8, 2019
Camp slams the Trump administration and international supporters for their attempts to foment a coup in Venezuela, noting that the potential move is all about getting access to oil and playing a clip of National Security Advisor John Bolton admitting it on Fox News.

10 LIES ABOUT JULIAN ASSANGE - APRIL 22, 2019
Following Assange's arrest in the United Kingdom, Camp harshly criticizes the authorities and media for their critiques of him and support for his arrest, while those he exposed for murder and torture remain free.

FIGURE 5.28 Camp's Trump-era highlights.

Nevertheless, attack pieces on Camp's work appeared on NPR and in *The New York Times*, and both suggested that the show was nothing more than Russian propaganda.[181] In response to these critiques and also to the fact that RT America had to register as a "foreign agent," Camp would later open his show by saying, "I'm an American in America covering American news for Americans" to underscore the fact that he was not simply a propagandist for Russia. He also stressed that he wrote all of his own material and never had any interference from the network in terms of content.

While the show's presence on RT America struck a nerve, and while the network itself was eventually shut down by the U.S. government after the Russian invasion of Ukraine, which ended the show, the real reason why Camp ruffled feathers was that his satire was far more edgy and bold than that found on most other satire news shows. As Camp himself put it in an episode of *Redacted Tonight* that addressed the issue of its ties to Russia,

> Being a born and bred American who just wants to make America a better country—that doesn't stop the assault against us. Because on this show we talk about redacted news; that is not okay for the ruling elite. And therefore, so many great anti-establishment programs must be branded with a neo-McCarthyist paintbrush. The corporatocracy doesn't have any logical or convincing arguments against what we're saying, so they just attack where we're saying it.[182]

As the title of the show made clear, its focus was on stories that had been "redacted" from other news coverage. In fact, unlike the slate of satirists who regularly skewered Trump, Camp's show tended to cover stories no one else was picking up. This meant that on many nights when Noah, Colbert, and Meyers covered the same news story, Camp was covering a story that was getting no attention. In one example from the 2016 election, Camp highlighted the fact that the media claimed Hillary Clinton won the first Democratic debate, even though Bernie Sanders won every poll.[183] After running down a series of polls that all had Sanders winning, Camp then showed a media pundit saying that the media elite determined that Clinton had won anyway. During the 2016 election, Camp repeatedly highlighted flaws in our democratic institutions, cronyism in the Democratic party, voter purges, and potential hacks of voting systems—all stories that were largely ignored by both the mainstream news and political comedians. His April 2016 episode, which looked at election fraud, broke news on the weaknesses in our electronic voting system.

This made Camp's work especially valuable in the Trump era, because he refused to stick to the script of the sorts of stories that get attention. Also, unlike many other political comedians, Camp didn't prioritize entertainment value when choosing which stories to cover. Instead, as a satirist who put activism above laughs, he covered the stories he believed were most socially significant. One perfect example of this was the fact that Camp was virtually the only political comedian to give the Transpacific Partnership (TPP) any attention on his show when the controversial trade deal was being debated in 2015. In fact, when Stewart did cover it, it was for three seconds to explain why it just wasn't a good story for making jokes.[184]

One of Camp's special skills is peeling back layers of doublespeak and deception and asking viewers to consider why they have become apathetic about issues of major public import. He doesn't just target the power elite and the media that cover them; he also calls on his audience to snap out of complacency. Astonished that the public wasn't taking the TPP more seriously, he said,

> All you need to ask yourself is: "Is there anything in my life that I want decided by hundreds of corporate lobbyists?"[185] And, if the answer is, "no, there is literally nothing in my life I want decided by corporate vulture fluffers," then . . . why would you want them deciding the largest issues of our time?[186]

Thus, Camp's style takes Stewart's characteristic outrage up a notch. His jokes tend to combine an incredibly sharp analysis of a political situation with humor that can be crass and often sexual. The juxtaposition of his critical insight alongside a gross or sexually explicit analogy is a powerful tactic to get viewers to pay attention and to laugh while thinking through a difficult issue.

Other signature Camp traits are his more global view on issues and his refusal to frame them according to American exceptionalist paradigms. Shortly after the Trump inauguration, he did a piece on the "real reason why the U.S. wants war with Iran."[187] He started off by saying,

> [L]et's cover one of the most important things that happened that only got a little bit of media coverage. Donald Trump seems to be gearing up for war with Iran already. In fact, he didn't just warn them. He didn't just caution them. He put them "on notice."

Camp then mocked that by saying, "He put them 'on notice.' I thought that was something only said by high school dance teams." But then Camp made his real point, "I would think Iran has probably been on notice since they realized they were surrounded by U.S. military bases."[188] He then suggested that folks shouldn't worry because, of course, the Democrats wouldn't support war with Iran, only to then cut to a headline with Hillary Clinton advocating war with Iran as well.

The key point is not just that no one was following the story the way that Camp was at the time; it is also that Camp was able to use the story to point out the realities of U.S. oligarchy and the disturbing ways in which establishment Democrats and the GOP—what Camp refers to as the "corporate government"—often hold astonishingly similar political views on foreign policy.

Of course, Camp wasn't focused only on "serious" political comedy. He also weighed in on Trump's outrageous, narcissistic behavior and his tiny hands, but even when Camp made easy jokes about Trump and his dangerous, loony antics, he always had a serious edge to his larger point. In one strong example, Camp covered Trump's speech at the United Nations during which Trump stated that he had accomplished more than any other president ever—a statement that led the UN audience to laugh and led Camp to retort that Trump "had accidentally turned the UN into night at the Apollo."[189] He then showed a tape of Trump bragging about increasing the military budget, only to express astonishment that Trump would

FIGURE 5.29 Lee Camp points to all of the military bases surrounding Iran.

Source: 'The REAL Reason the U.S. Wants War with Iran, Standing Rock News, Capitalism Failing," YouTube, *Redacted Tonight*, February 10, 2017, https://www.youtube.com/watch?v=65_GcK0g_VU. License free image.

boast about an increased military budget in front of the very same countries he would use that money to destroy.

Camp offered a critical perspective to the satire landscape covering the Trump era, because his tendency to not allow Trump to be the center of his focus allowed him to target the deeper structures of power, of which Trump was only one small, tiny-handed piece.

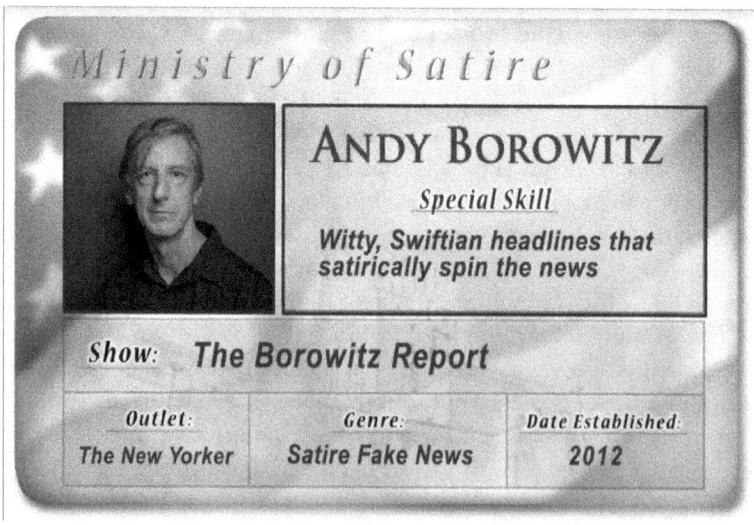

FIGURE 5.30 "Ministry of Satire" ID card for Andy Borowitz.

Design credit: Eric Spielvogel.

Much political satire takes the form of "fake" news, in which the satire stems from a made-up story that helps to parody reality. As explained in the previous chapter on the connections between satire and the news, this form of satire has become increasingly messy in an era in which propaganda news is almost impossible to discern from satirical fake news. But the hoax-based propaganda news isn't the only problem; the other problem is that the actual headlines themselves, based on reality, often seem so outlandish that they read like satire fake news as well.

While there are several well-known outlets for satirical fake news, most notably *The Onion*, without question it is the work of Andy Borowitz for *The New Yorker* that holds the spot of the most politically incisive satirical fake news of the Trump era. In the late 1990s, Borowitz, who had earlier made his name as the creator of *The Fresh Prince of Bel-Air*, began emailing his friends with satirical news parodies.[190] By 2001, the effort had morphed into a website, *The Borowitz Report*, which posted a new, 250-word piece each weekday. The site drew substantial attention, growing its readership into the millions and leading *The Daily Beast* to call Borowitz "America's Satire King" in 2008.[191] In 2012, *The New Yorker* acquired *The Borowitz Report*, giving Borowitz's unique brand of satirical comedy an even bigger platform.

Borowitz drew a following because he had a direct and incisive way of parodying absurd realities. One excellent example comes from a 2014 piece titled "Polar Vortex Causes Hundreds of Injuries as People Making Snide Remarks About Climate Change Are Punched in Face." It then opens,

> The so-called polar vortex caused hundreds of injuries across the Midwest today, as people who said "so much for global warming" and similar comments were punched in the face. Authorities in several states said that residents who had made ignorant comments erroneously citing the brutally cold temperatures as proof that climate change did not exist were reporting a sharp increase in injuries to the face and head regions.[192]

The piece offers an exaggerated, hyperbolic image of how those who accept climate science might react to climate deniers if they weren't civilized. It is a brilliant move that underscores the absurdity of climate change deniers by placing those behaviors in a parallel world in which they might be held accountable for saying dumb things.

Given that Borowitz made his brand by offering exaggerated, fake headlines, the political rise of Donald Trump was destined to pose a challenge for his signature style. Not long after the inauguration, Borowitz explained how hard Trump was making it for him to do his work. "We're living in an age that defies satire," said Borowitz in a CNN interview.

> You have a president of the United States who is a former game show host. That sounds like something that would happen on a Sharknado sequel. It's really tough to make a daily diet of comedy out of something that's already ridiculous.[193]

Borowitz acknowledged that the 2016 election was a real pivot point for his work and for the form and function of satire in general. Borowitz noted that, after 2016, he found that audiences were increasingly looking to him to offer insight into Trump and into politics more broadly.[194] They also turned to his work to feel less alone in their worldviews. With Trump, Borowitz often focused on his bombastic narcissism and overblown bragging about his business acumen. So, the parallel Trump-era headline to the previous one read, "Calling Earth a 'Loser,' Trump Vows to Make Better Deal with New Planet."[195] The thing was that it seemed possible that Trump could say something that outrageous. He certainly said similarly ridiculous things. It was this seesaw between Borowitz-style irony and Trump-era serious absurdity that made the work of Borowitz so important. And again, this is why satire has been able to engage with Trump in ways that the regular news media can't. Rather than take seriously a bombastic Trump line in order to unpack its lies and spin, as tends to happen on straight news, Borowitz goes after the exaggerated hubris itself by emulating it in a way that makes it even easier to see that Trump's claims are illogical farce rather than statements that should be taken seriously—even if his claims can and do have serious impact.

Like the satire of Jonathan Swift, Borowitz' style depends on exaggeration and on offering an absurd response to a real crisis with a deadpan tone that allows the absurd response to highlight the actual absurdities. By offering an exaggerated, ridiculous view of a problem, Borowitz emphasizes the way that the public has been told that an absurd solution to a crisis is a normal, reasonable plan. But, of course, in "Trumpland" everything was already an exaggerated, ludicrous parody, a fact that Borowitz claimed made his work in the Trump era significantly harder. Moreover, in the wake of news about the proliferation of propagandistic fake news and its potential influence on the 2016 election, *The New Yorker* decided to add a banner to all of Borowitz' pieces that stated "not the news," so that it could potentially avoid any un-ironic shares of his work. Borowitz has been clear that while his pieces are satirical parody, they are aimed at highlighting the truth. Using satire to get at the truth is exceedingly hard, though, when those you are satirizing so blatantly eschew the truth and claim to live in a world of "alternative facts."

Borowitz also hasn't been shy about speaking about the social benefits of satire, especially in the Trump era. Acknowledging that the audience for his jokes already agrees with his politics, Borowitz rightly notes that satire in moments of crisis works to keep "people sane." But he sees a further power in his work: that it can inspire people to act. "It can work," he explains.[196] He isn't delusional enough to think that he is going to persuade a Trump supporter to see the light; rather, he is hoping to use his comedy to motivate those who agree with him to get off the couch and do more.

> I'm a big believer in preaching to the choir. Comedy may be able to influence some people, but mainly what I'm trying to do is energize the people who already agree with me to get out there and do something to change the world a little bit.[197]

BOROWITZ'S TRUMP HIGHLIGHTS 2015 - 2019

1 **"NATION WITH CRUMBLING BRIDGES AND ROADS EXCITED TO BUILD A GIANT WALL" - AUGUST 21, 2015**
Shortly after Trump announces his campaign for president and his plan to build a wall on the southern border, Borowitz offers up a sharp take on the irrationality of the idea in a country with bigger issues.

2 **"CNN PREPARED TO CUT AWAY FROM DEBATE TO WHATEVER TRUMP IS DOING" - OCTOBER 13, 2015**
Borowitz takes aim at the media for its willingness to cover everything Trump does. The future President received billions in "free media" during the campaign.

3 **"TRUMP TO STEP AWAY FROM MAKING HIS BUSINESSES BANKRUPT TO FOCUS ON BANKRUPTING COUNTRY" - NOVEMBER 20, 2016**
After Trump's victory in the 2016 election, Borowitz goes after Trump's history of failed business ventures and hints at his likely failures as the nation's president.

4 **"PUTIN AGREES TO RECEIVE INTELLIGENCE BRIEFINGS IN TRUMP'S PLACE" - DECEMBER 13, 2016**
In the wake of controversy over Russian meddling in the 2016 election and support for Trump, Borowitz takes the joke further.

5 **"TRUMP SAYS HE HAS BEEN TREATED VERY UNFAIRLY BY PEOPLE WHO WROTE CONSTITUTION" - FEBRUARY 10, 2017**
After a tumultuous first few weeks as president, including the Muslim ban, Borowitz highlights the disregard that Trump has for the law and the U.S. Constitution.

6 **"TRUMP WARNS THAT DUMPING ROY MOORE COULD START DANGEROUS TREND OF BELIEVING WOMEN" - NOVEMBER 15, 2017**
During a heated special election for a Senate seat in Alabama, Borowitz offers a take on the GOP nominee, Roy Moore, a sexual preddator, who Trump supported.

7 **"MEXICO OFFERS TO PAY FOR TRUMP'S PSYCHIATRIC CARE" - APRIL 5, 2018**
Borowitz satirizes one of Trump's favorite lines about Mexico paying for his wall on the southern border, hinting at the President's instability in the White House.

8 **"TRUMP UNABLE TO STOP CARAVAN OF DEMOCRATIC WOMEN INVADING WASHINGTON" - NOVEMBER 7, 2018**
After the 2018 midterm elections saw Democrats take back the House, Borowitz turns Trump's concerns about a caravan around on him.

9 **"KAVANAUGH OFFERS TO PAY FOR WALL BY RECYCLING HIS EMPTIES" - JANUARY 10, 2019**
Borowitz combines two key controversies of Trump's presidency- the wall and new Supreme Court Justice Brett Kavanaugh- slyly hinting at Kavanaugh's comments, "I like beer" from his confirmation.

10 **"ERIS, GREEK GODDESS OF CHAOS, CONFIRMS THAT SHE WANTED TRUMP TO BE PRESIDENT" - FEBRUARY 1, 2019**
Borowitz jokingly implies that Trump is simply fulfilling the end-goal of bringing chaos to the United States and to the world.

FIGURE 5.31   Borowitz' Trump-era highlights.

FIGURE 5.32 "Ministry of Satire" ID card for Michael Moore.
Design credit: Eric Spielvogel.

Michael Moore's work as a political comedian defies summary because, first and foremost, he comes at satire primarily as a public intellectual and activist. While more than willing to engage in self-deprecating humor to relax his audience, in the end, Moore's comedy always has a larger point. Moore is without question one of the most important satirists in U.S. history, having created the format that later led to the current abundance of satire news shows that seem like versions of *The Daily Show*. It was Moore, though, who pioneered the format with *TV Nation* for the BBC from 1994 to 1995. He is also the reason why documentaries, especially satirical ones, screen regularly in movie theaters. His film about George W. Bush and the events of 9/11/2001, *Fahrenheit 9/11*, broke box office records and solidified his work as a satirical documentary filmmaker.

Moore rejects the label "political activist," describing it as redundant in a democracy: "I and you and everyone else has to be a political activist. If we're not politically active, it ceases to be a democracy."[198] That said, Moore regularly brings his signature style of ironic, satirical political insight into the public sphere. He attends marches, holds rallies, appears on cable news, uses *Twitter*, pens open letters, and more. While Moore already had a long and significant career as a political figure before Trump announced his campaign, there were a few key ways in which the rise of Trump and the larger political shifts in the United States affected Moore's style. At a basic level, Moore was both more invested in fostering political engagement and action and more concerned about the demise of our democratic institutions and the arrogant display of oligarchic power. These twin impulses of being both more politically optimistic and encouraging and more pessimistic and concerned governed much of his work in this period. This was all on display in the film Moore released as the nation was heading into the 2016 primaries, *Where to*

Invade Next, which tries to reimagine U.S. patriotism and rescue American exceptionalism from its right-wing, aggressive versions.

Where to Invade Next begins with the observation that the United States has not won a war since World War II. It then comically imagines the Department of Defense calling on Moore to step in and save our nation. His plan? Invade nations not to take them over, but to take their good ideas. We then see a hilariously ironic shot of Moore draped in the American flag on a ship, heading out on his quest. Moore then embarks on a tour of a series of European nations and one in Africa where he finds society getting it right. From debt-free education to paid leave, women's rights, prison reform, and delicious school lunches, Moore offers viewers a world in which people simply live better than we do here. In a brilliant move, Moore made his most patriotic film yet without shooting a single frame in the United States.

That doesn't mean, though, that the film doesn't offer glimpses into our own society, but these largely come from news footage of protests in Ferguson, MO, and elsewhere—not from Moore's camerawork. The contrast is stark. Abroad, Moore conquers other nations to "pillage" their good ideas. At home, we see a nation ripped apart by racism and torn by political division.

The American flag is literally everywhere in the film. And it works as an excellent motif. It is at once ironic and intensely patriotic. Most of the shots have Moore carrying the flag across airports into new countries and planting it strategically as he "claims" what he has found for America in a twist on the well-worn imperialist/militarist gesture. Reversing the link between the right and obsessive patriotism, now it is "lefty" Moore who brandishes the flag everywhere. At the heart of the film, though, is the question of what it might take to get U.S. citizens to really work to advance conditions in our country and to engage in politics productively, rather than in response to fear and hate. By the end of the film, *Where to Invade Next* refers as much to invading our apathetic political zeitgeist as it does to invading other nations.

When the film came out in early 2015, Trump was still a long shot, and the real political battle was between Bernie Sanders and Hillary Clinton. By October of 2016, the scene looked quite different. By then, the ticket was Trump versus Clinton, and Moore could see there was much to worry about. While pundits and politicians all seemed convinced that Trump couldn't win, Moore, who had a strong grasp of the views of voters from swing states like Michigan, didn't agree. In an effort to help boost Clinton's chances of winning, he released *Michael Moore in TrumpLand*, a film of a one-man stage performance Moore delivered on October 7, 2016, in Ohio. Billed as the film that Ohio Republicans tried to shut down, it follows Moore as he enters into "hostile territory" with the goal of influencing the November election.

TrumpLand at first comes off as a simple gesture to persuade Trump voters to think twice before casting their ballots—but that is just the surface. In fact, the film wasn't only aimed at convincing Trump supporters to reexamine their plans on Election Day; its real goal was to heal the nation after an election cycle that felt more like a civil war than a functional democracy. In keeping with Moore's more

MOORE'S TRUMP HIGHLIGHTS 2015 - 2018

1 WHERE TO INVADE NEXT - DECEMBER 23, 2015
In his first film in six years, Moore travels the globe and explores the social programs of seemingly more progressive states, uncovering along the way that almost all of the ideas, now dubbed "socialism," originated in the U.S.

2 TRUMP WILL WIN - JULY 2016
Months before his actual victory, and with all signs pointing to a Clinton victory, Moore lists five reasons Trump will win, including midwestern discontent, backlash from white men, and distrust of Hillary.

3 HOW TO STOP TRUMP FROM WINNING - AUGUST 4, 2016
As the 2016 election closed in, Moore took on the role of voter turnout activist in order to prevent a Trump victory. Moore encouraged individuals to get 50 people to the polls and act as a designated "precinct captain" for your neighborhood.

4 AN OPEN LETTER TO IVANKA - AUGUST 11, 2016
Moore writes a letter to Ivanka Trump, begging her to conduct an intervention with her father, who he hints is not just politically but also clinically insane.

5 MOORE IN TRUMPLAND - OCTOBER 2016
In a film released prior to the 2016 election, Moore travels to a conservative Ohio town and puts on a one-man show in front of likely Trump voters to better understand their commitment to the billionaire candidate and encourages them to vote for Clinton.

6 CALL TO MILLENNIALS - NOVEMBER 8, 2016
On Election Day 2016, Moore appeals to millennials and encourages them to turn out and vote to ensure that Trump doesn't win and prevent Baby Boomers and other older generations from winning again.

7 ANTI-TRUMP RALLY - JANUARY 19, 2017
On the day before Trump's inauguration, Moore holds a rally in New York denouncing the incoming president alongside celebrities including Alec Baldwin and Robert DeNiro.

8 10-POINT PLAN TO STOP TRUMP - FEBRUARY 21, 2017
Just a month into Trump's presidency, Moore calls on Americans to fight back against his politics by calling Congress, supporting groups challenging his actions, and running for office.

9 "THE TERMS OF MY SURRENDER" - AUGUST 10, 2017
Moore made his theatrical debut with a one-man show on Broadway, in which he offers commentary and analysis on the current political landscape in the age of Trump.

10 FAHRENHEIT 11/9 - SEPTEMBER 21, 2018
In an homage to his well known *Fahrenheit 9/11* film about the Bush administration, Moore dives into the presidency of Donald Trump and other hot button topics around the country.

FIGURE 5.33 Moore's Trump-era highlights.

politically positive take in *Where to Invade Next*, *Trumpland* doesn't viciously attack Trump and praise Clinton. Instead, it begins by showing respect for Trump supporters, by understanding their rage, and by acknowledging their views—including their hatred of Hillary Clinton. After humanizing Trump supporters, he humanizes Clinton. But rather than offering a whitewashed portrait of her, he begins by acknowledging that she is not perfect. Moore uses his ironic wit and his impressive storytelling skills to suggest that the real crisis in the nation isn't blue versus red; it's the lack of dialogue.

Speaking to assumed Trump voters, Moore tells them he understands them, but have they really thought this through? "You wanted to send a message. You had righteous anger and justifiable anger. Well, message sent. Good night, America. You've just elected the last President of the United States."[199] As if to further drive home the point, in late October 2016, Donald Trump sent out a tweet that included a four-minute audio recording that seemed to suggest that Moore was endorsing Trump.[200]

In response, Moore tweeted, "Look at this Orwellian tweet by Trump! Donald, u either haven't seen my movie or u are conning your followers. The clip u show [u] doctored."[202] But it gets even better, because Trump Jr. also tweeted the edited clip, to which Moore replied: "Hey everyone—Trump, Jr. & right wing thinks my movie called "TrumpLand" is pro-Trump! Haha. Pls don't tell them otherwise! #satire #irony."[203]

Trumpland, along with Moore's long list of public appearances and a series of open letters, was part of his efforts to raise awareness before the 2016 vote. Afterward, he didn't let up either, but his tone and mission shifted. In a rally held in Manhattan the day before the inauguration, Moore called for a political action campaign of "100 Days of Resistance": "As bad as we think it's going to be, it's going to be worse," he said. "We're in a dangerous moment in history where a malignant narcissist and a sociopath is in the Oval Office. But here is the good news," Moore went on.

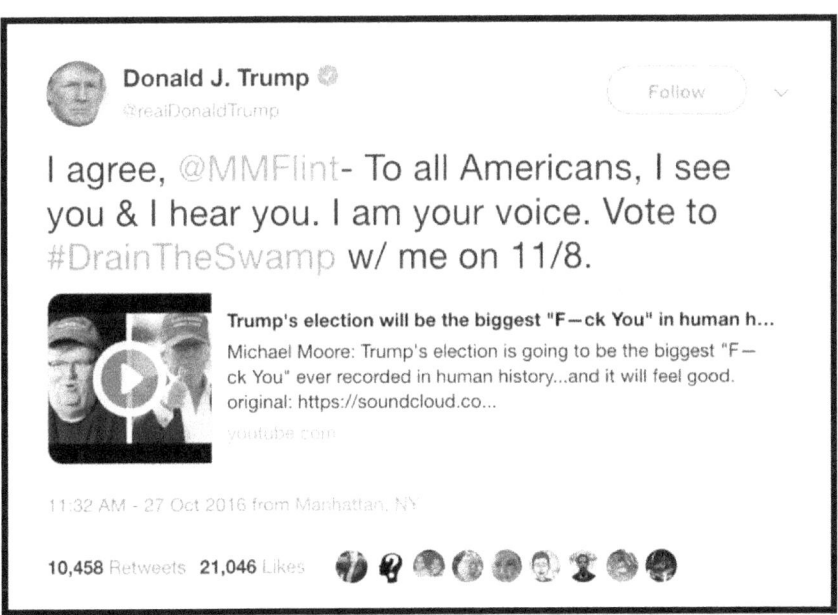

FIGURE 5.34 The Trump team tweets a doctored clip from *Trumpland*.[201]

Source: @realDonaldTrump, *Twitter* October 27, 2016, https://twitter.com/realdonaldtrump/status/791648889725450240. License free image.

FIGURE 5.35 Donald Trump, Jr., reinforces the idea that the right doesn't get irony.

Source: @MMFlint, *Twitter* October 26, 2016, https://twitter.com/MMFlint/status/791328954397384704. License free image.

> There's more of us than there are of them. He does not rule with a mandate. There is no mandate. Keep this in mind in your moments of despair. You are not alone. We are the majority. Don't give up. Wake up, brush teeth, make coffee, contact Congress. . . . That's the new morning routine.[204]

And as mentioned at the start of this chapter, he also suggested that one critical way to bring down Trump was with an "army of comedy."[205]

Moore took full advantage of the fact that, in the Trump era, mocking and satirical irony were not just accepted; they were the norm. It was a huge contrast from his earlier experiences. Moore's anti-Bush comments at the 2003 Academy Awards left him "abandoned by skittish Hollywood liberals, vilified by angry conservatives and victimized by hate mail and death threats."[206] But rather than give up and go into hiding, Moore went on to release *Fahrenheit 9/11*, a scathing, satirical look at the links between the Bush family, the Saudis, Osama bin Laden, and U.S. corporate interests.[207] Reaction to the film was so intense that Bill

O'Reilly likened Moore to Nazi propagandist Joseph Goebbels, Clint Eastwood threatened to kill him, and conservatives tried to block theatrical screenings of the film.[208]

Moore was one of the few political comedians to refuse to succumb to pressure in the Bush era and back down, a skill set that prepared him well to use satire to expose abuses of power, hypocrisy, and hubris in the Trump era. In fact, Moore decided to use his own personal story of deploying satire for political action in his Broadway show *The Terms of My Surrender*, which showed that Moore could take his skills from the screen to the stage. In the show, Moore highlights his own history of being politically active and engaged. Moore used the show not just to tell his own story, though. He also used it as a blueprint for civic engagement. He even bused his audience, at times, to the front of Trump Tower so they could practice protesting.

After his Broadway play, Moore then went on to release his most scathing indictment of the Trump era yet, *Fahrenheit 11/9*.[209] The film begins in Philadelphia on November 7, 2016—election eve. Images flash of euphoric Hillary Clinton supporters, expecting to see their candidate formally declared president. Then we see clips of various politicians and celebrities, who all smugly claim that Donald Trump is never going to win. It's a brilliant opening to a cautionary tale. Rather than starting with a focus on Trump, Moore opens by focusing on a deluded public who couldn't see what was coming.

From the opening moments of the film, Moore makes it clear that Trump is the symptom, not the disease. What makes Trump especially frightening, though, as Moore explains, is that he is not like the rest of the ruling class. Rather than hiding his abuses of power in the shadows, he takes the limelight. And, rather than trying to repress his megalomania, Trump basks in it. Even more, Trump is a master at manipulating the media and controlling the narrative. But most importantly, Trump doesn't believe that any rules apply to him, and he is obsessed with holding absolute power. This is why the title of the film references Moore's earlier work in *Fahrenheit 9/11*—the message is that if the Bush administration's response to 9/11 distressed you, then you should be truly terrified by what a Trump administration might make of a similar event.

To make the point clear, Moore goes back to the time that he appeared alongside Trump on Roseanne Barr's *The Roseanne Show* in 1998. Moore's *Roger and Me* came out in 1989 not long after Trump's *Art of the Deal* (1987). They both clearly represented radically different views about capitalism. So, when Trump saw Moore, he had good reason to think Moore might go after him, and he threatened to cancel the interview. In damage control mode, Barr's team asked Moore to play nice with Trump, and he conceded. Looking back on that moment, Moore reflects on the fact that Trump played him that day, that Trump got what he wanted from him. At the time, Moore had a reputation as someone who would bravely go after corporate corruption and abuses of power. Yet, as they prepped Moore for the Barr show, he was convinced to roll over for Trump. It was through that experience that Moore learned not to underestimate Trump—a lesson he repeated all through the 2016 election cycle as one of the lone voices who predicted Trump's win.

As Moore looks back on Trump's rise to power, he offers his audience lots of sharp, witty, satirical irony, but, ultimately, Moore's point is that Trump may be a joke, but there's nothing funny about him. As if to drive home the point, this is Moore's most chilling, least lighthearted film yet. Sure, he breaks up the tension with scenes like the one in which he posits that Gwen Stefani is the reason Trump decided to run, but these moments are flashes in a film that draws serious and detailed comparisons between the Trump administration and Nazi Germany.

At the heart of the film is the message that abusive systems of power depend on a public that is complacent, compromising, passive, and distracted. In order to draw out how we came to be a nation in which so few people vote and even fewer feel like their voices matter, Moore takes aim across the political spectrum. One of the most powerful aspects of the film is the way that Moore pulls no punches as he outs the establishment left and faults it for its complicity with corporate capital. Nancy Pelosi, Bill Clinton, and Barack Obama all come under fire as Moore reveals how they sold out the ideals of the Democratic Party to corporate backers. He even implicates himself, not only for his soft pedaling of Trump during the Barr interview but also for the various times that his own career has brushed up against the corrupt power elite in ways that feel altogether too chummy to him in hindsight. He even reveals that Jared Kushner hosted the after-party for the premiere of *Sicko* (2007), his documentary about the failures in our healthcare system.

One of the most moving elements of the film is the way in which Moore tells the story of the water crisis in his hometown of Flint, MI, and turns this personal and local tragedy into a warning for the nation as a whole. Moore documents how Michigan's Governor Rick Snyder put profit over the people of Flint when he replaced their clean water source with one that was contaminated with lead. The film offers chilling details of how the Snyder administration knowingly poisoned an entire city. Moore makes the case that the story of Flint is not one of isolated corruption and greed; it is the story of a nation that has allowed this sort of criminal behavior to be more than acceptable—routine. With scenes that connect Snyder and Trump, Moore shows how a willful disregard for human life and the total abandonment of any moral code are now common political practice. Moore works hard to drive home the point that the story of Flint is not an isolated incident or a tragic accident, but proof of the triumph of corporate capitalism over democratic ideals.

As Moore moves across the country, covering stories of families that have been left behind by a system designed to benefit the oligarchy, he also documents a rising resistance. From the teachers' strike in West Virginia to the teenage students of Parkland, FL, who organized the "March for Our Lives," to various young, progressive politicians, like Alexandria Ocasio-Cortez, Rashida Tlaib, and Michael

Hepburn, Moore reminds us that what we need isn't hope; it's action. Never one to leave his audience in despair, Moore offers his viewers a path to resistance. He makes it clear, though, that the only way that resistance will make a difference is if everyone who is frustrated with the system gets involved.

Unlike political comedians who fret over whether their comedy can make a difference or who sidestep the issue of political impact, Moore has always been consistent in his interest in using comedy, pranks, sarcasm, and satire to promote a progressive platform. For Moore, troping on Marshall McLuhan's famous dictum, the medium is the message, which explains why he launched a podcast, "Rumble with Michael Moore," prior to the 2020 election because it allowed him to offer an almost immediate way to connect with his audience.[210] Moore uses satire and comedy to blend humor with politics because he knows it works. And that is why his specific brand of political comedy is such an important feature of Trump-era satire. The impressive element of Moore's satire, though, is that it works across a range of satirical styles. While plenty of political comedians draw on a range of tactics to use comedy to reach their audience, Moore engages in a full-on, guerilla-style, multimedia assault on Trumpism.

★★★

The preceding discussions have been only highlights of some of the most visible satirists who worked to make "Donald Drumpf Again." There literally is no way to do justice to the full range of satirical material at our disposal. Randy Rainbow, *Mad Magazine*, Jim Jeffries, *South Park*, the regular installments of "Weekend Update" for *SNL* are all excellent examples of Trump satire—each offering its own unique contribution. What's more, there were several excellent Trump-era satirical projects that were short lived or canceled during the Trump era. Yet, even though they didn't stay on the air, they still managed to get in some very good digs at the political foibles of the time. Think, for example, of the work of Larry Wilmore, Jordan Klepper, Anthony Atamanuik, and Michelle Wolf in this regard. Bill Maher is perhaps the one comedian who was central in the post-9/11 years but less so in the Trump years, but that is mainly because his show didn't adapt to the particular ways that Trump and his team called for new approaches to satirizing them.

One additional category of Trump-era professional satire that must be highlighted here is the work of editorial cartoonists. Editorial cartooning has a long, illustrious history in the United States as a potent source of satirical wit used to spark social critique. It was a key element in the American Revolution and has historically been one of the strongest forms of satire in the country. While internet technologies had shifted some of the ways in which long-standing editorial cartooning for newspapers worked, it was still the case that when Trump was elected there were a significant number of editorial cartoonists working for print news, making a living by mocking the absurdities of our society. Cartoonists like Steve Sack, Jack Ohman, Joel Pett, Matt Wuerker, Mike Thompson, and Ann Telnaes used their art to mock Trump. The beauty of the editorial cartoon is that it offers its audience an image, often accompanied by brief text, that quickly and succinctly makes a satirical point. Unlike other forms of satire, editorial cartoons tend to reach a broader audience because their work is easily appreciated by a wide range of people and because they offer a sharp, distilled image that quickly conveys a point.

Trump, of course, had long been the subject of critical cartoons, especially in Gary Trudeau's *Doonesbury* as I explained in the second chapter of this book. As his political career took hold, though, he became a far bigger target.

Trump-era cartoons continued the tradition of using the genre to insult a target, often in a pointed, openly negative way, pulling no punches. And because they tend to offer relatively sharp critique, even for satire, it is no surprise that cartoonists are often accused of being offensive and incendiary in their work. It was still surprising though, when the *Pittsburgh Post-Gazette* decided to fire Rob Rogers after a 25-year career for doing cartoons critical of Trump.[211]

While Rogers lost his position, the cartoon critics of the Trump presidency kept on coming. Upholding a valued U.S. tradition of using artistic caricatures and sharp wit to expose abuses of power, hubris, and outright stupidity, the cartoonists went after Trump relentlessly.

FIGURE 5.36 This cartoon by Steve Sack perfectly illustrates the twisted logic of the Trump administration and shows how satire is effective at exposing the Trump team's hypocrisy.

Source: Steve Sack. Used with permission.

"Let's Make Donald Drumpf Again" 199

FIGURE 5.37 This cartoon by Joel Pett clearly suggests that Trump is a threat to both a free press and cartoonists.[212]

Source: Joel Pett. Used with permission.

The important takeaway is that Trump remains the most mocked president in U.S. history and that Trump-era satire had to bend, adapt, and adjust in order to use irony to help speak truth to power. It was so successful at making these adjustments that it often was more timely, relevant, and hard-hitting than the regular mainstream news. Even more importantly, sarcasm, snark, and satire were not the domain of professionals only—nor have they ever been. But, as I noted in my co-authored book *Is Satire Saving Our Nation*, the post-9/11 years saw a significant rise in what is best described as "citizen satire"—a form of satirical intervention similar to citizen journalism in that it is aided by contemporary technologies that make it easy for average citizens to spread their messages with impact.[213] This type of satire became especially powerful in the Trump years, as citizens engaged in satirical communications across a range of platforms.

It was virtually impossible, for example, to go to a protest and not see satirical protest signs. For example, many signs visible during the "Women's March" questioned Trump's masculinity in ways that were ironic and powerful.[214] See, for example, the image in Figure 5.38, which portrays Trump as the sexual slave of Putin, a move that was filled with irony for protesters fighting for women's rights and against misogyny.[215] In addition to citizens participating in protests, several political action groups sprung up after Trump was elected. Among them, one of

FIGURE 5.38 This photo shows the increase in sarcasm and sass at protests.

Source: Photo taken by Sociologist Kristen Barber for a study of masculinity in protest. Used with permission.

the most important was Indivisible. Indivisible was launched by former Democratic Congressional staffers who had witnessed the power of the Tea Party movement. They decided to create a guide to help Trump resisters that would focus on effective tactics for building momentum and having impact. Yet, there was one key difference they had in mind. Where the Tea Party traded on anger, fear, and hysteria to freak out its members, Indivisible mobilized its members by using laughtivism—a form of activism that recognizes the power of humor and comedy to incite change.[216] Thus, unlike the angry, scary rhetoric of the Tea Party that sought to gain support through fear, Indivisible used satirical activism—"missing" labels on milk cartons and on posters calling out their missing representatives, chickens at town halls to represent "chicken" leaders, cardboard cutouts of members of Congress, and empty suits and empty chairs to depict absent politicians refusing to engage with constituents. Some resisters even went so far as to buy billboards to make their satirical point.[217]

As Srdja Popovic explains, laughtivism helped bring down Serbian dictator Slobodan Milosevic, and it "breaks fear and builds confidence," thereby creating

FIGURE 5.39 This billboard calls out Paul Ryan for "running" from his constituents.
Source: @StopTheSpeaker, *Twitter*, https://twitter.com/StopTheSpeaker/status/834071437845680133. License free image.

a political mindset that can inspire revolutionary change and mobilize collective action.[218] There is little question that the Trump era saw a spike in laughtivism in this nation.

Memes and tweets were also fertile ground for citizen-generated, anti-Trump snark and sarcasm. Each time Trump tweeted, average citizens responded to him with snark and sarcasm—usually at a rate that far outpaced serious interactions with his tweets. The various ways in which citizens mocked Trump and his message were literally endless and examples abound. Some were mostly silly mockery.[219]

Other citizen satire tweets, though, used irony to expose the farce and folly of Trump's hubris, like the example in Figure 5.41 from Bob Vulfov, which brilliantly parodied Trump's narcissistic ego.[220]

Much was made of the fact that Trump used *Twitter* to speak directly to his base without the medium of the press, at least until he was banned from it. But less attention was paid to the fact that such a move allowed his critics to tweet right back at him. After almost every Trump tweet, the reply feed had

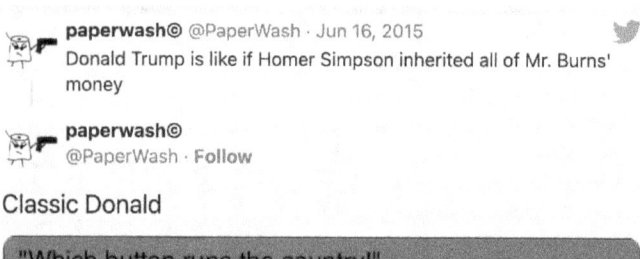

FIGURE 5.40   Silly tweet mocking Trump.

Source: @Paperwash, *Twitter*, 16 June 2015, https://twitter.com/PaperWash/status/610919222563196928. License free image.

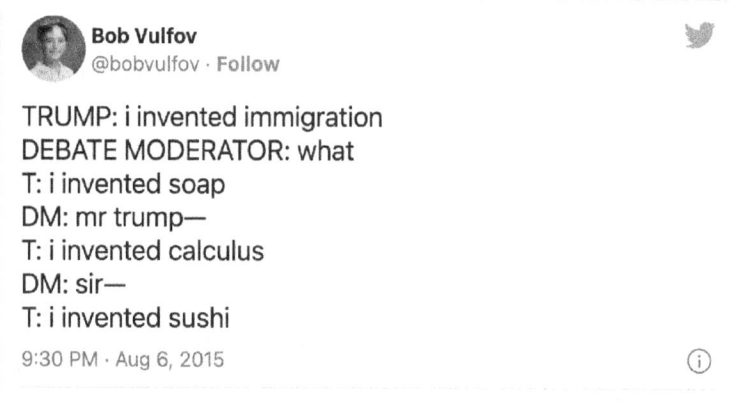

FIGURE 5.41   Satirical tweet mocking Trump.

Source: @bobvulfov, *Twitter*, 6 August 2015, https://twitter.com/bobvulfov/status/629464596152238080. License free image.

substantial snark presence, if it wasn't outright dominated by it. This is all to say that sarcasm and satire became increasingly part of the public idiom of political participation.

But, you might wonder, this increased degree of sarcasm and satire can't be good for the strength of our democratic institutions. Or can it? And, even more possibly, you may wonder if all of this joking isn't just a palliative that distracted us from the real horrors of Trump and his allies. I mean, laughing at a narcissistic authoritarian who seems hell-bent on destroying the very values our nation rests on can't be good, can it? Read the next chapter on the proof we have of the political effects of satire to find out.

Notes

1. "Donald Trump: Last Week Tonight with John Oliver (HBO)." *YouTube* video, posted by *Last Week Tonight* on February 28, 2016, 21:53, www.youtube.com/watch?v=DnpO_RTSNmQ&t=2s.
2. Locker, Melissa. "John Oliver Takes on Donald Trump on *Last Week Tonight*." *Time*, February 29, 2016, http://time.com/4240734/john-oliver-donald-trump-last-week-tonight/.
3. "Donald Trump: Last Week Tonight with John Oliver (HBO)." *YouTube* video, posted by *Last Week Tonight* on February 28, 2016, 21:53, www.youtube.com/watch?v=DnpO_RTSNmQ&t=2s.
4. Ibid.
5. Ibid.
6. Ibid.
7. Ibid.
8. Ibid.
9. Ibid.
10. Ibid.
11. Ibid.
12. Oliver, John. "Last Week Tonight." *HBO*, http://donaldjdrumpf.com.
13. "John Oliver Sells 35,000 'Make Donald Drumpf Again' Hats – Video." *The Guardian*, March 16, 2016, www.theguardian.com/us-news/video/2016/mar/16/john-oliver-sells-35000-make-donald-drumpf-again-hats-video.
14. See https://twitter.com/RealDonalDrumpf?ref_src=twsrc%5Egoogle%7Ctwcamp%5Eserp%7Ctwgr%5Eauthor.
15. Zorthian, Julia. "John Oliver's 'Donald Drumpf' Segment Broke HBO Records." *Time*, March 31, 2016, http://time.com/4277790/john-oliver-donald-drumpf-records/.
16. Nunberg, Geoffrey. *Talking Right: How Conservatives Turned Liberalism into a Tax-Raising, Latte-Drinking, Sushi-Eating, Volvo-Driving. "New York Times"-Reading, Body-Piercing, Hollywood-Loving, Left-Wing Freak Show*. Public Affairs, 2007.
17. Romano, Aja. "Michael Moore: Fight Donald Trump with 'an Army of Comedy'." *Vox*, January 20, 2017, www.vox.com/policy-and-politics/2017/1/20/14331072/michael-moore-alec-baldwin-we-stand-united-rally-comedy.
18. Credit Tamara Knoss.
19. For more on this, see Young, Dannagal G. *Irony and Outrage: The Polarized Landscape of Rage, Fear, and Laughter in the United States*. Oxford University Press, 2020.
20. Quinnipiac University. "QU Poll Release Detail." *QU Poll*, January 15, 2019, https://poll.qu.edu/national/release-detail?ReleaseID=2593.
21. See Fowler, James. "The Colbert Bump in Campaign Donations: More Truthful Than Truthy." *PS: Political Science and Politics*, vol. 41, no. 3, 2008, pp. 533–539. JSTOR, www.jstor.org/stable/20452245. Accessed 4 August 2022.

22 Quinnipiac University. "QU Poll Release Detail." *QU Poll*, January 15, 2019, https://poll.qu.edu/national/release-detail?ReleaseID=2593.
23 Boukes, Mark. "Agenda-Setting with Satire: How Political Satire Increased TTIP's Saliency on the Public, Media, and Political Agenda." *Political Communication*, vol. 36, no. 3, 2019, pp. 426–451, https://doi.org/10.1080/10584609.2018.1498816.
24 Johnson, Ted. "FCC Inspector General: John Oliver Segment Triggered System Slowdown, Not Bots." *Variety*, August 7, 2018, https://variety.com/2018/politics/news/john-oliver-fcc-triggered-slowdown-1202898328/.
25 Borum Chattoo, Caty and Lauren Feldman. *A Comedian and an Activist Walk into a Bar: The Serious Role of Comedy in Social Justice*. Foreword by Norman Lear. UC Press, 2020.
26 Wuerker, Matt. "Matt Wuerker's Editorial Cartoons." *CartoonistGroup*, April 18, 2019, www.theeditorialcartoons.com/store/add.php?iid=177308.
27 Gerson, Michael. "The Language of Hatred, Increasingly Normalized by Trump." *RealClearPolitics*, May 2, 2017, www.realclearpolitics.com/articles/2017/05/02/the_language_of_hatred_increasingly_normalized_by_trump_133757.html.
28 Talbot, Thaddeus. "You Have a Right to Know How Trump's Muslim Ban was Implemented. So We Sued." *ACLU*, April 13, 2017, www.aclu.org/blog/immigrants-rights/you-have-right-know-how-trumps-muslim-ban-was-implemented-so-we-sued?redirect=blog/speak-freely/you-have-right-know-how-trumps-muslim-ban-was-implemented-so-we-sued.
29 Goodman, Amy. "Stephen Colbert's Blistering Performance Mocking Bush and the Press Goes Ignored by the Media." *Democracy Now*, May 3, 2006, www.democracynow.org/2006/5/3/stephen_colberts_blistering_performance_mocking_bush.
30 Kurtzman, Daniel. "Colbert at the White House Correspondents' Dinner." *LiveAbout*, April 9, 2019, www.liveabout.com/stephen-colbert-white-house-correspondents-dinner-2734728.
31 Gajanan, Mahita. "Read Hasan Minhaj's Full Speech from the White House Correspondents' Dinner." *Time*, May 1, 2017, https://time.com/4761644/hasan-minhaj-white-house-correspondents-dinner-speech-transcript/.
32 Ibid.
33 Ibid.
34 Ibid.
35 Ibid.
36 Ibid.
37 Ibid.
38 Deerwester, Jayme. "Trump Tweets: 'Should Federal Election Commission And/or FCC' Look into 'SNL'?" *USA Today*, March 18, 2019, www.usatoday.com/story/life/tv/2019/03/18/trump-tweets-snl-federal-probe/3199989002/.
39 Stefansky, Emma. "Trump Steadfastly Refuses to Call Out Charlottesville White Supremacy." *Vanity Fair*, August 13, 2017, www.vanityfair.com/news/2017/08/trump-charlottesville-on-many-sides-white-supremacy.
40 Bradley, Laura. "Seth Meyers Attacks Trump on Charlottesville: 'He Is Not a President'." *Vanity Fair*, August 15, 2017, www.vanityfair.com/hollywood/2017/08/donald-trump-charlottesville-seth-meyers-colbert-late-night.
41 Ibid.
42 Ibid.
43 Ibid.
44 Kenny, Daniel J. "How John Oliver Usurped a Genre." *Harvard Political Review*, October 31, 2014, http://harvardpolitics.com/books-arts/john-oliver-usurped-genre/.
45 Ibid.
46 Garber, Megan. "John Oliver Pushes Comedy Further Toward Activism." *The Atlantic*, November 14, 2016, www.theatlantic.com/entertainment/archive/2016/11/john-oliver-activist-comedian/507599/.

47 Kenny, Daniel J. "How John Oliver Usurped a Genre." *Harvard Political Review*, October 31, 2014, http://harvardpolitics.com/books-arts/john-oliver-usurped-genre/.
48 Wilkinson, Alissa. "5 Years in, HBO's Last Week Tonight Is a Lot More Than 'Just Comedy'." *Vox*, February 17, 2019, www.vox.com/culture/2019/2/14/18213228/last-week-tonight-john-oliver-hbo-season-six.
49 Ibid.
50 "President-Elect Trump: Last Week Tonight with John Oliver (HBO)." *YouTube* video, posted by Last Week Tonight on November 13, 2016, 29:00, www.youtube.com/watch?v=-rSDUsMwakI&spfreload=5.
51 Ibid.
52 Garber, Megan. "John Oliver Pushes Comedy Further Toward Activism." *The Atlantic*, November 14, 2016, www.theatlantic.com/entertainment/archive/2016/11/john-oliver-activist-comedian/507599/.
53 Dekel, Jon. "The John Oliver Effect: How the Daily Show Alum Became the Most Trusted Man in America." *National Post*, February 18, 2015, https://nationalpost.com/entertainment/television/the-john-oliver-effect-how-the-daily-show-alum-became-the-most-trusted-man-in-america.
54 Ibid.
55 "Coal." *YouTube* video, posted by Last Week Tonight on June 19, 2017, www.youtube.com/watch?v=aw6RsUhw1Q8.
56 Ibid.
57 Ibid.
58 Crofts, Jamie Lynn. "This Coal Baron's Lawsuit Against John Oliver Is Plain Nuts." *ACLU*, August 2, 2017, www.aclu.org/blog/free-speech/coal-barons-lawsuit-against-john-oliver-plain-nuts.
59 Ibid.
60 For more on this see my *Colbert's America: Satire and Democracy*. Palgrave, 2011.
61 Abrams, Natalie. "Stephen Colbert Hopes Donald Trump Stays in Race (And Thinks He Can Win)." *Entertainment Weekly*, August 10, 2015, https://ew.com/article/2015/08/10/stephen-colbert-donald-trump/.
62 Colbert, Stephen. "Can't Wait to Get on Air September 8, Until Then: #dryTrumping." *Twitter*, August 10, 2015, 5:12 p.m., https://twitter.com/StephenAtHome/status/630894625796943872.
63 "Announcing: An Announcement!" *YouTube* video, posted by *The Late Show with Stephen Colbert* on June 16, 2015, www.youtube.com/watch?v=OFVC3qYGYiE.
64 Colbert, Stephen. "All You Can Trump Buffet." *The Late Show with Stephen Colbert*, September 8, 2015, www.cbs.com/shows/the-late-show-with-stephen-colbert/video/71AFD268-BDDC-CD28-0FD4-B0857418B28D/all-you-can-trump-buffet/.
65 Ibid.
66 Ibid.
67 Patterson, Thomas. "Pre-Primary News Coverage of the 2016 Presidential Race: Trump's Rise, Sander's Emergence, Clinton's Struggle." *Harvard Kennedy School Shorenstein Center on Media, Politics and Public Policy*, June 13, 2016, https://shorensteincenter.org/pre-primary-news-coverage-2016-trump-clinton-sanders/.
68 Ibid.
69 Garber, Megan. "How Donald Trump Beat Stephen Colbert at His Own Game." *The Atlantic*, September 23, 2015, www.theatlantic.com/entertainment/archive/2015/09/the-colbert-trump/406891/.
70 Krieg, Gregory. "Donald Trump Defends Size of His Penis." *CNN*, March 4, 2016, www.cnn.com/2016/03/03/politics/donald-trump-small-hands-marco-rubio/index.html.
71 Ibid.

72 "The 2016 Race Learns What's Below Rock Bottom." *YouTube* video, posted by The Late Show with Stephen Colbert on March 8, 2015, 4:17, www.youtube.com/watch?v=70iDoDAAfyQ&fbclid=IwAR3eDzK9t1OGrFaxNM4V3_68Z0QNgzt1rXaKzmSObesGs4VUNySXj5HUWNw.
73 Ibid.
74 Ibid.
75 Ibid.
76 "Donald Trump." *PublicFigureMedia*, February 2, 2019, https://publicfigure.com/2019/02/02/stephen-colbert-is-so-shocked-by-trumps-nyt-interview-that-he-does-an-extra-monologue/.
77 Kreps, Daniel. "See Stephen Colbert, Experts Help Blueprint Trump's Wall." *Rolling Stone*, June 25, 2018, www.rollingstone.com/tv/tv-news/see-stephen-colbert-experts-help-blueprint-trumps-wall-126108/.
78 Ibid.
79 "This Monologue Goes Out to You, Mr. President." *YouTube* video, posted by *The Late Show with Stephen Colbert* on May 2, 2017, www.youtube.com/watch?v=HaHwlSTqA7s.
80 Ibid.
81 Ibid.
82 Ibid.
83 "Colbert Report Writers—Truthiness and Pun Journals." *YouTube* video, posted by The Paley Center on November 7, 2009, www.youtube.com/watch?v=WvnHf3MQtAk&t=1m.
84 "The Word – Truthiness." *The Colbert Report*, Comedy Central, October 17, 2005, www.cc.com/video/63ite2/the-colbert-report-the-word-truthiness.
85 Sternberg, Adam. "Stephen Colbert Has America by the Ballots." *New York Magazine*, https://nymag.com/news/politics/22322/.
86 Niles, Emma and Robert Reich. "The 935 Lies They Told Us About Iraq." *Truthdig*, January 24, 2008, www.truthdig.com/articles/the-935-lies-they-told-us-about-iraq/.
87 "The Word: Trumpiness." *YouTube* video, posted by *The Late Show with Stephen Colbert* on July 19, 2016, www.youtube.com/watch?v=NqOTxl3Bsbw.
88 Milbank, Dana. "Does Trump's Great Gut Mean a Tiny Brain?" *The Washington Post*, November 28, 2018, www.washingtonpost.com/opinions/why-would-trump-need-brains-when-he-has-a-gut/2018/11/28/75bc6c38-f341-11e8-80d0-f7e1948d55f4_story.html.
89 "The Word: Trumpiness." *YouTube* video, posted by *The Late Show with Stephen Colbert* on July 19, 2016, www.youtube.com/watch?v=NqOTxl3Bsbw.
90 Houke, Curtis. "Samantha Bee's TBS Show Debuts with Vile Slam of 'Fish-Faced Horses★★★ Salesman' Cruz." *mrcTV*, February 9, 2016, www.mrctv.org/videos/samantha-bee-s-tbs-show-debuts-vile-slam-fish-faced-horses-salesman-cruz.
91 "Cruz 101 | Full Frontal with Samantha Bee | TBS." *YouTube* video, posted by *Full Frontal with Samantha Bee* on March 15, 2016, www.youtube.com/watch?v=cMgaqhTZBlg.
92 Niles, Emma and Robert Reich. "The 935 Lies They Told Us About Iraq." *Truthdig*, January 24, 2008, www.truthdig.com/articles/the-935-lies-they-told-us-about-iraq/.
93 Morris, Alex. "How Samantha Bee Crashed the Late-Night Boys' Club." *Rolling Stone*, June 25, 2018, www.rollingstone.com/tv/tv-news/how-samantha-bee-crashed-the-late-night-boys-club-104583/.
94 Houck, Curtis. "Bee Savages Scalia, 'Obstructionist A★★' McConnell; Wants Gavel to 'Plug Up Your Abortion Hole'." *mrcTV*, February 15, 2016, www.mrctv.org/videos/bee-savages-scalia-constitutional-mcconnell-wants-gavel-plug-your-abortion-hole.
95 Houck, Curtis. "Samantha Bee's TBS Show Debuts with Vile Slam of 'Fish-Faced, Horses★★★ Salesman' Cruz." *mrcTV*, February 9, 2016, www.newsbusters.org/blogs/nb/curtis-houck/2016/02/09/samantha-bees-tbs-show-debuts-vile-slam-fish-faced-horses-salesman.

96 Wilstein, Matt. "Samantha Bee Tears into 'Feckless C★nt' Ivanka Trump." *The Daily Beast*, May 31, 2018, www.thedailybeast.com/samantha-bee-tears-into-feckless-cunt-ivanka-trump.
97 Kreps, Daniel. "Samantha Bee Addresses Ivanka Controversy, Regrets 'One Bad Word'." *Rolling Stone*, June 25, 2018, www.rollingstone.com/tv/tv-news/samantha-bee-addresses-ivanka-controversy-regrets-one-bad-word-628364/.
98 Bradley, Laura. "Samantha Bee Says Her 'Feckless C—t' Apology Was Not Meant for Right-Wing Critics." *Vanity Fair*, August 24, 2018, www.vanityfair.com/hollywood/2018/08/samantha-bee-full-frontal-feckless-cunt-michelle-wolf-the-break-cancellation.
99 Houck, Curtis. "Samantha Bee's TBS Show Debuts with Vile Slam of 'Fish-Faced, Horses★★★ Salesman' Cruz." *mrcTV*, February 9, 2016, www.newsbusters.org/blogs/nb/curtis-houck/2016/02/09/samantha-bees-tbs-show-debuts-vile-slam-fish-faced-horses-salesman.
100 Morris, Alex. "How Samantha Bee Crashed the Late-Night Boys' Club." *Rolling Stone*, June 25, 2018, www.rollingstone.com/tv/tv-news/how-samantha-bee-crashed-the-late-night-boys-club-104583/.
101 Jones, Kipp. "*Daily Show* Alum Samantha Bee Debuts New Show Trashing GOP as 'Banquet of All-You-Can-Eat Crazy'." *Breitbart*, February 9, 2016, www.breitbart.com/entertainment/2016/02/09/samantha-bees-tbs-debut-mocks-cruzs-faith-blasts-trump-crazy-gop-attack/.
102 Bozell, Brent and Tim Graham. "Liberals Bewitched by Samantha Bee." *Newsbusters*, February 20, 2016, www.newsbusters.org/blogs/nb/brent-bozell/2016/02/20/bozell-graham-column-liberals-bewitched-samantha-bee.
103 "Sam Sits Down with Trump Supporters by the Sea Shore." *YouTube* video, posted by *Full Frontal with Samantha Bee* on March 15, 2016, www.youtube.com/watch?v=zWlUgI4cB4M&feature=youtu.be.
104 Holub, Christian. "Samantha Bee Interviews Trump Supporters." *Entertainment Weekly*, March 15, 2016, https://ew.com/article/2016/03/15/samantha-bee-interview-trump-supporters/.
105 "Life After Hate." *YouTube* video, posted by *Full Frontal with Samantha Bee* on August 14, 2017, www.youtube.com/watch?v=I5a5Yo4_eLM&feature=youtu.be; Leah, Rachel. "A Former Skinhead Reflects on Charlottesville: 'We Have a Massive and Dangerous Domestic Terrorist Threat'." *Salon*, August 16, 2017, www.salon.com/2017/08/16/a-former-skinhead-reflects-on-charlottesville-we-have-a-massive-and-dangerous-domestic-terrorist-threat/; Life After Hate, www.lifeafterhate.org/.
106 Bee, Samantha. "Full Frontal with Samantha Bee." *TBS*, www.tbs.com/shows/full-frontal-with-samantha-bee.
107 Mariotti, Renato, et al. "Meyers: Trump Wanted Me to Apologize On-Air for Making Fun of Him." *Politico*, May 8, 2018, www.politico.com/magazine/story/2018/05/08/seth-meyers-trump-whcd-jokes-apologize-218323.
108 Ibid.
109 Ibid.
110 "Sarah Palin and Hillary Address the Nation." *YouTube* video, posted by *Saturday Night Live* on September 23, 2013, www.youtube.com/watch?v=vSOLz1YBFG0.
111 Levere, Jane. "Seth Meyers and His Writing Team Talk Trump, 'A Closer Look' and YouTube." *Forbes*, October 31, 2017, www.forbes.com/sites/janelevere/2017/10/31/seth-meyers-and-his-writing-team-talk-trump-a-closer-look-and-youtube/#116f91ccd8fc.
112 Holmes, Jack. "Seth Meyers Had a Field Day with President Trump's Batsh★t Press Conference." *Esquire*, February 17, 2017, www.esquire.com/news-politics/videos/a53123/seth-meyers-trump-press-conference/.
113 "Kellyanne Conway On Trump's Silence to Quebec Attack: 'He Doesn't Tweet About Everything'." *HuffPost Video*, www.huffpost.com/entry/kellyanne-conway-on-trumps-silence-to-quebec-attack-he-doesnt-tweet-about-everything_n_5b579342e4b-07de723e98ccb.

114 Busis, Hillary. "Everything Trump Has Had Time to Tweet About Instead of the Quebec Attack." *Vanity Fair*, February 10, 2017, www.vanityfair.com/hollywood/2017/02/donald-trump-quebec-mosque-terrorist-attack-seth-meyers-twitter.

115 Dessem, Matthew. "Seth Meyers Lists All the Dumb Things Donald Trump Tweeted About This Weekend and It's Breathtaking." *Slate*, March 19, 2019, https://slate.com/culture/2019/03/seth-meyers-donald-trump-weekend-tweetstorm.html.

116 "Jimmy Kimmel Reveals Details of His Son's Birth & Heart Disease." *YouTube* video, posted by *Jimmy Kimmel Live* on May 1, 2017, www.youtube.com/watch?v=MmWWoMcGmo0.

117 Ibid.

118 Edgers, Geoff. "Late Show of Emotion." *The Washington Post*, March 1, 2018, www.washingtonpost.com/news/style/wp/2018/03/01/feature/jimmy-kimmel-might-be-americas-conscience-but-hell-still-do-anything-for-a-laugh/?utm_term=.ba973e8c34ce.

119 Ibid.

120 Ibid.

121 Jimmy Kimmel Live, "Facebook." October 10, 2017, www.facebook.com/watch/?v=10155734294473374.

122 Ibid.

123 Ibid.

124 Yahr, Emily. "Jimmy Kimmel Explains His Twitter Feud with Donald Trump Jr. Over Harvey Weinstein Jokes." *The Washington Post*, October 10, 2017, www.washingtonpost.com/news/arts-and-entertainment/wp/2017/10/10/jimmy-kimmel-explains-his-twitter-feud-with-donald-trump-jr-over-harvey-weinstein-jokes/?utm_term=.e25f1f432a15.

125 Kimmel, Jimmy. "Excellent Point Mr. President! You Should Quit That Boring Job—I'll Let You Have My Show All to Yourself #MAGA." *Twitter*, October 7, 2017, 7:41 a.m., https://twitter.com/jimmykimmel/status/916674867734355968.

126 Trump Jr., Donald. "Thoughts on Harvey Weinstein? #askingforafrined." *Twitter*, October 7, 2017, 11:03am.

127 Yahr, Emily. "Jimmy Kimmel Explains His Twitter Feud with Donald Trump Jr. Over Harvey Weinstein Jokes." *The Washington Post*, October 10, 2017, www.washingtonpost.com/news/arts-and-entertainment/wp/2017/10/10/jimmy-kimmel-explains-his-twitter-feud-with-donald-trump-jr-over-harvey-weinstein-jokes/?utm_term=.a2e6e6be2cda.

128 "Jimmy Kimmel Runs Through Donald Trump's Particularly Batshit Week." *Digg.com*, http://digg.com/video/kimmel-trump-racist-comments.

129 Kimmel, Jimmy. "Hey @realDonaldTrump u up?" *Twitter*, February 26, 2017, 10:50 p.m., https://twitter.com/jimmykimmel/status/836060793783267328.

130 "Person of the Year." *Time Magazine*, https://pbs.twimg.com/media/Eo_r9v4U8AMR0_a?format=jpg&name=medium.

131 Paterniti, Michael. "Jimmy Kimmel Doesn't Want to Cry." *GQ*, January 16, 2018, www.gq.com/story/jimmy-kimmel-is-seriously-funny.

132 Gibson, Megan. "Trevor Noah Faces Backlash Over Twitter History." *Time*, March 31, 2015, http://time.com/3764913/trevor-noah-twitter-backlash/.

133 Bakare, Lanre. "Trevor Noah: 'It's Easier to Be an Angry White Man Than an Angry Black Man'." *The Guardian*, April 2, 2016, www.theguardian.com/tv-and-radio/2016/apr/02/trevor-noah-on-replacing-jon-stewart-and-changing-the-daily-show.

134 Cuccinello, Hayley C. "Trevor Noah's 'Daily Show' Reaches 100th Episode, But Noah Is Still Struggling." *Forbes*, April 28, 2016, www.forbes.com/sites/hayleycuccinello/2016/04/28/trevor-noahs-daily-show-reaches-100th-episode-but-noah-is-still-struggling/#296e66052c24.

135 Ryan, Maureen. "Comedy Central's 'Daily Show' Has Lost Its Edge." *Variety*, March 30, 2016, https://variety.com/2016/voices/columns/comedy-central-daily-show-1201740385/.

136 Paskin, Willa. "Why Are Americans Ignoring Trevor Noah?" *Slate*, January 24, 2016, updated January 25, 2016, www.slate.com/articles/arts/cover_story/2016/01/why_america_isn_t_paying_attention_to_the_daily_show_with_trevor_noah_in.html.
137 Bakare, Lanre. "Trevor Noah: 'It's Easier to Be an Angry White Man Than an Angry Black Man'." *The Guardian*, April 2, 2016, www.theguardian.com/tv-and-radio/2016/apr/02/trevor-noah-on-replacing-jon-stewart-and-changing-the-daily-show.
138 Noah, Trevor. "Donald Trump: America's African President." *The Daily Show with Trevor Noah*, Comedy Central, October 1, 2015, www.cc.com/video-clips/qf2zhn/the-daily-show-with-trevor-noah-donald-trump-america-s-african-president.
139 "Satire." *Wikipedia*, September 28, 2019, https://en.wikipedia.org/wiki/Satire.
140 Braxton, Greg. "Trevor Noah Strikes a Nerve – and Ratings Gold – as He Steers *The Daily Show* into the Trump Era." *Los Angeles Times*, June 8, 2017, www.latimes.com/entertainment/tv/la-ca-st-sunday-conversation-trevor-noah-20170608-htmlstory.html.
141 "Crisis Actor Exposed!!! #TAMMYMUSTGO." *YouTube* video, posted by *The Daily Show with Trevor Noah* on February 22, 2018, www.youtube.com/watch?v=D6LddsrgqpM.
142 Bradley, Laura. "The Daily Show Identifies a Real 'Crisis Actor': Tomi Lahren." *Vanity Fair*, February 23, 2018, www.vanityfair.com/hollywood/2018/02/tomi-lahren-crisis-actor-trevor-noah-daily-show.
143 "Journalisming—Cable News Panels Are Sh★tshows." *The Daily Show with Trevor Noah* (Video Clip). Comedy Central, www.cc.com/video-clips/omzt3x/the-daily-show-with-trevor-noah-journalisming-cable-news-panels-are-sh-tshows.
144 "The 'Master Race' Needs to Play It Cool." *The Daily Show with Trevor Noah*, Comedy Central, www.cc.com/video-clips/alpfbe/the-daily-show-with-trevor-noah-the-master-race-needs-to-play-it-cool.
145 "Trevor Noah Eviscerates the Civility Argument." *YouTube* video, posted by *The Daily Show with Trevor Noah* on June 26, 2018, 6:30, www.youtube.com/watch?v=qljfObaUG2s.
146 Marr, Madeleine. "No Fake News: The Daily Show's Trump Presidential Twitter Library Is Headed to Miami." *Miami Herald*, October 22, 2018, www.miamiherald.com/miami-com/news/article225809845.html#storylink=cpy.
147 Ibid.
148 Ibid.
149 The Daily Show and Trevor Noah. *The Donald J. Trump Presidential Twitter Library*. Spiegel and Grau, 2018, p. xi.
150 Grothaus, Michael. "Trump Will Keep Tweeting from His Personal Twitter Account During His Presidency." *Fast Company*, January 16, 2017, www.fastcompany.com/4028797/trump-will-keep-tweeting-from-his-personal-twitter-account-during-his-presidency.
151 Maglio, Tony. "How Trevor Noah's 'Daily Show' Is Beating Jon Stewart's." *The Wrap*, November 1, 2015, updated December 8, 2015, www.thewrap.com/trevor-noah-first-month-daily-show-comedy-central-michele-ganeless-digital-tv-ratings-twitter/.
152 Chappelle, Dave. "8:46." *YouTube* video, posted by *Netflix Is a Joke* on June 12, 2020, www.youtube.com/watch?v=3tR6mKcBbT4.
153 Keishin Armstrong, Jennifer. "How Trevor Noah Conquered US Comedy." *BBC*, October 5, 2017, www.bbc.com/culture/story/20170918-how-trevor-noah-conquered-us-comedy.
154 "Donald Trump: The White ISIS." *The Daily Show with Trevor Noah*, Comedy Central, December 8, 2015, www.cc.com/video/0org9p/the-daily-show-with-trevor-noah-donald-trump-the-white-isis.
155 Ibid.
156 Ibid.
157 Ibid.

158 Ibid.
159 Lee, Traci G. "Comedian Hasan Minhaj to Congress on Guns: 'Is This What You Want Your Legacy to Be?'" *NBC News*, June 17, 2016, www.nbcnews.com/news/asian-america/comedian-hasan-minhaj-criticizes-congress-powerful-speech-orlando-n594486.
160 Gajanan, Mahita. "Read Hasan Minhaj's Full Speech from the White House Correspondents' Dinner." *Time*, May 1, 2017, https://time.com/4761644/hasan-minhaj-white-house-correspondents-dinner-speech-transcript/.
161 De Morawa, Lisa. "Netflix Launching 'Patriot Act with Hasan Minhaj' in October." *Deadline*, August 9, 2018, https://deadline.com/2018/08/hasan-minhaj-netflix-patriot-act-debut-october-28-1202443188/.
162 Rami, Trupti. "Hasan Minhaj Wants to Update Late-Night Comedy Model With 'Radioactive' Topics." *Vulture*, November 19, 2018, www.vulture.com/2018/11/hasan-minhaj-patriot-act-new-late-night-comedy-model.html.
163 Hennigan, Adrian. "Netflix's 'Patriot Act with Hasan Minhaj' Is Way Funnier and Fresher Than 'Last Week Tonight'." *Haaretz*, November 27, 2018, www.haaretz.com/us-news/.premium-netflix-s-patriot-act-with-hasan-minhaj-is-way-funnier-and-fresher-than-last-week-tonight-1.6696501.
164 Rami, Trupti. "Hasan Minhaj Wants to Update Late-Night Comedy Model with 'Radioactive' Topics." *Vulture*, November 19, 2018, www.vulture.com/2018/11/hasan-minhaj-patriot-act-new-late-night-comedy-model.html.
165 Ibid.
166 "Saudi Arabia | Patriot Act with Hasan Minhaj." *YouTube* video, posted by *Netflix Is a Joke* on October 28, 2018, www.youtube.com/watch?v=LUhbZdvtzcw.
167 Ibid.
168 Stewart, Ian. "Netflix Drops Hasan Minhaj Episode in Saudi Arabia at Government's Request." *NPR*, January 1, 2019, www.npr.org/2019/01/01/681469011/netflix-drops-hasan-minhaj-episode-in-saudi-arabia-at-governments-request.
169 "Immigration Enforcement | Patriot Act with Hasan Minhaj." *YouTube* video, posted by *Netflix Is a Joke* on November 25, 2018, www.youtube.com/watch?v=H1g3P3g_Css.
170 Grisar, P.J. "Stephen Miller High School Clips Prove Some Folks Don't Ever Grow Up." *The Forward*, November 27, 2018, https://forward.com/culture/414848/stephen-miller-high-school-clips-prove-some-folks-dont-ever-grow-up/.
171 Ibid.
172 "Civil Rights Under Trump | Patriot Act with Hasan Minhaj." *YouTube* video, posted by *Netflix Is a Joke* on March 3, 2019, www.youtube.com/watch?v=uKXIvfQnYEY.
173 Ibid.
174 Techler, Graham. "Hasan Minhaj's Patriot Act Remains Netflix's Best Talk Show in Its Second Season." *Paste Magazine*, February 12, 2019, www.pastemagazine.com/articles/2019/02/hasan-minhajs-patriot-act-remains-netflixs-best-ta.html.
175 Hill, Libby. "'Patriot Act with Hasan Minhaj' Will Move Further into Investigative Journalism." *IndieWire*, April 7, 2019, www.indiewire.com/2019/04/patriot-act-with-hasan-minhaj-dictators-netflix-emmys-fyc-1202056584/.
176 Ibid.
177 "Redacted Tonight." *RT*, "TV-Novosti." n.d., www.rt.com/shows/redacted-tonight-summary/.
178 Gupta, Prachi. "The John Oliver of Russia Today: I'm Making Comedy Out of the Darkest Issues in the World." *Salon*, October 6, 2014, www.salon.com/2014/10/06/im_making_comedy_out_of_the_darkest_issues_in_the_world_meet_the_john_oliver_of_russia_today/; Riffkin, Rebecca. "Americans' Trust in Media Remains at Historical Low." *Gallup*, September 28, 2015, https://news.gallup.com/poll/185927/americans-trust-media-remains-historical-low.aspx.
179 Johnstone, Caitlin. "Lee Camp Just Destroyed the Entire Establishment Narrative About RT." *Medium*, November 20, 2017, https://medium.com/@caityjohnstone/lee-camp-just-destroyed-the-entire-establishment-narrative-about-rt-b8c42870d942.

180 "Why I'm a Complete and Total Hypocrite – And Actually Really Proud of It." *YouTube* video, posted by *Redacted Tonight* on February 16, 2015, www.youtube.com/watch?v=d4PtD0R9WsA.

181 "Lee Camp: How to Create NPR's Propaganda – As Seen in a Hit Piece Against Me." *World Beyond War*, December 21, 2017, https://worldbeyondwar.org/lee-camp-create-nprs-propaganda-seen-hit-piece/.

182 "The Truth About RT America." *YouTube* video, posted by *Redacted Tonight* on November 18, 2017, 12:46, www.youtube.com/watch?v=u_YLPUvBcDM&feature=youtu.be&t=5m12s.

183 "New Proof the Media Is Lying to You About Hillary's Campaign." *YouTube* video, posted by Redacted Tonight on October 24, 2015, www.youtube.com/watch?v=SvP6edGhJvs.

184 McClennen, Sophia A. "Trevor Noah's Master Class: It's Not Just Fox News—This Is the Topic That Needs Noah, Oliver, Stewart." *Salon*, October 13, 2015, www.salon.com/2015/10/12/trevor_noahs_master_class_its_not_just_fox_news_this_is_the_topic_that_needs_noah_oliver_stewart/.

185 Ibid.

186 Ibid.

187 "The REAL Reason the U.S. Wants War with Iran, Standing Rock News, Capitalism Failing." *YouTube* video, posted by *Redacted Tonight* on February 10, 2017, 26:42, www.youtube.com/watch?v=65_GcK0g_VU.

188 Ibid.

189 "Trump's Hilarious Speech to the U.N." *YouTube* video, posted by *Redacted Tonight* on October 1, 2018, 5:27, www.youtube.com/watch?v=dGbTst3ii04.

190 "Andy Borowitz." *Wikipedia*, April 15, 2019, https://en.wikipedia.org/wiki/Andy_Borowitz.

191 Ibid.

192 Borowitz, Andy. "Polar Vortex Causes Hundreds of Injuries as People Making Snide Remarks About Climate Change Are Punched in Face." *The New Yorker*, January 6, 2014, www.newyorker.com/humor/borowitz-report/polar-vortex-causes-hundreds-of-injuries-as-people-making-snide-remarks-about-climate-change-are-punched-in-face.

193 Giuliani-Hoffman, Francesca. "Andy Borowitz: 'We're Living in an Age That Defies Satire'." *CNNMoney*, June 12, 2017, https://money.cnn.com/2017/06/12/media/andy-borowitz-interview-reliable-sources-podcast/index.html.

194 Adler, Paul. "Famed Writer Andy Borowitz Is the Sovereign of Satire." *Westchester Magazine*, February 28, 2018, www.westchestermagazine.com/Westchester-Magazine/March-2018/The-Sovereign-of-Satire/.

195 Borowitz, Andy. "Calling Earth a 'Loser,' Trump Vows to Make Better Deal with New Planet." *The New Yorker*, June 1, 2017, www.newyorker.com/humor/borowitz-report/calling-earth-a-loser-trump-vows-to-make-better-deal-with-new-planet.

196 Giuliani-Hoffman, Francesca. "Andy Borowitz: 'We're Living in an Age That Defies Satire'." *CNNMoney*, June 12, 2017, https://money.cnn.com/2017/06/12/media/andy-borowitz-interview-reliable-sources-podcast/index.html.

197 Adler, Paul. "Famed Writer Andy Borowitz Is the Sovereign of Satire." *Westchester Magazine*, February 28, 2018, www.westchestermagazine.com/Westchester-Magazine/March-2018/The-Sovereign-of-Satire/.

198 "Michael Moore." *Wikipedia*, July 24, 2019, https://en.wikipedia.org/wiki/Michael_Moore.

199 Moore, Michael, dir. "Michael Moore in Trumpland." 2016, www.imdb.com/title/tt6163356/.

200 Trump, Donald J. "I Agree @MMFlint- to All Americans, I See You & I Hear You. I am Your Voice. Vote to #DrainTheSwamp w/ Me on 11/8." *Twitter*, October 27, 2016, 7:32AM, https://twitter.com/realdonaldtrump/status/791648893725450240.

201 Ibid.
202 Moore, Michael. "Look at This Orwellian Tweet by Trump! Donald, U Either Haven't Seen My Movie or U Are Conning Your Followers. The Clip U Show U Doctored." *Twitter*, October 27, 2016, 7:18 p.m., https://twitter.com/mmflint/status/791826506800623616.
203 Moore, Michael. "Hey Everyone—Trump, Jr. & Right Wing Thinks My Movie Called 'TrumpLand' Is Pro-Trump! Haha. Pls Don't Tell Them Otherwise! #satire #irony." *Twitter*, October 26, 2016, 10:21 a.m., https://twitter.com/MMFlint/status/791328954397384704.
204 Romano, Aja. "Michael Moore: Fight Donald Trump with an Army of Comedy." *Vox*, January 20, 2017, www.vox.com/policy-and-politics/2017/1/20/14331072/michael-moore-alec-baldwin-we-stand-united-rally-comedy.
205 Moore, Michael. "As I've Said Many Times, It Will Be an Army of Comedy That Brings Him Down. His Skin Is So Thin, He Can't Handle the Humor or the Ridicule." *Twitter*, February 7, 2017, 3:10 am, https://twitter.com/mmflint/status/828878620563222528.
206 Strauss, Gary. "Moore Gets His Point Across." *USA Today*, June 24, 2004, www.spokesman.com/stories/2004/jun/24/moore-gets-his-points-across/.
207 Moore, Michael. "Fahrenheit 11/9." September 21, 2018, https://fahrenheit119.com/.
208 McClennen, Sophia A. "'American Sniper's' Biggest Lie: Clint Eastwood Has a Delusional Fox News Problem." *Salon*, January 27, 2015, www.salon.com/2015/01/26/american_snipers_biggest_lie_clint_eastwood_has_a_delusional_fox_news_problem/.
209 Moore, Michael. "Fahrenheit 11/9." September 21, 2018, https://fahrenheit119.com/.
210 "The Medium Is the Message." *Wikipedia*, September 18, 2019, https://en.wikipedia.org/wiki/The_medium_is_the_message.
211 Anderson, Nick. "Rob Rogers' Firing Is a Frightening Omen." *CNN*, June 23, 2018, www.cnn.com/2018/06/23/opinions/rob-rogers-cartoonists-matter-anderson-opinion/index.html.
212 Pett, Joel. "It's Standard Operating Procedure for Trump." *Kentucky*, May 2, 2019, www.kentucky.com/opinion/editorial-cartoons/joel-pett/article229956119.html?fbclid=IwAR3a9yyFReSaGxAUCRfIo_3eRnX-97hS_7HoCG9G-iRn688DcIojVbMM9iM.
213 McClennen, Sophia A. and Remy Maisel. *Is Satire Saving Our Nation? Mockery and American Politics*. Palgrave Macmillan, 2014.
214 Barber, Kristen. "Satire as Protest in the Women's March." *Gender & Society*, April 12, 2017, https://gendersociety.wordpress.com/2017/04/12/satire-as-protest-in-the-womens-march/.
215 Ibid.
216 McClennen, Sophia A. "Hitting Trump Where It Hurts: The Satire Troops Take Up Comedy Arms Against Donald Trump." *Salon*, February 11, 2017, www.salon.com/2017/02/11/hitting-trump-where-it-hurts-the-satire-troops-take-up-comedy-arms-against-donald-trump/.
217 Paul Ryan's Legacy. "Our Billboard Is Still Up in @SpeakerRyan's Hometown of Janesville: We're Alternating Locations for Max Visibility, https://secure.actblue.com/contribute/page/stopthespeaker?refcode=twitter . . ." *Twitter*, February 21, 2017, 8:05 a.m., https://twitter.com/StopTheSpeaker/status/834071437845680133/photo/1?ref_src=twsrc%5Etfw%7Ctwcamp%5Etweetembed&ref_url=https%3A%2F%2Fwww.salon.com%2F2017%2F03%2F26%2Fwe-are-relearning-democracy-5-ways-the-anti-trump-movement-indivisible-is-redefining-political-action%2F.
218 Popovic, Srdja and Mladen Jokic. "Why Dictators Don't Like Jokes." *Foreign Policy*, April 5, 2013, https://foreignpolicy.com/2013/04/05/why-dictators-dont-like-jokes/.

219 Paperwash. "Donald Trump Is Like if Homer Simpson Inherited All of Mr. Burns' Money." *Twitter*, June 16, 2015, 2:17 p.m., https://twitter.com/PaperWash/status/610919222563196928?ref_src=twsrc%5Etfw%7Ctwcamp%5Etweetembed&ref_url=https%3A%2F%2Fwww.buzzfeed.com%2Fjarrylee%2Flets-make-twitter-great-again.

220 Vulfov, Bob. "TRUMP: I Invented Immigration DEBATE MODERATOR: What T: I Invented Soap DM: mr Trump— T: I Invented Calculus DM: Sir— T: I Invented Sushi." *Twitter*, August 6, 2015, 6:30 p.m., https://twitter.com/bobvulfov/status/629464596152238080?ref_src=twsrc%5Etfw%7Ctwcamp%5Etweetembed&ref_url=https%3A%2F%2Fwww.buzzfeed.com%2Fjarrylee%2Flets-make-twitter-great-again.

6
THE JOKE'S ON YOU
The Power of Satire

On January 7, 2015, two brothers, Saïd and Chérif Kouachi, forced their way into the Paris offices of the French satirical weekly magazine *Charlie Hebdo*. They killed 12 people and injured 11 others. *Charlie Hebdo* had long been on an extremist hit list due to its controversial depictions of the prophet Mohammad. Later, Al Qaeda claimed responsibility for the attack, saying that it was "revenge for the honor" of Muhammad.[1]

The public response to the attacks was swift. Mass demonstrations were held globally, but especially in Paris. Participants honored free speech and held signs that read "Je suis Charlie" in solidarity with those murdered.[2] For many, the attacks symbolized a long-standing sense that cultural expressions were being censored in an era of increased social tensions. How could it make sense to murder someone who had mocked you? How was that level of violence an appropriate reaction to a characterization with which you disagreed? The early responses to the attacks focused on the idea that no one should die for a cartoon and that a strong defense of free speech meant supporting all forms of expression—even potentially offensive ones.

In a piece I wrote for *Salon* shortly after the attacks, I cautioned that it wouldn't be long before critics came after the dead satirists.[3] And I was right. *Charlie Hebdo* was condemned for being racist, for not being good satire, for being inflammatory, for participating in French Islamophobia, and maybe even for contributing to the actual context of violence that caused a number of those murdered to die.[4] After the rise of solidarity encapsulated by "Je suis Charlie," we soon had "Je ne suis pas Charlie." The questions asked were whether *Charlie Hebdo* participated in hate speech and images by demonizing Islam and whether those representations were so extreme that they actually incited violence. Also at stake was the question of whether it is ok to simply mock a group, even knowing in advance that the joke will feel like an insult to those connected to the cartoon. Is it ok to make fun of a group even if you know it will upset them when you do it?

DOI: 10.4324/9781003294177-6

In the aftermath of the attacks, much was made of the question of whether the cartoons depicting Islam in *Charlie Hebdo* had been too derogatory. Had the cartoons crossed a line? Alternatively, the attacks also led to debates about the limits of free speech. But at the center of concerns following the attacks was the question of the power of satire. Did the *Charlie Hebdo* cartoons have power and, if so, what kind?

Interestingly, those who muse on the power of satire tend to be negative. But the negativity takes two distinct forms. On the one hand, satire comes under critique because it is seen as a threat to faith in institutions, to trust in leaders, to commitment to political engagement, and so on. In these cases, it is seen as negative because it fosters a negative view of the world that is unfounded and that will lead to adverse social behaviors. On the other hand, there is the view that satire is negative because it doesn't do anything. Interestingly, this is the exact opposite charge. Here satire is bad because it is a distraction from real political action. It is bad because it makes us feel good when we should feel bad. To illustrate the stark differences between these views, consider these two quotes. According to P. J. O'Rourke, "Satire doesn't effect change."[5] Yet, in almost complete contrast, Arnold Zwicky writes that, "Satire in general is dangerous."[6]

One way we can note the power of satire is in the stark and extreme ways that those in power try to shut it down. In fact, in recent years we've seen a number of signs of the power of satire, certainly in the sense of its power to threaten, intimidate, and enrage those it mocks. In 2014, Egyptian satirist Bassem Youssef was forced off the air when the MBC network claimed that he might influence the Egyptian elections.[7] Then Jon Stewart released *Rosewater*, a film about an Iranian journalist imprisoned over a misunderstanding of satire.[8] Then, the Chinese government decided to ban puns, claiming that they breach "the law on standard spoken and written Chinese" and "make promoting cultural heritage harder."[9] Next, North Korea allegedly cyber-hacked Sony Pictures over the satirical film *The Interview*, leading many theaters to withdraw it from their screens.[10] Cartoonist Ramón Nse Esono Ebalé was detained in 2017 in Equatorial Guinea, targeted for his outspoken political art, which violated Equatorial Guinea's colonial-era defamation statute forbidding criticism of the president or other high-ranking officials.[11] He was jailed, locked up for "unflattering satirical drawings" of President Teodoro Obiang Nguema Mbasogo, the longest-serving dictator in Africa.[12] And these are just a few examples.

In Jon Stewart's endorsement of Egyptian comedian Bassem Youssef's book about his experiences being attacked for his satirical comedy, he writes, "Comedy shouldn't take courage, but it made an exception for Bassem."[13] Stewart, of course, is right. Comedy shouldn't take courage, but it often does, even in countries like the United States where, even though imprisonment or murder is less likely to befall the offending comedian, there are still myriad ways that those producing jokes are pressured and penalized. These sorts of clear and present violent threats to satirists differ in scope and intensity from threats that derive more from the fact that the satirist is often dependent on the media industry for a platform for their work. Bill Maher lost his show *Politically Incorrect* on ABC after making what some perceived as an insensitive comment after the 9/11 attacks. Colbert has come under FCC investigation for off-color remarks on his show.[14] *The Smothers Brothers* was eventually canceled because CBS found its content politically offensive.[15] There are countless examples of pressures faced by satirical comedians due to their content.

In the United States, the pressure often comes in the form of a lawsuit. For example, in 1983, Larry Flynt's *Hustler* magazine, known for its photos of nude women, crude humor, and satire, printed a parody ad. The butt of the joke was Jerry Falwell, the Christian fundamentalist televangelist who famously launched the Moral Majority, a group dedicated to advocating against abortion, pornography, homosexuality, and the loss of so-called family values. The *Hustler* ad was modeled on a Campari campaign that featured interviews with celebrities who spoke of their "first time," playing with the double entendre of first sex or a first taste of Campari.

In the Falwell parody, his "first time" is depicted as starting with a goat in an outhouse.[16] But soon, Falwell kicks out the goat and lets in his mother, because "Mom looked better than a Baptist whore with a $100 donation."[17] The ad suggests that he loses his virginity to his mom while they are both drunk off their "God-fearing asses on Campari."[18]

Falwell wasn't amused.

He sued Flynt, *Hustler*, and Flynt's distribution company for libel, invasion of privacy, and intentional infliction of emotional distress. The first two charges were unsuccessful, but Falwell won on the claim of intentional infliction of emotional distress, leading Flynt to appeal. Eventually the case landed in the Supreme Court.

In Justice Rehnquist's majority opinion, he stated, "The appeal of the political cartoon or caricature is often based on exploitation of unfortunate physical traits or politically embarrassing events—an exploitation often calculated to injure the feelings of the subject of the portrayal."[19] Rehnquist then cited the "intentionally injurious" cartoons of Thomas Nast, who launched a graphic vendetta against "Boss" Tweed, and suggested that this type of comedy is an important feature of political speech: "Despite their sometimes caustic nature, from the early cartoons portraying George Washington as an ass to the present day, graphic depictions and satirical cartoons have played a prominent role in public and political debate."[20]

Falwell lost and satire won. The Supreme Court decision helps to explain why the United States is one of the few countries on the planet that allows its citizens to mock those in power and not be punished for it. Up until the 1988 *Hustler* decision, the Supreme Court had not weighed in on the particular nature of satirical speech and its connection to potentially causing emotional distress. As Len Niehoff explained in a presentation at a symposium on "The State of Our Satirical Union" at the University of Minnesota, "For those who value freedom of expression, particularly in the form of satire, this outcome set an important and welcome precedent."[21]

When the decision was delivered over 30 years ago, likely no one imagined the deep ironies of the Trump era, when the president responded to being the most-mocked man on earth by becoming visibly undone and threatening his critics with lawsuits. During his campaign, Trump repeatedly brought up his desire to change U.S. libel laws to make it easier for him to sue newspapers.[22] "One of the things I'm going to do if I win," he told supporters at a rally,

> I'm going to open up our libel laws . . . [s]o when the New York Times writes a hit piece which is a total disgrace or when the Washington Post, which is there for other reasons, writes a hit piece, we can sue them and win money instead of having no chance of winning because they're totally protected.[23]

Thankfully, though, as Susan E. Seager explains, Trump may be a libel bully, but he is also a libel loser.[24] Thus far, Trump's speech-targeting lawsuits have failed, she explains, "because the First Amendment protects good-faith reporting about public figures (that is, published without actual malice) and immunizes subjective opinions and jokes, even if they are 'negative' and 'horrible,' as Trump complains."[25]

Yet, as the *Hustler* case proved, public figures can try to go after comedians who mock them for more than just libel. Falwell's attorneys added the claim of intentional infliction of emotional distress, and, if the Supreme Court had not rejected that as a valid claim, imagine the lawsuits a thin-skinned, litigious president like Trump could have launched at comedians. Trump wasn't just the most-mocked president in U.S. history; he also was the least able to take a joke.

Well before he won the election, Trump questioned whether he could shut down jokes coming at him from shows like *Saturday Night Live* (*SNL*), and he was threatening comedians with lawsuits. He regularly attempted to intimidate *Spy Magazine*. And there was the time that Trump sued Bill Maher in 2013 for failing to live up to an "unconditional offer" made on NBC's *Tonight Show*.[26] The suit took place in the midst of Trump's birther scandal when he kept offering money to President Barack Obama if he would produce his birth certificate. Riffing off the absurdity of Trump's birtherism, Maher offered to donate $5 million to charity if Trump provided a copy of his birth certificate proving that he was not "spawn of his mother having sex with an orangutan."[27]

As explained earlier, that seemed like a pretty obvious joke, yet Trump took him seriously and actually sent Maher a copy of his birth certificate and a list of charities he wanted to receive the money. When Maher didn't pay up, Trump sued him. Maher responded to the lawsuit with this retort: "This is known as parody, and it's a form of something we in the comedy business call a joke." "Just like we're the gun country, we're the joke country. We love our free speech and we love celebrities getting taken down a peg. So, Don, just suck it up like everybody else."[28]

Trump later dropped the suit, having been publicly shamed for even bringing it to begin with. But he did continue to threaten those who joked about him. During his political career, Donald Trump regularly complained that jokes against him were "unfair" or biased, and he wondered whether there should be some sort of "equal time" for views that favored him. While those ideas have no legal standing, there seems little doubt that Trump's rants that jokes about him are not fair resonate with his base.

What all these events have in common is the way that they prove the power of satire: its power to frustrate and enrage those who feel criticized by it and its power to spark public debate over the issues it raises. In a moment when much public discourse has been galvanized around simplistic and divisive talking points, satirists tend to muddy the waters and ask their audiences to think of things from a different view.

There is, of course, another side to the power of satire: its power to persuade and to potentially shape public opinion. When I opened this book, I pointed to the fact that the power of satire generally leads to concern and worry. For the most part, when folks worry over satire, they worry that it is making its audience too cynical. Or they worry that it serves as a distraction from "real" politics. Or they worry that it is supplanting the real news and skewing audience perceptions. Interestingly, for the most part, worries over satire are largely speculative. So, in order to make sense of what we should and shouldn't worry about with satire's rising influence, in what follows, I review the core issues that cause concern and highlight the actual research we have on these topics.

Does Satire Divide Us?

Despite the wide range of scholarly arguments in favor of the positive benefits to comedy, there has been a long tradition of denigrating comedy as antisocial, immature, scornful, and irrational. Plato, one of the most influential critics of laughter, described humor as an emotion that overrides rational self-control. Plato was also one of the first intellectuals to note the way in which humor can exacerbate social division. He writes in *The Republic* that the guardians of the state should avoid laughter, "for ordinarily when one abandons himself to violent laughter, his condition provokes a violent reaction."[29]

Similarly, Descartes, in *Passions of the Soul*, identifies three of the six basic emotions in laughter—wonder, love, (mild) hatred, desire, joy, and sadness. While he notes that there are other causes of laughter than hatred, he describes laughter as primarily an expression of scorn and ridicule:

> Derision or scorn is a sort of joy mingled with hatred, which proceeds from our perceiving some small evil in a person whom we consider to be deserving of it; we have hatred for this evil, we have joy in seeing it in him who is deserving of it; and when that comes upon us unexpectedly, the surprise of wonder is the cause of our bursting into laughter.[30]

Certainly, one can see his point in the various ways that Trump has been mocked for his physicality. One of the best examples of this was the anarchist group INDECLINE installing statues of then-candidate Trump naked and without testicles in New York, San Francisco, Cleveland, and Seattle.[31] While the statue was immensely gratifying to a number of onlookers, there is little question that it was exactly the sort of derisive, insulting humor Plato and Descartes thought was unbecoming.

For some, humor is entirely dependent on social divisions with hierarchies. Thomas Hobbes in *Treatise on Human Nature and That on Liberty and Necessity* suggested that humor is predicated on a sense of eminency in ourselves and infirmity in others: "It is no wonder therefore that men take heinously to be laughed at or derided, that is, triumphed over."[32] Such arguments frame humor as a strategy to attack the identities of others, a move designed to divide groups in a hostile way.

These criticisms of mocking humor coalesced into what is now known as "The Superiority Theory" of humor. Roger Scruton argues that, "If people dislike being laughed at, it is surely because laughter devalues its object in the subject's eyes."[33] Charles Gruner characterizes humor as a game with winners and losers and considers it essentially a competition.[34] The basic idea behind this theory is that humor depends on offering the jokester a superior position vis-à-vis their target.

The catch, though, as will be discussed in more detail later on the specific distinction of satirical humor, is that the question of whether a joke is funny is entirely dependent on whether one is associated with the butt of the joke—or whether one is doing the laughing. There is some comedy aimed at the human condition overall—we might think of bathroom humor as a good example. But most comedy is not designed to be consumed by all of humanity in the same way. This is especially true of satire. Satire almost always has a target distinct from its intended audience, the exception being, for example, general satire of the human condition.

In order to understand the power dynamic of a joke, consider that there are three main stakeholders: the jokester, the butt of the joke (and those who are sympathetic to the butt of the joke), and the audience. The structure of a satirical joke is naturally aggressive:

> [A] tendentious joke calls for three people: in addition to the one who makes the joke, there must be a second who is taken as the object of the hostile or sexual aggressiveness, and a third in whom the joke's aim of producing pleasure is fulfilled.[35]

As Deniz Göktürk points out, aggressive comedy challenges us to ask,

> Who is laughing with whom at whom, and why? What kinds of bonds are forged between the tellers of jokes and their listeners? Are hidden aggressions expressed indirectly through the joke? Who is the object of attack, or the butt of the joke?[36]

And as Judith Yaross Lee argues, "[W]hether a target takes an attack with good humor will depend on how sharply it stings—and whether the sting feels metaphorical or seems really to cut."[37]

But here is the real risk of satire in the Trump era. In an age of increased political polarization, where opposing groups often feel they have no common ground, satire that engages and amuses an audience is almost surely going to incense and enrage those who feel targeted. For instance, when a comedian like Stephen Colbert mocks Trump, it is the supporters of Trump who are as likely to be angry at a joke as the former president himself. Trump has shown thin skin, but it has also been his supporters who have bristled at Trump mockery. And, even more importantly, Trump's allies have used these jokes to confirm their sense that Colbert's audience devalues them. The point is that in each joke the butt is generally not alone. If one is mocking a figure of authority, for example, those who like that authority figure will feel targeted as well.

While satire does not create the divisions between social groups, there is little doubt that it heightens them. Perhaps more than any other genre of comedy, satire is the form of comedy most likely to produce extreme rewards and extreme risks. This is so because most humor, and especially satirical humor, tends to be boundary reinforcing, dividing between the "it getters" and the "allies of the butt of the joke" and, thereby, underscoring group affiliation in ways that are both community reinforcing and socially divisive. Göktürk underscores the fact that, while humor can have benefits to those in on the joke, there is little question that it highlights differences across social identities:

> We have inherited brains that are inherently sensitive to group affiliation. We find meaning in our lives through social identities, and we experience comfort with those who share these identities. However, when creating an "us," the brain seems to seek out a "them," bringing online a series of psychological processes—including fear and distrust—that colors our view of out-group members.[38]

Satire is often accused of elitism, because, at its core, it generally focuses on criticizing ideas the satirist characterizes as stupid, illogical, arrogant, or manipulative. It has a biting edge not found in the gentle silliness of comedy that allows everyone to laugh at their common humanity. The upside of satire is that it is especially effective at helping the audience critique the status quo and reject commonly held beliefs that are socially damaging. And, of course, not all satire has the same bite. Colbert's satirical comedy, for example, has far more of a playful edge than the searing mockery of Bill Maher or the righteous rage of Samantha Bee. But in the end, regardless of its edge, satire is about criticizing attitudes, beliefs, worldviews, and behaviors that the satirist wants to target. George A. Test argues in *Satire: Spirit and Art* that

> satire ultimately judges, it asserts that some person, group, or attitude is not what it should be. However restrained, muted, or disguised a playful judgment may be, whatever form it takes, such an act undermines, threatens, and perhaps violates the target, making the act an attack.[39]

The critical issue is that satire can often feel like "one-sided" comedy: what is community building for one group feels like harassment or bullying to the other. As Moira Smith argues, "[T]hese cases constitute both harassment and humor."[40] She points out that the preferred term today is "laughing with" someone, but that, in general, the laughter is more commonly "at" another, and often at another who is linked to a larger group identity. For Smith, certain comedy does not just reinforce boundaries; it heightens them depending on whether the stakeholder is laughing or "unlaughing." She cites the work of Michael Billig, who coined the term "unlaughter" to characterize "a display of not laughing when laughter might otherwise be expected, hoped for or demanded."[41] Those laughing are pitted against those unlaughing.

This means that certain group identities can feel like the target of the joke. These reactions were certainly on display in the Trump era, when even after he won the 2016 election, it often felt that his supporters were "sore winners." Their candidate had won, yet they still seemed to act like they were alienated, marginalized, discriminated victims. Much of this rhetoric has been stoked by alt-right, white nationalist narratives that suggest that conservatives are under constant attack. These views may be unfounded, but that does not keep the group from defining itself as a victim. In that context, satirical jokes aimed at Trump were likely to land among his supporters and produce a sense of rage.

Comedy has a public performative quality that puts group responses on display. Thus, it tends to have the potential to heighten meta-perceptions (i.e. how we perceive others to perceive us) and, therefore, to play a significant role in shaping views in-groups have of out-groups. In fact, as Nour Kteily, Gordon Hodson, and Emile Bruneau found in their study of the role of meta-dehumanization and intergroup conflict, it is often one group's ideas of how another group defines them that can have the most significant impact on potential intergroup conflict.[42] So, in the United States, the way in which conservatives use "liberal" as an epithet only heightens social polarization. Similarly, the phrase "MAGA Republican" used by a political comedian is likely to lead such a person to bristle. The point is that groups become extremely sensitive to their ideas of what other groups think of them. It is less a question of what they think of the other group and more a question of what they think the other group thinks about them.

This is all to say that one negative outcome of the power of satire is that it does heighten political division. There simply is no way around it. Because satirical jokes are aimed at abuses of power, hypocrisy, faulty logic, corruption, etc., they have a target. In the case of the Trump joke, he is the target and, by association, so too are his fans. But it's worse, because in the Trump era the potential boundary-heightening consequences of satire have been even higher due to the characteristics of the groups that support Trump. These perceptions can then be further heightened in communities that are already inclined to defensive, victimized, thought patterns, as seen in political ideologies such as social dominance orientation, right-wing authoritarianism, religious fundamentalism, and conservatism.

For instance, research by Dannagal Young, Benjamin Bogozzi, Abigail Goldring, Shannon Paulsen, and Erin Drouin found that conservatives had a lower ability to appreciate ironic and exaggerated humor than liberals.[43] Other research on political conservatives has found that they share psychological factors of fear and aggression, dogmatism and intolerance of ambiguity, uncertainty avoidance, a need for cognitive closure, and terror management.[44] This last feature, terror management, is linked to the idea that political conservatives are inclined to punish outsiders and those who threaten the status of cherished worldviews—a factor that seems to be on regular display in the aggressive actions of white nationalists.

What is important to understand here is that satire doesn't create these social factions. And as I'll describe in the closing section of this chapter, it has very positive effects for its audience. But, that said, there is no doubt that in an environment of increased political division, in which some political groups are highly sensitive to criticism, the jabs of satirical jokes will sting not just the target but those who like the target.

Does Satire Make Us Cynical? Does It Keep Us From Participating in Politics? Is Its Negativity Bad for Democracy?

Since the election of Donald Trump in 2016, public trust has waned across a range of institutions—especially government and the press. According to the Edelman Trust Barometer, from 2017 to 2018 the United States witnessed the steepest decline in public trust of institutions ever measured. Trust dropped 9 points among the general population and a whopping 23 points with the informed public, placing the United States last in a ranking of 28 countries.[45]

When assessed across party lines, the decline in trust is even more noteworthy. The Pew Research Center reports that the "share of Democrats expressing trust in government is among the lowest levels for members of the party dating back nearly six decades." As of May 2017, only 16 percent of Democrats and Democratic leaners said they were satisfied with the way things were going, down from 52 percent in October 2016.[46]

The reason public trust in institutions is measured regularly is due, at least in part, to the common assumption that a lack of trust—or cynicism—is a bad omen for a healthy democracy. A lack of trust, that is, a cynical attitude, the worry goes, leads to a lack of commitment to institutions. It results in fatalism, nihilism, and a general belief that everyone is corrupt, biased, and/or self-serving.

Those critical of the effects of cynicism on political engagement worry that being negative will adversely affect one's interest in advocating for political change. As Julian Baggini put it in *The Guardian*, "[T]he greatest slur against cynicism is that it nurtures a fatalistic pessimism, a belief that nothing can ever be improved."[47]

And while a lack of trust is also tied to skepticism and pessimism, it is often thought that the cynic is the worst of all—simply too negative and too critical and too untrusting to do anything but sow more distrust and ruin the whole enterprise.

A rise in cynicism, then, is often directly tied to concerns that citizens will be too negative to participate in politics. They will give up on fighting for change and focus, instead, on griping about everything they think is wrong.

From this viewpoint, the election of Donald Trump and the unprecedented rise in voter distrust in politics and the press were grim developments. As *US News and World Report* put it, Trump turned us into a nation of cynics, and "[o]ptimism, that all-American trait, appears to be waning."[48]

The increase in cynicism seemed to justify a negative view of satire because satire is commonly associated with cynicism. Critics of satire worry that satirists create cynics and thereby threaten the strength of democratic institutions by leading the public to give up on them. So, it would make sense that as Trump was elected, and as public trust in institutions waned at precisely the same time that satirical criticism of Trump abounded, there would be reason to worry that satire might deter voters from being engaged in a positive and productive way.

But what if the worries over the rise in cynicism as a negative and paralyzing response to Trump were unfounded? What if it turns out that being a cynic is actually a good sign for political engagement? And, what if the long-standing assumption that cynics are just grouchy naysayers is all wrong?

Here are three key things to keep in mind as we worry about satire and its potential to foster cynicism.

Cynicism Is Not the Same Thing as Apathy

Most who worry that cynicism will ruin our democracy conflate cynicism with apathy. They confuse a lack of trust in institutions (cynicism) with a lack of interest in doing anything about it (apathy). The common misperception is that the cynic is simply so negative that they give up on advocating for change. This assumption often leads to the idea that, if all we do is consume negative news, we will simply give up on politics altogether. But a 2012 research study on the ties between negative news and political engagement proved that assumption to be false.[49] In fact, the research team was able to show that there was no link whatsoever between cynicism and apathy.

Another study from a research team based at the University of Connecticut was able to refute the presumed link between cynicism and apathy.[50] In contrast, the researchers found that there is a positive relationship between political cynicism and political participation. They further showed that the cynic's tendency to think critically is a productive metric for indicating political involvement. This means that the more critical and skeptical the cynic is, the more likely they will be politically active.

J. Gregg Robinson did a research study on the rise in cynicism after the foreclosure crisis, which led him to further debunk the presumed ties between cynicism and apathy. Robinson's research demonstrates a valuable link between cynicism and anger and shows that the cynic's anger often motivates political action. "Anger at government is unlike indifference to it," he explains. "An angry person is still engaged with the object of anger. In politics, like love, the worst thing is not anger, but indifference."[51] His study explains that one of the decisive features of cynicism is anger, and anger directly leads to a desire to fight back.

Political Satire Creates Politically Active Cynics

The concern over the rise of the cynic is matched by concern over the rise of political satire in creating the cynic. Since 9/11, satire has become more socially significant in this nation, not only as a source of news but also as a major player in shaping political discourse. Remember that Jon Stewart was often described as the "most trusted man in America"—a sign for many that our nation was heading in the wrong direction and that satire was at least partially to blame.[52]

The fact that satire regularly highlights the flaws in political institutions leaves many to worry that it creates cynics who will detach from democracy. In a 2008 study, Jonathan Morris and Jody Baumgartner found a causal connection between young people aged 18–30 watching *The Daily Show* and cynicism toward the news media, which is consistent with their earlier research from 2006. Baumgartner and Morris also suggest that people who turned to Stewart on *The Daily Show* for news regularly may have suffered more from cynicism because Stewart went beyond "highlighting the shortcomings of elected officials, candidates, and political institutions" and focused exclusively on the negative, which "may lead viewers to believe that the system comprises only of [sic] bad apples and that it is poisoned beyond repair."[53]

In a study on audience effects in *Politics Is a Joke!* by S. Robert Lichter, Jody C. Baumgartner, and Jonathan S. Morris, they survey years of joke data and conclude that the inherent negativity of late-night humor "is helping late night television comics remake American political life."[54] While they don't focus uniquely on satirical comedy, their overall argument is that late-night humorists have had a direct effect on increased cynicism toward politics in the American public. Yet, they don't study the difference between derogatory mocking versus critically engaged satire as they correlate with cynicism.

But guess what? These worries that satire has a negative effect on democracy simply are not confirmed by research on political satire, cynicism, and political engagement. There is proof that exposure to satire makes people more cynical and increases negative attitudes toward politics. But, as I've argued in my research on satire and politics, satire can't make an audience cynical about something that doesn't deserve it.[55]

The most important finding, though, is not that satire increases cynicism; it is that satire develops politically active cynics. Research by Hoon Lee and Nojin Kwak shows that the emotionally stimulating platform tied to satirical comedy engages viewers and increases those viewers' desire to be politically active.[56]

In fact, research shows that consumers of political satire news tend to be more confident about their views. As was pointed out by *HuffPost Media* blogger and USC Annenberg School Professor Marty Kaplan in 2006, people who watched

The Daily Show when Stewart hosted were more confident about their political knowledge than those who relied on network news. He further pointed out that people who are more confident that they understand politics are more likely to participate in politics than those who don't trust their own understanding.

Another study by Hsuan-Ting Chen, Chen Gan, and Ping Sun showed that the link between cynical anger and political satire was directly tied to citizen engagement. The researchers found that when "people consider an issue personally important and anger serves as a motivating factor, exposure to cross-cutting political satire can transform people into active citizens."[57]

There's a catch, though. As Baumgartner and Brad Lockerbie have shown, not all political comedy is equally designed to lead the audience to action.[58] There is a marked difference, for example, between most late-night comedy and the specific genre of political satire. A mocking joke about Trump's ridiculous hair or his ill-fitting suits gets a laugh, for example, but it doesn't lead to any productive political outcome. Baumgartner and Lockerbie show that true political satire like that found on Comedy Central's *The Daily Show* or John Oliver's *Last Week Tonight* can, in fact, mobilize viewers to political action.[59]

Evidence also suggests that the angrier the satire, the better. This means that the edgy, sharp, and pissed-off political satire of Lee Camp on *Redacted Tonight* or Samantha Bee on *Full Frontal* was more likely to lead to politically productive cynicism.[60]

Not All Cynicism Is the Same

I've mentioned that since Trump was elected in 2016 cynicism has been on the rise, but I haven't yet covered the fact that Trump didn't just make his detractors cynical; he also actively cultivated a cynical base of supporters. In yet one more example of how the Trump era made hyperbole the norm, there was a rise in legitimately cynical Trump critics alongside a rise in irrational Trump-loving cynics, who trusted no one but him.

So just as we have to winnow out the real fake news (i.e. news that is purposefully misleading) from the fake-fake news (i.e. news called fake because the audience doesn't like it), we also have to critically evaluate the difference between legitimate cynics and fabricated ones. Legitimate cynics have a verifiable reason not to trust in something. Fabricated ones have been hyped up to freak out over nothing.

Baggini refers to intelligent cynicism.[61] For him, intelligent cynicism derives from a critical disposition to ask questions, reject the status quo, and resist rosy narratives that hide the truth of things. The catch, though, is that one of the pillars of the Trump agenda was the idea that his supporters couldn't trust anyone but him and those who support him. Steve Benen explains that sowing distrust and undermining public confidence in government and the media were a staple of the Trump presidency.[62] Whether casting doubt on crowd sizes, federal judges, experts, or scientists, Trump learned to weaponize cynicism to his benefit.

So, for all of the intelligent Trump-era cynics, there is an equally expanding group of irrational cynics who are also angry and who are also interested in advancing their agenda. This, of course, explains at least part of what happened at the January 6, 2021, insurrection.

This is all to say that, thanks to Trump, we have a prime opportunity to rethink the role of cynicism in politics in this country. Where once the legitimate cynic was ostracized for being too negative and too critical, we can now see that those habits of mind are essential features of political agency. Just because one has a negative view of politicians and the institutions they work for, doesn't mean they don't care, and doesn't mean they aren't ready to fight for change. Turns out that the rise in intelligent cynicism fostered by the consumption of political satire is not just an appropriate response to Trump; it might actually be a sign of optimism.

Does Satire Make Us Complicit? Does Satire Distract by Making Jokes of Something Serious?

One of the most common criticisms of political satire is the idea that the audience consumes satirical comedy, has a laugh, and then settles in on their couch in a negative stupor. Malcolm Gladwell accuses satire of functioning like a political analgesic.[63] For him, satirical comedy overshadows meaningful political debate. As one of the guests on his podcast dedicated to the negative effects of satire put it, "perhaps, instead of laughing about them, we should try to do something about them."[64] Steve Almond similarly worries about satire's ability to create an apathetic, unserious cynic in *Bad Stories*. "We are learning to see politics and media as a joke," he writes.[65]

The issue, though, is that these sorts of concerns need to be assessed within a particular context. There are no studies that show that consumption of political comedy leads directly to apathy, nor are there studies that correlate consumption of satire with a reduction in critical awareness of major social issues. In fact, as I've pointed out, most studies suggest the opposite trend.

Many of these worries about satire as a distraction stem from the work of Neil Postman, whose 1986 book *Amusing Ourselves to Death* posited that U.S. society displayed an addiction to amusement that acted as a diversion from legitimate political engagement.[66] The core idea of the book is the notion that the dystopic world created by Aldous Huxley in *Brave New World*, in which people focus on their own hedonistic pleasures and cede their rights, comes far closer to describing social ills than the stark authoritarian dystopia narrated by George Orwell in *1984*. Critical to Postman's argument is the idea that television serves as mindless distraction, and he specifically points to TV news as nothing more than entertainment programming that is designed to reduce the potential of a viewer to act on knowledge.

Postman, of course, makes a number of critical observations, and there is little doubt that entertainment television has mind-numbing effects. The key issue, though, is that Postman does not distinguish between types of television entertainment, and, even more importantly, he was writing in the 1980s, well before the internet age when viewers were able to interact critically with materials seen on screen in a far more active way. In fact, the passive person in front of the television is more the anomaly than the rule today. This is especially so in the realm of political satire in which viewers engage with material by sharing, commenting, and creating memes and other critical responses.

Even still, the worries that televised comedy is encouraging the public to simply sit back and do nothing continue to run strong. Indeed, during the Trump era, despite an overall increase in a range of forms of political action, there remains a significant—and valid—concern that the U.S. public is simply too politically apathetic. Perhaps the best example of this from the Trump era took place in the wake of the Charlottesville attacks, when Heather Heyer was mowed down by a white nationalist who drove his car into a crowd of protesters. After the attacks, Trump suggested that there were "many sides" to the story, a response that led many late-night comedians to skewer him for his lack of leadership, his missing moral compass, and his less-than-subtle support for racists. But the most infamous comedic response to the attacks took place on *SNL* when Tina Fey appeared on *SNL*'s "Weekend Update." As a graduate of the University of Virginia (UVA) where the attack took place, Fey showed up wearing a UVA sweatshirt. She started her bit talking about how disturbing Trump's response was and how concerning it was to see that more alt-right protests were scheduled across the country. But then she shifted to address the anxieties the public had over what it should do about the rising presence of alt-right violence: "I know a lot of us are feeling anxious and we are asking ourselves, 'What can I do? I am just one person.'"[67] She went on to say,

> I would urge people this Saturday, instead of participating in the screaming matches and potential violence, find a local business you support, like a Jewish American bakery or an African American run bakery, order a cake with the American flag on it, and just eat it.[68]

She then proceeded to stuff her face with cake while Colin Jost asked her how eating cake had any possibility of making any kind of difference. Fey went on a rant in which she reminded the audience that Native Americans were shot at while protesting, but under Trump white nationalists are being defended. She then, ironically, told the audience that when this sort of thing enrages them, they should just yell into their cake. When Jost mentioned that some of the rallies were being canceled, Fey replied, "See it is already working! Sheetcaking is a grassroots movement, Colin. Most of the women I know have been doing it once a week since the election."[69] She even gets Michael Che so riled up that he reaches for some cake to eat in protest too. As she closes, she states, "I really want to encourage all good, sane Americans to treat these rallies like a thoughtful movie with two female leads, don't show up. Let these morons scream into the empty air."[70]

The bit led to a tremendous backlash as Fey was accused of being tone deaf to her white privilege, and many expressed outrage that she would encourage folks not to do anything in response to public displays of hatred and racism. Folks took her ironic call to "sheetcaking" literally, eventually leading her to apologize for missing the mark, especially in her last statement. She later admitted she would have changed the last line of the bit, "If I could put one sentence back digitally, I would say to people, 'Fight them in every way except the way that they want.'"[71] Overall, though, the bit was a cautionary tale because it served as a reminder that, in the Trump era, the sort of irony Fey used in her bit was lost even on her intended audience. She was literally eating cake, a metaphor that should be a fairly obvious joking reference to Marie Antoinette's famous tone-deaf call to deal with a lack of bread among the French by having them "eat cake." For many, the joke was missed, and the ironic twist of suggesting that the audience should eat cake as a response to social injustice was taken seriously. Of course, the greatest irony of all is the fact that the public debate after the bit led to an active and productive engagement on the issue of how best to challenge and protest the rise of white nationalism, demonstrating, yet again, that satirical interventions can have productive political outcomes.

The "sheetcaking" controversy doesn't confirm that comedy makes us complicit or distracted, but it does prove that, in the Trump era, it became especially hard to make ironic jokes about serious issues.

Does Satire Warp Audience Perceptions?

Perhaps one of the most interesting facets of satirical power is its ability to offer the public framing narratives about public figures. When Stephen Colbert coined the term "truthiness" to describe the way in which the George W. Bush administration acted on what "felt true" rather than what was true, he didn't just coin a popular word; he offered the public a common vocabulary. Political satire since 9/11/2001 has had an increasing role in shaping public debates of current issues. In yet another example, Tina Fey's impersonation of Sarah Palin during the 2012 election had a measurable impact on negative views of the candidate.[72] Interestingly, the research shows that the negative impression of Palin that resulted from Fey's impersonation likely did not influence the outcome of the election overall, even if it was true that Palin's own reputation was hurt in the process.

If one thinks that it makes sense to have a negative view of Palin, then such an outcome is welcome. But research does show that the impact of the impersonation may have been a lot more powerful than may make us comfortable. For instance, one of Tina Fey's lines as Palin was that she could see Russia from her house. That line stuck in many audience members' minds to such a degree that they actually thought the candidate had said it, when she had not. Similarly, when Chevy Chase impersonated Gerald Ford as a bumbling spastic, despite the fact that Ford was quite athletic, Chase, also, affected perceptions of Ford. While the portrayal of Ford as uncoordinated did not have any direct impact on his likability, it is noteworthy that a characterization of him in such a manner had that much power.

Similarly, research shows that when candidates appear on a late-night comedy show, it can influence voter perceptions. One study showed that after George W.

Bush appeared on *The Late Show* with David Letterman, viewers adjusted their perceptions of his character traits. Interestingly, though, researchers also found that, despite the fact that Bush spoke with Letterman about a number of policy issues, it was voter assessments of his personality that shifted after the interview. Also interesting is the fact that the study found that the same adjustments did not occur for Al Gore when he appeared in late-night interviews, leading researchers to speculate that the extent to which an appearance on a late-night show for an interview has a greater chance of shifting voter perceptions if the candidate is lesser known.[73]

Knowledge of the candidate is one issue. Another critical issue is how knowledgeable the viewer of late-night comedy is prior to tuning in to hear the jokes. In a 2006 study, Dannagal Young and Russell M. Tisinger found that a viewer's political knowledge affected the extent to which their views would be influenced by late-night comedy monologues.[74] This finding, of course, makes perfect sense. Not all viewers of late-night comedy are the same. The degree to which a viewer is partisan and the degree to which they are already politically informed directly relate to the degree to which a comedy sketch can change their views.

In *Politics is a Joke!*, Lichter, Baumgartner, and Morris show that late-night comedy regularly fosters negative views for the audience.[75] But here is where the research falls a bit short. Their research combines all types of comedic interventions, failing to distinguish between satire and mockery or between silly humor and sharp ironic wit. In the case of the Ford impersonation, there was nothing political about Chevy Chase's bit; it was just goofy. Satirical comedy tends to go after ideas more than physicality and tends to be more about an ironic takedown than an insult. This means that not all comedy is equal, and the sort that is just insulting mockery can often leave negative impressions that are far more powerful than a satirical call to think critically about a person and their policies. Satire, unlike mockery, is not simply derisive and derogatory; it is typically aimed at flawed thinking, abuses of power, corruption, and malice rather than the target's character. When it goes after faulty logic, hypocrisy, immorality, and poor reasoning, it elevates the critical-thinking capacities of the audience.

Even more important is the question of how an audience member forms an opinion of a figure satirized. Do they only watch late-night comedy to develop their perspective? Or do they watch the political figure and form their own views? And do they also consult more traditional news outlets? Here is where the research is perhaps the most encouraging. Despite worries that viewers of satire news only watch comedy to get news, most research suggests that is not the case and that, in fact, those viewers who watch satire news tend to consume more political news overall. Research by Young and Tisinger on the habits of young viewers who tuned in to watch Jon Stewart and Stephen Colbert on Comedy Central showed that, rather than watching less "real" news, those viewers watched more. In fact, they found that viewers of satire news shows reported "consuming more (not less) political information from traditional sources, particularly online, and through talk radio."[76]

One important study by Lauren Feldman and Caty Borum Chattoo shows that comedy, not specifically satire, has a number of effects on audience perceptions that can influence the way they think about political issues. They show that comedy can get audience members to pay attention to an issue that they might have avoided.[77] The idea is that an audience is more likely to tune in to comedy than to a political talk show. And it makes a lot of sense because folks often prefer to be entertained by comedy than to consume depressing political debate programming. Mostly this seems like a good outcome, but we can see how some might speculate that the appeal of comedy could potentially have a negative impact if, say, the comedy then causes people to think that it is a waste of time to vote, for example.

Borum Chattoo and Feldman further show that comedy works as a "priming agent" and can reduce resistance to the message behind the comedy, though that may be less likely with satirical comedy. As they put it, "Humor, because of its ability to draw attention, may be particularly well suited for bringing people into contact with ideas that run counter to their own beliefs."[78] The catch here is that humor may occupy the mind with processing the joke, thereby lowering the mind's defense against the message inside the joke: "[W]ith humor, our attention and interest are directed at 'getting' the humor; we process the joke more deeply, not the persuasive arguments, thereby reducing our motivation and/or ability to counter-argue."[79] These arguments are consistent with Young's research, which found that late-night political jokes, compared to nonhumorous versions of the same jokes, produced more thoughts aimed at humor comprehension and appreciation and fewer negative thoughts directed at message arguments.[80] What this means is that one of the risks of satire is that its wit may distract the audience members and alter their thoughts about the issue being satirized. While I would argue that satire's edge and its boundary-heightening components have generally been shown not to radically alter audience predilections and existing confirmation bias, it is still important to note how the process of "getting a joke" can distract from the message of the joke and thereby influence public opinion.

Does Satire Offer an Easy Excuse for Bad Behavior?

"I was just kidding" is probably one of the most common refrains uttered when someone gets busted. Even President Donald Trump tried to back out of his infamous "pussy grabbing" comment by saying it had not been serious speech, but rather just "locker room banter."[81] The call of "just joking" has a long history, but there are a few key reasons why there has been an increase in what I call the "Colbert Defense."[82]

The Colbert Defense is what happens when a criminal, bigot, racist, jerk, or otherwise horrible person tries to back out of offensive behavior by calling it just an act, just a joke, or an example of satire. The goal of the Colbert Defense is to suggest that what was said or done wasn't to be taken seriously or literally, thereby allowing the offensive person to avoid taking responsibility for their actions.

So why is crying satire on the rise?

One clear factor is that satirists are more powerful in the public sphere than at any time in human history. But perhaps the most interesting part of the story is the way in which the cry of satire, sarcasm, and just plain joking is a consequence of a post-truth world.

To determine when speech is serious becomes harder and harder when your president is "the liar in chief" and the most popular news channel, Fox News, is only totally accurate 17 percent of the time.[83] When former Trump spokesperson Kellyanne Conway could utter the phrase "alternative fact" with a straight face, it became clear that legitimate, sincere, and accurate speech was no longer the norm.[84]

Even more bizarrely, satirists are commonly more trusted than journalists.[85] They also do a better job than the corporate news at speaking truth to power. This is why, in the Trump era, shows like *The Daily Show with Trevor Noah* and *The Late Show with Stephen Colbert* enjoyed better ratings.[86] Viewers tuned in for some comedy, but they also tuned in because the satire, snark, and sarcasm on those shows were more "serious" forms of speech than the sensationalist, hyperbolic, and hysterical discourse of the straight news.

The other key reason why there has been a rise in the Colbert Defense is that we are also operating in a world in which more and more people just don't get irony, parody, and comedic exaggeration. In her book *Irony and Outrage*, Young explains that major segments of the population simply can't process irony. Add to that the fact that Trump was already a bombastic parody and the alt-right "serious" news sites were already extreme exaggerations. This means that, when Trump was elected, the baseline for public discourse was already extremely saturated with over-the-top forms of communication. Satire depends on exaggeration and parody to point out the flaws and folly in what it is mocking. That is really hard to do if what you are making fun of already seems like a joke. Even master satirist Andy Borowitz has admitted that satire has been a really a hard register in which to work during the Trump era.[87]

While Trump may have been the gasbag-in-chief, it is worth remembering that we have long been living in an era in which the lines of serious speech and comedy have been blurred. Recall that 2012 GOP primary candidate Herman Cain tried to back out of a comment that he wanted to electrify the fence on the U.S.-Mexico border by saying that he was just kidding. In fact, he suggested that he "would bring a sense of humor to the White House, because America's too uptight!"[88] Cain's defense of his outrageous claim wasn't important because it was lame and stupid; it was important because Cain didn't seem to get the idea that we actually don't need any humor in the White House.

At the time, few, if any, journalists pointed out to Cain that the job of the president is to support the Constitution and exercise leadership in a democracy, not to be funny. Instead, it was Stephen Colbert on *The Colbert Report* who managed to reveal to the public the absurdity of the Cain campaign. In fact, Colbert offered an amazing parody of a Cain ad.[89] The parody was funny and smart, mostly because it didn't really stray much from the original. The original ad featured Cain's campaign chair smoking in a totally weird shot, and it closed with the candidate's super bizarre slow-motion smile. Colbert's parody ad basically mirrored the same things in a way that called even more attention to how odd Cain's entire campaign message was.[90]

In the wake of the Cain campaign, the cries of "just kidding" are literally a daily event, but let's consider a few more examples that help to make the case that attempts to use the Colbert Defense are on the rise. In one bizarre story, Philippine President Rodrigo Duterte claimed he was "being sarcastic" when he told troops that he would take the blame for them if they raped women while implementing martial law to battle Muslim militants.[91] The statement then led to a *Twitter* clash with Chelsea Clinton, who reminded Duterte that rape jokes simply aren't funny. "Duterte is a murderous thug with no regard for human rights. It's important to keep pointing that out & that rape is never a joke," she wrote.[92] But again, what is really weird is that Duterte seems to have absolutely no clue what sarcasm is. Even if we decide not to take his comment literally, there is no way it is an example of sarcasm.

Pundits also regularly try the Colbert Defense. Hate-speech diva Ann Coulter is always getting in trouble and then trying to back out of it by claiming that she didn't mean what she said. In one classic example, she came under fire for referring to John Edwards as a "faggot," to which she replied, "C'mon, it was a joke. I would never insult gays by suggesting that they are like John Edwards. That would be mean."[93] Coulter is often given a pass by those who say she is just a performer and therefore doesn't have to face consequences for what she says.

During his custody hearing, *InfoWars* pundit Alex Jones tried to suggest that he is not liable for things he says on his show because he is just a performance artist. Jones' attorney, David Minton, described Jones' work as "satire" and "sarcasm." And yet he certainly doesn't present himself as a satirist to his audience of over 3 million, a fact that later led him to lose a defamation case brought by parents of children killed in the Sandy Hook shooting.[94] So, the cry of satire in this instance was just a lot of hot air.

Accused criminals have tried the Colbert Defense too. A defender of the Penn State fraternity—Kappa Delta Rho—that allegedly operated two closed *Facebook* pages on which members posted pictures of nude, unconscious women, drug deals, and hazing explained away the behavior by saying it was just a no-big-deal part of everyday culture; it was satire. "It was a satirical group. It wasn't malicious whatsoever. It wasn't intended to hurt anyone. It wasn't intended to demean anyone. It was an entirely satirical group and it was funny to some extent."[95]

Even more disturbing is the story of a University of Maryland student who killed a young black man, Richard W. Collins. The accused student had been a member of a *Facebook* group filled with anti-black and sexist memes. And yet, when confronted about the content on the site, the site's administrator said it had been started as satire and was intended to make fun of the so-called alt-right.[96]

From criminals to politicians to pundits, the Colbert Defense has been on the rise and shows no signs of waning. This means that we need a clear way to distinguish between the various forms of obnoxious speech out there, like hate speech, as opposed to satire.

Here's a handy test:

- Is the person using irony to get at the truth or using invective to hide it?
- Do the comments punch up or down? That is, do they attack those more powerful or those who are weaker than the speaker?
- Do the comments poke fun at abuses of power, or do they justify them?
- Is the goal of the speech to point out folly or to create hysteria?
- Is the speech designed to protect sanity or foster insanity?
- Is it a champion of reason or fear?
- Is the speaker exaggerating to expose the truth or to freak everyone out?
- Does the speaker use humor to make the audience smarter, or do they use humor to belittle others?

In the end, the core question is, Is the speaker helping to make sense of the world and give a laugh at the same time? Or is the speaker lying, conniving, bullying, demeaning, and demoralizing? And remember this: satirists love language, and they play with it to make us smarter. The satire posers abuse language, twisting words to advance their position. In the end, being a satirist is not the same thing as being absurd, offensive, or dangerous.

Does Satire Have Any Power That Is Valuable to Democracy?

While, as explained earlier, satire can increase political polarization, incense those who feel insulted by its jokes, potentially exacerbate negative political views, distract an audience into softening to a potentially negative attitude toward political engagement, and serve as an excuse for bad behavior, there are also a number of measurable ways in which satire positively supports democracy. Here is a rundown of the positive effects of satire on democracy that we can prove.

Satire Informs the Public and Helps With Information Recall

Following the success of Jon Stewart and Stephen Colbert in raising awareness to a number of important news stories, researchers decided to try to determine whether viewers of these shows are more or less informed. While, as mentioned earlier, there is evidence that viewers can develop negative views of politicians from watching late-night comedy, it is also true that viewers of satire news regularly score highly when tested for accurate knowledge of public affairs. A 2007 Pew Research study found that viewers of *The Daily Show* and *The Colbert Report* demonstrated the highest knowledge of national and international affairs (Fox News viewers were near the bottom, below "online news discussion blogs" and above only "Local TV news" and "Network morning shows").[97] Reinforcing these findings, a 2012 Pew study found that people who only watched *The Daily Show* fared about as well as those who only watched Sunday news shows. Their knowledge of issues was only bested by NPR listeners. Even more noteworthy, Fox News viewers scored lower in knowledge than those with no news exposure at all, although those who watched just CNN or MSNBC fared only slightly better than those with no exposure to news.[98] As described throughout this book, one reason satire viewers scored so well is due to the way in which the news is covered on satire shows. The packaging of the information, the ability to question the status quo, and the refusal to show "balance" when covering an outrageous story are among some of the reasons why viewers of these shows do better when tested on their knowledge of issues. But there is another major reason why satire news may be better suited as a medium for educating an audience: the humor effect. Research shows that humor works as a highly effective way of engaging memory.[99] Teachers, for example, have long known that use of a silly mnemonic device will help students to recall important information. The key is that the mind likes to remember humor.

When consuming comedy, the mind is more open to remembering information, and it will then have greater information recall.[100] In fact, research shows that, when information is packaged with comedy, the mind displays increased attention and increased encoding (i.e. it is stored in memory better). Moreover, humor reduces negative emotions, energizes the brain, and increases interest—activities that all help the mind to remember information delivered with comedy. And, as I'll explain in the next chapter, those habits became especially handy in the Trump era.

Satire Speaks Truth to Power

The goal of satire is to use irony to expose lies, hypocrisy, bluster, bullying, arrogance, evil, and corruption. Satire is literally designed to critique institutions of power and abusive leaders and to expose their flaws. Democracy depends on an active and engaged citizenry. It also depends on citizens who are willing to fight to improve the system, and that requires that citizens understand all that is wrong with it. I conducted a research study with Serbian activist Srdja Popovic that proved that adding satire to activism—i.e. engaging in laughtivism—had a 100 percent success rate in reframing the narratives of abusive power.[101] Those who engage in abuses of power are inherently ironic, because they say they are being honest or fair or just or accountable when they are doing the opposite. When an individual reveals those lies with satire, they are almost always successful at showing the public the truth behind the lies.

While satire may be linked to cynicism, as explained previously, the cynic who consumes satire is engaged and ready to fight for change. This means that as public trust in institutions wanes, public trust in satire may well increase. Researchers were able to show, for example, that both Jon Stewart and Stephen Colbert scored high in trust.[102][103] John Oliver similarly has been called "one of the most trusted names in journalism."[104] Because satirists openly display their bias and are not attempting to be straight journalists, they often seem more trustworthy to viewers than reporters. Perhaps even more importantly, satire is highly effective at speaking truth to power, because rather than telling viewers what to think, the satirist calls on viewers to question what they are being told.

Satire Creates a Sense of Community and Offers a Shared Narrative

As explained earlier, satire is connected to heightened social divisions because jokes have a target and an intended audience. Satirical interventions divide between the "it getters" and those connected to the butt of the joke. However, concerns that satire heightens polarization are counterbalanced by the ways in which satire helps to build a sense of community. One of the significant ways that satire performed a public function in the aftermath of 9/11/2001 and into the Trump era was the way that it helped audiences to feel less alone. Democracies depend on a sense of the collective, on a shared mission and political action that moves beyond individual interest.

There are various ways in which satire works to help build community. The first and most obvious is that it creates a public forum for discussing an issue. When Jimmy Kimmel addresses his audience to talk about healthcare, for example, he opens the door for public debate among like-minded individuals who care about how to make healthcare in the United States better. Similarly, when Stephen Colbert coins the word "truthiness," he offers the public an easy and portable word it can use to diagnose existing social ills.

Research by Feldman and Chattoo further shows how comedy works to break down social barriers, creating new alliances among disparate members of society. They analyze the role that comedy plays in the "contact hypothesis," which "proposes that positive interactions between members of diverse social groups can reduce prejudice, by providing the opportunity to learn more."[105] "Additionally," they explain, "the diminishment function of humor can be used to signal that any perceived social divide is not as consequential as one may have originally assumed."[106] Thus, they point out that,

> when mediated comedy positively portrays marginalized social groups and does so in a way that unmasks rather than minimizes racial and cultural differences, it can help foster a sense of understanding of and commonality with these groups among majority audiences.[107]

Young similarly shows in *Irony and Outrage* that humor has a community-building function because not only does it make the comedian look good, but it also builds an affective connection with their audience.

As Stephen Duncombe explains in *Dream: Re-imagining Progressive Politics in an Age of Fantasy*, for decades, left-wing politics abandoned engaging with the sorts of spectacle that can build populist momentum.[108] Thus, the ability to engage the public in a broad collective fashion was taken over by the negative, fear-based politics of the right. These were the tactics on display with the founding of the Tea Party, and they were especially visible at Trump rallies and, most notably, the January 6, 2021, insurrection. Duncombe, though, points to the particular power of satire to offer a left-wing version of collective engagement and fantasy building. Part of that process requires shared symbols, vocabularies, and messages that work across communities to help build a collective political project. According to Duncombe, "Donald Trump's presidency has shown how this is done, albeit to ends that are deplorable. Abandoning logic and truth, the Fabulist in Chief conjures up spectacle to energize his base."[109] Promotion for his book reminds readers that, "Matching the right in this fashion does not mean adopting its values. Rather Duncombe sets out what he calls a politics of 'ethical spectacle'."[110] Satire does an exceptionally strong job of offering a counter spectacle to Trump. Using wit and humor, the satirist provides a comedic intervention that offers the viewers an opportunity to collectively laugh together and think through the crisis in a positive and productive way.

Satire Engages the Public, Entertains Citizens, and Energizes Activism

Perhaps one of the most encouraging features of satire's ability to foster a healthy democracy is its role in energizing citizens and encouraging political participation. In direct contrast to the concerns that satire leads to apathy and distraction, several studies have confirmed that satire consumers are politically active. A study from 2008 showed, for example, that exposure to political comedy shows was "positively associated with some forms of political participation."[111] Another study from 2011 that focused on the effects of watching Jon Stewart showed that, "*The Daily Show* and late-night comedy in general are part of a diet of healthy political characteristics and behaviors, all of which correlate positively with political participation, discussion, and debate viewing."[112]

But there's more. Political satire is an especially effective tool for entertaining the citizenry. Research on citizenship shows that a critical way to foster active citizens is with entertainment. Similar to the ideas of Duncombe, Liesbet van Zoonen argues that it is both possible and necessary to see political participation and involvement as fun in her book *Entertaining the Citizen*.[113] Van Zoonen explains that the overlap and intersection between politics and entertainment are nothing new. She also shows that when political involvement is fun, it can reach a broader audience and attract citizens to become active. These sorts of patterns were observed by scholars who have watched how political satirists like Stephen Colbert and John Oliver have drawn audiences to become involved in issues. Both Colbert and Oliver have encouraged viewers to engage in cyber-citizenship, and they have also both been able to spur viewers to donate to causes and write to politicians. The 2010 rally organized by Stewart and Colbert in advance of the midterm elections drew a crowd of over 200,000. In addition, the Comedy Central live broadcast reportedly drew 2,000,000 total viewers, with an additional 570,000 live video streams on the internet.[114]

Satire doesn't just entertain and engage the citizen; it also energizes activism and helps increase its efficacy. Serbian activist Srdja Popovic coined the term "laughtivism." He explains that "humor is infusing the arsenal of the 21st-century protestor" because "it works."[115] When protests are launched using humor as a tactic, it "breaks fear and builds confidence." Popovic also claims that it adds a "cool factor," making it attractive to be a part of a movement. But perhaps most importantly, he points out that humor tends to incite clumsy reactions from a movement's opponents:

> The best acts of laughtivism force their targets into lose-lose scenarios, undermining the credibility of a regime no matter how they respond. These acts move beyond mere pranks; they help corrode the very mortar that keeps most dictators in place: Fear.[116]

Popovic has studied the rising use of humor as a component of activism and protest, showing that such tactics can expand the base of participants in a movement:

> [P]rotestors understand that humor offers a low-cost point of entry for ordinary citizens who don't consider themselves particularly political, but are sick and tired of dictatorship. Make a protest fun, and people don't want to miss out on the action.[117]

Our research together further confirms this—67 percent of the laughtivist cases we studied increased the base of supporters for a movement.[118]

Evidence of the rising presence of satirical protest, or laughtivism, abounds in the Trump era. One need only think of the "pussy hats" that many protesters wore at the "Women's March." In fact, as explained in the previous chapter, at any progressive rally today, there are legions of satirical, sarcastic, and snarky signs. Using satire as a protest tactic isn't just fun; it is effective. It helps to engage participants and make the act of protesting not just pleasurable but also memorable.

Satire Helps to Foster Critical Thinking

A healthy democracy needs an informed and engaged citizenry. Citizens not only need to have correct information; they also need to have sophisticated reasoning skills to make informed decisions. Because satire depends on irony, on using words in ways that are different from their literal meaning, it is directly connected to some of the most sophisticated thought processes. Satire is also designed to encourage the public to question the status quo, to detect BS, and to resist logical fallacies. Research shows that the consumption of satire can stimulate critical thinking.[119] Rebecca Glazier points out that, "[V]iewers of late-night satire are more informed about candidates and issue positions (Young 2004), and they are more knowledgeable about politics in general (Pew Research Center 2007) compared to those who do not view these programs."[120] It isn't just that consumers of satire are more informed and better at critical thinking; they are also more confident in their knowledge. In a 2006 study, Baumgartner and Morris found that viewers of *The Daily Show* had increased confidence in their ability to understand politics.[121]

Much satire news, for instance, juxtaposes news clips with witty analysis. That blending is highly complex and requires sophisticated analytical skills on the part of the audience. Even a headline from an Andy Borowitz piece for *The New Yorker* asks the reader to process a complex ironic joke. It simply isn't possible to understand and engage with satire without thinking critically. Glazier explains that, by its nature, satire is difficult to understand. This means that critically engaging with satire requires higher-level thinking skills. All of these habits of the mind are extremely productive for a healthy democracy. In fact, as I'll explain in the concluding chapter, it may well be satire's connection to higher-order thinking that was its most important contribution to our democracy during the Trump presidency.

Satire Increases Citizen Confidence and Inspires Action

This last point may be the most significant one to drive home for those who are inherently skeptical about the role that satire can play in a democracy. There are reams of research to show that satire doesn't just make us smarter; it gets us engaged and active. Work by Young shows that satire increases confidence and a sense of political efficacy—two notions critical to political engagement. Believing that one has "political efficacy" means being confident in one's "capacity to participate in political life (internal political efficacy) and the sense that the system will be responsive to one's voice (external political efficacy)."[122] Young's study revealed that viewing satire contributed to individuals' "confidence in their ability to understand and participate in politics, which then increased the likelihood of their participating."[123] Even more importantly, she documents that her research is not a matter of isolated findings: "Numerous studies have confirmed this link between viewing satire and being confident in one's ability to understand and participate in political life."[124] She further adds that her research confirms a range of other politically "healthy" consequences of viewing satire, including talking about politics, following politics, and paying attention to current events.[125]

Other research has confirmed the "gateway" function of satire: after being exposed to an issue through satire, the audience seeks further information and potentially acts on what it learns. Most of this work is connected to Matt Baum's "gateway hypothesis," which posits that exposure to "soft news" formats might increase attention to foreign affairs. The idea is that these types of formats draw a wider audience, which includes those who might not be drawn to straight political reporting. According to Baum, "[C]onsuming soft news influences the attitudes of politically inattentive individuals."[126] Further research by Cao and Brewer shows a significant positive relationship between exposure to candidate interviews on late-night or political comedy shows and knowledge about campaigns.[127]

But, again, the critical point is that the viewers aren't just smarter and more informed; they are more active and engaged. Numerous studies have shown that the audiences for satire, especially *The Daily Show with Jon Stewart*, participated in politics at a higher rate than the general voting-eligible public.[128] Moreover, Moy, Xenos, and Hess found that late-night comedy viewers in general, which was not specifically limited to satire viewers, demonstrated increased intentions to vote.[129] Other research has differentiated between satire and late-night comedy in general to show that satire viewers have a measurable increase in political activity. For example, Baumgartner and Lockerbie used data from the American National Election Studies and found that viewers of Comedy Central satire programming (*The Daily Show* and *The Colbert Report*) demonstrated more political behaviors (attending political rallies, discussing politics, contributing to a political party, wearing political buttons) than late-night comedy viewers of shows like *Late Night with David Letterman*.[130]

Perhaps one of the most exciting avenues of research into the effects of satire is its role in political activism. In her book *Humour in Political Activism*, Majken Sorenson analyzes a series of ways in which humor has a positive effect on political action.[131] She studies a series of cases and demonstrates how humor can be highly effective at building a culture of resistance, especially because it is very effective at reducing both fear and apathy. Similarly, Amber Day's research in *Satire and Dissent* shows that, "[A]ffirmation and reinforcement fulfill an integral community-building function, which is a crucial component of nurturing a political movement."[132] Satire as part of a political action has other benefits as well. Sorenson, Popovic in *Blueprint for Revolution*, and Popovic and myself in *Pranksters vs. Autocrats* show, for example, how the role of ironic humor can be highly effective for building a political movement.[133] For example, Sorenson explains that things that appear meaningless to the outsider (like humor) might contribute significantly to higher morale and energy within the movement, and this, in turn, has the potential to lead to more energy to spend on other types of activism. Moreover, research shows that infusing ironic humor into activism also helps the activists themselves deal with setbacks, reprisals, and violence. Sorenson explains that when she was actively involved in a campaign that used humor, "The humour was good to make us stick together and to confront the fear and anxiety, because it was possible to change a dramatic situation like beating up [by police] into something funny."[134]

Whether individuals engage in an army of satire, as Michael Moore called for, or just engage in the everyday habits of an active citizen, research repeatedly confirms that satire plays a positive role in advancing democracy. Jeffrey Jones has further argued that exposure to political satire is positively correlated to increased political participation and that it cultivates the characteristics of an engaged citizenry. Similarly, my work with Remy Maisel in *Is Satire Saving Our Nation?* documents a series of ways in which political satire builds political engagement among audiences by creating a community of active and involved citizens.[135] More importantly, we now have literally decades of research that documents the positive social impact of satire, and, thus far, there simply is no significant proof that any of the negative outcomes satire skeptics worry about actually happen. In the next and final chapter, I'll run down what may well be the best gift satire gives to a democracy—an active and engaged mind.

Notes

1. Vick, Karl. "Al-Qaeda Group Claims Responsibility for Paris Terror Attack." *Time*, January 9, 2015, https://time.com/3661650/charlie-hebdo-paris-terror-attack-al-qaeda/.
2. Devichand, Mukul. "How the World Was Changed by the Slogan 'Je Suis Charlie'." *BBC*, January 3, 2016, www.bbc.com/news/blogs-trending-35108339.
3. McClennen, Sophia A. "They'll Come for 'The Daily Show' Next: Why Satirists Always Threaten Fundamentalists." *Salon*, 2015, www.salon.com/test/2015/01/09/theyll_come_for_jon_stewart_next_why_satirists_always_threaten_fundamentalists/.
4. Lakritz, Naomi. "Lakritz: Charlie Hebdo Controversy Is About Good Taste, Not Fear." *Calgary Herald*, 2015, https://calgaryherald.com/opinion/columnists/lakritz-charlie-hebdo-controversy-is-about-good-taste-not-fear; Kludt, Tom. "Not Everyone Is Celebrating Charlie Hebdo's Satire." *CNN*, 2015, https://money.cnn.com/2015/01/08/media/charlie-hebdo-paris-manhunt/; Sparrow, Jeff. "We Can Defend Charlie Hebdo Without Endorsing It." *ABC*, 2015, www.abc.net.au/news/2015-01-09/sparrow-we-should-support-charlie-hebdo,-not-endorse-it/6007836; Handelzats, Michael. "Drawing New Conclusions After Charlie Hebdo Attack." *Haaretz*, 2015, www.haaretz.com/life/books/.premium-cartoonists-must-draw-new-conclusions-after-attack-1.5359013.
5. Shackle, Samira. "The NS Interview – PJ O'Rourke." *New Statesman*, 2012, www.newstatesman.com/north-america/2012/01/barack-obama-interview-tea.
6. Zwicky, Arnold. "The Dangers of Satire." *Language Log*, 2008, http://languagelog.ldc.upenn.edu/nll/?p=369.
7. Hill, Evan. "Egyptian Satirist Youssef Ends TV Show." *Aljazeera America*, 2016, http://america.aljazeera.com/blogs/scrutineer/2014/6/3/egyptian-satiristyoussefendstvshow.html#commentsDiv.
8. McClennen, Sophia A. "Jon Stewart's War on Propaganda: Cruz Sound as Dogmatic as Fundamentalist Iranians." *Salon*, 2014, www.salon.com/test/2014/11/17/jon_stewarts_war_on_propaganda_hannity_cruz_sound_as_dogmatic_as_fundamentalist_iranians/.
9. Branigan, Tania. "China Bans Wordplay in Attempt at Word Control." *The Guardian*, 2014, www.theguardian.com/world/2014/nov/28/china-media-watchdog-bans-wordplay-puns.
10. Laughland, Oliver. "FBI Director Stands by Claim That North Korea Was Source of Sony Cyber-Attack." *The Guardian*, 2015, www.theguardian.com/world/2015/jan/07/fbi-director-north-korea-source-sony-cyber-attack-james-comey.
11. "Free Ramon Esono Ebale." *Voice Project*, http://voiceproject.org/campaign/free-ramon-esono-ebale/.
12. "Equatorial Guinea: Political Cartoonist Arrested." *Human Rights Watch*, 2017, www.hrw.org/news/2017/09/19/equatorial-guinea-political-cartoonist-arrested.
13. "Promotional Materials" for Bassem Youssef, *Revolution for Dummies: Laughing Through the Arab Spring*. Harper Collins, 2017.
14. Statt, Nick. "FCC Opens Investigation into Stephen Colbert's Controversial Trump Insult." *The Verge*, 2017.
15. Muldaur, Maureen. dir. "Smothered: The Censorship Struggles of the Smothers Brothers Comedy Hour." 2002, https://www.documentarysite.com/2010/12/10/smothered-the-censorship-struggles-of-the-smothers-brothers-comedy-hour/.
16. "Hustler Magazine v. Falwell." *Wikipedia*, 2019, https://en.wikipedia.org/wiki/Hustler_Magazine_v._Falwell.
17. Ibid.
18. Ibid.
19. Hustler Magazine, Inc., et al. v. Falwell, 485, U.S. 46, 46–57 (4th Cir. 1988), http://law2.umkc.edu/faculty/projects/ftrials/conlaw/hustler2.html.
20. Ibid.
21. Niehoff, Leonard N. "Of Bee Stings, Mud Pies, and Outhouses: Exploring the Value of Satire Through the Theory of Useful Untruths." *The State of Our Satirical Union*, conference paper, University of Minnesota, April 20, 2018, https://drive.google.com/

file/d/12JRwLy9ByHzf_QdEaD9H6S7ypuOsvFPr/view; "The State of Our Satirical Union," University of Minnesota, 2018, https://cla.umn.edu/hsjmc/news-events/news/state-our-satirical-union.
22. Gold, Hadas. "Donald Trump: We're Going to 'Open Up' Libel Laws." *Politico*, 2016, www.politico.com/blogs/on-media/2016/02/donald-trump-libel-laws-219866.
23. Ibid.
24. Seager, Susan. "Donald Trump Is a Libel Bully but Also a Libel Loser." *Media Law Resource Center*, www.medialaw.org/index.php?option=com_k2&view=item&id=3470.
25. Ibid.
26. Gardner, Eriq. "Why Donald Trump Is Likely to Lose a Lawsuit Against Bill Maher (Analysis)." *The Hollywood Reporter*, 2013, www.hollywoodreporter.com/thr-esq/why-donald-trump-is-lose-417806.
27. Ibid.
28. Ibid.
29. Plato. *The Republic of Plato*. Translated by Benjamin Jowett. Henry Frowde, Oxford University Press, 1888. *Project Gutenberg EBook*, www.gutenberg.org/files/55201/55201-h/55201-h.htm.
30. Descartes, René. *Delphi Collected Works of René Descartes*. Delphi Publishing, 2017, art. 178–179.
31. Sidahmed, Mazin. "Anarchist Group Installs Nude Donald Trump Statues in New York City." *The Guardian*, 2016, www.theguardian.com/us-news/2016/aug/18/nude-donald-trump-statues-new-york-indecline.
32. Hobbes, Thomas. *The Treatise on Human Nature and that on Liberty and Necessity*. J. McCreery. Black-Horse-Court, 1812.
33. Scruton, Roger and Peter Jones. "Laughter." *Aristotelian Society Supplementary Volume*, vol. 56, no. 1, July 11 1982, pp. 197–228, 208, https://doi.org/10.1093/aristoteliansupp/56.1.197.
34. Gruner, Charles R. *The Game of Humor*. Routledge, 1999.
35. Freud, Sigmund. *Jokes and Their Relation to the Unconscious*. W. W. Norton & Company, 1990, p. 118.
36. Göktürk, Deniz. "Jokes and Butts: Can We Imagine Humor in a Global Public Sphere?" *PMLA/Publications of the Modern Language Association of America*, vol. 123, no. 5, 2008, pp. 1707–1711, https://doi.org/10.1632/pmla.2008.123.5.1707.
37. Yaross Lee, Judith. "Assaults of Laughter." *Studies in American Humor*, vol. 1, no. 1, April 1, 2015, pp. v–xiv, https://doi.org/10.5325/studamerhumor.1.1.v: p.v.
38. Göktürk, Deniz. "Jokes and Butts: Can We Imagine Humor in a Global Public Sphere?" *PMLA/Publications of the Modern Language Association of America*, vol. 123, no. 5, 2008, pp. 1707–1711, https://doi.org/10.1632/pmla.2008.123.5.1707.
39. Ibid., p. 5.
40. Smith, Moira. "Humor, Unlaughter, and Boundary Maintenance." *The Journal of American Folklore*, vol. 122, no. 484, 2009, pp. 148–171, 162. *JSTOR*, www.jstor.org/stable/20487675.
41. Ibid.
42. Bruneau, Emile, et al. "They See Us as Less Than Human: Meta-Dehumanization Predicts Intergroup Conflict via Reciprocal Dehumanization." *Journal of Personality and Social Psychology*, vol. 110, no. 3, 2016, p. 343.
43. Young, Dannagal, et al. "Psychology, Political Ideology, and Humor Appreciation: Why Is Satire so Liberal?" *Psychology of Popular Media Culture*, vol. 8, 2017, https://doi.org/10.1037/ppm0000157.
44. Maclay, Kathleen. "Researchers Help Define What Makes a Political Conservative." *UCBerkeleyNews*, 2003, www.berkeley.edu/news/media/releases/2003/07/22_politics.shtml.
45. "2018 Edelman Trust Barometer." *Edelman*, 2018, www.edelman.com/sites/g/files/aatuss191/files/2018-10/2018_Edelman_Trust_Barometer_Global_Report_FEB.pdf.

46 "Public Trust in Government Remains Near Historic Lows as Partisan Attitudes Shift." *Pew Research Center*, 2017, www.people-press.org/2017/05/03/public-trust-in-government-remains-near-historic-lows-as-partisan-attitudes-shift/.
47 Baggini, Julian. "In Praise of Cynicism." *The Guardian*, 2013, www.theguardian.com/world/2013/jul/10/in-praise-of-cynicism.
48 Walsh, Kenneth. "A Nation of Cynics." *U.S. News*, 2018, www.usnews.com/news/the-report/articles/2018-01-05/president-trump-is-leading-a-nation-of-cynics.
49 Pinkleton, Bruce, et al. "Perceptions of News Media, External Efficacy, and Public Affairs Apathy in Political Decision Making and Disaffection." *Journalism & Mass Communication Quarterly*, Sage Journals, 2012, https://journals.sagepub.com/doi/abs/10.1177/1077699011428586?journalCode=jmqc&.
50 Fu, Hanlong, et al. "Reconsidering Political Cynicism and Political Involvement: A Test of Antecedents." *American Communication Journal*, 2011, http://ac-journal.org/journal/pubs/2011/summer/Cynicism_Proof.pdf.
51 Robinson, J. Gregg. "Political Cynicism and the Foreclosure Crisis." *Social Justice*, vol. 40, no. 3(133), 2014, pp. 99–118, 111. *JSTOR*, www.jstor.org/stable/24361651. Accessed 14 July 2022.
52 Riggio, Ronald. "Why Jon Stewart Is the Most Trusted Man in America." *Psychology Today*, 2009, www.psychologytoday.com/us/blog/cutting-edge-leadership/200907/why-jon-stewart-is-the-most-trusted-man-in-america.
53 Baumgartner, Jody C. and Jonathan S. Morris. "Stoned Slackers or Super Citizens? The Daily Show Viewing and Political Engagement of Young Adults." *The Stewart/Colbert Effect: Essays on the Real Impact of Fake News*, ed. Amarnath Amarasingam. McFarland, 2011, pp. 63–78, 64.
54 Lichter, Robert S., et al. *Politics Is a Joke!* Routledge, 2014, p. 9.
55 McClennen, Sophia A. and Remy Maisel. *Is Satire Saving Our Nation? Mockery and American Politics*. Palgrave Macmillan, 2014.
56 Lee, Hoon and Nojin Kwak. "The Affect Effect of Political Satire: Sarcastic Humor, Negative Emotions, and Political Participation." *Mass Communication and Society*, vol. 17, no. 3, pp. 307–328, https://doi.org/10.1080/15205436.2014.891133.
57 Chen, Hsuan-Ting, et al. "How Does Political Satire Influence Political Participation? Examining the Role of Counter- and Pro-Attitudinal Exposure, Anger, and Personal Issue Influence." *International Journal of Communication*, University of Southern California, 2017, https://ijoc.org/index.php/ijoc/article/view/6158.
58 Baumgartner, Jody and Brad Lockerbie. "Maybe It *Is* More Than a Joke: Satire, Mobilization, and Political Participation." *Social Science Quarterly*, vol. 99, 2018, pp. 1060–1074, https://doi.org/10.1111/ssqu.12501.
59 Ibid.
60 Robinson, J. Gregg. "Political Cynicism and the Foreclosure Crisis." *Social Justice*, vol. 40, no. 3(133), 2014, pp. 99–118. *JSTOR*, www.jstor.org/stable/24361651.
61 Baggini, Julian. "In Praise of Cynicism." *The Guardian*, 2013, www.theguardian.com/world/2013/jul/10/in-praise-of-cynicism.
62 Benen, Steve. "Trump Takes Aim at Public's Trust in Democratic Institutions." *MSNBC*, 2018, www.msnbc.com/rachel-maddow-show/trump-takes-aim-public-trust-democratic-institutions.
63 Gladwell, Malcolm. "The Satire Paradox—Revisionist History by Malcolm Gladwell." *YouTube* video, posted by Revisionist History, June 23, 2021, www.youtube.com/watch?v=V-EgIxRwjDA.
64 Ibid.
65 Almond, Steve. *Bad Stories: What the Hell Just Happened to Our Country*. Red Hen Press, 2018, p. 84.
66 Postman, Neil. *Amusing Ourselves to Death: Public Discourse in the Age of Show Business*. Penguin Books, 2006.
67 Vitto, Laura. "Tina Fey Knows She 'Screwed Up' in Her Charlottesville Sheet-Cake Segment for SNL." *Mashable*, 2018, https://mashable.com/2018/05/05/tina-fey-sheet-cake-charlottesville-sketch-letterman/.

68 Ibid.
69 "Weekend Update: Tina Fey on Protesting After Charlottesville – SNL." *YouTube* video, posted by *Saturday Night Live* on August 18, 2017, www.youtube.com/watch?v=iVvpXZxXWZU.
70 Ibid.
71 Vitto, Laura. "Tina Fey Knows She 'Screwed Up' in Her Charlottesville Sheet-Cake Segment for SNL." *Mashable*, 2018, https://mashable.com/2018/05/05/tina-fey-sheet-cake-charlottesville-sketch-letterman/.
72 Baumgartner, Jody, et al. "The Fey Effect: Young Adults, Political Humor, and Perceptions of Sarah Palin in the 2008 Presidential Campaign." *The Public Opinion Quarterly*, 2012. *JSTOR*, www.jstor.org/stable/41345969?seq=1#page_scan_tab_contents.
73 Moy, Patricia, et al. "Priming Effects of Late-Night Comedy." *International Journal of Public Opinion Research*, Oxford Academic, 2005, https://academic.oup.com/ijpor/article/18/2/198/674427.
74 Young, Dannagal G. and Russell M. Tisinger. "Dispelling Late-Night Myths: News Consumption Among Late-Night Comedy Viewers and the Predictors of Exposure to Various Late-Night Shows." *Harvard International Journal of Press/Politics*, vol. 11, no. 3, July 2006, pp. 113–134, https://doi.org/10.1177/1081180X05286042.
75 Lichter, Robert S., et al. *Politics Is a Joke!* Routledge, 2014.
76 Young, Dannagal G. and Russell M. Tisinger. "Dispelling Late-Night Myths: News Consumption Among Late-Night Comedy Viewers and the Predictors of Exposure to Various Late-Night Shows." *Harvard International Journal of Press/Politics*, vol. 11, no. 3, 2006, pp. 113–134, https://doi.org/10.1177/1081180X05286042.
77 Borum Chattoo, Caty and Lauren Feldman. *A Comedian and an Activist Walk into a Bar: The Serious Role of Comedy in Social Justice*. Foreword by Norman Lear. UC Press, 2020, p. 41.
78 Ibid., p. 45.
79 Ibid., p. 56.
80 Young, Dannagal G. *Irony and Outrage: The Polarized Landscape of Rage, Fear, and Laughter in the United States*. Oxford University Press, 2020, p. 45.
81 Paquette, Danielle. "Why the Most Outrageous Part of Donald Trump's 'Hot Mic' Comments isn't the Vulgar Language." *The Washington Post*, 2016, www.washingtonpost.com/news/wonk/wp/2016/10/07/the-real-issue-with-donald-trump-saying-a-man-can-do-anything-to-a-woman/?utm_term=.267f40080a94.
82 McClennen, Sophia A. "Enough with 'The Colbert Defense': Why Criminals, Bigots and Jerks Cry 'Satire!' When Exposed." *Salon*, Salon.com, June 17, 2017, www.salon.com/2017/06/17/enough-with-the-colbert-defense-why-criminals-bigots-and-jerks-cry-satire-when-exposed/.
83 Stuart, Tessa. "Donald Trump: Liar in Chief." *Rolling Stone*, 2017, www.rollingstone.com/politics/politics-features/donald-trump-liar-in-chief-115517/; "Fox's Profile." *PunditFact*, www.politifact.com/punditfact/tv/fox/.
84 Todd, Chuck. "Conway: Press Secretary Gave 'Alternative Facts'." *NBC*, 2017, www.nbcnews.com/meet-the-press/video/conway-press-secretary-gave-alternative-facts-860142147643.
85 Poniewozik, James. "Jon Stewart, the Fake Newsman Who Made a Real Difference." *Time*, 2015, https://time.com/3704321/jon-stewart-daily-show-fake-news/.
86 McClennen, Sophia A. "Stephen Colbert and Trevor Noah Step Up: Donald Trump Made *The Daily Show* and Out of Character Colbert Relevant Again." *Salon*, 2017, www.salon.com/test/2017/04/08/trevor-noah-and-stephen-colbert-step-up-donald-trump-made-the-daily-show-and-out-of-character-colbert-relevant-again/.
87 "Andy Borowitz: Trump 'Defies Satire'." *CNN*, 2017, https://money.cnn.com/video/news/2017/06/11/reliable-sources-andy-borowitz-trump-political-satire.cnnmoney/index.html.
88 Kavanaugh, Jim. "Cain: America's Too Uptight!" *CNN*, 2011, http://edition.cnn.com/2011/POLITICS/09/12/debate.cain.humor/index.html?utm_source=huffingtonpost.com&utm_medium=referral&utm_campaign=pubexchange_article.

89 Colbert, Stephen. "Herman Cain's Campaign Ad." *The Colbert Report*, Comedy Central, October 25, 2011, www.cc.com/video-clips/3uz7qn/the-colbert-report-herman-cain-s-campaign-ad.
90 Colbert, Stephen. "The Colbert Report." *Comedy Central*, 2011, www.cc.com/video-clips/3uz7qn/the-colbert-report-herman-cain-s-campaign-ad.
91 "Duterte Claimed His Rape Joke was Just Sarcasm." *The New York Post*, 2017, https://nypost.com/2017/06/01/duterte-claims-his-rape-joke-was-just-sarcasm/.
92 Clinton, Chelsea. "Hi Kevin-Duterte Is a Murderous Thug with No Regard for Human Rights: It's Important to Keep Pointing That Out & That Rape Is Never a Joke." *Twitter*, May 26, 2017, 10:57 p.m., https://twitter.com/chelseaclinton/status/868209548213051392.
93 "Coulter Under Fire for Anti-Gay Slur." *CNN*, 2007, http://edition.cnn.com/2007/POLITICS/03/04/coulter.edwards/.
94 Borchers, Callum. "Alex Jones Should Not Be Taken Seriously, According to Alex Jones' Lawyers." *The Washington Post*, 2017, www.washingtonpost.com/news/the-fix/wp/2017/04/17/trump-called-alex-jones-amazing-joness-own-lawyer-calls-him-a-performance-artist/?utm_term=.4b17f63d0e33; Quantcast, www.quantcast.com/user/login?forward=/infowars.com.
95 Otterbein, Holly. "Police: PSU Frat Posted Photos of Nude Unconscious Women on Facebook." *Philadelphia Magazine*, 2015, www.phillymag.com/news/2015/03/17/police-psu-frat-posted-photos-of-nude-unconscious-women-on-facebook/; Otterbein, Holly. "Member of Penn State's Kappa Delta Rho Defends Fraternity." *Philadelphia Magazine*, 2015, www.phillymag.com/news/2015/03/18/member-of-penn-states-kappa-delta-rho-defends-fraternity/.
96 Fausset, Richard and Serge Kovaleski. "Officials Decline to Call Fatal Stabbing of Black Student a Hate Crime." *The New York Times*, 2017, www.nytimes.com/2017/05/22/us/black-student-stabbed-maryland.html?_r=0.
97 "Survey: Daily Show/Colbert Viewers Most Knowledgeable, Fox News Viewers Rank Lowest." *Think Progress*, 2007, http://thinkprogress.org/default/2007/04/16/11946/daily-show-fox-knowledge/#.
98 Beaujon, Andrew. "Survey: NPR's Listeners Best-Informed, Fox Viewers Worst-Informed." *Poynter*, 2012, www.poynter.org/latest-news/mediawire/174826/survey-nprs-listeners-best-informed-fox-news-viewers-worst-informed/.
99 "The Humor Effect: How Laughing Helps You Remember." *Effectiviology*, https://effectiviology.com/humor-effect/.
100 Borum Chattoo, Caty and Lauren Feldman. *A Comedian and an Activist Walk into a Bar: The Serious Role of Comedy in Social Justice*. Foreword by Norman Lear. UC Press, 2020, p. 42.
101 See *Pranksters versus Autocrats* where we study 44 cases of dilemma actions. All of the examples of laughtivism we studied were effective at reframing the narrative. Popovic, Srdja and Sophia A. McClennen. *Pranksters vs. Autocrats: Why Dilemma Actions Advance Nonviolent Activism*. Cornell University Press, 2020.
102 McCarthy, Niall. "Americans Trust Jon Stewart More Than Bloomberg and the Economist." *Forbes*, 2015, www.forbes.com/sites/niallmccarthy/2015/02/11/americans-trust-jon-stewart-more-than-bloomberg-and-the-economist-infographic/#3fad46523526.
103 Kakutani, Michkito. "Is Jon Stewart the Most Trusted Man in America." *The New York Times*, 2008, www.nytimes.com/2008/08/17/arts/television/17kaku.html.
104 Rivera, Kamila. "Why Does John Oliver Feel Like the Only Person We Can Trust on TV." *Showbiz Cheatsheet*, 2019, www.cheatsheet.com/entertainment/why-does-john-oliver-feel-like-the-only-person-we-can-trust-on-tv.html/.
105 Borum Chattoo, Caty and Lauren Feldman. *A Comedian and an Activist Walk into a Bar: The Serious Role of Comedy in Social Justice*. Foreword by Norman Lear. UC Press, 2020, p. 48.

106 Ibid., p. 49.
107 Ibid., p. 50.
108 Duncombe, Stephen. *Dream: Re-Imagining Progressive Politics in an Age of Fantasy*. The New Press, 2007.
109 Duncombe, Stephen. *Dream or Nightmare*. OR Books, 2019, www.stephenduncombe.com/dreampolitik/.
110 Ibid.
111 Brewer, Paul. "Political Comedy Shows Public Participation in Politics." *International Journal of Public Opinion Research*, 2008, p. 90, www.academia.edu/424545/Political_Comedy_Shows_and_Public_Participation_In_Politics.
112 Young, Dannagal G. and Sarah Esralew. "Jon Stewart a Heretic? Surely You Jest: Political Participation and Discussion Among Viewers of Late-Night Comedy Programming." *The Stewart/Colbert Effect: Essays on the Real Impact of Fake News*, ed. Amarnath Amarasingam. McFarland, 2011, pp. 99–116.
113 Van Zoonen, Liesbet. *Entertaining the Citizen: When Politics and Popular Culture Converge*. Rowman & Littlefield, 2005.
114 "'Sanity' Rally Seen By 2 Million TV Viewers." *Boston.com*, 2010, http://archive.boston.com/ae/tv/articles/2010/11/01/sanity_rally_seen_by_2_million_tv_viewers/.
115 Popovik, Srdja and Mladen Joksic. "Why Dictators Don't Like Jokes." *Foreign Policy*, 2013, https://foreignpolicy.com/2013/04/05/why-dictators-dont-like-jokes/.
116 Ibid.
117 Ibid.
118 Popovic, Srdja and Sophia A. McClennen. *Pranksters vs. Autocrats: Why Dilemma Actions Advance Nonviolent Activism*. Cornell University Press, 2020, p. 49.
119 Glazier, Rebecca. "Using Satire to Stimulate Critical Thinking in the Political Science Classroom." *APSA*, 2011, Annual Meeting Paper, SSRN, https://ssrn.com/abstract=1903286; *ResearchGate*, 2019, www.researchgate.net/publication/228212448_Using_Satire_to_Stimulate_Critical_Thinking_in_the_Political_Science_Classroom.
120 Glazier, Rebecca. "The Teacher: Satire and Efficacy in the Political Science Classroom." *PS: Political Science and Politics*, www.rebeccaglazier.net/wp-content/uploads/2013/06/Glazier-Satire-and-Efficacy-PS-2014.pdf.
121 Baumgartner, Jody and Jonathan S. Morris. "The Daily Show Effect: Candidate Evaluations, Efficacy, and American Youth." *American Politics Research*, vol. 34, no. 3, May 2006, pp. 341–367, https://doi.org/10.1177/1532673X05280074.
122 Young, Dannagal G. *Irony and Outrage*. Oxford University Press, p. 187.
123 Ibid.
124 Ibid.
125 Ibid.
126 Baum, Matthew. "Soft News and Political Knowledge: Evidence of Absence or Absence of Evidence?" *Political Communication*, vol. 20, 2003, pp. 173–190, https://doi.org/10.1080/10584600390211181.
127 Cao, Xiaoxia and Paul R. Brewer, "Political Comedy Shows and Public Participation in Politics." International Journal of Public Opinion Research, vol. 20, no. 1, Spring 2008, pp. 90–99, https://doi.org/10.1093/ijpor/edm030.
128 Young, Dannagal G. "Theories and Effects of Political Humor: Discounting Cues, Gateways, and the Impact of Incongruities." *The Oxford Handbook of Political Communication*, August 2017, www.oxfordhandbooks.com/view/10.1093/oxfordhb/9780199793471.001.0001/oxfordhb-9780199793471-e-29.
129 Moy, P., Xenos, M.A. and Hess, V.K. "Communication and Citizenship: Mapping the Political Effects of Infotainment." *Mass Communication & Society*, vol. 8, 2005, pp. 111–131.
130 Baumgartner, Jody and Brad Lockerbie. "Maybe It *Is* More Than a Joke: Satire, Mobilization, and Political Participation." *Social Science Quarterly*, vol. 99, 2018, https://doi.org/10.1111/ssqu.12501.

131 Sørensen, Majken Jul. *Humour in Political Activism: Creative Nonviolent Resistance*. Palgrave Macmillan, 2016.
132 Day, Amber. *Satire and Dissent: Interventions in Contemporary Political Debate*. Indiana University Press, 2011, p. 146.
133 Popović, Srdja and Matthew Miller. *Blueprint for Revolution: How to Use Rice Pudding, Lego Men, and Other Nonviolent Techniques to Galvanize Communities, Overthrow Dictators, or Simply Change the World*. Spiegel & Grau, 2015.
134 Sørensen, Majken Jul. *Humour in Political Activism: Creative Nonviolent Resistance*. Palgrave Macmillan, 2016, p. 96.
135 McClennen, Sophia A. and Remy Maisel. *Is Satire Saving Our Nation? Mockery and American Politics*. Palgrave Macmillan, 2014.

7
THE LAST LAUGH
Satire's Secret Weapon

Thirty-odd years ago, one of the most famous public service announcement ad campaigns was launched. "This is your brain on drugs" featured a man asking the audience if it understood the dangers of drug use.[1] He then held up an egg and said, "This is your brain." He motioned to a frying pan, "This is drugs." He then cracked the egg into the pan and as the egg fried said, "This is your brain on drugs."[2]

What does your brain look like when it is on Trump? Most attention to the negative consequences of the Trump presidency tends to focus on the dismantling of federal agencies, the gutting of public policies, the divisive and aggressive politics, the cronyism, racism, and elitism, the corruption, and the assault on facts. What is often missed is the overall ways in which Trumpism has had a collective effect on how the nation thinks. Policies can be undone, but mindsets less so. Thus, the real threat to our nation caused by the Trump era may well be the mind warp it caused and continues to cause.[3] This is not only true for those who exhibit extreme belief bias and simply accept everything they hear on Fox News or Newsmax or from the Trump camp; it is also a problem for those of us who would like to remain critically analytical.

We now have significant evidence that the Trump era created a cognitive load— a mental exhaustion of the nation—one so significant that fake news headlines or false statements can be taken as true if repeated enough. One study by Gordon Pennycook, Tyrone Cannon, and David Rand on the cognitive processing of fake news stories showed that, "[I]ncreased perceptions of accuracy for repeated fake news headlines occurs [sic] even when the stories are labeled as contested by fact checkers, or are inconsistent with the reader's political ideology."[4] The point is that an ongoing barrage of misinformation can get to us all, wear us down, and impede our judgment.

Some critics have found an apt comparison between the Trump era and George Orwell's *1984*. While the dystopian novel has a lot of insight to offer us, it can't

DOI: 10.4324/9781003294177-7

actually capture the cognitive effects of Trumpism, and that is because the Trump team did not just brainwash us or numb our brains with newspeak; it actually implemented, consciously or not, a complex, five-point strategy poised to make our minds shut down critical thinking. Each of these tactics has a special impact on cognitive functioning.

An Epidemic of Lies

The lying of Trump was legendary. But we paid less attention to the cognitive impact of processing an endless stream of lies. As Maria Konnikova wrote in *Politico* back in 2017, all presidents lie, but Trump was in a category of his own, with a whopping 70 percent of his statements coming in as false.[5]

The lies are certainly bad, especially when they are the basis for policy, but Konnikova explains that one of the most pernicious effects of a serial liar is cognitive: "When we are overwhelmed with false, or potentially false, statements, our brains pretty quickly become so overworked that we stop trying to sift through everything."[6] For Konnikova, the frightening reality is that Trump's endless lying runs the risk of colonizing the brains of those who never even supported him. She cites research that shows that the brain has to first accept a lie as true in order to analyze it, and then refute it. Over time, the brain tires of that process and slowly starts to accept the lies as true. She refers to a fascinating, if disheartening, 2015 study that showed that if people repeated the phrase "The Atlantic Ocean is the largest ocean on Earth" enough times, the Atlantic Ocean started to seem like the largest ocean on Earth.[7] Eventually, if we are overloaded with constant lies, our brains become too exhausted to reject the lie. Before we know it, claims that are obviously false, like allegations of massive voter fraud during an election, can seem true.[8]

But there's more. Trump's fabrications are a special type of lying. He is what CNN called the "gaslighter in chief."[9] Gaslighting depends on the creation of a parallel universe that blurs any real connection to the truth, and it is a common practice for narcissists. "The techniques include saying and doing things and then denying it, blaming others for misunderstanding, disparaging their concerns as oversensitivity, claiming outrageous statements were jokes or misunderstandings, and other forms of twilighting the truth."[10] Gaslighting is an especially abusive form of lying. Psychologists explain that it "can lead to the victim losing all trust in their own judgment and reality."[11] It results in self-doubt, angst, turmoil, and guilt.

Trump also excels at bullshit, which is its own separate category of lying. Here, the liar actually has no idea whatsoever what is actually true. They just make things up, state them with confidence, and refuse to accept any correction. That process also takes a significant toll on the mind of the person listening to all of the bullshit.

In his first 406 days as president, Trump made 2,436 misleading or false claims, an average of six per day.[12] Most analyses of Trump's false statements, like the running tab kept by *The Washington Post*, lumped his lies together with his bullshit—and that was a mistake. As Gordon Pennycook explains, "The difference between bullshit and lying is that bullshit is constructed without any concern for the truth.

It's designed to impress rather than inform. And then lying, of course, is very concerned with the truth—but subverting it."[13] Understood this way, it seems clear that Trump bullshits as much as, if not more than, he lies. Even better, he admits to—even gloats about—his constant bullshitting. In one example, he bragged that he just made up assertions of trade imbalances between the United States and Canada when talking to Canadian Prime Minister Justin Trudeau.[14]

An Assault On Logic

Critical thinking doesn't just require facts; it requires the ability to reason, deduce, infer, and analyze. Those skills have also been under attack in the Trump era, too. Melissa McCarthy's impersonation of Press Secretary Sean Spicer, during which she ranted to the press that she was just "using [their] words" when in fact the words she was using were not coming from the press but rather from the Trump camp, reminds us that circular logic, tautology, and flawed thinking dominated the arguments made by the Trump White House.[15]

Jet Heer explains that fact-checking Trump is simply not sufficient to understand the cognitive effects of his statements. According to Heer, "Fact-checking Trump is vitally important, but it doesn't go far enough. Unless we analyze how he's attacking not just facts but also logic, we can't measure the full damage he's doing and respond accordingly."[16] Heer keys into the fact that Trump contradicts himself constantly and that he uses "kettle logic," a practice whereby mutually incompatible concepts are fused together at the same time. To illustrate how Trump uses kettle logic, Heer points out that, during the 2016 campaign, Trump variously said that he opposed the Iraq War before it started; that he opposed Obama's withdrawal from Iraq; that America should have taken Iraqi oil; that he opposed putting more boots on the ground; *and* that America should re-invade Iraq.[17,18,19]

Contradictions, though, are only the tip of the illogical iceberg for Trump. Trump and his allies practice an ongoing and incessant assault on all forms of logic. And without logic, we can't get any real thinking done of any kind.

The Trump team offered an ongoing lesson in a range of examples of poor logic. Trump excels, for example, at the red herring—the deliberate use of a distraction to avoid actually answering a question or explaining oneself. Trump regularly distracts and deflects when asked a clear and specific question. When asked about his lewd behavior in the wake of the "pussy grabbing" scandal, for example, Trump responded by offering a red herring and talking about ISIS.[20]

Then there is faulty reasoning that inaccurately links cause and effect. One example is Trump's claim that China has created the climate change "hoax" so that it can beat us in manufacturing. Over and over, it has been the case that Trump doesn't just have his facts wrong; he can't make sense of them either.

Flaws in logic have taken place outside of the Trump camp, too. During the Republican primary leading up to the 2016 election, the mainstream media kept treating him like a legitimate candidate—a move that displayed the poor logic of a false equivalency.[21]

Flawed logic offers a special form of cognitive toll because it suggests that it makes sense to process information in a particular, yet illogical, way. These sorts of deceptions can take many forms, but, as John Oliver has pointed out, one of the Trump team's favorites is "whataboutism."[22] "It implies that all actions regardless of context share a moral equivalency," says Oliver.[23] "And since nobody is perfect, all criticism is hypocritical and everyone should do whatever they want."[24] Trump practiced whataboutism, for example, when he suggested that there were "many sides" to blame when a neo-Nazi intentionally drove a car into a mass of people and killed protestor Heather Heyer in Charlottesville.

But it's even worse. Brendan Nyhan and Jason Reifler conducted one of the most revealing—and depressing—studies of truth, logic, and politics.[25] They showed that when conservatives hold a false belief and are shown irrefutable evidence to the contrary, rather than change their mind, they actually cling more tenaciously to their misinformed belief. They found that Republicans held more firmly to their false beliefs about the Iraq War when exposed to correcting information. They practiced "motivated reasoning" and were skeptical of any information that contradicted their ideas. They simply wouldn't listen to any source of information from outside their bubble.

The Blustering Bully

There is a lot of research on the long-term effects of bullying on children who grow up to be anxious and depressed adults. But increasing attention is turning to the effects of bullying on adults.[26] Much of that work has looked at workplace bullying and the psychological distress it causes.[27]

Now we have to contend with the reality that Trump created a government defined by bullying and bluster.[28] Before, during, and after the 2016 election, Trump showed all of the signs of a malignant narcissist, and that is the quintessential bully personality.[29] His *Twitter* rants, when he still had a *Twitter* account, may have been one of the most visible signs of this behavior, but it is a pervasive and ongoing feature of his politics and persona.

Trump also surrounded himself with bullies: from Steve Bannon to Sean Spicer to Kellyanne Conway to Roger Stone, the Trump team consistently used a tactic of bluster and bully to shout down, silence, shame, and attack their critics. As Jeb Lund explained for *Esquire*, Trump's "team is a hammer, and every problem, including you, is shaped like a nail. They have no sympathy."[30]

If there was one constant in the entire array of Trump positions, from the Muslim ban,[31] to eliminating EPA references to climate change,[32] to Immigration and Customs Enforcement (ICE) raids,[33] to making up terrorist attacks that didn't happen,[34] it was bullying, the type of bullying that destroys lives and incites fear. The endless litany of derogatory nicknames Trump uses to address his critics is yet another blatant example of his bully persona.

As we can note in the rise of white nationalist groups who put their racism on display in an increasingly aggressive fashion and who followed Trump's call to violently storm the Capitol on January 6, 2021, in an effort to overturn the 2020 election, there is significant evidence to show that Trump started an epidemic of bullying. In schools, in workplaces, and in communities, Trump-inspired intimidation is out of control. The psychological impact of this sort of harassment is anxiety, hopelessness, fear, and anger.

The Society of the Spectacle

French theorist Guy Debord published *The Society of the Spectacle* in 1967. One of his famous theses was, "All that once was directly lived has become mere representation."[35] For Debord, the society of the spectacle meant that the social relationship between people was mediated by images. But even more importantly, he argued that passive identification with the spectacle supplants genuine activity.[36]

Writing 50 years ago, Debord accurately imagined life under the first reality TV president. Then, almost 20 years after Debord, Neil Postman wrote *Amusing Ourselves to Death*, a study that argued for Aldous Huxley's vision of a dystopian world, in which people voluntarily sacrifice rights because they are too distracted by hedonist consumption to resist.[37] For Postman, control of the population would come from our substitution of entertainment for civic engagement. Postman was especially worried about the role that television was playing in shaping public perceptions.

Both Debord and Postman recognized that the mass-mediated spectacle would have dire consequences for democracy and political action. Psychological research also confirms that constantly watching media spectacles has a negative effect on the brain.[38] Consumption of an endless stream of spectacle makes it harder for the brain to connect details to a larger context, and it leads to attention deficits and distractibility.

The Trump presidency was the first openly and unabashedly spectacle-driven administration in U.S. history. It depended on destroying the public's ability to see the bigger picture, and it relied on substituting bluster for substance and glitz for reality. It functioned as that shiny object we can't stop watching. The longer we were mesmerized by it, the more our critical thinking suffered.

As Amanda Taub and Brendan Nyhan explain, "[S]ocial science research suggests that Mr. Trump's alternative version of reality may appeal to his supporters."[39] According to Taub and Nyhan, "Partisan polarization is now so extreme in the United States that it affects the way that people consume and understand information—the facts they believe, and what events they think are important."[40]

The Endless Barrage

Remember when there was speculation that Trump would win but would immediately outsource his duties as president?[41] No one could have imagined that after only one month in office there would be such a violent flurry of executive orders and other devastating policy decisions. And certainly no one imagined that after he lost the 2020 election he would still be exhausting us with a daily onslaught of corruption, graft, unethical behavior, and malevolent policy platforms.

As Jon Stewart put it when he appeared as a guest on *The Late Show with Stephen Colbert* early in the Trump presidency, "The presidency is supposed to age the President, not the public."[42]

The endless barrage of Trump is overwhelming. As Frank Bruni put it in the *New York Times*, Trump "has succeeded at nothing so much as devising an analogue to the shock-and-awe military campaign: It's the appall-and-anesthetize political strategy."[43] It leaves the public numb, in shock, exhausted, and brain-dead.

Folks often decide to take a break from the news, only to find out something horrible has happened while they looked away. It's cognitively exhausting.

After the 2016 election, doctors reported patients coming in and asking for medications to help with Trump anxiety.[44] The Trump administration led to additional medications prescribed, extra ER visits, delayed procedures, missed work, and more—and this was all before the increased medical needs brought on by the COVID-19 pandemic. Even without the intended destruction of the Affordable Care Act, and not even counting the major medical fallout from COVID, there was proof that the nation suffered "a major medical toll from [Trump's 2016] election."[45]

This is all to say that, in the end, perhaps one of the most significant effects of the Trump presidency may well be on the order of cognitive functioning, critical thinking, and rational thought. We can hear our brains sizzling in the Trump frying pan, and it's the sound of the nation collectively cooking its mind.

Taken together, the preceding five strategies were destined to severely mess with our heads. This is your brain on Trump, and it is not pretty. As dire as this all may seem, there are, however, as the next section explains, ways to fight back and keep our minds from burning out completely.

Strategies to Fight Trump-Era Brain Rot

In an appendix to George Orwell's dystopian novel *1984*, he describes "The Principles of Newspeak," the official language of the authoritarian regime in his novel: "Newspeak was designed not to extend but to diminish the range of thought."[46] As mentioned earlier, for many, *1984* served as a guide to the Trump era.[47] But it was not just the lies and the alternate reality of Trump that sparked parallels to Orwell's novel, it was also the fact that his administration threatened to diminish our range of thought. As I have explained, the Trump era was designed to create massive cognitive fatigue. In fact, unlike the grim world of *1984*, the Trump brain rot is far more complex than Orwell's dystopia. It included five main strategies, which, as I've described, were a real threat to our mental capacities.

Since Trump's 2016 election and in the wake of the "big lie," there has been considerable attention to how best to form a productive resistance to his platform, policies, and outsized personality. There have been debates over the pros and cons of marches[48] and the strengths and limits of uniting around the Democratic Party,[49] but there has been much less attention to the fact that any real resistance requires us to be at our cognitive best.

There are a number of critical ways that we can work to strengthen our cognitive skills in the face of a daily assault on advanced thinking. Continuing, for example, to offer rational arguments in the face of irrational ones is key. Seeking ways to let off steam and escape from a state of anxiety is critical as well. We know, for instance, that exercise is a great way to keep the mind nimble. Research on ways to defend the brain from dementia and Alzheimer's Disease correlates with research on how to survive the alienating effects of authoritarianism: both approaches agree that, for the mind to thrive, we need to socialize and develop affective relationships. A number of studies indicate that maintaining strong social connections prevents cognitive decline.[50] All of the research on ways to develop, strengthen, and maintain cognitive ability concurs that we need to constantly seek new ways to challenge our minds.[51] Playing games, doing crosswords or Sudoku, and doing puzzles are all standard recommendations to keep our minds active.

But, what is perhaps more fun to consider since the 2016 election is the fact that much research points to the cognitive benefits of swearing. *Psychology Today* reports that scholars are amassing research that shows that anger is a potent form of social communication[52] and that it fuels optimism, creative brainstorming, and problem-solving by focusing the mind and mood in highly refined ways.[53] It also explains that anger is the polar opposite of fear, sadness, disgust, and anxiety. "When the gall rises, it propels the irate toward challenges they otherwise would flee and actions to get others to do what they, the angry, wish."[54]

In another article published in *Psychology Today*, Neel Burton explains that swearing is extremely good for the mind.[55] It reduces pain, it helps give us a greater sense of control, it is a form of nonviolent retribution, and it helps build fun bonds with our peers. Another scientific study showed that people who swear are smart.[56] Angry swearing helps us to sharpen our minds, build our community, and activate the mental joy of humor—all actions that help to defend the brain against the dulling effects of Trumpland. This all means that an angry, well-timed swear may be a powerful antidote to Trump-era brain rot. And swears that are creative, sarcastic, and sassy are the best of all.

In fact, we have ample evidence that many have resorted to creative swearing to deal with Trump. In one well-known example after Trump arrived in Scotland back in 2016 and commended the Scots "for taking their country back," his mistaken interpretation of their referendum on nationalism was met with a flurry of invectives. One of the best was a tweet that referred to Trump as a "tiny fingered, Cheeto-faced, ferret wearing shitgibbon."[57] That insult went viral.

But talking back should take multiple forms, and in certain contexts the best talking back includes sass, snark, and sarcasm. We have often heard the phrase, "Sarcasm is the body's natural response to stupid." Except it isn't just a response to stupid; it is actually a marker of intelligence. And that's where the secret weapon of satire comes in. It may just be the case that consuming and producing satire is one of the most effective ways to resist the cognitive load that will surely be part of the Trump legacy.

The Secret Weapon of Satire

In a National Rifle Association (NRA) TV ad, a man stands in front of a TV screen that airs a series of clips. Among them is a shot of John Oliver saying the words "National Rifle Association" and another is a shot of Alec Baldwin impersonating Donald Trump on *Saturday Night Live* (*SNL*). The rest of the shots are from talk shows, pundits, or cable news reporting. As the clips roll, the man takes a sledgehammer to the TV and smashes it. Then a slogan appears: "The truth is our greatest weapon."[58]

It is a stunningly stupid ad. But it does offer a window into two very different ways of thinking, one that pits the right-wing brain against the left.

Think about it: what better way for the NRA to expose its penchant for aggressive hyperbole and its snowflake logic than to have a man sledgehammer a TV and equate that act with the "truth"? According to the NRA's logic, its weapon is the truth, which is a sledgehammer that it will use to destroy anything or anyone who says things it doesn't like. This is the ad it uses to suggest it is being misrepresented as a group of aggressive lunatics. Its irrationality is only outdone by its irony.

It's also stunning for its decision to target Oliver and Baldwin, because it does suggest the very real ways that political comedians feel like a threat to the right. No one needs reminding of Donald Trump's incessant agitation over Alec Baldwin's impersonations of him on *SNL*. Recall that Trump wasn't just upset at the way that he was being presented as a bombastic fool (hardly a creative stretch); Trump also suggested that folks were "forced" to watch the impersonations,[59] that the comedy was "one-sided" and "biased,"[60] and that he deserved "equal time."[61]

But one of the best examples of the right-wing witch hunt over late-night comedy came from House Intelligence Committee Chair Devin Nunes, who didn't take kindly to a sketch Stephen Colbert did on *The Late Show* that mocked him. Colbert traveled to Washington, D.C., to grill lawmakers about the investigation into the Trump campaign's possible collusion with Russia.[62] While there, he released his own redacted memo about Nunes. Nunes later called into Neil Cavuto's *Fox Business* show and called Colbert's jokes a "danger" to the country.[63] "Conservatives in this country are under attack," Nunes said. "They attack people who are trying to get to the truth."[64]

While it would be a stretch to consider late-night comedians dangerous to anything, they do pose a threat to the right-wing's version of the truth and the mindset required to accept it. And that's why the right keeps targeting them. Clearly, those on the right, like Trump himself, don't like being ridiculed. But that isn't the main reason why these comedians are viewed as a threat. Instead, the real challenge comedians pose is to the right-wing version of the "truth"—a truth that is actually grounded in lies, bullshit, and faulty logic. And what really makes the right's antagonistic attitude toward comedians interesting is the fact that the comedians aren't just challenging right-wing truth claims; they are thwarting the cognitive processes that lead us to accept right-wing falsehoods as true.

The problem with the culture of lies—besides the cognitive toll it takes on all of us—is that it may well be closely tied to a decline in democratic values. A study released by the Democracy Voter Study Group found that there is an alarming level of support for authoritarian rule among U.S. voters.[65] Trump himself has displayed no fondness for democracy, but we now know that only a slim majority of Americans (54 percent) consistently express a pro-democratic position. In addition, the highest levels of support for authoritarian leadership come from those who are disaffected, disengaged from politics, deeply distrustful of experts, culturally conservative, and have negative attitudes toward racial minorities. That is also the same demographic that doesn't like political satire and may even consider it "dangerous" to the nation.

After the election, Michael Moore talked about the political value of using an army of comedy to bring down Trump.[66] And, as I explained in the previous chapter, we have ample evidence to suggest that political satire and comedic resistance can have tremendous political impact. We know that satire has direct and positive benefits for democracy, but much less attention has been given to its cognitive benefits. Yet, as I will argue here in my conclusion, it may well be the cognitive benefits of satire that are its secret weapon. Democracies depend not just on active, informed, and energized citizens but also on citizens who can exhibit advanced cognitive skills.

So, if the right's "greatest weapon" is a distorted, illogical, twisted truth; the left's is satire. One shuts the brain down; the other lights it up.

There is considerable proof that those who consume and produce satire are more creative, more intelligent, and more able to handle nuance and complexity. This is all to say that satire isn't just fun and mobilizing; it is also linked to being clever and more critically reflective. Satirical comedy does more than just poke at a thin-skinned narcissist like Trump; practicing satire and processing irony actually make one smarter, more intellectually nimble, and more creative.

Scholars who look at the political effects of satire often focus on the target of the joke rather than the structure of it. That is to say that they look at the content and not the form. For example, when trying to understand why there is far more satire from the left than the right, a common assumption is that the reason for this is the content of the satire. As Stephen Colbert once famously explained when asked why there were no right-wing satire shows, "Going after the status quo is not necessarily a conservative thing to do; it's antithetical to the idea of conservatism. Comedy is all about change. So, it's going to be a challenge for them."[67]

There is certainly some truth to this, but, as research by Dannagal Young, Benjamin Gagozzi, Abigail Goldring, Shannon Poulsen, and Erin Drouin shows, it is actually the structure and form of satire that most vex conservatives.[68] In fact, their research demonstrates that the partisan breakdown over satire is far more closely related to different ways of thinking than it is to tolerance for questioning the status quo. As they explain it, there is an ideological breakdown between minds that enjoy effortful thinking and those that don't. What's more, study after study has shown that these habits do break down across party lines. One study from 1996 found that, "[I]ndividuals high, in contrast to low, in need for cognition tend to have active, exploring minds; through their sense and intellect, they reach and draw out information from their environments."[69] Other studies conducted since the turn of the millennium confirm these trends and show that the need for cognitive challenge—understood as effortful, complex thinking—tends to be higher for political liberals than for conservatives.[70]

There are basically two core structures to satire: exaggeration and irony. And to further complicate things, these forms are often combined, as they were, for example, in Alec Baldwin's impersonations of Trump for *SNL*. Exaggeration is simply taking a concept and magnifying its traits. Exaggeration can yield interesting cognitive effects because it asks the brain to understand the gap between the original and the exaggeration. That process tends to have the added benefit of asking the mind to consider the magnified traits. So, for example, when Baldwin exaggerates Trump's hubris, he asks the audience to reflect on the original hubris itself.

Sarcasm and irony operate differently, and they are considered to be harder to cognitively process. Both types of communication depend on the ability to understand inverted meaning. What is said literally is not what is meant. So, for example, if it is a cold, slushy day and one is asked how one likes the weather, if the answer is, "I love it when it is warm like this," then the listener knows that the speaker does not mean what was said. That is sarcasm.

Sarcasm is a subset of irony, which includes a wide range of ways that meaning can be delivered with an inversion of ideas. It would be ironic, for example, for an expert on how to avoid shark bites to be bitten by a shark. That example is not sarcastic, nor is it satirical, but it still requires the mind to process opposing ideas. And, in fact, it is an example of what we call situational irony. As I've explained throughout this book, satire and sarcasm tend to deploy rhetorical/creative irony—that is, irony through the inverted meanings of words and symbols—and they often use creative irony to expose situational irony. In one classic example, Colbert, when he was in character on *The Colbert Report*, used to like to ask conservative guests on his show, "George Bush: great president or greatest president?" The irony, of course, was that Colbert did not think Bush was great at all. This line also offers an excellent example of how satire can mock faulty logic, because Colbert offers a false choice, neither of which he actually agrees with.

Irony is hard to understand. It is even hard for experts who spend their whole lives analyzing it. Research has shown that some people just don't get it. They miss the intended meaning altogether, as was the case with conservatives who watched *The Colbert Report* and missed the fact that Colbert was playing the character of a right-wing pundit.[71]

The cognitive complexity in processing satire comes from the fact that the brain has to take in information and then process its meaning in a way that differs from what was initially perceived. That process can be cognitively exhausting, and it explains the way that more complex irony, like a Harold Pinter play, will be appreciated much less often than easier irony, like a John Oliver pun. But all irony requires a sharp, nimble mind. And it requires the brain to work. In fact, scientific research proves that those who regularly use and accurately detect sarcasm are smarter than those who don't.[72] In a piece for *Salon*, Francesca Gino explained that snark and sarcasm are valuable in fostering intelligence and creativity: "Because the brain must think creatively to understand or convey a sarcastic comment, sarcasm may lead to clearer and more creative thinking."[73] And, as Srdja Popovic explains in *Blueprint for Revolution*, the use of laughtivism for nonviolent protest encourages creativity.[74]

There is a growing body of work that uses imaging studies to show that many parts of the brain are involved in processing sarcasm. Katherine P. Rankin conducted a neurological study that determined that the detection of sarcasm requires advanced abilities to appreciate context and "figure[e] out what others are thinking."[75] Li Huang, Francesca Gino, and Adam Galinsky did a study that found that, "[B]oth the construction and interpretation of sarcasm lead to greater creativity because they activate abstract thinking."[76] Overall, a number of studies have shown that, "Sarcasm seems to exercise the brain more than sincere statements do. Scientists who have monitored the electrical activity of the brains of test subjects exposed to sarcastic statements have found that brains have to work harder to understand sarcasm."[77]

The creativity linked to processing irony and sarcasm is directly linked to the fact that those who produce and consume irony and sarcasm need to be open to ambiguity, nuance, and layered meaning, and they need to accept communication that does not offer simple closure. As the study by Young et al. found, there is a real partisan breakdown when it comes to these cognitive processes. Conservatives prefer closure and don't tolerate ambiguity well. Conservatives "often report a higher threat salience than do liberals, a tendency that often translates into greater psychological need to reduce uncertainty."[78]

Those who enjoy and create satire don't just break down across party lines; there may be a significant cognitive difference in how those who regularly consume satire handle lies and those who don't. While more research is needed to fully make the case, there seem to be two main reasons why satire consumers may be better at detecting falsehoods than those who don't consume this type of humor.

One of the big differences has to do with the types of cognitive activities people enjoy. Satire lovers enjoy using their reflective cognitive abilities, which are effortful, typically deliberative, and require working memory, over intuitive cognitive abilities, which don't require higher-order cognitive skills. When I interviewed Gordon Pennycook about the potential of satire to serve as a defense against Trump-era falsehoods, he remained skeptical that satire could strengthen mental fitness as a defense against falsehoods, serving—if you will—as a mental gym to strengthen the mind, but he did acknowledge that there may well be an overlap between people who are both willing and able to think analytically and satire viewers. "People do break down," he explained, "according to the degree that they are willing and eager to engage in analytic reasoning."[79]

Pennycook et al. explained that theories of reasoning break down between intuitive thinking and analytic thinking. The first type is autonomously cued, whereas the second requires effortful thinking. We can see this breakdown in types of jokes, where a silly slapstick stunt is processed intuitively and a John Oliver monologue requires analytical thinking. As Chin explains, processing satire demands "mental gymnastics," where the mind is able "to see beyond the literal meaning of the words and understand that the speaker may be thinking of something entirely different."[80] This process develops what cognitive scientists call "theory of mind," where the brain is able to process a range of cues, such as tone of voice, body language, and context, in highly nuanced ways.

But here is one of the more interesting parts of this research: the mind that likes to process satire doesn't just have the cognitive ability to do it; it also has the willingness. As Pennycook et al. explain, "[T]o be a good reasoner, one must have both the capacity to do whatever computation is necessary (i.e., cognitive ability, intelligence) and the willingness to engage deliberative reasoning processes (i.e., analytic cognitive style; thinking disposition)."[81]

A number of studies have suggested that those who support right-wing ideology are more susceptible to bullshit,[82] more governed by belief bias, and less tolerant of irony and humorous exaggeration.[83] But, as the recent studies on fake news processing show, both the left and the right can fall for fake news. The critical difference, then, isn't simply left or right political views, but analytical or intuitive thinkers.

One of the key reasons why satire may prove to be an important secret weapon in the age of Trump is the connections between how the brain processes irony and how it processes a lie. As I mentioned earlier, when the brain encounters a lie, it must first accept it as true and then refute it. Research shows that ultimately the brain tires of this process, which is why repetition that the Atlantic Ocean is the largest ocean will eventually convince the mind to accept that falsehood as true. As I've explained, the barrage of lies in the Trump era is truly of concern for the health of our democracy. The cognitive overload is real, and its negative effects on advanced higher-order thinking are a threat to an active and engaged citizenry. This is all to show that there is now proof that the mainstreaming of bullshit and lies in the Trump era is indeed rotting our brains. It was first thought that one way to prevent the spread of false information would be to flag it by third-party fact-checking, but the study just cited showed that that effort did not sufficiently help.

And that's where the comedians come in. Thus far, there have been no studies that have compared the cognitive processing of satire with the cognitive processing of falsehoods. But there is significant corollary research to show that it may well be true that the best cognitive defense against Trump-era falsehoods is satirical comedy. We know, for instance, that those who consume sarcasm are smarter,[84] more creative, and better at reading context.[85] All useful tools to process lies.

The really remarkable part of this story, and the one that is most relevant in the Trump age of lies, is that the process for understanding irony is remarkably similar to that of processing a lie. In both cases, the brain has to be able to distinguish between what is said and what is true. And in both cases, the brain has to reconcile ambiguity, incongruence, and the misuse of words. It further has to process tone, context, and body language to infer meaning. As Young et al. explain, the brain first has to process irony literally, then use context to adjust meaning and understand the irony.[86] And, in contrast to the way that the mind tires of processing lies and BS, when the mind processes irony, it doesn't get tired of doing it. It doesn't lose its skills of distinguishing between what was said and what was meant. Even more importantly, it enjoys the experience of processing the irony.

We knew back when Jon Stewart and Stephen Colbert were on Comedy Central that their viewers were among the most informed on issues of any group consuming news.[87] But now the role of satire in informing the public may be even more important—satirists may be the one thing that is reliably keeping analytical thinkers engaged. It's important to note that sarcastic statements are like a true lie. "You're saying something you don't literally mean, and the communication works as intended only if your listener gets that you're insincere," explains Richard Chin.[88]

What is perhaps most interesting about the way in which satire works as a foil for Trump-era mental manipulations is that satire is designed to go after the three main ways our brains are constantly being duped: lies, bullshit, and faulty logic. In one example of satire mocking a Trump lie, Colbert called out Trump for claiming that his State of the Union Address had the highest number of viewers in history.[89] Colbert remained stunned that Trump needed to lie about his numbers and then decided to respond by using ironic exaggeration: "So let me just say right now, in advance, congratulations to President Trump on winning the Super Bowl. Well played. . . . Also, you make a great Black Panther."[90] This example shows how satire is effective at honing skills of skepticism, a necessary practice to detect bullshit. There is a real corollary between satire consumers and skeptics—a trend that further explains habits of the mind that help to defend against Trump-era cognitive fatigue.

But here is another critical twist to the story. We know that fake news headlines, Trump bullshit, and the NRA's skewed logic do in fact get cognitive traction even among those of us not predisposed to accept those falsehoods. Yet, those viewers who watch satire and other types of ironic comedy do not lose the ability to detect the ways that these comedians use creative deception to be funny. Why do we get tired of processing lies, but not of processing ironic comedy? And are satire consumers better at detecting falsehoods?

That's where pleasure comes in. To process ironic humor cognitively involves pleasure. There is a cognitive reward for processing a joke that leads to laughter or amusement or a sense of self-satisfaction. Jokes engage both analytical and affective cognitive processes. Watching Samantha Bee or Colbert or Oliver dissect falsehoods is both analytically engaging and fun. The element of fun may be part of the reason why we keep getting the joke but get worn down by incessant lies. When lies in the form of ironic statements are processed through comedy, we don't lose the ability to detect them as false. Colbert talks about how satire "alleviates fog off of the mind," and Egyptian comedian Bassem Youssef reminds us that we can't be afraid when we are laughing at a joke. The positive affect connected to consuming and processing satire not only helps the mind to remember the joke; it also serves as a salve against the cognitive fatigue of living in an atmosphere of lies, bullying, and bullshit.

While satire is not typically belly laugh humor; it is still funny. It offers the mind a unique combination in which it has to actively use reasoning skills while receiving pleasure. Research also shows that humor "reduces or eliminates the combination of fear and/or anger called 'stress'," which, as explained earlier, blossomed in the Trump era. Studies confirm that when we are confronted with stress, if "we shift to the play mode of humor, our heart rate, blood pressure, and muscle tension decrease, as do levels of epinephrine, norepinephrine, and cortisol."[91]

This special power of satire may well explain why satirical comedians keep being attacked as a danger to the NRA, the Trump agenda, and right-wing extremism. Each time a comedian ironically makes fun of the right-wing mindset, they help to engage our analytical thinking in a fun and powerful way.

In 1907, the *Journal of Psychology* said of humor that,

> Perhaps its largest function is to detach us from our world of good and evil, of loss and gain, and to enable us to see it in proper perspective. It frees us from vanity, on the one hand, and from pessimism, on the other, by keeping us larger than what we do, and greater than what can happen to us.[92]

As we confront a world that seems to be dominated by a culture of greed, narcissism, bullying, and corruption, satire doesn't just keep our minds sharp; it offers us a whole other way to see the world.

This is all to show that satire may well be using irony to seriously keep us all sane. This book has shown that Trump may be a joke, but the satire about him isn't.

Notes

1 "This Is Your Brain on Drugs." *Wikipedia*, July 30, 2019, https://en.wikipedia.org/wiki/This_Is_Your_Brain_on_Drugs.
2 Ibid.
3 McClennen, Sophia A. "Beware the Trump Brain Rot: The Cognitive Effects of This Administration's Actions Could Be Disastrous." *Salon*, February 25, 2017, www.salon.com/2017/02/25/beware-the-trump-brain-rot-the-cognitive-effects-of-this-administrations-actions-could-be-disastrous/.
4 Pennycook, Gordon, et al. "Prior Exposure Increases Perceived Accuracy of Fake News." *Journal of Experimental Psychology: General*, vol. 147, no. 12, 2018, pp. 1865–1880, https://doi.org/10.1037/xge0000465.
5 Konnikova, Maria. "Trump's Lies vs. Your Brain." *Politico*, February 2017, www.politico.com/magazine/story/2017/01/donald-trump-lies-liar-effect-brain-214658.
6 Ibid.
7 Dahl, Melissa. "Even People Who Know Better Fall for Lies if They Hear Them Enough." *The Cut*, November 30, 2015, www.thecut.com/2015/11/why-even-people-who-know-better-fall-for-lies.html.
8 Reich, Robert. "Trump's Dangerous Lies About Voter Fraud." *Newsweek*, February 17, 2017, www.newsweek.com/robert-reich-trump-dangerous-lies-voter-fraud-557897.
9 Ghitis, Frida. "Donald Trump Is 'Gaslighting' All of Us." *CNN*, January 16, 2017, www.cnn.com/2017/01/10/opinions/donald-trump-is-gaslighting-america-ghitis/.

10. Ibid.
11. Canonville, Christine. "What Is Gaslighting?: The Effects of Gaslighting on Victims of." *The Roadshow for Therapists, Narcissist Behavior*, December 21, 2018, https://narcissisticbehavior.net/the-effects-of-gaslighting-in-narcissistic-victim-syndrome/.
12. Kelly, Meg and Glenn Kessler. "Analysis | President Trump Has Made 2,436 False or Misleading Claims so Far." *The Washington Post*, August 15, 2018, www.washingtonpost.com/news/fact-checker/wp/2018/03/02/president-trump-made-2436-false-or-misleading-claims-so-far/.
13. Resnick, Brian. "Why People Fall for Bullshit, According to a Scientist." *Vox*, December 3, 2015, www.vox.com/science-and-health/2015/12/3/9844480/why-people-believe-bullshit-science.
14. Rozsa, Matthew. "President Trump Admits to the World That He Makes Things Up to America's Allies." *Salon*, March 15, 2018, www.salon.com/2018/03/15/president-trump-admits-to-the-world-that-he-makes-things-up-to-americas-allies/.
15. Rosen, Christopher. "Melissa McCarthy Plays Unhinged Sean Spicer in Biting 'SNL' Sketch." *EW.com*, February 6, 2017, http://ew.com/tv/2017/02/05/snl-melissa-mccarthy-sean-spicer/.
16. Heer, Jeet. "Trump's Lies Destroy Logic as Well as Truth." *The New Republic*, November 28, 2016, https://newrepublic.com/article/139025/trumps-lies-destroy-logic-well-truth.
17. Nguyen, Tina. "Donald Trump's Contradictory Iraq War Position Implodes." *Vanity Fair*, February 19, 2016, www.vanityfair.com/news/2016/02/donald-trump-iraq-war.
18. Mak, Tim. "Trump Wants to Re-Invade Iraq; Bomb Things." *The Daily Beast*, April 14, 2017, www.thedailybeast.com/articles/2015/08/11/trump-wants-to-re-invade-iraq-bomb-things.html.
19. Heer, Jeet. "Trump's Lies Destroy Logic as Well as Truth." *The New Republic*, November 28, 2016, https://newrepublic.com/article/139025/trumps-lies-destroy-logic-well-truth.
20. McClennen, Sophia A. "'Because ISIS': Whoever Wins the Presidential Election, the Middle East Loses." *Salon*, October 11, 2016, www.salon.com/2016/10/11/because-isis-whoever-wins-the-presidential-election-the-middle-east-loses/.
21. Krugman, Paul. "The Falsity of False Equivalence." *The New York Times*, September 26, 2016, http://krugman.blogs.nytimes.com/2016/09/26/the-falsity-of-false-equivalence/?_r=0.
22. "The Danger of 'WhatAbout-ism' Arguments by John Oliver." *YouTube* video, posted by Josh Olin on November 16, 2017, www.youtube.com/watch?v=RS82JNd0YzQ.
23. Ibid.
24. Ibid.
25. Nyhan, Brendan and Jason Reifler. "When Corrections Fail: The Persistence of Political Misperceptions." *Political Behavior*, vol. 32, no. 2, 2010, pp. 303–330, https://doi.org/10.1007/s11109-010-9112-2.
26. "Adult Bullying." *Bullying Statistics*, July 7, 2015, www.bullyingstatistics.org/content/adult-bullying.html.
27. "Workplacebullying.org." *Workplace Bullying Institute*, www.workplacebullying.org/individuals/problem/being-bullied/.
28. Shafer, Jack. "Trump the Bully." *Politico*, January 27, 2017, www.politico.com/magazine/story/2017/01/trump-the-bully-214698.
29. McAdams, Dan P. "The Narcissist." *The Atlantic*, January 18, 2018, www.theatlantic.com/magazine/archive/2016/06/the-mind-of-donald-trump/480771/.
30. Lund, Jeb. "Stop Waiting for Trump to Start Making Sense." *Esquire*, January 11, 2017, www.esquire.com/news-politics/news/a52214/trump-bullies/.
31. Sargent, Greg. "Trump Is Set to Introduce a New 'Muslim Ban': This One Is Nonsense, too." *The Washington Post*, April 6, 2019, www.washingtonpost.com/blogs/plum-line/wp/2017/02/21/trump-is-set-to-introduce-a-new-muslim-ban-this-one-is-nonsense-too/?utm_term=.e911e480ded8.
32. Volcovici, Valerie. "Trump Administration Tells EPA to Cut Climate Page from Website: Sources." *Reuters*, January 25, 2017, www.reuters.com/article/us-usa-trump-epa-climatechange-idUSKBN15906G.

33 Rein, Lisa, et al. "Federal Agents Conduct Immigration Enforcement Raids in at Least Six States." *The Washington Post*, February 11, 2017, www.washingtonpost.com/national/federal-agents-conduct-sweeping-immigration-enforcement-raids-in-at-least-6-states/2017/02/10/4b9f443a-efc8-11e6-b4ff-ac2cf509efe5_story.html?utm_term=.c126fdf4fa65.
34 Ibid.
35 Debord, Guy. *The Society of the Spectacle*. Zone Books, 1967, p. 12.
36 Ibid., p. 2.
37 Postman, Neil. *Amusing Ourselves to Death: Public Discourse in the Age of Show Business*. Penguin Books, 2006.
38 Blaszczak-Boxe, Agata. "Too Much TV Really Is Bad for Your Brain." *LiveScience*, December 2, 2015, www.livescience.com/52959-television-cognitive-function.html.
39 Taub, Amanda and Brendan Nyhan. "Why People Continue to Believe Objectively False Things." *The New York Times*, March 22, 2017, www.nytimes.com/2017/03/22/upshot/why-objectively-false-things-continue-to-be-believed.html?rref=collection/sectioncollection/upshot&action=click&contentCollection=upshot®ion&module=package&version=highlights&contentPlacement=1&pgtype=sectionfront&_r=0.
40 Ibid.
41 Rubin, Jennifer. "He Won: Now What Does Donald Trump Do?" *The Washington Post*, November 9, 2016, www.washingtonpost.com/blogs/right-turn/wp/2016/11/09/he-won-now-what-does-donald-trump-do/?utm_term=.6cacd2003de3.
42 Ortiz, Erik. "Jon Stewart Reunites with Stephen Colbert, Mocks Trump's Executive Orders." *NBCNews.com*, February 1, 2017, www.nbcnews.com/pop-culture/tv/jon-stewart-reunites-stephen-colbert-mocks-trump-s-executive-orders-n715306.
43 Bruni, Frank. "Donald Trump Will Leave You Numb." *The New York Times*, February 18, 2017, www.nytimes.com/2017/02/18/opinion/sunday/donald-trump-will-leave-you-numb.html.
44 Ofri, Danielle. "Americans' Election-Induced Anxiety isn't Abating: Should Doctors Be Treating It?" *Slate Magazine*, January 19, 2017, www.slate.com/articles/health_and_science/medical_examiner/2017/01/americans_are_experiencing_election_induced_medical_symptoms.html.
45 Ibid.
46 Orwell, George. *1984*. Signet, 1961, p. 187.
47 Gopnik, Adam. "Orwell's '1984' and Trump's America." *The New Yorker*, January 27, 2017, www.newyorker.com/news/daily-comment/orwells-1984-and-trumps-america.
48 "Do Street Protests Still Work?" *NPR*, The Bryant Park Project, March 18, 2008, www.npr.org/templates/story/story.php?storyId=88461838.
49 Davidson, Lawrence. "Is There a Future for the Democratic Party?" *CounterPunch.org*, January 16, 2017, www.counterpunch.org/2017/01/16/is-there-a-future-for-the-democratic-party/.
50 "Prevention." *Alzheimer's Disease and Dementia, Alzheimer's Association*, n.d., www.alz.org/research/science/alzheimers_prevention_and_risk.asp#social.
51 Kravetz, Dennis. "10 Ways to Boost Your Cognitive Fitness and Longevity." *The Huffington Post*, July 2, 2013, www.huffingtonpost.com/dennis-kravetz/10-ways-to-boost-your-cognitive-fitness_b_3195153.html.
52 Rogers, Joann. "Go Forth in Anger." *Psychology Today*, March 11, 2014, www.psychologytoday.com/articles/201403/go-forth-in-anger?collection=163107.
53 "Optimism." *Psychology Today*, n.d., www.psychologytoday.com/basics/optimism.
54 Ibid.
55 Burton, Neel. "Hell Yes: The 7 Best Reasons for Swearing." *Psychology Today*, June 21, 2019, www.psychologytoday.com/blog/hide-and-seek/201205/hell-yes-the-7-best-reasons-swearing.
56 Tejada, Chloe. "Swearing Is a Sign of High Intelligence: Well, F★Ck." *HuffPost*, September 27, 2016, www.huffingtonpost.ca/2016/09/27/swear-words-intelligence_n_12213206.html.

57 Zimmer, Ben. "A Hero for Our Time: We Found the Man Behind the Priceless Trump Insult 'S–gibbon'." *Slate Magazine*, February 13, 2017, https://slate.com/culture/2017/02/the-origin-of-the-trump-insult-shitgibbon-revealed.html.
58 Hart, Benjamin. "The NRA's Greatest Weapon Is the Truth. or a Giant Hammer. One of the Two." *New York Intelligencer*, February 12, 2018, https://nymag.com/intelligencer/2018/02/the-nras-greatest-weapon-is-either-truth-or-a-giant-hammer.html.
59 Jensen, Erin. "Trump Rips 'Alex Baldwin' on Twitter, Says 'Terrible Impersonation' Was 'Agony' to Watch." *USA Today*, March 2, 2018, www.usatoday.com/story/life/entertainthis/2018/03/02/trump-rips-alec-baldwin-his-impersonation-twitter-agony-those-who-were-forced-watch/388067002/.
60 "Trump on Alec Baldwin's Hollywood Reporter Interview: 'SNL' Is 'Agony for Those Forced to Watch'." *The Hollywood Reporter*, March 2, 2018, www.hollywoodreporter.com/news/trump-responds-alec-baldwin-calling-snl-impression-agony-1090165.
61 Ibid.
62 Stern, Marlow. "Stephen Colbert Goes to Washington to Grill Congressmen on Trump-Russia." *The Daily Beast*, The Daily Beast Company, March 3, 2018, www.thedailybeast.com/stephen-colbert-goes-to-washington-in-search-of-trump-russia-answers.
63 Ibid.
64 Ibid.
65 Drutman, Lee, et al. "Follow the Leader." *Democracy Fund Voter Study Group*, March 2018, www.voterstudygroup.org/publications/2017-voter-survey/follow-the-leader.
66 Romano, Aja. "Michael Moore: Fight Donald Trump with 'an Army of Comedy'." *Vox*, January 20, 2017, www.vox.com/policy-and-politics/2017/1/20/14331072/michael-moore-alec-baldwin-we-stand-united-rally-comedy.
67 Colbert, Stephen. "Forum." *The Institute of Politics at Harvard University*, December 1, 2006, http://iop.harvard.edu/forum/.
68 Young, Dannagal G., et al. "Psychology, Political Ideology, and Humor Appreciation: Why Is Satire so Liberal?" *Psychology of Popular Media Culture*, vol. 8, no. 2, 2019, pp. 134–147.
69 Cacioppo, John T., et al. "Dispositional Differences in Cognitive Motivation: The Life and Times of Individuals Varying in Need for Cognition." *Psychological Bulletin*, vol. 119, 1996, pp. 197–253, 243.
70 For more, see Young, Dannagal G. *Irony and Outrage*. Oxford University Press.
71 LaMarre, Heather L., et al. "The Irony of Satire." *The International Journal of Press/Politics*, vol. 14, no. 2, April 1, 2009, p. 212.
72 Chin, Richard. "The Science of Sarcasm? Yeah, Right." *Smithsonian.com*, November 14, 2011, www.smithsonianmag.com/science-nature/the-science-of-sarcasm-yeah-right-25038/.
73 McClennen, Sophia A. "The Resistance Is All in Your Head: 6 Ways to Fight Trump Brain Rot." *Salon*, March 4, 2017, www.salon.com/2017/03/04/the-resistance-is-all-in-your-head-6-ways-to-fight-trump-brain-rot/.
74 Popovic, Srdja and Matthew Miller. *Blueprint for Revolution: How to Use Rice Pudding, Lego Men, and Other Non-Violent Techniques to Galvanize Communities, Overthrow Dictators, or Simply Change the World*. Scribe Publications, 2015.
75 Hurley, Dan. "The Science of Sarcasm (Not That You Care)." *The New York Times*, June 3, 2008, www.nytimes.com/2008/06/03/health/research/03sarc.html.
76 Huang, Li, et al. "The Highest Form of Intelligence: Sarcasm Increases Creativity for Both Expressers and Recipients." *Organizational Behavior and Human Decision Processes*, vol. 131, November 2015, pp. 162–177.
77 Chin, Richard. "The Science of Sarcasm? Yeah, Right." *Smithsonian.com*, November 14, 2011, www.smithsonianmag.com/science-nature/the-science-of-sarcasm-yeah-right-25038/#0tDr8L5CLumRX7Ku.99.
78 Young, Dannagal G., et al. "Psychology, Political Ideology, and Humor Appreciation: Why Is Satire So Liberal?" *Psychology of Popular Media Culture*, vol. 8, no. 2, 2017, p. 136, https://doi.org/10.1037/ppm0000157.

79 Interview with Gordon Pennycook, March 1, 2017.
80 Chin, Richard. "The Science of Sarcasm? Yeah, Right." *Smithsonian.com*, November 14, 2011, www.smithsonianmag.com/science-nature/the-science-of-sarcasm-yeah-right-25038/#JsryQi26GjCssbXC.99.
81 Pennycook, Gordon, et al. "On the Reception and Detection of Pseudo-Profound Bullshit." *Judgment and Decision Making*, vol. 10, no. 6, 2015, pp. 549–563, http://journal.sjdm.org/15/15923a/jdm15923a.html.
82 Resnick, Brian. "Why People Fall for Bullshit, According to a Scientist." *Vox*, December 3, 2015, www.vox.com/science-and-health/2015/12/3/9844480/why-people-believe-bullshit-science.
83 Young, Dannagal G., et al. "Psychology, Political Ideology, and Humor Appreciation: Why Is Satire So Liberal?" *Psychology of Popular Media Culture* 8, no. 2, 2019, pp. 134–147, https://doi.org/10.1037/ppm0000157.
84 Chin, Richard. "The Science of Sarcasm? Yeah, Right." *Smithsonian.com*, November 14, 2011, www.smithsonianmag.com/science-nature/the-science-of-sarcasm-yeah-right-25038/.
85 Gino, Francesca. "The Surprising Benefits of Sarcasm." *Scientific American*, November 17, 2015, www.scientificamerican.com/article/the-surprising-benefits-of-sarcasm/.
86 Young, Dannagal G., et al. "Psychology, Political Ideology, and Humor Appreciation: Why Is Satire So Liberal?" *Psychology of Popular Media Culture* 8, no. 2, 2019, p. 135.
87 "Survey: Daily Show/Colbert Viewers Most Knowledgeable, Fox News Viewers Rank Lowest." *ThinkProgress*, April 16, 2007, https://thinkprogress.org/survey-daily-show-colbert-viewers-most-knowledgable-fox-news-viewers-rank-lowest-854e2c6d917d/.
88 Chin, Richard. "The Science of Sarcasm? Yeah, Right." *Smithsonian.com*, November 14, 2011, www.smithsonianmag.com/science-nature/the-science-of-sarcasm-yeah-right-25038/.
89 Bradley, Laura. "Stephen Colbert won't Let Trump Get Away with That Ratings Lie." *Vanity Fair*, February 2, 2018, www.vanityfair.com/hollywood/2018/02/trump-state-of-the-union-ratings-colbert.
90 Ibid.
91 Morreall, John. "Philosophy of Humor." *Stanford Encyclopedia of Philosophy*, September 28, 2016, https://plato.stanford.edu/entries/humor/.
92 Ibid.

WORKS CITED

Abrams, Brian. *Obama: An Oral History*. Little A, 2018.
Abrams, Natalie. "Stephen Colbert Hopes Donald Trump Stays in Race (And Thinks He Can Win)." *Entertainment Weekly*, August 10, 2015, https://ew.com/article/2015/08/10/stephen-colbert-donald-trump/.
Adgate, Brad. "The Ratings Bump of Donald Trump." *Forbes*, April 18, 2018, www.forbes.com/sites/bradadgate/2018/04/18/the-ratings-bump-of-donald-trump/#7cf77d937ec1.
Adler, Paul. "Famed Writer Andy Borowitz Is the Sovereign of Satire." *Westchester Magazine*, February 28, 2018, www.westchestermagazine.com/Westchester-Magazine/March-2018/The-Sovereign-of-Satire/.
Allcott, Hunt and Matthew Gentzkow. "Social Media and Fake News in the 2016 Election." *Journal of Economic Perspectives*, vol. 31, no. 2, Spring 2017, pp. 211–236, https://web.stanford.edu/~gentzkow/research/fakenews.pdf.
Almond, Steve. *Bad Stories: What the Hell Just Happened to Our Country*. Red Hen Press, 2018.
Alter, Rebecca. "Alec Baldwin Holds Up a 'You're Welcome' Sign on *SNL*." *Vulture*, November 8, 2020, www.vulture.com/2020/11/no-thanks-alec-baldwin-holds-a-youre-welcome-sign-on-snl.html.
Anderson, Nick. "Rob Rogers' Firing Is a Frightening Omen." *CNN*, June 23, 2018, www.cnn.com/2018/06/23/opinions/rob-rogers-cartoonists-matter-anderson-opinion/index.html.
Armstrong, Jennifer Keishin. "How Trevor Noah Conquered US Comedy." *BBC*, October 5, 2017, www.bbc.com/culture/story/20170918-how-trevor-noah-conquered-us-comedy.
Associated Press. "Trump Likely to Be Most Mocked President by Late Night, Study Finds." *The Hollywood Reporter*, May 5, 2017, www.hollywoodreporter.com/news/trump-be-mocked-president-by-late-night-study-finds-1000499.
Baggini, Julian. "In Praise of Cynicism." *The Guardian*, July 10, 2013, www.theguardian.com/world/2013/jul/10/in-praise-of-cynicism.
Bai, Matt. "How Gary Hart's Downfall Forever Changed American Politics." *The New York Times*, September 18, 2014, www.nytimes.com/2014/09/21/magazine/how-gary-harts-downfall-forever-changed-american-politics.html.

Bakare, Lanre. "Trevor Noah: 'It's Easier to Be an Angry White Man Than an Angry Black Man.'" *The Guardian*, April 2, 2016, www.theguardian.com/tv-and-radio/2016/apr/02/trevor-noah-on-replacing-jon-stewart-and-changing-the-daily-show.

Baldwin, Alec and Kurt Anderson. *You Can't Spell America Without Me*. Penguin, 2017.

Balluck, Kyle. "Trump: 'Unfair' Coverage Should Be Tested in Courts." *The Hill*, December 16, 2018, https://thehill.com/homenews/administration/421574-trump-unfair-coverage-should-be-tested-in-courts.

Barber, Kristen. "Satire as Protest in the Women's March." *Gender & Society*, April 12, 2017, https://gendersociety.wordpress.com/2017/04/12/satire-as-protest-in-the-womens-march/.

Barton, Chris. "Seth Meyers Calls Trump a 'Lying Racist' Over His Charlottesville News Conference." *Los Angeles Times*, Tribune, August 1, 2017, www.latimes.com/entertainment/la-et-entertainment-news-updates-august-seth-meyers-calls-trump-a-lying-1502978870-htmlstory.html.

———. "Revisiting Comedy Central's 'Roast of Donald Trump,' When 'President Trump' Was a Punchline and Trump Could Take a Joke." *Los Angeles Times*, April 27, 2018, www.latimes.com/entertainment/tv/la-et-donald-trump-roast-20180425-story.html.

Baum, Matthew. "Soft News and Political Knowledge: Evidence of Absence or Absence of Evidence?" *Political Communication*, vol. 20, 2003, pp. 173–190, https://doi.org/10.1080/10584600390211181.

Baumgartner, Jody C. and Brad Lockerbie. "Maybe It *Is* More Than a Joke: Satire, Mobilization, and Political Participation." *Social Science Quarterly*, vol. 99, no. 3, 2018, pp. 1060–1074, https://doi.org/10.1111/ssqu.12501.

Baumgartner, Jody C. and Jonathan S. Morris. "The Daily Show Effect: Candidate Evaluations, Efficacy, and American Youth." *American Politics Research*, vol. 34, no. 3, May 2006, pp. 341–367, https://doi.org/10.1177/1532673X05280074.

———. "Stoned Slackers or Super Citizens? The Daily Show Viewing and Political Engagement of Young Adults." *The Stewart/Colbert Effect: Essays on the Real Impact of Fake News*, edited by Amarnath Amarasingam. McFarland, 2011, pp. 63–78.

Baumgartner, Jody C., et al. "The Fey Effect: Young Adults, Political Humor, and Perceptions of Sarah Palin in the 2008 Presidential Election Campaign." *Public Opinion Quarterly*, vol. 76, no. 1, 2012, pp. 95–104, https://academic.oup.com/poq/article-abstract/76/1/95/1894315.

———. "Did the Road to The White House Run Through Letterman? Chris Christie, Letterman, and Other-Disparaging Versus Self-Deprecating Humor." *Journal of Political Marketing*, vol. 17, no. 3, 2018, pp. 282–300, www.tandfonline.com/doi/abs/10.1080/15377857.2015.1074137.

Baym, Geoffrey D. *From Cronkite to Colbert: The Evolution of Broadcast News*. Paradigm, 2010.

Beaujon, Andrew. "Survey: NPR's Listeners Best-Informed, Fox Viewers Worst-Informed." *Poynter*, 2012, www.poynter.org/latest-news/mediawire/174826/survey-nprs-listeners-best-informed-fox-news-viewers-worst-informed/.

Beckwith, Ryan Teague. "Watch President Obama Troll Donald Trump in 2011." *Time*, August 10, 2015, https://time.com/3991301/donald-trump-barack-obama/.

Benen, Steve. "Trump Takes Aim at Public's Trust in Democratic Institutions." *MSNBC*, February 5, 2018, www.msnbc.com/rachel-maddow-show/trump-takes-aim-public-trust-democratic-institutions.

Berman, Lea and Jeremy Bernard. "The Best Joke George W. Bush Ever Told in Office." *Time*, January 9, 2018, https://time.com/5094914/president-jokes/.

Bissel, Tom. "The Tragicomedy of Donald Trump on Saturday Night Live." *Harper's Magazine*, September 13, 2017, https://harpers.org/archive/2017/10/whos-laughing-now/.

Blanc, Jarrett and Jeff Greenfield. "Meyers: Trump Wanted Me to Apologize On-Air for Making Fun of Him." *Politico*, May 8, 2018, www.politico.com/magazine/story/2018/05/08/seth-meyers-trump-whcd-jokes-apologize-218323.
Blaszczak-Boxe, Agata. "Too Much TV Really Is Bad for Your Brain." *Live Science*, December 2, 2015, www.livescience.com/52959-television-cognitive-function.html.
Branigan, Tania. "China Bans Wordplay in Attempt at Word Control." *The Guardian*, November 28, 2014, www.theguardian.com/world/2014/nov/28/china-media-watchdog-bans-wordplay-puns.
Brenan, Megan. "Americans Remain Distrustful of Mass Media." *Gallup*, September 20, 2020, https://news.gallup.com/poll/321116/americans-remain-distrustful-mass-media.aspx.
Borchers, Callum. "Alex Jones Should Not Be Taken Seriously, According to Alex Jones' Lawyers." *The Washington Post*, April 17, 2017, www.washingtonpost.com/news/the-fix/wp/2017/04/17/trump-called-alex-jones-amazing-joness-own-lawyer-calls-him-a-performance-artist/?utm_term=.4b17f63d0e33; Quantcast, www.quantcast.com/user/login?forward=/infowars.com.
Borowitz, Andy. "Cheney Receives Heart Transplant; Bush Still on Waiting List for Brain." *The New Yorker*, June 15, 2012, www.newyorker.com/humor/borowitz-report/cheney-receives-heart-transplant-bush-still-on-waiting-list-for-brain.
———. "Polar Vortex Causes Hundreds of Injuries as People Making Snide Remarks About Climate Change Are Punched in Face." *The New Yorker*, January 6, 2014, www.newyorker.com/humor/borowitz-report/polar-vortex-causes-hundreds-of-injuries-as-people-making-snide-remarks-about-climate-change-are-punched-in-face.
———. "Calling Earth a 'Loser,' Trump Vows to Make Better Deal with New Planet." *The New Yorker*, June 1, 2017, www.newyorker.com/humor/borowitz-report/calling-earth-a-loser-trump-vows-to-make-better-deal-with-new-planet.
———. "Trump Voters Celebrate Massive Tax Cut for Everyone but Them." *The New Yorker*, November 16, 2017, www.newyorker.com/humor/borowitz-report/trump-voters-celebrate-massive-tax-cut-for-everyone-but-them.
———. "Nazis Feeling Neglected After Republicans' Embrace of Child Molesters." *The New Yorker*, December 5, 2017, www.newyorker.com/humor/borowitz-report/nazis-feeling-neglected-after-republicans-embrace-of-child-molesters.
———. "Americans Startled by Spectacle of President Who Can Speak English." *The New Yorker*, April 25, 2018, www.newyorker.com/humor/borowitz-report/americans-startled-by-spectacle-of-president-who-can-speak-english.
———. "Kavanaugh Offers to Pay for Wall by Recycling His Empties." *The New Yorker*, January 10, 2019, www.newyorker.com/humor/borowitz-report/kavanaugh-offers-to-pay-for-wall-by-recycling-his-empties.
Boukes, Mark. "Agenda-Setting with Satire: How Political Satire Increased TTIP's Saliency on the Public, Media, and Political Agenda." *Political Communication*, vol. 36, no. 3, 2019, pp. 426–451, https://doi.org/10.1080/10584609.2018.1498816.
Bozell, Brent and Tim Graham. "Liberals Bewitched by Samantha Bee." *Newsbusters*, February 20, 2016, www.newsbusters.org/blogs/nb/brent-bozell/2016/02/20/bozell-graham-column-liberals-bewitched-samantha-bee.
Bradley, Laura. "Seth Meyers Attacks Trump on Charlottesville: 'He Is Not a President'." *Vanity Fair*, August 15, 2017, www.vanityfair.com/hollywood/2017/08/donald-trump-charlottesville-seth-meyers-colbert-late-night.
———. "The *Daily Show* Identifies a Real 'Crisis Actor': Tomi Lahren." *Vanity Fair*, February 23, 2018, www.vanityfair.com/hollywood/2018/02/tomi-lahren-crisis-actor-trevor-noah-daily-show.

———. "Samantha Bee Says Her 'Feckless C--t' Apology Was Not Meant for Right-Wing Critics." *Vanity Fair*, August 24, 2018, www.vanityfair.com/hollywood/2018/08/samantha-bee-full-frontal-feckless-cunt-michelle-wolf-the-break-cancellation.

———. "Stephen Colbert Won't Let Trump Get Away with That Ratings Lie." *Vanity Fair*, February 2, 2018, www.vanityfair.com/hollywood/2018/02/trump-state-of-the-union-ratings-colbert.

Braxton, Greg. "Trevor Noah Strikes a Nerve – and Ratings Gold – as He Steers *The Daily Show* into the Trump Era." *Los Angeles Times*, June 8, 2017, www.latimes.com/entertainment/tv/la-ca-st-sunday-conversation-trevor-noah-20170608-htmlstory.html.

Brewer, Paul and Xiaoxia Cao. "Political Comedy Shows Public Participation in Politics." *International Journal of Public Opinion Research*, vol. 20, no. 1, 2008, pp. 90–99, www.academia.edu/424545/Political_Comedy_Shows_and_Public_Participation_In_Politics.

Bruneau, Emile, et al. "They See Us as Less Than Human: Meta-Dehumanization Predicts Intergroup Conflict Via Reciprocal Dehumanization." *Journal of Personality and Social Psychology*, vol. 110, no. 3, 2016, pp. 343–370, https://psycnet.apa.org/doiLanding?doi=10.1037%2Fpspa0000044.

Bruni, Frank. "Donald Trump Will Leave You Numb." *The New York Times*, February 18, 2017, www.nytimes.com/2017/02/18/opinion/sunday/donald-trump-will-leave-you-numb.html.

Burton, Neel. "Hell Yes: The 7 Best Reasons for Swearing." *Psychology Today*, June 21, 2019, www.psychologytoday.com/blog/hide-and-seek/201205/hell-yes-the-7-best-reasons-swearing.

Busis, Hillary. "Everything Trump Has Had Time to Tweet About Instead of the Quebec Attack." *Vanity Fair*, February 10, 2017, www.vanityfair.com/hollywood/2017/02/donald-trump-quebec-mosque-terrorist-attack-seth-meyers-twitter.

Byrne, Deirdre. "Sarah Cooper, That Woman from TikTok Lip-Syncing to Trump, Grew Up in Rockville." *MyMCM*, July 16, 2020, www.mymcmedia.org/sarah-cooper-that-woman-from-tiktok-lip-syncing-to-trump-grew-up-in-rockville/.

Cacioppo, John T., et al. "Dispositional Differences in Cognitive Motivation: The Life and Times of Individuals Varying in Need for Cognition." *Psychological Bulletin*, vol. 119, 1996, pp. 197–253.

Canonville, Christine. "What Is Gaslighting?: The Effects of Gaslighting on Victims of." *The Roadshow for Therapists, Narcissist Behavior*, December 21, 2018, https://narcissisticbehavior.net/the-effects-of-gaslighting-in-narcissistic-victim-syndrome/.

Carter, Graydon. "A Joke Certainly, but No Laughing Matter." *Vanity Fair*, April 2017, https://archive.vanityfair.com/article/2017/4/a-joke-certainly-but-no-laughing-matter.

———. "The Trump Presidency Is Already a Joke." *Vanity Fair*, March 22, 2017, www.vanityfair.com/news/2017/03/graydon-carter-trump-presidency-is-already-a-joke.

Cassino, Dan, et al. "What You Know Depends on What You Watch." *Public Mind Poll*, Fairleigh Dickinson University, May 3, 2012, http://publicmind.fdu.edu/2012/confirmed/.

Charity, Justin. "Here's a Smart Blog About 'Covfefe', Which Is Dumb." *The Ringer*, May 2017, www.theringer.com/2017/5/31/16043182/donald-trump-twitter-covfefe-memes-media-292870104291.

Chattoo, Caty Borum and Lauren Feldman. *A Comedian and an Activist Walk into a Bar: The Serious Role of Comedy in Social Justice*. Foreword by Norman Lear. UC Press, 2020.

Chen, Hsuan-Ting, et al. "How Does Political Satire Influence Political Participation? Examining the Role of Counter- and Pro- Attitudinal Exposure, Anger, and Personal Issue Influence." *International Journal of Communication*, vol. 11, 2017, p. 19, https://ijoc.org/index.php/ijoc/article/view/6158.

Chin, Richard. "The Science of Sarcasm? Yeah, Right." *Smithsonian.com*, November 14, 2011, www.smithsonianmag.com/science-nature/the-science-of-sarcasm-yeah-right-25038/.

Cohen, Bernard C. *The Press and Foreign Policy*. Princeton University Press, 1963, p. 13.

Confessore, Nicholas and Karen Yourish. "$2 Billion Worth in Free Media for Donald Trump." *The New York Times*, March 15, 2016, www.nytimes.com/2016/03/15/upshot/measuring-donald-trumps-mammoth-advantage-in-free-media.html.

Covucci, David. "Hell Is the Aftermath of the White House Correspondents Dinner." *The Daily Dot*, April 30, 2018, www.dailydot.com/layer8/white-house-correspondents-dinner-takes/.

Crofts, Jamie Lynn. "This Coal Baron's Lawsuit Against John Oliver Is Plain Nuts." *ACLU*, August 2, 2017, www.aclu.org/blog/free-speech/coal-barons-lawsuit-against-john-oliver-plain-nuts.

Cuccinello, Hayley C. "Trevor Noah's *Daily Show* Reaches 100th Episode, But Noah Is Still Struggling." *Forbes*, April 28, 2016, www.forbes.com/sites/hayleycuccinello/2016/04/28/trevor-noahs-daily-show-reaches-100th-episode-but-noah-is-still-struggling/#296e66052c24.

Dahl, Melissa. "Even People Who Know Better Fall for Lies If They Hear Them Enough." *The Cut*, November 30, 2015, www.thecut.com/2015/11/why-even-people-who-know-better-fall-for-lies.html.

Daily Show and Trevor Noah. *The Donald J. Trump Presidential Twitter Library*. Spiegel and Grau, 2018.

Davidson, Lawrence. "Is There a Future for the Democratic Party?" *CounterPunch.org*, January 16, 2017, www.counterpunch.org/2017/01/16/is-there-a-future-for-the-democratic-party/.

Day, Amber. *Satire and Dissent: Interventions in Contemporary Political Debate*. Indiana University Press, 2011.

Debord, Guy. *The Society of the Spectacle*. Zone Books, 1967.

Deerwester, Jayme. "Trump Tweets: 'Should Federal Election Commission And/or FCC' Look into 'SNL'?" *USA Today*, March 18, 2019, www.usatoday.com/story/life/tv/2019/03/18/trump-tweets-snl-federal-probe/3199989002/.

De Haldevang, Max. "Sean Spicer Just Claimed That Hitler 'Was Not Using Gas on His Own People'." *Quartz*, April 11, 2017, https://qz.com/955858/sean-spicer-donald-trumps-press-chief-claimed-that-hitler-was-not-using-gas-on-his-own-people/.

Dekel, Jon. "The John Oliver Effect: How the Daily Show Alum Became the Most Trusted Man in America." *National Post*, February 18, 2015, https://nationalpost.com/entertainment/television/the-john-oliver-effect-how-the-daily-show-alum-became-the-most-trusted-man-in-america.

Delmacy, Nick. "Why Do so Many Men Imitate Women for Comedy but Not the Other Way Around?" *Cypher Avenue*, 2014, https://cypheravenue.com/why-do-so-many-men-imitate-women-for-comedy-but-not-the-other-way-around/.

De Moraes, Lisa. "No FCC Fine for Stephen Colbert's Late-Night Donald Trump C★★★ Holster Crack." *Deadline*, May 23, 2017, https://deadline.com/2017/05/stephen-colbert-donald-trump-fcc-no-fine-mouth-cock-holster-monologue-1202101084/.

———. "Jimmy Kimmel: President Donald Trump Is Completely Unhinged." *Deadline*, August 15, 2017, https://deadline.com/2017/08/jimmy-kimmel-donald-trump-unhinged-news-conference-charlottesville-neo-nazis-white-supremacists-video-1202149926/.

———. "Jimmy Kimmel Mocks Donald Trump's Reality TV Pact with Kim Jong Un." *Deadline*, June 13, 2018, https://deadline.com/2018/06/jimmy-kimmel-donald-trump-kim-jong-un-summit-video-1202409518.

———. "Netflix Launching 'Patriot Act with Hasan Minhaj' in October." *Deadline*, August 9, 2018, https://deadline.com/2018/08/hasan-minhaj-netflix-patriot-act-debut-october-28-1202443188/.

Denning, Steve. "Chief Justice Roberts Requests Tenth Circuit to Investigate Kavanaugh Ethics Questions." *Forbes*, October 13, 2018, www.forbes.com/sites/stevedenning/2018/10/11/chief-justice-roberts-requests-tenth-circuit-to-investigate-kavanaugh-ethics-questions/#126491a01877.

Descartes, René. *Delphi Collected Works of René Descartes*. Delphi Publishing, 2017.

Dessem, Matthew. "Seth Meyers Lists All the Dumb Things Donald Trump Tweeted About This Weekend and It's Breathtaking." *Slate*, March 19, 2019, https://slate.com/culture/2019/03/seth-meyers-donald-trump-weekend-tweetstorm.html.

Devichand, Mukul. "How the World Was Changed by the Slogan 'Je Suis Charlie'." *BBC*, January 3, 2016, www.bbc.com/news/blogs-trending-35108339.

Dewey, Caitlin. "Facebook Fake-News Writer: 'I Think Donald Trump Is in the White House Because of Me'." *The Washington Post*, November 17, 2016, www.washingtonpost.com/news/the-intersect/wp/2016/11/17/facebook-fake-news-writer-i-think-donald-trump-is-in-the-white-house-because-of-me/?noredirect=on&utm_term=.d6f54bff1cbd.

Donovan, Laura. "Trump on WHCD Jokes Against Him: 'Is There Anyone Else They Could Talk About?'" *Yahoo News*, May 1, 2011, https://news.yahoo.com/news/trump-whcd-jokes-against-him-anyone-else-could-203203408.html.

Dovere, Edward-Isaac. "Meyers, Trump Wanted Me to Apologize On-Air for Making Fun of Him." *Politico*, May 8, 2018, www.politico.com/magazine/story/2018/05/08/seth-meyers-trump-whcd-jokes-apologize-218323/.

Drutman, Lee, et al. "Follow the Leader." *Democracy Fund Voter Study Group*, March 2018, www.voterstudygroup.org/publications/2017-voter-survey/follow-the-leader.

Dukore, Bernard Frank. *Where Laughter Stops: Pinter's Tragicomedy*. University of Missouri Press, 1976.

Duncombe, Stephen. *Dream: Re-Imagining Progressive Politics in an Age of Fantasy*. The New Press, 2007.

———. *Dream or Nightmare*. OR Books, 2019, www.stephenduncombe.com/dreampolitik/.

Edgers, Geoff. "Late Show of Emotion." *The Washington Post*, March 1, 2018, www.washingtonpost.com/news/style/wp/2018/03/01/feature/jimmy-kimmel-might-be-americas-conscience-but-hell-still-do-anything-for-a-laugh/?utm_term=.ba973e8c34ce.

El-Ghobashy, Tamer. "Jon Stewart Is This Generation's Cronkite: Poll." *NBC*, July 27, 2009, www.nbcnewyork.com/news/archive/NATLJon-Stewart-is-The-Most-Trusted-Name-in-News-Poll.html.

Emerson, Sarah. "Boomers Share the Most Fake News on Facebook, Study Finds." *Vice*, January 9, 2019, https://motherboard.vice.com/en_us/article/439z8g/boomers-share-the-most-fake-news-on-facebook-study-finds?utm_source=vicefbus&fbclid=IwAR0q4IioJlQrXn3ik4CK9TeTtd670UFq4ZJY4bi1pVWzss7vdCDC41sOjEA.

"Equatorial Guinea: Political Cartoonist Arrested." *Human Rights Watch*, September 19, 2017, www.hrw.org/news/2017/09/19/equatorial-guinea-political-cartoonist-arrested.

Even, Dan. "FACT CHECK: Did MAD Magazine Lampoon Donald Trump in 1992?" *Snopes.com*, June 28, 2017, www.snopes.com/fact-check/did-mad-magazine-publish-a-trump-cartoon-in-1992/.

Fahrenthold, David. "Trump Said He'd Give Away $5 Million- or Maybe $50 Million- for Proof Obama Was Born in the U.S. Will He Pay It?" *The Washington Post*, September 16, 2016, www.washingtonpost.com/news/post-politics/wp/2016/09/16/

trump-said-hed-give-away-5-million-or-maybe-50-million-for-proof-obama-was-born-in-the-u-s-will-he-pay-it/?utm_term=.f24d5301afa4.

———. "A Time Magazine with Trump of the Cover Hangs in His Golf Clubs: It's Fake." *The Washington Post*, June 27, 2017, www.washingtonpost.com/politics/a-time-magazine-with-trump-on-the-cover-hangs-in-his-golf-clubs-its-fake/2017/06/27/0adf96de-5850-11e7-ba90-f5875b7d1876_story.html?utm_term=.0ed208c038e7.

Fausset, Richard and Serge Kovaleski. "Officials Decline to Call Fatal Stabbing of Black Student a Hate Crime." *The New York Times*, 2017, www.nytimes.com/2017/05/22/us/black-student-stabbed-maryland.html?_r=0.

Feirstein, Bruce. "Trump's War on 'Losers': The Early Years." *Vanity Fair*, August 12, 2015, www.vanityfair.com/news/2015/08/spy-vs-trump.

Firzli, Nicolas J. "Understanding Trumponics." *Analyse Financiere*, January 26, 2017, http://analysefinanciere.org/2017/01/26/understanding-trumponics/.

Fisher, Marc and Will Hobson. "Donald Trump Masqueraded as a Publicist to Brag About Himself." *The Washington Post*, May 3, 2016, www.washingtonpost.com/politics/donald-trump-alter-ego-barron/2016/05/12/02ac99ec-16fe-11e6-aa55-670cabef46e0_story.html.

Flood, Brian. "'SNL' Is Tougher on Trump Than Past Presidents, But NBC Won't Let Up Anytime Soon, Experts Say." *Fox News*, December 7, 2018, www.foxnews.com/entertainment/snl-is-tougher-on-trump-than-past-presidents-but-nbc-wont-let-up-anytime-soon-critics-say.

Forgey, Quint. "Trump Vilifies 'Dishonest' Press at Michigan Rally." *Politico*, April 28, 2018, www.politico.com/story/2018/04/28/trump-michigan-rally-media-press-559197.

Foster, Thomas. *How to Read Literature like a Professor: A Lively and Entertaining Guide to Reading Between the Lines*. Harper, 2017.

Fowler, James H. "The Colbert Bump in Campaign Donations: More Truthful than Truthy." *PS: Political Science and Politics*, vol. 41, no. 3, 2008, pp. 533–539. JSTOR, www.jstor.org/stable/20452245. Accessed 4 August 2022.

Framke, Caroline. "How Late Night with Seth Meyers Became the Calm in a Political Comedy Storm." *Vox*, August 25, 2017, www.vox.com/culture/2017/8/25/16189952/seth-meyers-interview-trump-2017.

"Free Ramon Esono Ebale." *Voice Project*, http://voiceproject.org/campaign/free-ramon-esono-ebale/.

Freud, Sigmund. *Jokes and Their Relation to the Unconscious*. W. W. Norton & Company, 1990.

Fu, Hanlong, et al. "Reconsidering Political Cynicism and Political Involvement: A Test of Antecedents." *American Communication Journal*, 2011, http://ac-journal.org/journal/pubs/2011/summer/Cynicism_Proof.pdf.

Gajanan, Mahita. "Read Hasan Minhaj's Full Speech from the White House Correspondents' Dinner." *Time*, May 1, 2017, https://time.com/4761644/hasan-minhaj-white-house-correspondents-dinner-speech-transcript/.

Garber, Megan. "How Donald Trump Beat Stephen Colbert at His Own Game." *The Atlantic*, September 23, 2015, www.theatlantic.com/entertainment/archive/2015/09/the-colbert-trump/406891/.

———. "John Oliver Pushes Comedy Further Toward Activism." *The Atlantic*, November 14, 2016, www.theatlantic.com/entertainment/archive/2016/11/john-oliver-activist-comedian/507599/.

Gardner, Eriq. "Why Donald Trump Is Likely to Lose a Lawsuit Against Bill Maher." *The Hollywood Reporter*, February 4, 2013, www.hollywoodreporter.com/thr-esq/why-donald-trump-is-lose-417806.

———. "Donald Trump Withdraws Bill Maher Lawsuit." *The Hollywood Reporter*, September 12, 2019, www.hollywoodreporter.com/thr-esq/donald-trump-withdraws-bill-maher-432675.

Gerson, Michael. "The Language of Hatred, Increasingly Normalized by Trump." *RealClearPolitics*, May 2, 2017, www.realclearpolitics.com/articles/2017/05/02/the_language_of_hatred_increasingly_normalized_by_trump_133757.html.

Ghitis, Frida. "Donald Trump Is 'Gaslighting' All of Us." *CNN*, January 16, 2017, www.cnn.com/2017/01/10/opinions/donald-trump-is-gaslighting-america-ghitis/.

Gibson, Megan. "Trevor Noah Faces Backlash Over Twitter History." *Time*, March 31, 2015, http://time.com/3764913/trevor-noah-twitter-backlash/.

Giuliani-Hoffman, Francesca. "We're Living in An Age That Defies Satire." *CNN Money*, June 12, 2017, https://money.cnn.com/2017/06/12/media/andy-borowitz-interview-reliable-sources-podcast/index.html.

Gladwell, Malcolm. "Being Nice isn't Really so Awful." *The New Yorker*, December 10, 2013, www.newyorker.com/books/page-turner/being-nice-isnt-really-so-awful.

———. "The Satire Paradox—Revisionist History by Malcolm Gladwell." *Revisionist History, YouTube*, June 23, 2021, www.youtube.com/watch?v=V-EgIxRwjDA.

Glazier, Rebecca. "Using Satire to Stimulate Critical Thinking in the Political Science Classroom." *APSA*, 2011, Annual Meeting Paper, SSRN, https://ssrn.com/abstract=1903286; *ResearchGate*, 2019, www.researchgate.net/publication/228212448_Using_Satire_to_Stimulate_Critical_Thinking_in_the_Political_Science_Classroom.

———. "The Teacher: Satire and Efficacy in the Political Science Classroom." *PS: Political Science and Politics*, vol. 47, no. 4, pp. 867–872, www.rebeccaglazier.net/wp-content/uploads/2013/06/Glazier-Satire-and-Efficacy-PS-2014.pdf.

Göktürk, Deniz. "Jokes and Butts: Can We Imagine Humor in a Global Public Sphere?" *PMLA/Publications of the Modern Language Association of America*, vol. 123, no. 5, 2008, pp. 1707–1711, https://doi.org/10.1632/pmla.2008.123.5.1707.

Gold, Hadas. "Donald Trump: We're Going to 'Open Up' Libel Laws." *Politico*, 2016, www.politico.com/blogs/on-media/2016/02/donald-trump-libel-laws-219866.

Goldman, Russell. "Donald 'Bombshell' Fails to Blow Up." *ABC News*, October 24, 2012, http://abcnews.go.com/Politics/OTUS/donald-trump-fails-drop-bombshell-offers-cash-obama/story?id=17553670.

Gonyea, Don and Domenico Montanaro. "Donald Trump's Been Saying the Same Thing for 30 Years." *NPR*, January 20, 2017, www.npr.org/2017/01/20/510680463/donald-trumps-been-saying-the-same-thing-for-30-years.

Goodman, Amy. "Stephen Colbert's Blistering Performance Mocking Bush and the Press Goes Ignored by the Media." *Democracy Now*, May 3, 2006, www.democracynow.org/2006/5/3/stephen_colberts_blistering_performance_mocking_bush.

Gopnik, Adam. "Orwell's '1984' and Trump's America." *The New Yorker*, January 27, 2017, www.newyorker.com/news/daily-comment/orwells-1984-and-trumps-america.

———. "Trump and Obama: A Night to Remember." *The New Yorker*, June 19, 2017, www.newyorker.com/news/daily-comment/trump-and-obama-a-night-to-remember.

Graham, David. "The Many Scandals of Donald Trump, a Cheat Sheet." *The Atlantic*, January 23, 2017, www.theatlantic.com/politics/archive/2017/01/donald-trump-scandals/474726/.

Grimbaum, Michael. "Trump Strategist Stephen Bannon Says Media Should 'Keep Its Mouth Shut'." *The New York Times*, January 26, 2017, www.nytimes.com/2017/01/26/business/media/stephen-bannon-trump-news-media.html.

Grisar, P.J. "Stephen Miller High School Clips Prove Some Folks Don't Ever Grow Up." *The Forward*, November 27, 2018, https://forward.com/culture/414848/stephen-miller-high-school-clips-prove-some-folks-dont-ever-grow-up/.

Grothaus, Michael. "Trump Will Keep Tweeting from His Personal Twitter Account During His Presidency." *Fast Company*, January 16, 2017, www.fastcompany.com/4028797/trump-will-keep-tweeting-from-his-personal-twitter-account-during-his-presidency.

Gruner, Charles R. *The Game of Humor*. Routledge, 1999.

Guardian Staff. "South Park Creators to Back Off Trump Jokes: 'Satire Has Become Reality'." *The Guardian*, February 2, 2017, www.theguardian.com/tv-and-radio/2017/feb/02/south-park-donald-trump-mr-garrison.

Gunther, Richard, et al. "Trump May Owe His 2016 Victory to 'Fake News', Study Suggests." *The Conversation*, February 15, 2018, https://theconversation.com/trump-may-owe-his-2016-victory-to-fake-news-new-study-suggests-91538.

Gupta, Prachi. "The John Oliver of Russia Today: 'I'm Making Comedy Out of the Darkest Issues in the World'." *Salon*, October 6, 2014, www.salon.com/2014/10/06/im_making_comedy_out_of_the_darkest_issues_in_the_world_meet_the_john_oliver_of_russia_today/.

Haberman, Maggie and Alexander Burns. "Donald Trump's Presidential Run Began in an Effort to Gain Stature." *The New York Times*, March 12, 2016, www.nytimes.com/2016/03/13/us/politics/donald-trump-campaign.html.

Hakola, Outi J. "Political Impersonations on *Saturday Night Live* During the 2016 U.S. Presidential Election." *European Journal of American Studies*, vol. 12, no. 2, 2017, pp. 1–20, http://journals.openedition.org/ejas/12153.

Hall, Sean. *This Means This, This Means That*. Laurence King Publishing, 2007.

Handelzats, Michael. "Drawing New Conclusions After Charlie Hebdo Attack." *Haaretz*, 2015, www.haaretz.com/life/books/.premium-cartoonists-must-draw-new-conclusions-after-attack-1.5359013.

Harris, Robert. "The Purpose and Method of Satire." *VirtualSalt*, November 22, 2018, www.virtualsalt.com/satire.htm.

Hart, Benjamin. "The NRA's Greatest Weapon Is the Truth/Or a Giant Hammer: One of the Two." *New York Intelligencer*, February 12, 2018, https://nymag.com/intelligencer/2018/02/the-nras-greatest-weapon-is-either-truth-or-a-giant-hammer.html.

Hart, Kim. "Here Are the Election Facebook Ads Russia Bought." *Axios*, November 1, 2017, www.axios.com/dems-release-russia-bought-facebook-ads-2505026286.html.

Heer, Jeet. "Trump's Lies Destroy Logic as Well as Truth." *The New Republic*, November 28, 2016, https://newrepublic.com/article/139025/trumps-lies-destroy-logic-well-truth.

Hennigan, Adrian. "Netflix's 'Patriot Act with Hasan Minhaj' Is Way Funnier and Fresher Than 'Last Week Tonight'." *Haaretz*, November 27, 2018, www.haaretz.com/us-news/.premium-netflix-s-patriot-act-with-hasan-minhaj-is-way-funnier-and-fresher-than-last-week-tonight-1.6696501.

Hill, Evan. "Egyptian Satirist Youssef Ends TV Show." *Aljazeera America*, 2016, http://america.aljazeera.com/blogs/scrutineer/2014/6/3/egyptian-satiristyoussefendstvshow.html#commentsDiv.

Hill, Libby. "'Patriot Act with Hasan Minhaj' Will Move Further into Investigative Journalism." *IndieWire*, April 7, 2019, www.indiewire.com/2019/04/patriot-act-with-hasan-minhaj-dictators-netflix-emmys-fyc-1202056584/.

Hirschorn, Michael. "The End of Irony—9/11 Encyclopedia—September 11 10th Anniversary." *New York Magazine*, August 27, 2011, http://nymag.com/news/9-11/10th-anniversary/irony/.

Hobbes, Thomas. *The Treatise on Human Nature and That on Liberty and Necessity*. J. McCreery, Black-Horse-Court, 1812.

Holmes, Jack. "Seth Meyers Had a Field Day with President Trump's Batsh★t Press Conference." *Esquire*, February 17, 2017, www.esquire.com/news-politics/videos/a53237/seth-meyers-trump-press-conference/.

Holub, Christian. "Samantha Bee Interviews Trump Supporters." *Entertainment Weekly*, March 15, 2016, https://ew.com/article/2016/03/15/samantha-bee-interview-trump-supporters/

Houke, Curtis. "Samantha Bee's TBS Show Debuts With Vile Slam of 'Fish-Faced Horses★★★ Salesman' Cruz." *mrcTV*, February 9, 2016, www.mrctv.org/videos/samantha-bee-s-tbs-show-debuts-vile-slam-fish-faced-horses-salesman-cruz.

———. "Bee Savages Scalia, 'Obstructionist A★★' McConnell; Wants Gavel to 'Plug up Your Abortion Hole'." *mrcTV*, February 15, 2016, www.mrctv.org/videos/bee-savages-scalia-constitutional-mcconnell-wants-gavel-plug-your-abortion-hole.

Howard, Adam. "How 'Saturday Night Live' Has Shaped Our Politics." *NBCNews.com*, September 30, 2016, www.nbcnews.com/pop-culture/tv/how-saturday-night-live-has-shaped-american-politics-n656716.

Huang, Li, et al. "The Highest Form of Intelligence: Sarcasm Increases Creativity for Both Expressers and Recipients." *Organizational Behavior and Human Decision Processes*, vol. 131, November 2015, pp. 162–177.

Hurley, Dan. "The Science of Sarcasm (Not That You Care)." *The New York Times*, June 3, 2008, www.nytimes.com/2008/06/03/health/research/03sarc.html.

"Hustler Magazine v. Falwell." *Wikipedia*, 2019, https://en.wikipedia.org/wiki/Hustler_Magazine_v._Falwell.

Itzkoff, Dave. "Jimmy Kimmel on Health Care, National Tragedies and Twitter Feuds." *The New York Times*, October 15, 2017, www.nytimes.com/2017/10/15/arts/television/jimmy-kimmel-politics.html.

Jensen, Erin. "Trump Rips 'Alex Baldwin' on Twitter, Says 'Terrible Impersonation' Was 'Agony' to Watch." *USA Today*, March 2, 2018, www.usatoday.com/story/life/entertainthis/2018/03/02/trump-rips-alec-baldwin-his-impersonation-twitter-agony-those-who-were-forced-watch/388067002/.

Johnson, Ted. "FCC Inspector General: John Oliver Segment Triggered System Slowdown, Not Bots." *Variety*, August 7, 2018, https://variety.com/2018/politics/news/john-oliver-fcc-triggered-slowdown-1202898328/.

Johnstone, Caitlin. "Lee Camp Just Destroyed the Entire Establishment Narrative About RT." *Medium*, November 20, 2017, https://medium.com/@caityjohnstone/lee-camp-just-destroyed-the-entire-establishment-narrative-about-rt-b8c42870d942.

Jones, Chris. "Alec Baldwin Gets Under Trump's Skin." *The Atlantic*, May 2017, www.theatlantic.com/magazine/archive/2017/05/alec-baldwin-gets-under-trumps-skin/521433/.

Jones, Jeffrey P. *Entertaining Politics: Satiric Television and Political Engagement*. Rowman & Littlefield, 2010.

Jones, Kipp. "'Daily Show' Alum Samantha Bee Debuts New Show Trashing GOP as 'Banquet of All-You-Can-Eat Crazy'." *Breitbart*, February 9, 2016, www.breitbart.com/entertainment/2016/02/09/samantha-bees-tbs-debut-mocks-cruzs-faith-blasts-trump-crazy-gop-attack/.

Kakutani, Michiko. "Is Jon Stewart the Most Trusted Man in America." *The New York Times*, August 17, 2008, www.nytimes.com/2008/08/17/arts/television/17kaku.html.

Keane, Erin. "From Truthiness to Post-Truth, Just in Time for Donald Trump: Oxford Dictionaries' Word of the Year Should Scare the Hell Out of You." *Salon*, November 19, 2016, www.salon.com/test/2016/11/19/from-truthiness-to-post-truth-just-in-time-for-donald-trump-oxford-dictionaries-word-of-the-year-should-scare-the-hell-out-of-you/.

Kelly, Meg and Glenn Kessler. "President Trump Has Made 2,436 False or Misleading Claims so Far." *The Washington Post*, August 15, 2018, www.washingtonpost.com/news/fact-checker/wp/2018/03/02/president-trump-made-2436-false-or-misleading-claims-so-far/.

Kenny, Daniel J. "How John Oliver Usurped a Genre." *Harvard Political Review*, October 31, 2014, http://harvardpolitics.com/books-arts/john-oliver-usurped-genre/.
Kludt, Tom. "Not Everyone Is Celebrating Charlie Hebdo's Satire." *CNN*, January 8, 2015, https://money.cnn.com/2015/01/08/media/charlie-hebdo-paris-manhunt/.
Konnikova, Maria. "Trump's Lies vs. Your Brain." *Politico*, February 2017, www.politico.com/magazine/story/2017/01/donald-trump-lies-liar-effect-brain-214658.
Kravetz, Dennis. "10 Ways to Boost Your Cognitive Fitness and Longevity." *The Huffington Post*, July 2, 2013, www.huffingtonpost.com/dennis-kravetz/10-ways-to-boost-your-cognitive-fitness_b_3195153.html.
Kreps, Daniel. "Samantha Bee Addresses Ivanka Controversy, Regrets 'One Bad Word'." *Rolling Stone*, June 25, 2018, www.rollingstone.com/tv/tv-news/samantha-bee-addresses-ivanka-controversy-regrets-one-bad-word-628364/.
———. "See Stephen Colbert, Experts Help Blueprint Trump's Wall." *Rolling Stone*, June 25, 2018, www.rollingstone.com/tv/tv-news/see-stephen-colbert-experts-help-blueprint-trumps-wall-126108/.
Krieg, Gregory. "Donald Trump Defends Size of His Penis." *CNN*, March 4, 2016, www.cnn.com/2016/03/03/politics/donald-trump-small-hands-marco-rubio/index.html.
Krugman, Paul. "The Falsity of False Equivalence." *The New York Times*, September 26, 2016, http://krugman.blogs.nytimes.com/2016/09/26/the-falsity-of-false-equivalence/?_r=0.
Kurtzman, Daniel. "Colbert at the White House Correspondents' Dinner." *LiveAbout*, April 9, 2019, www.liveabout.com/stephen-colbert-white-house-correspondents-dinner-2734728.
Lacapria, Kim. "Donald Trump 'Fifth Avenue' Comment." *Snopes*, January 24, 2016, www.snopes.com/fact-check/donald-trump-fifth-avenue-comment/.
Lakritz, Naomi. "Charlie Hebdo Controversy Is About Good Taste, Not Fear." *Calgary Herald*, January 13, 2015, https://calgaryherald.com/opinion/columnists/lakritz-charlie-hebdo-controversy-is-about-good-taste-not-fear.
LaMarre, Heather L., et al. "The Irony of Satire." *The International Journal of Press/Politics*, vol. 14, no. 2, April 1, 2009, p. 212.
Laughland, Oliver. "FBI Director Stands by Claim That North Korea Was Source of Sony Cyber-Attack." *The Guardian*, January 7, 2015, www.theguardian.com/world/2015/jan/07/fbi-director-north-korea-source-sony-cyber-attack-james-comey.
Leah, Rachel. "A Former Skinhead Reflects on Charlottesville: 'We Have a Massive and Dangerous Domestic Terrorist Threat'." *Salon*, August 16, 2017, www.salon.com/2017/08/16/a-former-skinhead-reflects-on-charlottesville-we-have-a-massive-and-dangerous-domestic-terrorist-threat/; Life After Hate, www.lifeafterhate.org/.
Lee, Hoon and Nojin Kwak. "The Affect Effect of Political Satire: Sarcastic Humor, Negative Emotions, and Political Participation." *Mass Communication and Society*, vol. 17, no. 3, pp. 307–328, https://doi.org/10.1080/15205436.2014.891133.
Lee, Judith Yaross. "Assaults of Laughter." *Studies in American Humor*, vol. 1, no. 1, April 2015, pp. v–xiv. https://doi.org/10.5325/studamerhumor.1.1.v.
Lee, Traci G. "Comedian Hasan Minhaj to Congress on Guns: 'Is This What You Want Your Legacy to Be?'" *NBC News*, June 17, 2016, www.nbcnews.com/news/asian-america/comedian-hasan-minhaj-criticizes-congress-powerful-speech-orlando-n594486.
Levere, Jane. "Seth Meyers and His Writing Team Talk Trump, 'A Closer Look' and YouTube." *Forbes*, October 31, 2017, www.forbes.com/sites/janelevere/2017/10/31/seth-meyers-and-his-writing-team-talk-trump-a-closer-look-and-youtube/#116f91ccd8fc.
Lewis, Charles. "Truth and Lies in the Trump Era." *The Nation*, October 13, 2017, www.thenation.com/article/truth-and-lies-in-the-trump-era/.

Libit, Daniel. "The Inside Story of Donald Trump's Comedy Central Roast Is Everything You Thought It Would Be." *The Huffington Post*, October 11, 2016, www.huffingtonpost.com/entry/the-inside-story-of-donald-trumps-comedy-central-roast-is-everything-you-thought-it-would-be_us_57fbed42e4b0e655eab6c191.

Lichter, Robert, et al. *Politics Is a Joke: How TV Comedians are Remaking Political Life*. Routledge, 2018.

Little, Becky. "How Gary Hart's Sex Scandal Betrayed His Character." *History, A&E Television Network*, November 7, 2018, www.history.com/news/gary-hart-scandal-front-runner.

Littleton, Cynthia. "Melissa McCarthy returns to 'SNL' as a 'Calm' White House Press Secretary Sean Spicer." *Business Insider*, February 12, 2017, www.businessinsider.com/snl-melissa-mccarthy-donald-trump-white-house-press-secretary-sean-spicer-2017-2.

Locker, Melissa. "John Oliver Takes on Donald Trump on Last Week Tonight." *Time*, February 29, 2016, http://time.com/4240734/john-oliver-donald-trump-last-week-tonight/.

Lorenz, Taylor, et al. "TikTok Teens and K-Pop Stans Say They Sank Trump Rally." *The New York Times*, June 21, 2020, www.nytimes.com/2020/06/21/style/tiktok-trump-rally-tulsa.html.

Lowndes, Joseph. "Far-Right Extremism Dominates the GOP: It Didn't Start–and End–with Trump." *The Washington Post*, November 8, 2021, www.washingtonpost.com/outlook/2021/11/08/far-right-extremism-dominates-gop-it-didnt-start-wont-end-with-trump/.

Lund, Jeb. "Stop Waiting for Trump to Start Making Sense." *Esquire*, January 11, 2017, www.esquire.com/news-politics/news/a52214/trump-bullies/.

Maclay, Kathleen. "Researchers Help Define What Makes a Political Conservative." *UCBerkeleyNews*, July 22, 2003, www.berkeley.edu/news/media/releases/2003/07/22_politics.shtml.

Maglio, Tony. "How Trevor Noah's *Daily Show* Is Beating Jon Stewart's." *The Wrap*, November 1, 2015, updated December 8, 2015, www.thewrap.com/trevor-noah-first-month-daily-show-comedy-central-michele-ganeless-digital-tv-ratings-twitter/.

Mahler, Jonathan. "CNN Had a Problem: Donald Trump Fixed It." *The New York Times*, April 4, 2017, www.nytimes.com/2017/04/04/magazine/cnn-had-a-problem-donald-trump-solved-it.html.

Mariotti, Renato, et al. "Meyers: Trump Wanted Me to Apologize On-Air for Making Fun of Him." *Politico*, May 8, 2018, www.politico.com/magazine/story/2018/05/08/seth-meyers-trump-whcd-jokes-apologize-218323.

Marks, Andrea. "'I Have to Pinch Myself': Sarah Cooper's Rapid Rise from Trump TikToker to Netflix Star." *Rolling Stone*, October 27, 2020, www.rollingstone.com/tv/tv-features/sarah-cooper-interview-everythings-fine-1081258/.

Marr, Kendra. "Donald Trump, Birther?" *Politico*, March 17, 2011, www.politico.com/story/2011/03/donald-trump-birther-051473.

Marr, Madeleine. "No Fake News: The Daily Show's Trump Presidential Twitter Library Is Headed to Miami." *Miami Herald*, October 22, 2018, www.miamiherald.com/miami-com/news/article225809845.html#storylink=cpy.

Martin, Michel. "Former White House Press Secretary Uncomfortable with Spicer's First Briefing." *NPR*, January 22, 2017, www.npr.org/2017/01/22/511103584/former-white-house-press-secretary-uncomfortable-with-spicers-first-briefing.

Mazza, Ed. "Every Critic, Every Detractor, Will Have to Bow Down to President Trump." *The Huffington Post*, September 23, 2016, www.huffingtonpost.com/entry/omarosa-bown-to-president-trump_us_57e47e34e4b0e80b1ba15296.

———. "Don Lemon Can't Stop Laughing as Old Paul Manafort Clip Comes Back to Haunt Trump." *Huffington Post*, November 30, 2018, www.huffingtonpost.com/entry/don-lemon-laughing-paul-manafort-donald-trump_us_5c00ed2ee4b0249dce737c53.

McAdams, Dan P. "The Narcissist." *The Atlantic*, January 18, 2018, www.theatlantic.com/magazine/archive/2016/06/the-mind-of-donald-trump/480771/.

McAndrew, Frank T. "Politicians Don't Seem to Laugh at Themselves as Much Anymore." *The Conversation*, August 21, 2019, https://theconversation.com/politicians-dont-seem-to-laugh-at-themselves-as-much-anymore-122103.

McCarthy, Niall. "Americans Trust Jon Stewart More Than Bloomberg and the Economist." *Forbes*, 2015, www.forbes.com/sites/niallmccarthy/2015/02/11/americans-trust-jon-stewart-more-than-bloomberg-and-the-economist-infographic/#3fad46523526.

McClennen, Sophia A. *Colbert's America: Satire and Democracy*. Palgrave Macmillan, 2011.

———. "Jon Stewart's War on Propaganda: Cruz Sound as Dogmatic as Fundamentalist Iranians." *Salon*, November 17, 2014, www.salon.com/test/2014/11/17/jon_stewarts_war_on_propaganda_hannity_cruz_sound_as_dogmatic_as_fundamentalist_iranians/.

———. "Stephen Colbert Schooled Fox News Hard: Comedy, Bill O'Reilly and the Exposure of Right-Wing Patriotism Lies." *Salon*, December 12, 2014, www.salon.com/2014/12/12/stephen_colbert_schooled_fox_news_hard_comedy_bill_oreilly_and_the_exposure_of_right_wing_patriotism_lies/.

———. "They'll Come for *The Daily Show* Next: Why Satirists Always Threaten Fundamentalists." *Salon*, January 9, 2015, www.salon.com/test/2015/01/09/theyll_come_for_jon_stewart_next_why_satirists_always_threaten_fundamentalists/.

———. "'American Sniper's' Biggest Lie: Clint Eastwood Has a Delusional Fox News Problem." *Salon*, January 27, 2015, www.salon.com/2015/01/26/american_snipers_biggest_lie_clint_eastwood_has_a_delusional_fox_news_problem/.

———. "Trevor Noah's Master Class: It's Not Just Fox News—This Is the Topic That Needs Noah, Oliver, Stewart." *Salon*, October 12, 2015, www.salon.com/2015/10/12/trevor_noahs_master_class_its_not_just_fox_news_this_is_the_topic_that_needs_noah_oliver_stewart/.

———. "'Because ISIS': Whoever Wins the Presidential Election, the Middle East Loses." *Salon*, October 11, 2016, www.salon.com/2016/10/11/because-isis-whoever-wins-the-presidential-election-the-middle-east-loses/.

———. "Don't Blame Jon Stewart for Donald Trump: Comedy Central Didn't Make America Fall for 'Fake News' and 'Post-Truth'." *Salon*, December 31, 2016, www.salon.com/2016/12/31/dont-blame-jon-stewart-for-donald-trump-comedy-central-didnt-make-america-fall-for-fake-news-and-post-truth/.

———. "Hitting Trump Where It Hurts: The Satire Troops Take Up Comedy Arms Against Donald Trump." *Salon*, February 11, 2017, www.salon.com/2017/02/11/hitting-trump-where-it-hurts-the-satire-troops-take-up-comedy-arms-against-donald-trump/.

———. "Beware the Trump Brain Rot: The Cognitive Effects of This Administration's Actions Could Be Disastrous." *Salon*, February 25, 2017, www.salon.com/2017/02/25/beware-the-trump-brain-rot-the-cognitive-effects-of-this-administrations-actions-could-be-disastrous/.

———. "Stephen Colbert and Trevor Noah Step Up: Donald Trump Made *The Daily Show* and Out of Character Colbert Relevant Again." *Salon*, April 2017, www.salon.com/test/2017/04/08/trevor-noah-and-stephen-colbert-step-up-donald-trump-made-the-daily-show-and-out-of-character-colbert-relevant-again/.

---. "Degeneration Nation: It Takes a Village of Idiots to Raise a Kakistocracy Like Donald Trump's." *Salon*, May 30, 2017, https://twitter.com/Phil_Lewis_/status/869797513427116033.

---. "Enough with 'The Colbert Defense': Why Criminals, Bigots and Jerks Cry 'Satire!' When Exposed." *Salon*, June 17, 2017, www.salon.com/2017/06/17/enough-with-the-colbert-defense-why-criminals-bigots-and-jerks-cry-satire-when-exposed/.

---. "Forget Fake News – Alt-Right Memes Could Do More Damage to Democracy." *Salon*, July 8, 2017, www.salon.com/2017/07/08/forget-fake-news-alt-right-memes-could-do-more-damage-to-democracy/.

---. "Trump's Ironic Effect on Political Satire." *Film Quarterly*, vol. 75, no. 2, 2021, pp. 27–37, https://doi.org/10.1525/FQ.2021.75.2.27.

---. "The Joke Is on You: Satire and Blowback." *Political Humor in a Changing Media Landscape: A New Generation of Research*, edited by Jody C. Baumgartner and Amy B. Becker. Lexington Books, 2018, pp. 137–156.

McClennen, Sophia A. and Remy Maisel. *Is Satire Saving Our Nation? Mockery and American Politics*. Palgrave Macmillan, 2014.

Milbank, Dana. "Does Trump's Great Gut Mean a Tiny Brain?" *The Washington Post*, November 28, 2018, www.washingtonpost.com/opinions/why-would-trump-need-brains-when-he-has-a-gut/2018/11/28/75bc6c38-f341-11e8-80d0-f7e1948d55f4_story.html.

Mitchell, Amy, et al. "Political Polarization and Media Habits." *Pew Research Center*, October 21, 2014, www.journalism.org/2014/10/21/political-polarization-media-habits/.

Moore, Michael. "Fahrenheit 11/9." September 21, 2018, https://fahrenheit119.com/.

Morreall, John. "Philosophy of Humor." *Stanford Encyclopedia of Philosophy*, September 28, 2016, https://plato.stanford.edu/entries/humor/.

Morris, Alex. "How Samantha Bee Crashed the Late-Night Boys' Club." *Rolling Stone*, June 25, 2018, www.rollingstone.com/tv/tv-news/how-samantha-bee-crashed-the-late-night-boys-club-104583/.

Moy, Patricia, et al. "Communication and Citizenship: Mapping the Political Effects of Infotainment." *Mass Communication & Society*, vol. 8, no. 2, 2005, pp. 111–131.

---. "Priming Effects of Late-Night Comedy." *International Journal of Public Opinion Research*, vol. 18, no. 2, 2006, pp. 198–210, https://academic.oup.com/ijpor/article/18/2/198/674427.

Muldaur, Maureen, dir. "Smothered: The Censorship Struggles of the Smothers Brothers Comedy Hour." 2002, https://www.documentarysite.com/2010/12/10/smothered-the-censorship-struggles-of-the-smothers-brothers-comedy-hour/.

National Annenberg Election Survey. "*Daily Show* Viewers Knowledgeable About Presidential Campaign." September 21, 2014, www.naes04.org and www.techdirt.com/articles/20141113/06034829128/yet-another-study-shows-us-satire-programs-do-better-job-informing-viewers-than-actual-news-outlets.shtml.

Nededog, Jethro. "Trevor Noah Rips Apart Donald Trump's Anti-immigration Views in Profanity-filled Rant." *Business Insider*, September 15, 2016, www.businessinsider.com/trevor-noah-donald-trump-immigration-rant-2016-9.

Nesbit, Jeff. "Donald Trump Is the First True Reality TV President." *Time*, December 9, 2016, http://time.com/4596770/donald-trump-reality-tv/.

Niehoff, Leonard N., "Of Bee Stings, Mud Pies, and Outhouses: Exploring the Value of Satire Through the Theory of Useful Untruths." *The State of Our Satirical Union*, Conference paper, University of Minnesota, April 20, 2018, https://drive.google.com/file/d/12JRwLy9ByHzf_QdEaD9H6S7ypuOsvFPr/view.

Niles, Emma and Robert Reich. "The 935 Lies They Told Us About Iraq." *Truthdig*, January 24, 2008, www.truthdig.com/articles/the-935-lies-they-told-us-about-iraq/.

Nunberg, Geoffrey. *Talking Right: How Conservatives Turned Liberalism into a Tax-Raising, Latte-Drinking, Sushi-Eating, Volvo-Driving, "New York Times"-Reading, Body-Piercing, Hollywood-Loving, Left-Wing Freak Show*. Public Affairs, 2007.

Nussbaum, Emily. "The TV That Created Donald Trump." *New Yorker*, July 24, 2017, www.newyorker.com/magazine/2017/07/31/the-tv-that-created-donald-trump.

Nuzzi, Olivia. "Kellyanne Conway Is a Star." *New York Magazine*, March 18, 2017, http://nymag.com/intelligencer/2017/03/kellyanne-conway-trumps-first-lady.html?gtm=bottom&gtm=bottom.

Nyhan, Brendan and Jason Reifler. "When Corrections Fail: The Persistence of Political Misperceptions." *Political Behavior*, vol. 32, no. 2, 2010, pp. 303–330, https://doi.org/10.1007/s11109-010-9112-2.

Ofri, Danielle. "Americans' Election-Induced Anxiety isn't Abating: Should Doctors Be Treating It?" *Slate Magazine*, January 19, 2017, www.slate.com/articles/health_and_science/medical_examiner/2017/01/americans_are_experiencing_election_induced_medical_symptoms.html.

Ortiz, Erik. "Jon Stewart Reunites with Stephen Colbert, Mocks Trump's Executive Orders." *NBCNews.com*, February 1, 2017, www.nbcnews.com/pop-culture/tv/jon-stewart-reunites-stephen-colbert-mocks-trump-s-executive-orders-n715306.

Orwell, George. *1984*. Signet, 1961.

Otterbein, Holly. "Police: PSU Frat Posted Photos of Nude Unconscious Women on Facebook." *Philadelphia Magazine*, 2015, www.phillymag.com/news/2015/03/17/police-psu-frat-posted-photos-of-nude-unconscious-women-on-facebook/

Pallotta, Frank. "Jimmy Fallon Responds to Trump: 'Why Are You Tweeting at Me?'" *CNNMoney*, June 26, 2018, https://money.cnn.com/2018/06/26/media/jimmy-fallon-trump-response/index.html.

Paquette, Danielle. "Why the Most Outrageous Part of Donald Trump's 'Hot Mic' Comments isn't the Vulgar Language." *The Washington Post*, October 7, 2016, www.washingtonpost.com/news/wonk/wp/2016/10/07/the-real-issue-with-donald-trump-saying-a-man-can-do-anything-to-a-woman/?utm_term=.267f40080a94.

Parker, Ryan. "'Simpsons' Writer Who Predicted Trump Presidency in 2000: 'It Was a Warning to America'." *The Hollywood Reporter*, June 26, 2019, www.hollywoodreporter.com/live-feed/simpsons-writer-who-predicted-trump-876295.

Paskin, Willa. "Why Are Americans Ignoring Trevor Noah?" *Slate*, January 24, 2016, updated January 25, 2016, www.slate.com/articles/arts/cover_story/2016/01/why_america_isn_t_paying_attention_to_the_daily_show_with_trevor_noah_in.html.

Paterniti, Michael. "Jimmy Kimmel Doesn't Want to Cry." *GQ*, January 16, 2018, www.gq.com/story/jimmy-kimmel-is-seriously-funny.

Patterson, John. "Dr. Strangelove: No 6 Best Comedy Film of All Time." *The Guardian*, October 18, 2010, www.theguardian.com/film/2010/oct/18/dr-strangelove-kubrick-comedy.

Patterson, Thomas. "Pre-Primary News Coverage of the 2016 Presidential Race: Trump's Rise, Sander's Emergence, Clinton's Struggle." *Harvard Kennedy School Shorenstein Center on Media, Politics and Public Policy*, June 13, 2016, https://shorensteincenter.org/pre-primary-news-coverage-2016-trump-clinton-sanders/.

———. "News Coverage of the 2016 General Election: How the Press Failed the Voters." *Harvard Kennedy School Shorenstein Center on Media, Politics, and Public Policy*, December 7, 2016, https://shorensteincenter.org/news-coverage-2016-general-election/.

———. "News Coverage of Donald Trump's First 100 Days." *Harvard Kennedy School Shorenstein Center on Media, Politics, and Public Policy*, May 18, 2017, https://shorensteincenter.org/news-coverage-donald-trumps-first-100-days/.

Pengelly, Martin. "'They Hate Your Guts': Trump Attacks Democrats and Media at Michigan Rally." *The Guardian*, April 29, 2018, www.theguardian.com/us-news/2018/apr/29/donald-trump-michigan-rally.

Pennycook, Gordon, et al. "On the Reception and Detection of Pseudo-Profound Bullshit." *Judgment and Decision Making*, vol. 10, no. 6, 2015, pp. 549–563.

———. "Prior Exposure Increases Perceived Accuracy of Fake News." *Journal of Experimental Psychology. General*, vol. 147, no. 12, 2018, pp. 1865–1880, https://doi.org/10.1037/xge0000465.

Pine, D. W. "The Stories Behind Donald Trump's TIME Covers." *Time*, January 19, 2021, https://time.com/5928282/donald-trump-time-covers/.

Pinkleton, Bruce, et al. "Perceptions of News Media, External Efficacy, and Public Affairs Apathy in Political Decision Making and Disaffection." *Journalism & Mass Communication Quarterly*, vol. 89, no. 1, 2012, pp. 23–29, https://journals.sagepub.com/doi/abs/10.1177/1077699011428586?journalCode=jmqc&.

Plato. *The Republic of Plato*. Translated by Benjamin Jowett. Henry Frowde, Oxford University Press, 1888. *Project Gutenberg EBook*, www.gutenberg.org/files/55201/55201-h/55201-h.htm.

Poniewozik, James. "Jon Stewart, the Fake Newsman Who Made a Real Difference." *Time*, 2015, https://time.com/3704321/jon-stewart-daily-show-fake-news/.

Popovic, Srdja and Mladen Jokic. "Why Dictators Don't Like Jokes." *Foreign Policy*, April 5, 2013, https://foreignpolicy.com/2013/04/05/why-dictators-dont-like-jokes/.

Popovic, Srdja and Sophia A. McClennen. *Pranksters vs. Autocrats: Why Dilemma Actions Advance Nonviolent Activism*. Cornell University Press, 2020.

Popovic, Srdja and Matthew Miller. *Blueprint for Revolution: How to Use Rice Pudding, Lego Men, and Other Nonviolent Techniques to Galvanize Communities, Overthrow Dictators, or Simply Change the World*. Spiegel & Grau, 2015.

Postman, Neil. *Amusing Ourselves to Death: Public Discourse in the Age of Show Business*. Penguin Books, 2006.

Pramuk, Jacob. "Trump: 'President Barack Obama Was Born in The United States. Period'." *CNBC*, September 16, 2016, www.cnbc.com/2016/09/16/trump-president-obama-was-born-in-the-united-states-period.html.

"President Trump Is Making Satire Great Again." *The Economist*, February 11, 2017, www.economist.com/united-states/2017/02/11/president-trump-is-making-satire-great-again.

"Public Knowledge of Current Affairs Little Changed by News and Information Revolutions." *Pew Research Center*, April 15, 2017, www.people-press.org/2007/04/15/public-knowledge-of-current-affairs-little-changed-by-news-and-information-revolutions/.

Quinnipiac University. "QU Poll Release Detail." *QU Poll*, January 15, 2019, https://poll.qu.edu/national/release-detail?ReleaseID=2593.

Rami, Trupti. "Hasan Minhaj Wants to Update Late-Night Comedy Model with 'Radioactive' Topics." *Vulture*, November 19, 2018, www.vulture.com/2018/11/hasan-minhaj-patriot-act-new-late-night-comedy-model.html.

Randall, Eric. "The 'Death of Irony,' and Its Many Reincarnations." *The Atlantic*, September 9, 2011, www.theatlantic.com/national/archive/2011/09/death-irony-and-its-many-reincarnations/338114/.

Read, Max. "Can Facebook Solve Its Macedonian Fake-News Problem?" *New York Magazine*, November 4, 2016, http://nymag.com/intelligencer/2016/11/can-facebook-solve-its-macedonian-fake-news-problem.html.

Reich, Robert. "Trump's Dangerous Lies About Voter Fraud." *Newsweek*, February 17, 2017, www.newsweek.com/robert-reich-trump-dangerous-lies-voter-fraud-557897.

Rein, Lisa, et al. "Federal Agents Conduct Immigration Enforcement Raids in at Least Six States." *The Washington Post*, February 11, 2017, www.washingtonpost.com/national/federal-agents-conduct-sweeping-immigration-enforcement-raids-in-at-least-6-states/2017/02/10/4b9f443a-efc8-11e6-b4ff-ac2cf509efe5_story.html?utm_term=.c126fdf4fa65.

Resnick, Brian. "Why People Fall for Bullshit, According to a Scientist." *Vox*, December 3, 2015, www.vox.com/science-and-health/2015/12/3/9844480/why-people-believe-bullshit-science.

Ridley, Matt. "It's Time for a Bonfire of the Regulatory Quangos That Are Destroying Our Democracy." *The Telegraph*, September 16, 2019, www.telegraph.co.uk/opinion/.

Riffkin, Rebecca. "Americans' Trust in Media Remains at Historical Low." *Gallup*, September 28, 2015, https://news.gallup.com/poll/185927/americans-trust-media-remains-historical-low.aspx.

Riggio, Ronald. "Why Jon Stewart Is the Most Trusted Man in America." *Psychology Today*, July 24, 2009, www.psychologytoday.com/us/blog/cutting-edge-leadership/200907/why-jon-stewart-is-the-most-trusted-man-in-america.

Rivera, Kamila. "Why Does John Oliver Feel Like the Only Person We Can Trust on TV." *Showbiz Cheatsheet*, 2019, www.cheatsheet.com/entertainment/why-does-john-oliver-feel-like-the-only-person-we-can-trust-on-tv.html/.

Roberts, Roxanne. "I Sat Next to Donald Trump at the Infamous 2011 White House Correspondents' Dinner." *The Washington Post*, April 28, 2016, www.washingtonpost.com/lifestyle/style/i-sat-next-to-donald-trump-at-the-infamous-2011-white-house-correspondents-dinner/2016/04/27/5cf46b74-0bea-11e6-8ab8-9ad050f76d7d_story.html?noredirect=on&utm_term=.0ca400193f5f.

Robinson, Gregg J. "Political Cynicism and the Foreclosure Crisis." *Social Justice*, vol. 40, no. 3(133), 2014, pp. 99–118, 111. *JSTOR*, www.jstor.org/stable/24361651. Accessed 14 July 2022.

Robinson, Joanna. "S.N.L.: Could Matt Damon's Crazed Impression Hurt Brett Kavanaugh?" *Vanity Fair*, September 30, 2018, www.vanityfair.com/hollywood/2018/09/snl-matt-damon-brett-kavanaugh-impression-trump.

Rogers, Joann. "Go Forth in Anger." *Psychology Today*, March 11, 2014, www.psychology-today.com/articles/201403/go-forth-in-anger?collection=163107.

Romano, Aja. "Michael Moore: Fight Donald Trump with 'an Army of Comedy'." *Vox*, January 20, 2017, www.vox.com/policy-and-politics/2017/1/20/14331072/michael-moore-alec-baldwin-we-stand-united-rally-comedy.

Rosen, Christopher. "Melissa McCarthy Plays Unhinged Sean Spicer in Biting 'SNL' Sketch." *EW.com*, February 6, 2017, http://ew.com/tv/2017/02/05/snl-melissa-mccarthy-sean-spicer/.

Rottenberg, Josh. "Anthony Atamanuik and James Adomian Have Turned 'Trump vs Bernie' into a Comedy Hit." *Los Angeles Times*, April 29, 2016, www.latimes.com/entertainment/tv/la-ca-st-trump-sanders-show-20160501-story.html.

Rozsa, Matthew. "Donald Trump's Watching a Lot of Television and It's Worrying His Aides: Reports." *Salon*, January 25, 2017, www.salon.com/control/2017/01/24/donald-trump-is-addicted-to-the-media-and-its-worrying-his-aides/.

———. "President Trump Admits to the World That He Makes Things Up to America's Allies." *Salon*, March 15, 2018, www.salon.com/2018/03/15/president-trump-admits-to-the-world-that-he-makes-things-up-to-americas-allies/.

Rubin, Jennifer. "He Won: Now What Does Donald Trump Do?" *The Washington Post*, November 9, 2016, www.washingtonpost.com/blogs/right-turn/wp/2016/11/09/he-won-now-what-does-donald-trump-do/?utm_term=.6cacd2003de3.

"Russia Spent $1.25 Million Per Month on Ads, Acted Like an Ad Agency: Muller." *AdAge*, February 16, 2018, https://adage.com/article/digital/russia-spent-1-25m-ads-acted-agency-mueller/312424/.

Rutenberg, Jim. "Colbert, Kimmel and the Politics of Late Night." *The New York Times*, September 24, 2017, www.nytimes.com/2017/09/24/business/colbert-kimmel-and-the-politics-of-late-night.html.

Ryan, Maureen. "Comedy Central's *Daily Show* Has Lost Its Edge." *Variety*, March 30, 2016, https://variety.com/2016/voices/columns/comedy-central-daily-show-1201740385/.

Sargent, Greg. "Trump Is Set to Introduce a New 'Muslim Ban'. This One Is Nonsense, too." *The Washington Post*, April 6, 2019, www.washingtonpost.com/blogs/plum-line/wp/2017/02/21/trump-is-set-to-introduce-a-new-muslim-ban-this-one-is-nonsense-too/?utm_term=.e911e480ded8.

Scherer, Michael. "Birtherism Is Dead, but the Birther Industry Continues." *Time*, April 27, 2011, http://swampland.time.com/2011/04/27/birtherism-is-dead-but-the-birther-industry-continues/.

Schneider, Christian. "Conservatives Should Not Surrender in Entertainment Wars." *Milwaukee Journal Sentinel*, June 14, 2018, www.jsonline.com/story/opinion/columnists/christian-schneider/2018/06/14/conservatives-should-not-surrender-comedy-war/701802002/.

Scruton, Roger and Peter Jones. "Laughter." *Aristotelian Society Supplementary Volume*, vol. 56, no. 1, 1982, pp. 197–228, https://doi.org/10.1093/aristoteliansupp/56.1.197.

Seager, Susan. "Donald Trump Is a Libel Bully but also a Libel Loser." *Media Law Resource Center*, Fall 2016, www.medialaw.org/index.php?option=com_k2&view=item&id=3470.

Second Nexus Staff. "We Need to Talk About How Donald Trump's Policies Are Harming Disabled Americans." *Second Nexus*, January 16, 2018, https://secondnexus.com/news/politics/trump-policies-harm-disabled/.

Segarra, Lisa Marie. "Stephen Colbert to Rex Tillerson: 'Nobody Calls Our President a Moron Except Me'." *Time*, October 5, 2017, http://time.com/4970357/stephen-colbert-to-rex-tillerson-nobody-calls-our-president-a-moron-except-me/.

Shackle, Shamira. "PJ O'Rourke." *New Statesman*, January 9, 2012, https://web.archive.org/web/20120115055927/www.newstatesman.com/north-america/2012/01/barack-obama-interview-tea.

Shafer, Jack. "Trump the Bully." *Politico*, January 27, 2017, www.politico.com/magazine/story/2017/01/trump-the-bully-214698.

Shaw, Jazz. "Even John Kasich Has Noticed That *The Daily Show with Trevor Noah* Is Tanking." *Hot Air*, March 31, 2016, https://hotair.com/archives/2016/03/31/even-john-kasich-has-noticed-that-the-daily-show-with-trevor-noah-is-tanking/.

Sidahmed, Mazin. "Anarchist Group Installs Nude Donald Trump Statues in New York City." *The Guardian*, August 18, 2016, www.theguardian.com/us-news/2016/aug/18/nude-donald-trump-statues-new-york-indecline.

Siegel, Lee. "How Jon Stewart, Stephen Colbert Blazed a Trail for Trump." *Colombia Journalism Review*, December 22, 2016, www.cjr.org/special_report/trump_jon_stewart_stephen_colbert.php.

Silverman, Craig. "This Analysis Shows How Viral Fake Election News Stories Outperformed Real News on Facebook." *Buzzfeed News*, November 16, 2016, www.buzzfeednews.com/article/craigsilverman/viral-fake-election-news-outperformed-real-news-on-facebook#.emA15rzd0.

Simon, Johnny. "'Turn the Lights Off': How the White House Hides from a Crisis, in Photos." *Quartz*, May 10, 2017, https://qz.com/980272/after-trump-fires-fbi-director-comey-photos-of-sean-spicer-hiding-in-the-shadows/.

Sims, David. "Alec Baldwin's Scarier, Nastier Donald Trump." *The Atlantic*, October 3, 2016, www.theatlantic.com/entertainment/archive/2016/10/alec-baldwin-donald-trump-snl/502610/.

———. "Why Comedy Central's 'The President Show' Might Just Work." *The Atlantic*, April 28, 2017, www.theatlantic.com/entertainment/archive/2017/04/why-the-president-show-might-just-work/524757/.

Skolnik, Jon. "Trump Tried to Get Justice Department to Stop 'SNL' and 'Jimmy Kimmel Live' From Mocking Him: RPT." *Salon*, June 22, 2021, www.salon.com/2021/06/22/trump-tried-to-get-justice-department-to-stop-snl-and-jimmy-kimmel-live-from-mocking-him-rpt/.

Slobin, Sarah. "The Truth About the Crowd at Trump's Inauguration, in One Photo." *Quartz*, January 22, 2017, https://qz.com/891784/the-truth-about-the-crowd-at-trumps-inauguration-in-one-photo/.

Smith, Moira. "Humor, Unlaughter, and Boundary Maintenance." *The Journal of American Folklore*, vol. 122, no. 484, 2009, pp. 148–171. *JSTOR*, www.jstor.org/stable/20487675.

Sørensen, Majken Jul. *Humour in Political Activism: Creative Nonviolent Resistance*. Palgrave Macmillan, 2016.

Sparrow, Jeff. "We Can Defend Charlie Hebdo Without Endorsing It." *ABC*, January 8, 2015, www.abc.net.au/news/2015-01-09/sparrow-we-should-support-charlie-hebdo,-not-endorse-it/6007836.

Statt, Nick. "FCC Opens Investigation into Stephen Colbert's Controversial Trump Insult." *The Verge*, May 5, 2017, www.theverge.com/2017/5/5/15564230/stephen-colbert-trump-insult-fcc-investigation-obscenity-laws.

Stefansky, Emma. "Trump Steadfastly Refuses to Call Out Charlottesville White Supremacy." *Vanity Fair*, August 13, 2017, www.vanityfair.com/news/2017/08/trump-charlottesville-on-many-sides-white-supremacy.

Stelter, Brian. "CNN Severs Ties with Jeffrey Lord." *CNN Business*, August 10, 2017, https://money.cnn.com/2017/08/10/media/jeffrey-lord-cnn-ties/index.html.

Stern, Marlow. "Stephen Colbert Goes to Washington to Grill Congressmen on Trump-Russia." *The Daily Beast*, March 3, 2018, www.thedailybeast.com/stephen-colbert-goes-to-washington-in-search-of-trump-russia-answers.

Sternberg, Adam. "Stephen Colbert Has America by the Ballots." *New York Magazine*, October 6, 2006, https://nymag.com/news/politics/22322/.

Stewart, Ian. "Netflix Drops Hasan Minhaj Episode in Saudi Arabia at Government's Request." *NPR*, January 1, 2019, www.npr.org/2019/01/01/681469011/netflix-drops-hasan-minhaj-episode-in-saudi-arabia-at-governments-request.

Strause, Jackie. "Comedy Central Launches Weekly Trump-Aimed Late-Night Show." *The Hollywood Reporter*, April 3, 2017, www.hollywoodreporter.com/live-feed/president-show-comedy-central-launches-weekly-trump-aimed-late-night-show-990727.

Stuart, Tessa. "Donald Trump: Liar in Chief." *Rolling Stone*, April 11, 2017, www.rollingstone.com/politics/politics-features/donald-trump-liar-in-chief-115517/.

Suebsaeng, Asawin and Adam Rawnsley. "Trump Wanted His Justice Department to Stop 'SNL' From Teasing Him." *The Daily Beast*, June 22, 2021, www.thedailybeast.com/trump-wanted-his-justice-department-to-stop-snl-from-teasing-him.

Swift, Art. "Americans' Trust in Mass Media Sinks to New Low." *Gallup*, September 14, 2016, https://news.gallup.com/poll/195542/americans-trust-mass-media-sinks-new-low.aspx.

Taibbi, Matt. *Hate Inc: Why Today's Media Makes Us Despise One Another*. OR Books, 2020.

Talbot, Thaddeus. "You Have a Right to Know How Trump's Muslim Ban Was Implemented: So We Sued." *ACLU*, April 13, 2017, www.aclu.org/blog/immigrants-rights/you-have-right-know-how-trumps-muslim-ban-was-implemented-so-we-sued?redirect=blog/speak-freely/you-have-right-know-how-trumps-muslim-ban-was-implemented-so-we-sue.

Taub, Amanda and Brendan Nyhan. "Why People Continue to Believe Objectively False Things." *The New York Times*, March 22, 2017, www.nytimes.com/2017/03/22/upshot/why-objectively-false-things-continue-to-be-believed.html?rref=collection/sectioncollection/upshot&action=click&contentCollection=upshot&region=ion&module=package&version=highlights&contentPlacement=1&pgtype=sectionfront&_r=0.

Techler, Graham. "Hasan Minhaj's Patriot Act Remains Netflix's Best Talk Show in Its Second Season." *Paste Magazine*, February 12, 2019, www.pastemagazine.com/articles/2019/02/hasan-minhajs-patriot-act-remains-netflixs-best-ta.html.

Tejada, Chloe. "Swearing Is a Sign of High Intelligence. Well, F★Ck." *HuffPost*, September 27, 2016, www.huffingtonpost.ca/2016/09/27/swear-words-intelligence_n_12213206.html.

"Today's Journalists Less Prominent." *Pew Research Center*, March 8, 2007, www.people-press.org/2007/03/08/todays-journalists-less-prominent/.

Todd, Chuck. "Conway: Press Secretary Gave 'Alternative Facts'." *NBC*, 2017, www.nbcnews.com/meet-the-press/video/conway-press-secretary-gave-alternative-facts-860142147643.

Velasquez-Manoff, Moises. "Trump Ruins Irony, too." *The New York Times*, March 20, 2017, www.nytimes.com/2017/03/20/opinion/trump-ruins-irony-too.html.

Vick, Karl. "Al-Qaeda Group Claims Responsibility for Paris Terror Attack." *Time*, January 9, 2015, https://time.com/3661650/charlie-hebdo-paris-terror-attack-al-qaeda/.

Vitto, Laura. "Tina Fey Knows She 'Screwed Up' in Her Charlottesville Sheet-Cake Segment for SNL." *Mashable*, 2018, https://mashable.com/2018/05/05/tina-fey-sheet-cake-charlottesville-sketch-letterman/.

Volcovici, Valerie. "Trump Administration Tells EPA to Cut Climate Page from Website: Sources." *Reuters*, January 25, 2017, www.reuters.com/article/us-usa-trump-epa-climatechange-idUSKBN15906G.

Walsh, Kenneth. "A Nation of Cynics." *U.S. News*, 2018, www.usnews.com/news/the-report/articles/2018-01-05/president-trump-is-leading-a-nation-of-cynics.

Wan, William. "The Surprisingly Dark, Twisted History of Presidential Impersonators in America." *The Washington Post*, June 27, 2016, www.washingtonpost.com/news/post-nation/wp/2016/06/27/the-surprisingly-dark-twisted-history-of-presidential-impersonators-in-america/?utm_term=.35a2894a71a7.

Warren, James. "Satirist Andy Borowitz Explains the Fine Art of Lampooning Trump." *Poynter*, October 31, 2017, www.poynter.org/news/satirist-andy-borowitz-explains-fine-art-lampooning-trump.

Watkins, D. "Dear Hard-Working White People: Congratulations, You Played Yourself." *Salon*, Salon Media Group, November 20, 2016, www.salon.com/2016/11/20/dear-hard-working-white-people-congratulations-you-played-yourself/.

White, Rose. "Do We Trust Comedians More than Journalists?" *Mediums*, June 12, 2016, https://medium.com/@rosekellywhite/do-we-trust-comedians-more-than-journalists-1a4b46a6588b.

Wilkinson, Alissa. "5 Years in, HBO's Last Week Tonight Is a Lot More Than 'Just Comedy'." *Vox*, February 17, 2019, www.vox.com/culture/2019/2/14/18213228/last-week-tonight-john-oliver-hbo-season-six.

Wilstein, Matt. "Alec Baldwin Goes High as Donald Trump Goes Low in SNL Twitter Battle." *Daily Beast*, January 15, 2017, www.thedailybeast.com/alec-baldwin-goes-high-as-donald-trump-goes-low-in-snl-twitter-battle.

———. "Samantha Bee Tears into 'Feckless C✶nt' Ivanka Trump." *The Daily Beast*, May 31, 2018, www.thedailybeast.com/samantha-bee-tears-into-feckless-cunt-ivanka-trump.

———. "Why 'The President Show' Star Can't Go Out in Public as Trump Anymore." *Daily Beast*, July 10, 2022, www.thedailybeast.com/why-the-president-show-star-cant-go-out-in-public-as-trump-anymore.

Winfrey, Graham. "Michael Moore, Robert De Niro, Alec Baldwin and More Lead Anti-Trump Rally in NYC." *IndieWire*, January 19, 2017, www.indiewire.com/2017/01/michael-moore-robert-de-niro-alec-baldwin-anti-trump-rally-1201770862/.

Yahr, Emily. "Jimmy Kimmel Explains His Twitter Feud with Donald Trump Jr. Over Harvey Weinstein Jokes." *The Washington Post*, October 10, 2017, www.washingtonpost.com/news/arts-and-entertainment/wp/2017/10/10/jimmy-kimmel-explains-his-twitter-feud-with-donald-trump-jr-over-harvey-weinstein-jokes/?utm_term=.e25f1f432a15.

———. "Read Jimmy Kimmel's Emotional Monologue That Begs Trump to Address Gun Control." *The Washington Post*, February 16, 2018, www.washingtonpost.com/news/arts-and-entertainment/wp/2018/02/16/read-jimmy-kimmels-emotional-monologue-that-begs-trump-to-address-gun-control/?noredirect=on&utm_term=.dd84d1b27d3c.

Young, Dannagal G. "Theories and Effects of Political Humor: Discounting Cues, Gateways, and the Impact of Incongruities." *The Oxford Handbook of Political Communication*, August 2017, www.oxfordhandbooks.com/view/10.1093/oxfordhb/9780199793471.001.0001/oxfordhb-9780199793471-e-29.

———. *Irony and Outrage: The Polarized Landscape of Rage, Fear, and Laughter in the United States*. Oxford University Press, 2020.

Young, Dannagal G. and Sarah Esralew. "Jon Stewart a Heretic? Surely You Jest: Political Participation and Discussion Among Viewers of Late-Night Comedy Programming." *The Stewart/Colbert Effect: Essays on the Real Impact of Fake News*, edited by Amarnath Amarasingam. McFarland, 2011, pp. 99–116.

Young, Dannagal G. and Russell M. Tisinger. "Dispelling Late-Night Myths: News Consumption Among Late-Night Comedy Viewers and the Predictors of Exposure to Various Late-Night Shows." *Harvard International Journal of Press/Politics*, vol. 11, no. 3, 2006, pp. 113–134, https://doi.org/10.1177/1081180X05286042.

Young, Dannagal G., et al. "Psychology, Political Ideology, and Humor Appreciation: Why Is Satire so Liberal?" *Psychology of Popular Media Culture*, vol. 8, no. 2, 2017, pp. 134–147, https://doi.org/10.1037/ppm0000157.

Youssef, Bassem. "Promotional Materials." *Revolution for Dummies: Laughing Through the Arab Spring*. Harper Collins, 2017.

Zimmer, Ben. "A Hero for Our Time: We Found the Man Behind the Priceless Trump Insult 'S—Gibbon'." *Slate Magazine*, February 13, 2017, https://slate.com/culture/2017/02/the-origin-of-the-trump-insult-shitgibbon-revealed.html.

Zoonen, Liesbet van. *Entertaining the Citizen: When Politics and Popular Culture Converge.* Rowman & Littlefield, 2005.

Zorthian, Julia. "John Oliver's 'Donald Drumpf' Segment Broke HBO Records." *Time*, March 31, 2016, http://time.com/4277790/john-oliver-donald-drumpf-records/.

Zwicky, Arnold. "The Dangers of Satire." *Language Log*, 2008, http://languagelog.ldc.upenn.edu/nll/?p=369.

INDEX

Note: Page numbers in *italic* indicate a figure on the corresponding page.

#FireColbert 152
#MAGA 46, 166
@RealDonaldDrumpf parody account 129
@realDonaldTrump *see* Trump's tweets
@RealHumanPraise *118*
1984 (Orwell) 226, 247, 252
4Chan 103
4th wall *56*
8:46 176
9/11: Al Qaeda 214; Bush and 72–74; Colbert and 152; democracy and 1–2; *Fahrenheit 9/11* 190, 194–195; first responders and *115*, 115; Fox News and 88; Maher and 197, 216; Minhaj and 180; Moore and 190, 194–195; news media and 106; *The Onion* and 111; politics and 134; Republican party and 72, 74, 194; satire following 1–2, 111–112, 130, 134, 199, 224, 228, 235; Stewart and 73, 115, 224; truth and 152, 180

ABC: *Good Morning America* 35; *Jimmy Kimmel Live!* 164; *Politically Incorrect* 216; *see also* Kimmel, Jimmy
Abel, Jon xi
absurdity 4
abuses of power 170; corporate America and 76, 182; satire's use of irony to expose 70, 73, 119, 159, 221, 230, 233, 234; Trump and 194–196, 199

Academy Awards 194
Access Hollywood tape 66–67, *67*, 95, 166
ACLU (American Civil Liberties Union) 145
activism xiv–xv; active citizenship 18, 225, 236, 239; celebrity 62, 78; direct viewer appeals to 142–144; laughtivism 200–201, 234, 237, 257; "political activist" label 190, 239; satire and 133, 182, 184, 236–237, 239; *TikTok* and 68; *see also* protest
Adomian, James 54
Affleck, Ben 164
Affordable Care Act 45, *114*, 252
African American community 158, 227
Agnew, Spiro 105, 107
Ailes, Roger 101
"all sides" of an issue 10, 45, 119
"All You Can Trump Buffet" 147
Almond, Steve 14–17, 226
Al Qaeda 214; *see also* 9/11
"alternative facts" 12, 13, 62, 68, 106, 108, 153, 231
Alternet 78
alt-right media 18, 104, 105, 107, 173, 221, 231, 232; *Breitbart* 104, 106, 107, 158; Charlottesville "Unite the Right" rally 138, 159, 164, 227, 250; *InfoWars* 105, 232; Newsmax 247; views of Hitler 62, 78
Alvarez, Jose xi

America (The Book): A Citizen's Guide to Democracy Inaction 114
American Civil Liberties Union (ACLU) 145
American exceptionalism 185, 191
American Idol 34
American Media 96
American National Election Studies 239
"Americans Startled by Spectacle of President Who Can Speak English" 15
Amusing Ourselves to Death (Postman) 226, 251
Anderson, Kurt 62
"Announcing an Announcement" 53, 147
anti-satire critiques 15–17
apathy 142, 172, 223–224, 236, 239
Apprentice, The 6, 34, 40–41, 53, 55, 91–92, 96, 160; *see also Celebrity Apprentice, The*
"army of comedy" xiv, 78, 131–132, 139, 194, 239, 255; *see also* "Satire League"
Art of the Deal, The 31, 195
Atamaniuk, Anthony 53–54, *54*
Atlantic City *see* bankruptcies *under* Trump, Donald
Atlantic magazine: "Can Satire Save the Republic?" issue 6–7, *6*; on Oliver's fight against apathy 142, *143*; on Trump impersonations 6–7, *6*, 52, 55
Austin, Rick 43
autocrats 4

baby boomers 104
Bad Stories (Almond) 14, 16–17, 226
Baggini, Julian 222, 225
Bai, Matt 95
Baldwin, Alec: coverage of 45, 66; impersonation of Trump by 2, 6–10, *6*, *10*, 50, 52–53, 55–62, 64, 256; other appearances of 62, 131; reaction of the right to 254
Bannon, Steve 62, 107–108, 138, 178, 250
Baron Cohen, Sacha (Ali G) 32–33, *33*
Barr, Roseanne 91, 195
Baumgartner, Jody C., 224–225, 229, 238
Baum, Matt 238
BBC 90, 99, 190
Becker, Amy xi
Beck, Glenn *114*
Bee, Samantha *132*, 153–159, *153*, *156*, *157*; on Ivanka Trump 72–73, *73*, 155–156, *157*; "Not the White House Correspondents' Dinner" 72, *156*
Begala, Paul *114*

belief bias 247, 258
Belkind, Myron 93
Benen, Steve 225
Bernstein, Carl 95
bias: belief bias 247, 258; civility and 174; confirmation 230; cynicism and 222; Equal Time Rule *9*, 9, 46, 61, 165–166, 217, 254; fake news and 13, 15; liberal bias in late-night comedy 5; in the media 61, 105, 107; satire's open display of 234; Trump's complaints of media bias *9*, 9, 61, 119–120, *120*, 217, 254
Biden, Joseph (Joe) 4, 9, 168, *169*
"big lie" 45, 252–253
Billig, Michael 221
bin Laden, Osama 194
Bissell, Tom 6
"Bitter Irony, A" (Strick) 70
black comedy 164
Black Lives Matter 176
Blaze, The 173
Blitzer, Wolf *111*, *113*
Blueprint for Revolution (Popovic and Miller) 239, 257
Boggess, Larry xi
Bogozzi, Benjamin 222
Bornstein, Harold *12*
Borowitz, Andy xi, 5, 15, 68, 70–71, 110–111, 231, 238; as "Satire League" member 186–188, *186*, *189*
Boukes, Mark 134
"Bowling Green Massacre" 68
brain rot 16, 19, 252–254
Brave New World (Huxley) 226
Breitbart 104, 106, 107, 158
Brewer, Paul 239
Brokaw, Tom *113*, 114
Bruneau, Emile 221
Bruni, Frank 252
Brzezinski, Mika 11, *11*
Buchanan, Pat *36*
bullying: satire and xiv, 5, 31, 68–70, 234; in the Trump administration 108, 120–121; Trump as bully *69*, 74–75, 95, 130, 217, 250–251
Burnett, Mark 34, 91–92
Burns, Alexander 24
Burton, Neel 253
Bush, Billy 67
Bush, George W.: 9/11 and 72–74, *114*; Colbert and 3, 10, 53, 73–74, 106, 136–137, 152, 256; "democracy" and 18; *Fahrenheit 9/11* 190, 194–195; impersonation of *156*; Iraq War and 9,

130, 136, 152; on *The Late Show* with David Letterman 228–229; Moore and 194–195; news media and 73–74; paid versus earned media *98*; satire and 18, 72; thinking with gut and 228; truth and 106, 137, 152, 228
Bush, Jeb 97, 163

cable news 11–12, 103, 105–106; 24/7 news cycle 16, 90, 105; punditry and 174; satirical takedowns of 109–110; Trump and his representatives on 88, 101
"Cable News Panels Are Sh*itshows" (Lydic) 174
Cain, Herman 231–232
Camp, Lee 76, 109, 154, *182*, 182–186, *183*, *186*, 225
Cannon, Tyrone 247
"Can Satire Save the Republic?" 6–7, *6*
Cao, Xiaoxia 239
Capra, Frank 4
Carlin, George 76
Carlson, Tucker 15, 74, *114*, 115
Carson, Johnny 94
Carter, Bill 45
Carter, Graydon 7, 44, 72–73, 129
Carter, Jimmy 4
cartoons *see* editorial cartoons
Cavuto, Neil 254
CBS: *Face the Nation* 69, 151; news on 99; *Survivor* 34, 92; *The Smothers Brothers Comedy Hour* 17, 216; *see also* Colbert, Stephen; *Late Show, The*
Celebrity Apprentice, The 23, 34, 35, 92; *see also Apprentice, The*
Cenac, Wyatt 88, *89*
Chapman, Matthew 100
Chappelle, Dave 176
Charity, Justin 85
Charlie Hebdo attack 214–215
Charlottesville "Unite the Right" rally 138, 159, 164, 227, 250
Chase, Chevy 58, 228–229
Chattoo, Caty Borum xi, 134, 229–230, 235
Che, Michael 52, 227
Cheney, Dick 72, 74
Chen Gan 225
Chen, Hsuan-Ting 225
Cher 131
child sex-trafficking allegations 15, 103, 104
Chin, Richard 258, 259
citizens and citizenship: active citizenship 13, 16–18, 61, 225, 236, 239; birther conspiracy 29, 35–38, 92–93, 217; "citizen satire" 199, 201; protests and 201; satire and citizen engagement 225, 236–239; speaking truth to power xiv, 133, 234–235; on social media 12–13, *12*, 66; *see also* activism; protest
Citizens United 118
civility 174, *175*
civil liberties/civil rights 181; dystopian worlds and 226, 251; free press 23, 61, 62, 92, 108, 136–137, *199*; free speech 23, 37, 119, 136–138, 214–215, 217; of migrant workers 146; protecting 144; Trump and 181; voting 138, 144, *149*; women's rights xiii, 180, 199–200
Clark, Yvette *117*
climate change 187, 249, 250
Clinton, Bill 45, 133, 195
Clinton, Chelsea 232
Clinton, Hillary: 2016 presidential election 52, *56*, 98, *98*, *99*, 101, *117*, 195; Camp on 184–185; conspiracy theories about 15, 103, 166; "lock her up" chants 98; McKinnon's impersonation of 55, 57, 59; Sanders and 191–192; Trump supporters' hatred of 78, 192
"Closer Look, A" segments 142, 161–162
CNBC *115*
CNN 105, 106; Borowitz on 187–188; calling Trump "gaslighter in chief" 248; Conway on 68, 162–163; coverage of Trump 99, 101; *Crossfire* 15, *114*, 115; firing of Jeffrey Lord 109; Lemon's open mocking 120; Meyers on 44; mocking of 110–111, *111*; sensationalism of 137, 148; viewership *112*, 234; under Zucker's management 94
cognitive dissonance 45
cognitive science 19, 258
Cohen, Bernard 100
Cohen, Leonard 58
Cohen, Michael 26, 96, 160
Colbert Report, The: audience 112–113, *112*, 170–171, 229, 233–234, 259; "Better Know a District" segments *117*; Cain campaign and 231–232; civic education and 133–134, 142; "Colbert Bump" and 133–134; "Colbert nation" 116, 142; *The Daily Show* and 109, 147; Fox News and 44, *118*; language and 3, 69–70, 73; satire and 69–70, 146–147, 170–171; top 10 moments *117–118*; "The Word" segments 152; *see also* Colbert, Stephen

Colbert's America: Satire and Democracy (McClennen) xi
Colbert, Stephen *132*, 145–153, *146, 149, 151*; @RealHumanPraise *118*; 9/11 and 152; activism and 236–237, 239; "All You Can Trump Buffet" 147; "Announcing an Announcement" 53, 147; Bush and 3, 10, 53, 73–74, 106, 136–137, 152, 256; CBS and 14, 45, 147; "Colbert Defense" 230–232; as *Daily Show* correspondent 147; FCC investigation into 70, 152, 216; Fox News and 44, *118*; impact on polls 94; impersonation of 53; interview with Minhaj 180; interview with Stewart 252; interview with Trump 148; language and 3, 69–70, 73; *The Late Show* and 14, 45, 109, 119, 145–153, *146, 149, 151*, 231; on-air persona 109, 116–117, 146, 147, 256; O'Reilly vs. 109, *149*; as parody of punditry 106, 109, 115–116, 146–147; presidential campaigns *117*; Rally to Restore Sanity 16, 236–237; right-wing witch hunt of 254; satirical tradition and 3, 146–147, 170–171, 220, 259; Stewart and 14–16, 37, 109, 113–114, 116–117, 119, 134, 259; Super PAC 97, 106, *118*, 146; Trump-era highlights *149*; on Trump's birther conspiracy 37; "truthiness" and 15, 106, 137, *117*, 152–153, 228, 235; tweets of *118*; visit to Iraq *117*; White House Correspondents' Association dinner and 136; on *YouTube* 147; *see also Colbert Report, The*
Cold War 17
Collins, Richard W., 232
Columbia Journalism Review, The 14
Comedian and an Activist Walk into a Bar, A (Feldman and Chattoo) 134
comedy: black comedy 164; "contact hypothesis" 235; deadpan 164, 176, 188; dick jokes 142, 150; "gateway hypothesis" 238; "getting" the jokes xv, 170, 230, 259; goofball comedy 45, 78, 148; group identity and humor 219–221; "locker room" humor 67, 168, 230; observational comedy 164, 171; "playing it straight" 10, 18, 76; self-deprecating jokes 4, 19n6, 25, 47n11, 165, 190; stand-up comedy xv, 150, 160, 176; "Superiority Theory" of humor 219; tragicomedy 5, 88–89; zingers 77, 150

Comedy Central 106, 109, 115–116, 119, 170; *@midnight* 54; 2011 roast of Trump 40–43, *42*; political behavior and 239, 259; *The President Show* 54, *54*; Rally to Restore Sanity and/or Fear 16, 236–237; targeting Fox News 44–45; *see also Colbert Report, The*; *Daily Show, The*
confirmation bias 230
conspiracy theories: birtherism 29, 35–38, 92–93, 217; about Hillary Clinton 15, 103, 166; Pizzagate 104
"contact hypothesis" 235
Conway, Kellyanne: "alternative facts" 108, 153, 231; "Bowling Green Massacre" 68; on CNN 68, 101, *102*, 162–163; impersonations of 59, 62
Cooper, Anderson 94, *113*, 121
Cooper, Sarah 64–68, *65, 67*
Coulter, Ann 105, 232
Couric, Katie *113*, 114
covfefe 85–86, *86, 87*
COVID-19 5, 176, 252
Cramer, Jim *115*
creative irony 3–4, 70, 73, 256
"crisis actors" 173
critical thinking: satire and 2, 13, 15–16, 111–112, 131–132, 171–172, 229, 237–238, 249–250; satirical vs. propagandistic fake news 12–15, 18, 100–104, 111–112, 122n16, 186, 188; Trump as threat to 13, 248–252
Cronkite, Walter 88, 94, 101, 106, *113*, 114
"crooked media" 54
Cruz, Ted 98, *98*, 148, 154
Cummings, Whitney 41
"c word" 72, 156–157
cyber-citizenship *see* social media
cynicism 2, 15–16, 215, 218, 222–226, 234

Da Ali G Show (with Sacha Baron Cohen) 32–33, *33*
Daily Beast, The 61, 187
Daily Show, The: 9/11 and *114*; during the 2016 election 77, 168–174, *172*; audience 112–113, *112, 113*, 233–234; Bee as correspondent on 154; Colbert as correspondent on 147; *The Colbert Report* and 14, 233; early days of 76–77, 106; "Indecision 2000" *114*; with Jon Stewart 14, 88–89, *89*, 106, 109, 225; Minhaj as correspondent on 135, 177; news media and 109, 120, 231; Noah as correspondent on 120, 171; Oliver

as correspondent on 88–89, *89*, 140; Oliver guest hosting 38, 40; politics and 224–225, 236, 238–239; "Rally to Restore Sanity" 16, 236–237; satire and 109–111, 170–171, 224–225; top 10 moments *114–115*; transition to Noah as host 76–77, 168–170; with Trevor Noah 77, 171–176, *172*, *174*, 231; *see also* Noah, Trevor; Stewart, Jon
Dalai Lama 142
Damon, Matt 62–63, *63*, 164
Day, Amber 239
deadpan 164, 176, 188
Debord, Guy 251
DeGeneres, Ellen 165
democracy 1–2; after 9/11 1–2; autocracy vs. 4; conversation and democratic deliberation 78; cynicism and 222–226; patriotism and 131; political activism and 190; role of the press in 116–117; satire and 1–2, 14–16, 18–19, 131, 133–134, 139, 203, 222–226, 233–239; Trump's disrespect of democratic institutions 76, 145, 150; truth and 108
Democracy Voter Study Group 255
Democratic National Committee (DNC): in the 2016 primaries 184; conspiracy theories about 103–104; corporate backers of 196; coverage during the 2016 election 99, 133–134; elevation of Trump's visibility 28–29; Hart sex scandal 95; jokes about 154; Republican outrage vs. Democratic irony 90; vulnerability to slanted news 104
De Niro, Robert 62
Department of Justice 4
"deplorables" 77
Descartes, René 218–219
Detroit Free Press 8
Dickerson, John 69, 151
dick jokes 142, 150
Di Leo, Jeffrey xi
Dobbs, Lou *113*
Doctors Without Borders *149*
"Donald J Trump Twitter Library" 174–175
Doonesbury 30–31, 34, *35*, 38, *39*, 198
Dr. Strangelove, Or How I Learned to Stop Worrying and Love the Bomb 17
dramatic irony 3–5
Dream: Reimagining Progressive Politics in an Age of Fantasy (Duncombe) 235–236
Dreamers 99
Drouin, Erin 222, 255

Drudge, Matt 105
Drumpf (Donald) 129–130, 133, 139–140, *141*, 144, *149*
Duncombe, Stephen xi, 235–236
Duterte, Rodrigo 232

Eastwood, Clint 195
Ebalé, Ramón Nse Esono 215
echo chambers 16
Economist, The 68
Edelman Trust Barometer 222
editorial cartoons x–xi, *8*, *135*, 197–198, *198*, *199*, 216; depicting fake news *110*; depicting Trump *8*, *135*, *199*; *Doonesbury* 30–31, 34, *35*, 38, *39*, 198; *Mad* magazine *32*, 32, 197
Edwards, John 232
elections *see* democracy; midterm elections; presidential elections
Emmy Awards 62
Entertaining Politics (Jones) 94
Entertaining the Citizen (van Zoonen) 236
Equal Time Rule *9*, 9, 46, 61, 165–166, 217, 254
Equatorial Guinea 215
Esquire 250
"ethical spectacles" 236
Everything's Fine (with Sarah Cooper) 66
exaggeration: irony and 5, 18, 30, 68, 74, 256, 259; not "getting" 231, 258; satire and 120, 188
extremist views 16; of the alt-right 107, 260; *Charlie Hebdo* attack 214; inverting Islamophobia 178; of Trump 59, 76, 158, 177

Facebook 105; comedians on 162; fake news on 91, 102–104; racism and sexism on 232; Russian interference in the 2016 election 102–103; Trump on 67
Face the Nation 69, 151
fact-checking 104, 143, 153, 249
Fahrenheit 11/9 78, 91, 101, 195
Fahrenheit 9/11 190, 194–195
Fairleigh Dickinson University 113
Fairness Doctrine 9, 104, 105
fake news 1, 100–109, *110*; in the 2016 election 13, 90–91, 103–104; cognitive processing of 247; as critique of mainstream news 100–109; cynicism and 225; on *Facebook* 91, 102–104; five meanings of the phrase 102–109, 122n16; for-profit fake news 103–104; propagandistic fake news 12–15, 18,

100–104, 111–112, 122n16, 187, 188; from Russia 14, 102–103; satirical 109–121, 187; Trump's allegations against mainstream press 11, 13, 151
Fallon, Jimmy: jokes about Trump 45, 78, 148; Meyers and 24; Trump impersonation by 7–8, 55, 59, 63–64, *64*, 168; *see also Tonight Show, The*
false equivalency 249
Falwell, Jerry 216–217
family separation policy 72, *149*, 155–156, *156*
"Fathers and Sons" 160
FCC (Federal Communications Commission) 70, 134, 138, 152, 216
fecklessness 72, 155–156, 157
Feldman, Lauren xi, 134, 229–230, 235
Ferrell, Will *156*
Fey, Tina 55, 155, 160, 227–228
"fifth estate" 119
figurative irony 4
Film Quarterly xi
Financial Times 99
First Amendment 23, 135–137, 178, 217
First Responders Health Care Bill 115
flattery 59
Fleischer, Ari 107–108
Floyd, George 176
Flynt, Larry 216
Ford, Gerald 58, 228, 229
"fourth estate" 117
Fox & Friends 25, 94, 166, 181
Fox Business 254
Fox News: accuracy of 231; the alt-right and 104; Colbert and 44, *118*; creation 105; evil or stupid? 88–89, *89*; Islamophobia of 137; Noah and 173, 175; opinion vs. fact and 231; "patriotism" and 88; reality and 88; Stewart and 44, 77; as target of satire 44, 77, 88; Trump administration officials on 181, 231; Trump's appearance after the 2011 WHCAD 25; Trump's relationship with 25, 67, 88, 90, 99; truth and 231; viewership 90, 113, *113*, 233–234; *see also* O'Reilly, Bill
free press 23, 61, 62, 92, 108, 136–137, *199*
free speech 23, 37, 119, 136–138, 214–215, 217
Frontline 143
Frye, David 58
Full Frontal with Samantha Bee 72, 142, 154–155, 158–159, 225; *see also* Bee, Samantha

Gagozzi, Benjamin 255
Galinsky, Adam 257
Gallup 101, *102*
gaslighting 108, 145, 248
"gateway hypothesis" 238
Gentile, Sal 162
Germany 99, 196
Gerson, Michael 136
"getting" the joke xv, 170, 230, 259
Gibson, Charles *113*, 114
Gino, Francesca 257
Giuliani, Rudolph *117*
Gladwell, Malcolm 14, 226
Glazier, Rebecca 237–238
Goebbels, Joseph 195
Göktürk, Deniz 219–220
Golden Globes *161*
Goldring, Abigail 222, 255
Good Morning America 35
goofball comedy 45, 78, 148
GOP *see* Republican Party (GOP)
Gopnik, Adam 44
Gore, Al *114*, 229
Gottfried, Gilbert 41
government shutdown (2019) 133
GQ magazine 168
Graff, Rhona 42
Graham, Katharine 23
Greaney, Dan xi, 38
Grosz, Peter 54
Ground Zero mosque 88
group identity 219–221
Gruner, Charles R. 219
Guardian, The 73, 171, 222
gun violence 37, *156*, 173, 178, 217; "March for Our Lives" 196; Marjory Stoneman Douglas shooting 76, 165, 173, 196; Pulse Nightclub shooting *156*; Sandy Hook shooting 232

Haberman, Maggie 24
hair (Trump's) 7, 24, 26, 31, 40–41, 150, 225
Hakola, Outi J. 59
Hall, Arsenio 133
Hall, Sean 3
Hammond, Darrell 34–35, *36*, 52, 55, 59
Handler, Chelsea 78, 155
hands (Trump's) 31, 129, 148, 185
Hanks, Tom 57
Hannity, Sean 107
Harpers 6
Harris, Kamala 168, *169*
Harris, Robert 69
Hart, Gary 95
Hartmann, Phil *36*

Harvard Lampoon xi
Harvard's Shorenstein Center on Media, Politics and Public Policy 97, 99, 148
Hate, Inc. (Taibbi) 90
HBO *see Last Week Tonight*; Maher, Bill; Oliver, John
Heer, Jeet 249
Hepburn, Michael 196–197
Hess, V.K. 239
Heyer, Heather 227, 250
high-order thinking 16, 19, 238, 258
Hirschorn, Michael 74
Hitchcock, Peter xi
Hitler 62, 78
hoaxes xiv, 103–104, 122n16, 187, 249
Hobbes, Thomas 219
Hodson, Gordon 221
Holt, Lester 52
Horace 171–172
Horner, Paul 103–104
Hot Air 77
Huang, Li 227
Huckabee Sanders, Sarah 10–11, 75, 174
Huffington Post, The 41–42
human rights *see* civil liberties/civil rights
Hume, Brit 113
humor *see* comedy; impersonations; satire
Hurricane Maria 156
Hustler magazine 216–217
Huxley, Aldous 226, 251
hyperbole 13, 15, 18, 31, 68–69, 74, 119, 225, 254

identity 219–221
"I'm fucking Ben Affleck" 164
Immigration and Customs Enforcement (ICE) 250
impersonations 7–8; Atamaniuk's Trump 53–54; Baldwin's Trump 6–9, *6, 10*, 52–62, 64, *56, 57, 60*; Colbert's Trump 53; Damon's Kavanaugh 62–63, *63;* Fallon's Trump 7–8, 63, *64*; Fey's Palin 55; Hammond's Trump 34–35, 55; impersonating an impersonation 58–63; McCarthy's Spicer 2, 62, *66*, 66, 121, 249; McKinnon's many impersonations 55, 57, 58–59, 62, 66; mockery in 7–8, 58–59; parody and 58–59; of presidents 58–59; on *Saturday Night Live* (*SNL*) 2, 18, 34–35, *36*, 52–53, 55; of Trump on social media 64–68, *65*
inauguration (of Trump) 61–62; coverage of 120; crowd size 62, 107, 108, 121; protests of 62, 193
INDECLINE 218–219
Indivisible 200

InfoWars 105, 232
Ingraham, Laura 105
insult comedy 164
Internet Research Agency 103
Interview, The 215
Iran 185, *186*, 215
Iraq War: allegations of treason during 130; Brian Williams's false claim of 101; Bush's false statements about 106, 136, 152, 250; Colbert's visit to Iraq *117*; irony and 72; satire and 9; Trump's statements about 249
irony 2–7, *8*; bitter irony of Trump 70–79; creative irony 3–4, 70, 73, 256; dramatic irony 3–5; exaggeration and 5, 18, 30, 68, 74, 256, 259; figurative irony 4; ironic irony 5; ironic wordplay 75; of Kimmel's sincerity 168; reality and 3–6; Republican outrage vs. Democratic irony 90; rhetorical irony 3, 70, 73, 256; satire's use of irony to expose abuse 70, 73, 119, 159, 221, 230, 233, 234; situational irony 3–5, 70, 136, 256; *see also* language; rhetoric
Irony and Outrage (Young) 90, 231, 235
Islamophobia 137, 177, 214
Is Satire Saving Our Nation? (McClennen and Maisel) x, xi, *3*, 6, 199, 239
It's a Wonderful Life (Frank Capra) 4

James, Lebron *161*
January 6, 2021, insurrection 226, 236, 251
Jay Z 129
Jeffries, Jim 197
Jennings, Peter 113
Jimmy Kimmel Live! 164
Jobs, Steve 77
Johnstone, Caitlin 182
jokes *see* comedy
Jones, Alex 15, 104, 105, 107, 232
Jones, Jeffrey 94, 239
Jones, Van 44
Jost, Colin xi, 227
journalism *see* news media
Journal of Psychology 260
Juvenal 171–172

Kaine, Tim *56*
kakistocracy 45, 88
Kaplan, Marty 224–225
Kappa Delta Rho fraternity 232
Kavanaugh, Brett 62–63, *63*, 111
Kenny, Daniel 142
"kettle logic" 249
Khashoggi, Jamal 180
Killam, Taran *36*

Kim Jong Un 35
Kimmel, Billy 165
Kimmel, Jimmy 164–168, *164*, *166*, *167*; on "covfefe" 85, *88*; effect of Trump on 76, 164–165; jokes about Trump 35, 85, *88*, 168, *169*; on Obamacare 45, 165, 235; on *Twitter* 46, *46*, 85, *88*, 165–166, *166*, 168, *169*; on *YouTube* 166; *The Man Show* 164
King, Larry 26, 28, 41, 44
Klepper, Jordan x, 173, 197
Knoss, Tamara xi
Konnikova, Maria 248
Koppel, Ted *113*
Kouachi, Saïd and Chérif 214
Kteily, Nour 221
Kubrick, Stanley 17
Kushner, Jared *8*, 196
Kwak, Nojin 224
Kyl, Jon *118*

Lahren, Tomi *172*, 173, 176
Lampanelli, Lisa 40
language: Bee's "full frontal" language 72, 155–157, *157*; body language 258–259; "c word" 72, 156–157; divisiveness and 7, 132, 220; humor and 178; Merriam Webster's mocking of Trump 85, *87*; Orwellian "newspeak" 108, 248, 252; satire and 233; "scare quotes" 74; Trump's command of 31, 70, 74–75, *156*; truth and 75; wordplay 2, 74, *75*; *see also* comedy; irony; rhetoric
Last Week Tonight (with John Oliver) 18, 38, 106, 127, 144, 225
Late Night (with Seth Meyers) 23–26, 138, 160, 162, 165.
Late Show, The (with Stephen Colbert) 14, 24, 45, 53, 94, 109, 145–148; Minhaj's appearance on 180; mocking Devin Nunes 254; monologue on "Trumpiness" 153; Oliver's appearance on 129; ratings 231; Stewart's appearance on 252, 254
Late Show with David Letterman 229, 239
LA Times 41
Lauer, Matt 101, *113*
laughtivism 200–201, 234, 237, 257
Lee, Hoon 224
Lee, Judith Yaross 219
Lehrer, Jim *113*
Lemon, Don 120
Leno, Jay 37

Letterman, David 109, 145–146, 165, 229, 239
Lewandowsky, Corey 103
Lewinsky, Monica 52
libel 95–96, 137, 216–217
Lichter, Robert 224, 229
"Life After Hate" 159
Limbaugh, Rush 104, 105, 107, *112*, *113*
lip-syncing 66
Lockerbie, Brad 225, 229
"locker room" humor 67, 168, 230
"lock her up" 98
Lord, Jeffrey 109
Lund, Jeb 250
Lydic, Desi 173–174

Macedonia 103
MacFarlane, Seth 40, 41
Macron, Emmanuel 15
Maddow, Rachel 121
Mad magazine *32*, 32, 197
Mad Money 115
Maher, Bill 37, 40, 197, 216, 217, 220
mainstream news media *see* alt-right media; news media
Maisel, Remy x, *3*, 6, 199, 239
"Make America Great Again" (MAGA) 54, 98; #MAGA 46, 166; "MAGA Republican" 221
"Make Donald Drumpf Again" 129–130, 133, 139, *141*, 144, *149*
Malaysian Airlines flight 110, *111*
Manafort, Paul 107, 120
Manigault, Omarosa 43
Man Show, The 164
Maples, Marla *36*
"March for Our Lives" 196
Marjory Stoneman Douglas shooting 76, 165, 173, 196
masculinity: of the *Access Hollywood* tape 66–67, *67*, 95, 166; in *Dr. Strangelove* 17; "locker room" humor 67, 168, 230; questioning Trump's 199–200; toxic 31, 57, 66, 166–168
"Master Race Needs to Play It Cool, The" 174
Matlin, Marlee 41
Mbasogo, Teodoro Obiang Nguema 215
MBS (Mohammed bin Salman) 180
McCain, John 55
McCarthy, Melissa 2, 62, *66*, 66, 121, 249
McCaughey, Betsey *114*
McConnell, Mitch 155

McKinnon, Kate 55, 57, 58–59, 62, 66
McLuhan, Marshall 197
media *see* news media
"medium is the message, the" 197
Meet the Press 28, 44, *113*
megalomania 31, 34, *35*, 93, 167, 174
memes 168, 201, 227, 232
"mental gymnastics" 258
Merriam Webster 85, *87*
meta-perception 221
Meyers, Seth 139–140, 159–164, *159*, *161*, *163*; at the 2011 WHCAD 10–11, 23–26, 37, 40, 41, 43–46, 96, 134–135, 159–160; "A Closer Look" segments 142, 161–162; on CNN 44; Fallon and 24; *Late Night* (with Seth Meyers) 23–26, 28–29, 138, 160, *161*, 162, 165; not apologizing to Trump 96; on *Saturday Night Live* (*SNL*) 4, 43, 160; Trump-era highlights *161*; on Trump's support of the alt-right 138–139; on *YouTube* 162
Michael Moore in TrumpLand 78, 191–193, *193*
midterm elections: in 2010 16, 146, 236–237; in 2018 61–62, 78, 94, 121, 151
millennials 14, 173, 174
Miller, Steve 181, *181*
Milosevic, Slobodan 200–201
Minhaj, Hasan *132*, *177*; on *The Daily Show* 135, 173, 176–178; as host of the White House Correspondents' Association Dinner (WHCAD) 136–139; *Patriot Act* 142; Radio & Television Correspondents' Association Dinner 178; shows with Netflix 178–182, *181*; Trump-era highlights *179*
Ministry of Satire 134–139; *see also* "Satire League"
Minton, David 232
Mirren, Helen 66–67, *67*
Mitchell, Andrea 11, *11*
mockery; in impersonations 7–8, 58–59; satire vs. mockery 2, 7–8, 171–172, 229; of Trump by average citizens 64, 201; of Trump by comedians 29, 31, 40, 68–69, 82, 74–75, 150–152
Modest Proposal, A (Swift) 69, 188
Moonves, Les 101
Moore, Michael x, xiii–xv, 190–197, *190*, *192*, *193*, *194*; 9/11 and 190, 194–195; Bush and 194–195; call for an "army of comedy" xiv, 78, 131–132, 139, 194, 239, 255; *Fahrenheit 11/9* 78, 91, 101, 195; *Fahrenheit 9/11* 190, 194–195; *Michael Moore in TrumpLand* 78, 191–193, *193*; *Roger and Me* 195; *Where to Invade Next* 191–192
Moral Majority 216
Morris, Jonathan S., 224–225, 229, 238
Moy, Patricia 239
Mr. Nutterbutter 144–145, *145*
MSNBC 11, 94, 96, 105, 137, 234
Mueller, Robert 102–103
Murray, Bob 144–145, *145*
Murray, Hugh xi
Muslim Americans 135–138; *see also* Islamophobia; Minhaj, Hasan
"Muslim ban" 136–137, 178, 250

narcissism: gaslighting and 248–249; millennial 14; of Trump 8, 38, 44, 52, 54, 65, 174, 185, 188, 193, 201, 203, 250
Nast, Thomas 216
National Enquirer, The 96
National Institutes of Health 165
National Mall 16, 146
National Press Club 93
National Rifle Association (NRA) 178, 254, 259, 260
national security 67, 75
Native Americans 227
NBC: *Apprentice, The* 6, 34, 40–41, 53, 55, 91–92, 96, 160; *The Celebrity Apprentice* 23, 34, 35, 92; CNBC *115*; *Meet the Press* 28, 44, *113;* MSNBC 11, 94, 96, 105, 137, 234; Peacock 155; *The Tonight Show* 24, 37, 45, 176, 217; *The Voice* xiv; *see also Late Night* (with Seth Meyers); *Saturday Night Live* (*SNL*)
neoliberalism: attack on 131, 158, 221; liberal bias in late-night comedy 5; news media and 90, 105, 107
Nesbitt, Jeff 88–89
Netflix 178–182, *181*
Newsbusters 157–158
NewsHour with Jim Lehrer 112
Newsmax 247
news media: during the 2016 presidential election 96–100, *98*, *99*, *100*; 24/7 cable news cycle 16, 90, 139; 9/11 and 106; as "crooked" 54; key media moments before 2016 *105–106*; neoliberalism and 90, 105–107; polarization and 78,

90, 105, 251; public trust in 11–12, 101–102, *102*, 137, 222–223; reality and 88–89, 91–92, 94, 100–101; social media and 88, 106; Trump's relationship with 12–14, 18, 85–100, *98*, *99*; watchdog role of 117, 119; *see also* alt-right media; cable news; social media; *specific networks and correspondents*
"newspeak" 108, 248, 252
Newsweek 117
New York Times Magazine 95
New York Times, The 94, 98–99, *115*, 252
New Yorker, The 5, 15, 44, 91; *see also* Borowitz, Andy
Niehoff, Len 216
Nixon, Richard 58, 95, 105, 107, 131
Noah, Trevor 76–78, *132*, 169–176, *170*, *172*, *175*; on civility 174, *175*; as *Daily Show* correspondent 120, 171; "Donald J. Trump Twitter Library" *172*, 174–175; Fox News and 173, 175; insights into American racism 176; Lahren and *172*, 173, 176; transition to hosting *The Daily Show* 76–77, 168–170; Trump as the "White ISIS" *172*, 177–178; Trump-era highlights *172*
North Korea 35, 75, 215
"Not the White House Correspondents' Dinner" 72, *156*
NPR 26, 90, *112*, 184, 234
nuance 7, 15, 18–19, 29, 255, 258
Nunberg, Geoffrey 131
Nunes, Devin 254
Nussbaum, Emily 91
Nyhan, Brendan 250, 251

Obama, Barack: attacks on 105; birther conspiracy 29, 35–38, 92–93, 217; immigration reform and 99–100, *100*; joke at the 2011 WHCAD 18, 23–25, 28–29; as a sellout 196; withdrawal from Iraq 249
Obamacare (Affordable Care Act) 45, *114*, 252
observational comedy 164, 171
Ocasio-Cortez, Alexandria 196
O'Donnell, Rosie 36
Ohman, Jack 197
Olbermann, Keith 54, *113*
Oliver, John 11, 127–130, *132*, *128*, 140–145, *140*, *141*, *145*; as *Daily Show* correspondent 88–89, *89*, 140; as *Daily Show* guest host 38, *40*; battle against apathy 142, 143; calling out "whataboutism" 250; "Donald Trump is America's back mole" 18, 127; fight against apathy 142, 143; *Last Week Tonight* 18, 38, 106, 127, 144, 225; *Late Show* appearance 129; "Make Donald Drumpf Again" 129–130, 133, 140, *141*, 144, *149;* public trust in 234; responsibility for Trump's candidacy 38, *40;* spurring citizen action 134, 141–145, 236; as a target of the right 254; Trump-era highlights *149*; tweets with Trump 128, *128*; on YouTube 130, 144
Onion, The 68, 110–111, 187
Oprah Winfrey Show, The 27–28, 44
O'Reilly, Bill 101, 107, *113*, *116*, 137, 195; Colbert and 109; satire and 109; Stewart and 115, *115*; *see also* Fox News
O'Reilly Factor, The 112
O'Rourke, P. J., 215
Orwell, George: *1984* 226, 247–248, 252; "newspeak" 108, 248, 252; Trump presidency as Orwellian dystopia 108, 193, 247–248
Oteri, Cheri 36
Out Front with Erin Burnett 56

Palin, Sarah 55, 155, 160, 228
Parker, Trey 68
parody 2–5, 8, 187–188, 216–217, 231–232; hoax vs. parody 103–104; impersonations and 58–59; of the news 110–111; parody accounts on *Twitter* 129; parodying a parody 134, 139, 171
Paskin, Willa 171
Passions of the Soul (Descartes) 218–219
Paste Magazine 181
Patriot Act 142, 179–181; *see also* Minhaj, Hasan
patriotism 88, 131, 190–191
Patterson, John 17
Patterson, Thomas 97–99
Paul, Rand 173
PBS 43, 90, *112*
Peabody Award 178
Peacock (NBC) 155
Pecker, David 96
Pelosi, Nancy *117*, 196
Pence, Mike 54, *56*, 62, *149*
Pennycook, Gordon 247, 248–249, 257–258
People magazine 92
Pett, Joel x–xi, *110*, 197, *199*
Pew Research Center 90, 112–114, *112*, 222, 233–234, 238
Philippines 232

Pinter, Harold 256–257
Pittsburgh Post-Gazette 198
Pizzagate 104
Plato 218–219
Plouffe, David 29
plural society 137
polarization 13, 16, 78; news media consumption and 78, 90, 105, 251; satire and 134, 220–221, 233, 235
political action committees (PACs) 97, 106, *118*, 146
political apathy *see* apathy
political cynicism *see* cynicism
"political efficacy" 238
Political Humor in a Changing Media Landscape: A New Generation of Research (Baumgartner and Becker) xi
Politically Incorrect 216
Politico 43, 62, 248
Politics Is a Joke! (Lichter et al.) 224, 229
polls: Colbert's impact on 94; on public trust 11–12, 90, 101, *102*, 106, 114; on Sanders 184; scandal and 95; on Trump 25, 54, 133, 148
Popovic, Srdja x 200–201, 234, 237, 239, 257
populism 54, 89, 235–236; *see also* alt-right media; Tea Party movement
Postman, Neil 226–227, 251
post-truth world 5, 15, 231
Poulsen, Shannon 222, 255
Pranksters vs. Autocrats (Srdja and McClennen) x, 239, 244n101
presidential elections: 1969 Nixon-Agnew campaign 105, 107; the "big lie" about 2020 45, 252–253; coverage of the Democratic National Committee (DNC) in 2016 99, 133–134; *The Daily Show* during the 2016 election 77, 168–174, *172*; earned media vs. paid media 97–98, *98*; fake news in the 2016 election 13, 90–91, 103–104; Hillary Clinton in 2016 52, *56*, 98, *98*, *99*, 101, *117*, 195; January 6, 2021, insurrection 226, 236, 251; Russian interference in the 2016 election 102–103; Super PACs 97, 106, *118*, 146; voter ID laws 144, *149*; *see also* primaries (presidential)
President Show, The 54, *54*
primaries (presidential): Democratic National Committee (DNC) in 2016 14, 28–29, 54, *98*, 154, 184, 190–191; Republican Party (GOP) in 2012 231; Republican Party (GOP) in 2016 86, 91, 147–148, 154, 31, 37–38, 173, 249–250; Super Tuesday 127, 132
propaganda: of corporate media 182; propagandistic fake news 12–15, 18, 100–104, 111–112, 122n16, 187, 188; Russian 14, 102–103; *see also* fake news
ProPublica 143
protest: ironic wordplay and 75; "March for Our Lives" 196; sarcasm at 199, *200*, 201, 203, 237; satire at 199–200, *199*; Trump's inauguration 62, 193; "Women's March" 199, *200*, 237; *see also* public trust
Psychology Today 253
public trust: Edelman Trust Barometer 222; Gallup poll on 101, *102*; gaslighting and 248; in government institutions 215, 223, 234; lack of trust 225; in the news media 11–12, 101–102, *102*, 137, 222–223; in satirists 11–12, 234; *see also* activism; apathy; cynicism
Puerto Rico 142
Pulitzer Prize winning cartoonist *110*
Pulse Nightclub shooting *156*
punditry: anti-satire 16; Colbert's parody of 106, 109, 115–116, 146–147; normalizing Trump 28, 93, 191; rise in 13, 101, 105, 174; use of the "Colbert Defense" 232
Putin, Vladimir 70, 151–152, 199

racism: *Charlie Hebdo* attack and 214; Islamophobia 137, 177, 214; Noah's insights into American racism 176; of Trump 41, 52, 55, 77, 130, 138–139; of Trump administration officials 178; of Trump supporters 158, 174, 176, 250–251; white nationalism 107, 130, 176, 178, 221–222, 227–228, 250–251; white privilege 227–228
Radio & Television Correspondents' Association Dinner 178
Rainbow, Randy 64, 196
Rally to Restore Sanity and/or Fear 16, 236–237
Ramos, Jorge 11, 148
Rand, David 247
Rather, Dan 108, *113*, 114
ratings: of *The Apprentice* 92; of cable news 94, 96, 101; of *The Daily Show* 171, 231; of late-night talk shows 45, 148, 150, 165, 231; of *Saturday Night Live* (*SNL*) 55; ratings over reality 101; Trump's relationship to 34–35, 94, 96
Reagan, Ronald 4, 162

reality: gaslighting 108, 145, 248; irony and 3–6; nation's ability to process 13–14; news media and 88–89, 91–92, 94, 100–101; politics and; satire and 30, 37, 59–61, 68, 127, 187; spectacle and 251; *see also* fake news; language; rhetoric
reality TV xiii, 3–4, 14, 15, 91–92; Trump as "Reality TV Buffoon" *30*, 34–35, *35*
Redacted Tonight 182–184, 225
Reddit 103, 106
Rehnquist, William 216
Reifler, Jason 250
Remnick, David 68
Republican Party (GOP): 2008 presidential election 160; 2012 presidential primary 231; 2016 presidential primary 86, 91, 147–148, 154, 31, 37–38, 173, 249–250; 9/11 and 72, 74, 194–195; Fairness Doctrine and 9; jokes about 154; "MAGA Republicans" 221; news media polarization and 90, 99–101, 104, 107, 250; as part of "corporate government" 185; Republican outrage vs. Democratic irony 90; satire and the Republican mindset 133, 158; Supreme Court vacancies and 155; Tea Party movement 130, 200, 236; Trump's place in 24, 29, 37–38, 89, 129, 149
Republic, The (Plato) 218
rhetoric: divisive rhetoric of the right 107, 132, 200, 221; hyperbole 13, 15, 18, 31, 68–69, 74, 119, 225, 254; rhetorical irony 3, 70, 73, 256; Trump's racist 158; *see also* language
Rice, Donna 95
Rich, B. Ruby xi
Rich, Seth 103
"Ridiculist, The" 121
roasts *see* 2011 roast of Trump *under* Comedy Central; White House Correspondents' Association Dinner (WHCAD)
Roberts, Roxanne 25
Robinson, Gregg 223–224
Roger and Me 195
Rogers, Rob 198
Rolling Stone 154
Roseanne Show, The 41, 91, 195
Rose, Charlie 101
Rosewater 140, 215
Ross, Jeffrey 41
Roston, Michael 90
RT America 182–184
Rubio, Marco 31, *98*, 148, 154

Ruffalo, Mark 62
Ruffin, Amber 155
Russert, Tim 28, 44, *113*
Russia 14, 102–103
Ryan, Maureen 171
Ryan, Paul *201*

Sack, Steve xi, 197, *198*
Salman, Mohammed bin (MBS) 180
Salon 182, 214, 257
Sanders, Bernie 14, 54, *98*, 154, 184, 191
Sanders, Sarah Huckabee 10, 75, 174
Sandy Hook shooting 232
sarcasm 2, 4, 16, 129–130, 253, 256–259; bullying and 69, 74; in classical satire 171; as defense for poor behavior 232; at protests 199, *200*, 201, 203, 237; in satirical fake news 109, 111, 115; in straight news 121; as a subset of irony 256
satire 1–6, *3*; after 9/11 1–2, 111–112, 130, 134, 199, 224, 228, 235; activism and 133, 182, 184, 236–237, 239; as antidote to brain rot 16, 19, 252–254; anti-satire critiques 15–18; apathy and 222–226, 236, 239; audience perceptions and 228–230; bullying and xiv, 5, 31, 68–70, 234; Bush and 18, 72; citizen engagement and 236–237, 238–239; "citizen satire" 199, 201; classical 171–172; on *The Colbert Report* 69–70, 146–147, 170–171; community and shared narrative through 235–236; as complicity and distraction 226–228; critical thinking and 2, 13, 15–16, 111–112, 131–132, 171–172, 229, 237–238, 249–250; cynicism and 2, 15–16, 215, 218, 222–226, 234; on *The Daily Show* 109–111, 170–171, 224–225; dealing with Trump's absurdity 4, 14–15; defined 2–3, *3*; democracy and 1–2, 14–16, 18–19, 131, 133–134, 139, 203, 222–226, 233–239; distinguishing satirists from jerks 71; divisiveness of 218–222; downside of 18–19; exaggeration and 120, 188; excusing bad behavior 230–233; exposing abuses of power through irony 70, 73, 119, 159, 221, 230, 233, 234; Fox News as target of 44, 77, 88; "gateway" function of 238; Horatian vs. Juvenalian 171–172; information flow and 233–234; irony and 2–5; mockery vs. 172, 229; open

display of bias 234; polarization and 134, 220–221, 233, 235; power of 214–218; at protests 199–200, *199*; as radical by nature 76; reality and 30, 37, 59–61, 68, 127, 187; the Republican mindset and 133, 158; satire vs. mockery 2, 7–8, 171–172, 229; satirical news vs. fake news 15; secret weapon of 254–260; speaking truth to power xiv, 121, 132, 133, 199, 231, 234–235; Stewart and 14–16, 171; Trump's relationship to 5–6, 9–10; watchdog role of 119, 133; *see also* activism; impersonations; parody
Satire and Dissent (Day) 239
"Satire League" 130–134, *131*, *132*, 139–140; *see also* Ministry of Satire
Saturday Night Live (*SNL*): 40th anniversary special 25–26; impersonations on 2, 18, 34–35, *36*, 52–53, 55; long history of mocking Trump 53; Meyers on 4, 25–26, 43, 160; ratings 55; "sheetcaking" 227–228; Trump hosting 8, *36*, 43, 160; Trump's complaints about 4, 8, *9*, 56, *57*, 61, 119, *120*, 138, 217, 254; "Weekend Update" segments 160, 197, 227
Saudi Arabia 180, 194
Sawyer, Diane *113*
Scalia, Antonin 155
Scarborough, Joe 94
"scare quotes" 74
Scotland 253
Scruton, Roger 219
Seager, Susan E. 217
self-deprecating jokes 4, 19n6, 25, 47n11, 165, 190
Sessions, Jeff 62, 66
sexism 31, 41
sex scandals 95
Sharknado 187
Sharpton, Al 62
Shaw, Bernard 89
"sheetcaking" 227–228
Shorenstein Center at Harvard 97, 99, 148
Showtime 33
Siegel, Lee 14–15
"silent majority" 105
Silverman, Sarah 155
Simpsons, The xi, 38
Sinclair Media 105
Siri 59
situational irony 3–5, 70, 136, 256
Smith, Moira 221
Smothers Brothers Comedy Hour, The 17, 216

snark 16, 109, 158, 199, 201, 231, 237, 253, 257
Snoop Dogg 40–42
Snyder, Mike 32
Snyder, Rick 196
social media 12–13; fake news and 1; late-night comedy on 162, 175–176; memes 168, 201, 227, 232; news media and 88, 106; *TikTok* 64–68; Trump supporters on 12–13, 177; *see also* Facebook; Twitter
Society of the Spectacle, The (Debord) 251
"soft news" 238
Sony Pictures cyber-attack 215
Sørensen, Majken 239
South Park 68, 197
spectacle 89, 235–236, 251; politics of "ethical spectacle" 236; Trump as xiv, 5–6, 30, 34, 38, 88–89, 93, 236
Spicer, Sean 11, *11*, 62, *66*, 66, 75, 107–108, 121, 249, 250
Spielvogel, Eric xi
Spy magazine 30, 31, 34, 40, 62, 129, 217
stand-up comedy xv, 150, 160, 176
State of the Union Address (2018) 101, 259
Stefani, Gwen xiv, 196
Stern, Howard 164
Stewart, Jon: Bush and 73, 115, 224; Colbert 14–16, 37, 109–110, 113–114, 116–117, 119, 134, 259; Cramer and *115*; on *Crossfire* 15, *114*, 115; *The Daily Show* and 76–77, 106, 109–110, 116–117, 146, 168; Fox News and 115, *115*, *116*; journalism and 15, *114*, 115, *115*, *116*; *Late Show* appearance 252, 254; as most trusted newsman 106, 113–115, *113*, 224; O'Reilly and 115, *115*, *116;* patriotism and 134; Rally to Restore Sanity 16, 236–237; *Rosewater* 140, 215; satire and 14–16, 171; on stupidity vs. evil 88–89, *89*; top ten moments *114*–*115*; on Youssef 215; *see also Daily Show, The*
Stinnett, Gina xi
Stone, Roger 250
Strick, James 70
Strong, Cecily *36*
Sudeikis, Jason *36*
Sun, Ping 225
"Superiority Theory" of humor 219
Super PACs 97, 106, *118*, 146
Super Tuesday 127, 132
Supreme Court: *Bush v. Gore 114*; *Citizens United 118*; *Hustler* ruling 216–217; on

the "Muslim ban" 136; vacancies 62–63, *63*, 111, *128*, 129, 155
Survivor 34, 92
Swift, Jonathan 69, 188
Syria 77, 136

Taibbi, Matt 90
Taksler, Sara x
Talking Right (Nunberg) 131
Tapper, Jake 101, *102*, 121
Taub, Amanda 251
TBS 154, 155; *see also Full Frontal with Samantha Bee*
Tea Party movement 130, 200, 236
Telecommunications Act of 1996 105
Telnaes, Ann 197
Terms of My Surrender, The 195
terrorism 72, 136, 250; *see also* 9/11
"Terrorism Awareness Project" 181
"theory of mind" 258
The Situation 40
"This is your brain on drugs" public service announcement 247
Thompson, Mike x, *8*, 197
Thrush, Glenn 101
TikTok 64–68
Time magazine 88–89, 96, *97*, 106, 114, 130, 168, *169*
Tisinger, Russell M., 229
Tlaib, Rashida 196
Todd, Chuck 24, 108, 163
Tonight Show, The 24, 37, 45, 176, 217
toxic masculinity 31, 57, 66, 166–168
tragicomedy 5, 88–89
Transpacific Partnership (TPP) 184–185
Treatise on Human Nature and That on Liberty and Necessity (Hobbes) 219
Trudeau, Gary 34, 198
Trudeau, Justin 249
Trump, Donald xiii–xv; 2011 Comedy Central roast of 40–43, *42*; 2018 State of the Union Address 101, 259; as the Absurd Politician 38–40, *39*, *40*; abuses of power by 194–195, 199; *Access Hollywood* tape 66–67, *67*, 95, 166; as "America's back mole" 18, 127; *The Apprentice* 6, 34, 40–41, 53, 55, 91–92, 96, 160; as assault on critical thinking 13, 248–252; avoiding Vietnam 72; Baldwin's impersonation of 2, 6–10, *6*, *10*, 50, 52–53, 55–62, 64, 256; bankruptcies of 42, 91, 95, 129; behavior at security briefings 59–60; "big lie" 45, 252–253; birtherism and 29, *30*, 35–38, 92–93, 217; bitter irony of Trump 70–79; as the Bragging Businessman *30*, 31–33, *32*, *33*; bullying of *69*, 74–75, 95, 108, 120–121, 130, 217, 250–251; *Celebrity Apprentice, The* 23, 34, 35, 92; civil liberties and 181; command of the English language 31, 70, 74–75, *156*; complaints about *Saturday Night Live* (*SNL*) 4, 8, *9*, 56, *57*, 61, 119, *120*, 138, 217, 254; complaints of media bias *9*, 9, 61, 119–120, *120*, 217, 254; Democratic National Committee (DNC) role in elevating Trump's visibility 28–29; disrespect of democratic institutions 76, 145, 150; early presidential aspirations 26–29, *27*; the endless barrage 251–252; epidemic of lies 248–249; extremist views of 59, 76, 158, 177; on *Facebook* 67; Fallon's impersonation of 7–8, 55, 59, 63–64, *64*, 168; family separation policy 72, *149*, 155–156, *156*; feud with Rosie O'Donnell *36*; Fox News and 25, 67, 88, 90, 99; as the Future Flop *30*; as "gaslighter in chief" 248; hair jokes 7, 24, 26, 31, 40–41, 150, 225; hosting *Saturday Night Live* (*SNL*) 8, *36*, 43, 160; impeachments of 132; interview with Colbert 148; as a joke xiii–xv; jokes about over the decades 29–40, *30*; *Late Night* (with Seth Meyers) and 160, 165; as a media junkie 90; megalomania of 31, 34, *35*, 93, 167, 174; mockery by average citizens 64, 201; mockery of 29, 31, 40, 68–69, 82, 74–75, 150–152; as the most mocked president 72, 199, 217; narcissism of 8, 38, 44, 52, 54, 65, 174, 185, 188, 193, 201, 203, 250; not "getting" jokes 42–43; as Orwellian 108, 193, 247–248; place in the Republican Party (GOP) 24, 29, 37–38, 89, 129, 149; polls on 25, 54, 133, 148; punditry's role in normalizing 28, 93, 191; questioning Trump's masculinity 199–200; racism of 41, 52, 55, 77, 92, 130, 138–139, 178; as the Reality TV Buffoon *30*, 34–35, *35*; relationship to ratings 34–35, 94, 96; relationship to satire 5–6, 9–10; relationship with the news media 12–14, 18, 85–100, *98*, *99*; representatives on cable news 88, 101, 181, 231; small hands of 7, 24, 26, 31, 40–41, 150, 225; as spectacle xiv, 5–6, 30, 34, 38, 88–89, 93, 236; statements about the Iraq War 249; United Nations

speech 185, *161*; as "White ISIS" 172, 177–178; *see also* Trump's tweets; *Twitter*
Trump, Donald Jr. *8*, 165–166, 193, *194*
Trump, Eric 103
Trump Foundation 95
"Trumpiness" 152–153
Trump, Ivana 41, *36*, 95
Trump, Ivanka *8*, 41, 72, *73*, 78, 155–156, *157*
Trump, Melania *36*, 41, 68
"Trumponomics" 34
Trump's tweets 4, 13, 18, 55, 59–60; average citizens responding to 12–14, *12*, 85, *202*; against comedians 4, *9*, 24, *57*, 61–62, *120*, 128, 165, *166*; covfefe 85–86, *86*, *87*, *88*; depictions of 59–60; diplomacy via 75; "Donald J. Trump Twitter Library" *172*, 174–175; "fake news" in *12*; full archive of 21; speaking directly to his base 201; a weekend of topics mentioned in *163*
Trump supporters: hatred of Clinton 78, 192; racism of 158, 174, 177, 250–251; rallies and 68, 236; on social media 12–13, 177; *see also* alt-right media; fake news
Trump Tower 41, 78, 92–93, 195
Trump University 34
"Trump vs. Bernie" tour 54
trust *see* public trust
truth: 9/11 and 152, 180; Bush and 106, 137, 152, 228; democracy and 108; Fox News and 231; language and 75; post-truth world 5, 15, 231; speaking truth to power xiv, 121, 132, 133, 199, 231, 234–235
"truthiness" 15, 106, 137, *117*, 152–153, 228, 235
TV Nation 190
Twitter 106; @RealDonaldDrumpf parody account 129; @RealHumanPraise *118;* "Colbert nation" 116, 142; comedians' presence on 168, 175–176; "Donald J. Trump Twitter Library" *172*, 174–175; Russian disinformation on 102–103; *see also* Trump's tweets

United Kingdom 99
United Nations 185
"Unite the Right" rally in Charlottesville 138, 159, 164, 227, 250
Univisión 11
"unlaughter" 221

"unpresidented" 2
US News and World Report 223

Vanity Fair 7, 62, 72–73
van Zoonen, Liesbet 236
Variety 171
Velazquez-Manoff, Moises 74
Vietnam 17, 72
View, The 35
Viviano, Sam 32
Voice, The xiv
voter ID laws 144, *149*
Vox 45, 142–143
Vulfov, Bob 201, *202*
Vulture 179

Wallace, Chris 57
Wall Street Journal, The 99
Walters, Barbara *113*
Warren, Elizabeth 138
Washington, George 216
Washington Post, The 25, 70, 92, 95, 96, 99, 153, 180, 217, 248
Watergate 58, 95
Webber, Julie xi
"Weekend Update" segments 160, 197, 227
Weinstein, Harvey 166
Welch, Edgar Maddison 104
Westmoreland, Lynn *117*
Wexler, Robert *117*
Weymouth, Lally 23
"whataboutism" 250
Where to Invade Next 191–192
White House Correspondents' Association Dinner (WHCAD) 134–136; in 2006 53, 73; in 2011 23–26, 29, 37, 43–44, 134–135, 159–160; in 2017 135–137, 178; in 2018 10–12, *11*, 18, 41; "Not the White House Correspondents' Dinner" 72, *156*
"White ISIS" *172*, 177–178
white nationalism 107, 130, 176, 178, 221–222, 227–228, 250–251
white privilege 227–228
Who Is America? (with Sacha Baron Cohen) 33
Wikipedia 142
Wilkinson, Alissa 142–143
Williams, Brian 101, 106, *113*, 114
Williams, Zoe 73
Wilmore, Larry 154, 197
Winfrey, Oprah 27–28, 44
Wolf, Michelle 10–11, *11*, 41, 155, 197
"Women's March" 199, *200*, 237

Wood, Roy 173–174
Woodruff, Bob *113*
Woodward, Bob 95
Wrap, The 176
Wuerker, Matt xi, *135*, 197

Xenos, M.A. 239

You Can't Spell America Without Me (Baldwin and Anderson) 62
Young, Dannagal xi, 90, 222, 229, 231, 235, 238, 255, 257, 259

Young, Mark Leiren xi
Youssef, Bassem x, 215, 259
YouTube: alt-right media on 104; Colbert's use of 147; Kimmel's use of 166; Meyers' use of 162; Oliver's use of 130, 144; in Saudi Arabia 180; Trump parodies on 64

zingers 77, 150
Zoonen, Liesbet van 236
Zorn, Chris xi
Zucker, Jeff 91, 94
Zwicky, Arnold 215

For Product Safety Concerns and Information please contact our EU representative GPSR@taylorandfrancis.com
Taylor & Francis Verlag GmbH, Kaufingerstraße 24, 80331 München, Germany

www.ingramcontent.com/pod-product-compliance
Lightning Source LLC
Chambersburg PA
CBHW051350290426
44108CB00015B/1954